Vergil and Classical Hexameter Poetry

VERGIL

AND CLASSICAL HEXAMETER POETRY

A Study in Metrical Variety

by

George E. Duckworth

The University of Michigan Press
Ann Arbor

PREFACE

This study of Latin hexameter poetry results in part from my efforts in recent years to arouse greater interest among my students in the perfection of Vergilian meter, in part from a growing conviction that new and valuable criteria might be developed to define more clearly the metrical procedures not only of Vergil but of other hexameter poets as well. My investigations into the frequencies of the metrical schemata (or "patterns," the term I prefer) and the manner in which they are used took at first the form of charts and percentage tables, and these I have translated, I hope, in such a way that my findings will be meaningful and of value to teachers and students of Latin poetry on all academic levels.

I planned and began this book some years ago, but several significant discoveries (e.g., the Catullan nature of Vergil's famous Fourth *Eclogue*, the surprising manner in which *Aeneid* X-XII differ metrically from the remainder of the epic, and Horace's increasing interest in variety, which culminates in the *Ars Poetica* and dates this poem after the other *Epistles*) seemed to justify more immediate publication. I therefore wrote a series of articles in which I discuss and compare the metrical techniques of the many hexameter poets from Ennius (239-169 B.C.) to Arator and Corippus (c. 550 A.D.). These articles have appeared in the *Transactions of the American Philological Association, Vergilius, Latomus,* and other classical journals, but the earliest articles did not have the benefit of my later investigations, and lacked much comparative material of value which can now be included. Also, the articles contained considerable scholarly discussion and numerous lists of statistical details which have been eliminated from the present book, since it is directed to a somewhat wider public. I trust, however, that all relevant frequencies and percentages have been included.

Much of the pioneer work on the frequencies of the metrical patterns, especially that by M. W. Drobisch a century ago and by J. La Roche a generation later, is now antiquated, being based on texts no longer in common use; it appears in foreign journals not readily accessible to many teachers, and furthermore is not free from many inaccuracies. It has seemed advisable, therefore, to scan again the hexameter poets and compile new frequency tables as a basis for my studies in metrical repetition and variety. My statistics for the hexameter poets from Ennius through the Silver Age, and including Nemesianus and Serenus in the third century A.D., are based on the scansions of the complete extant works of each poet, even when, as in the case of Vergil, Ovid's *Metamorphoses,* Statius, and Silius Italicus, the total number of verses for each ranges from twelve to fourteen thousand. But for the late period, with eighteen writers to be considered, many of them minor and known only to specialists, such a procedure seemed unnecessary and inadvisable. My statistics for the Late Empire, therefore, are based on a liberal sampling of each of the poets, usually from a thousand to two thousand verses, but about thirty-five hundred in the case of Claudian whose output is unusually large and who is considered the best of the hexameter poets after Statius. For this late period I have preferred to scan complete works or books rather than shorter and incomplete sections from a larger variety of poems.

Occasional inaccuracies and typographical errors are almost inevitable in a work of this nature. I have checked and rechecked all statistical material as carefully as possible, and I trust that the mistakes which remain will in no way affect the validity of my major conclusions concerning the metrical practices of the various poets, their similarities and differences, and the authenticity (or non-authenticity) of many controversial poems.

The five chapters of Part I, "Patterns and Procedures: the Vergilian Norm," describe the nature of the hexameter patterns (sixteen in number, exclusive of spondaic verses), variety in sixteen-line units, repeat clusters and repeated patterns, shift in fourth-foot texture in repeated patterns, and combinations of opposite and reverse patterns in adjacent lines. The new criteria concerning variety and repetition established in Part I provide the basis for the metrical "fingerprinting" of the various poets in Part II and are illustrated primarily from Vergil's *Aeneid,* which I consider the metrical norm for comparison with the other poets. Since *Aeneid* IV, the tragic story of Dido and Aeneas, is undoubtedly one of the best known and most beloved books of Vergil's epic, I draw my illustrations, whenever possible, from this source. Also, I compare in Part I Vergil's procedure with that of many other poets, both Greek and Latin.

Part II, "Facts and Findings: from Ennius to the Age of Justinian," is, in essence, a metrical history of Latin hexameter poetry and shows the developments and changes during a period of 750 years. The various chapters reveal the influence of earlier poets on those of later periods, e.g., Cicero on Vergil and Horace, Catullus LXIV on *Eclogue* IV of Vergil, Ovid on much of Silver Latin poetry (but not on Lucan or Silius Italicus, who are more indebted to Vergil), Horace and perhaps Lucilius on Juvenal, Valerius Flaccus on Claudian, and Vergil on many of the late Christian poets. The metrical analyses help to indicate the authenticity or spuriousness of several works of uncertain authorship, e.g., the hexameter poems of the *Appendix Vergiliana*, the *Halieutica* usually assigned to Ovid, the *Laus Pisonis*, the *Ilias Latina*, and the late *De providentia Dei*. Part II also contains several metrical comparisons with Greek hexameter poetry: Ennius and Homer, Catullus and Callimachus, Vergil's *Eclogues* and the *Idylls* of Theocritus, Catullus and Cyprian and the late Greek poets Quintus of Smyrna, Nonnus, and Musaeus.

The three Appendices discuss the dactylic nature of Ovid's elegiac poetry, a rare type of first-foot dactyl (three words), and a metrical comparison of the *Thirteenth Book of the Aeneid* by the Renaissance poet Maphaeus Vegius with the *Aeneid* of Vergil.

The two synoptic Tables (I and II) are designed to give the most significant frequencies and percentages for all the Latin hexameter poets discussed in this volume. Table III presents the relevant frequencies and percentages for the Greek hexameter poets mentioned both in Part I and Part II.

The Bibliography lists the editions of the poets on which my statistics are based (also the line totals of each) and gives more detailed information concerning the many books and articles to which I refer in an abbreviated form in the footnotes.

I am indebted to several colleagues and friends for their helpful suggestions concerning the Greek and Latin poets, and I wish to express my gratitude especially to Miss Elisabeth Case, formerly of the University of Michigan Press, now of the Cambridge University Press; her interest and encouragement during my metrical investigations have contributed immeasurably to the present form of this volume. I deeply appreciate a grant from the Princeton University Research Fund which has made the publication of the book possible.

George E. Duckworth

Princeton
May 1, 1969

CONTENTS

CONTENTS

PART 1

PATTERNS AND PROCEDURES:
THE VERGILIAN NORM

Chapter 1

THE HEXAMETER PATTERNS

The meter which appears most frequently in Greek and Latin poetry is the dactylic hexameter; totaling in the extant literature over 250,000 verses, it is predominantly the meter of epic poetry, from Homer to Musaeus, from Ennius to Corippus, but it is used also for pastoral (e.g., the *Idylls* of Theocritus, the *Eclogues* of Vergil and Calpurnius Siculus), scientific verse (e.g., the *Phaenomena* of Aratus, the *Astronomica* of Manilius), hymns, such as the *Homeric Hymns* and the *Hymns* of Callimachus, panegyrics and invectives (cf. Claudian and Sidonius in the Late Roman Empire), short epics, or *epyllia* (e.g., Catullus LXIV and the *Ciris*), and it provides the longer line of the Greek and Roman elegiac couplet.[1]

The dactylic hexameter is a quantitative verse consisting of long and short syllables; each line has six feet, with either a dactyl ($-\cup\cup$) or a spondee ($--$) in each of the first four feet; the fifth foot is regularly a dactyl, and the sixth foot is composed of two syllables, either a spondee or a trochee ($-\cup$) with the final syllable treated as long by the rule of *syllaba anceps*.

A spondee may occur in the fifth foot, in which case the verse is called "spondaic";[2] such spondaic lines are much less frequent in Latin poetry than in Greek, as the following list will indicate (one spondaic verse every *x* lines):

Homer:	19.4[3]
Aratus, *Phaenomena:*	6.9
Callimachus, *Hymns:*	15.1
Quintus of Smyrna:	14.3[4]
Vergil, *Aeneid:*	409.5
Horace, *Satires* and *Epistles:*	4,081.0
Ovid, *Metamorphoses:*	323.5
Silius Italicus:	2,033.8

The major exceptions in Latin hexameter poetry are Catullus LXIV, one spondaic verse every 13.6 lines, the *Ciris*, 35.7, Petronius, 58.8, and Avienus, *Aratea*, 64.7. Catullus LXIV and the *Ciris* were undoubtedly influenced by Callimachus, but Avienus' preference for spondaic verses is scarcely to be explained by the influence of Aratus, since the *Aratea* of Cicero and Germanicus Caesar show no such high frequency: Cicero, one spondaic verse every 480.0 lines, Germanicus, one every 170.3. Avienus has even more spondaic verses in his *Descriptio orbis terrae*, one every 48.0 lines.

It has been said that "infinite variety is possible in the grouping of the dactyls and the spondees which go to make up the verse."[5] This statement is perhaps true if we consider the distribution of caesuras and diaereses (inner metric) and the variety in sound effects; it is not true in respect to the actual grouping of the dactyls and the spondees, the outer metric of the verse.[6] There is here no "infinite variety." If we exclude the spondaic lines, we have only sixteen possible patterns; with the spondaic verses added, the number of possible patterns increases to thirty-two, but, since spondaic verses are so rare in Latin hexameter poetry, I shall deal only with the sixteen patterns which have a dactyl in the fifth foot.

The sixteen variations in the first four feet were arranged by Drobisch in four groups of four patterns each.[7] If we denote a dactylic foot by *d*, a spondaic foot by *s*, these four groups begin with *ds, dd, sd,* and *ss,* each of these combinations being followed by *ss, ds, sd,* and *dd;* the list of the sixteen possibilities is thus:

dsss	*ddss*	*sdss*	*ssss*
dsds	*ddds*	*sdds*	*ssds*
dssd	*ddsd*	*sdsd*	*sssd*
dsdd	*dddd*	*sddd*	*ssdd*

Such an arrangement, however, seems less easy to remember than the following: a progression from all spondees or dactyls through the various combinations to the opposite pattern. Since Latin poetry favors the spondee, I shall begin with all spondees in the first four feet; this arrangement gives us five groups instead of four, but will, I believe, have mnemonic merit, especially as the second eight are the opposites of the first eight,[8] in reverse order.

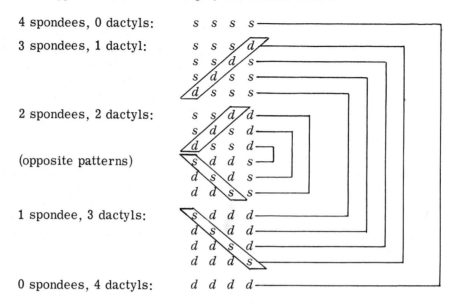

4 spondees, 0 dactyls: s s s s

3 spondees, 1 dactyl: s s s d
                          s s d s
                          s d s s
                          d s s s

2 spondees, 2 dactyls: s s d d
                          s d s d
                          d s s d

(opposite patterns)   s d d s
                          d s d s
                          d d s s

1 spondee, 3 dactyls: s d d d
                          d s d d
                          d d s d
                          d d d s

0 spondees, 4 dactyls: d d d d

The diagonal lines inserted above to indicate the shifting of dactyls and spondees should also help the reader to keep in mind the sixteen possible combinations of the hexameter patterns.[9]

A preponderance of spondees produces a verse that is slow, stately, and solemn. Among the most effective of the type *ssss* are perhaps *Aen.* VIII, 452:

illi inter sese multa vi bracchia tollunt,

where one can hear the Cyclopes working at their anvils, and III, 658, the description of Polyphemus:

monstrum horrendum, informe, ingens, cui lumen ademptum,

where the strange and horrible are emphasized; similar are IV, 181, and VII, 78:

monstrum horrendum, ingens, cui quot sunt corpore plumae,
id vero horrendum ac visu mirabile ferri.

Fear and anxiety are stressed in such *ssss* verses as I, 92; II, 559; IV, 279:

extemplo Aeneae solvuntur frigore membra;
at me tum primum saevus circumstetit horror.
at vero Aeneas aspectu obmutuit amens.

Dactylic verses are light, graceful, and rapid. In II, 790 *(ddds)* and 791 *(dddd)* the dactyls reproduce the swiftness with which the phantom of Creusa disappears:

haec ubi dicta dedit, lacrimantem et multa volentem
dicere deseruit, tenuisque recessit in auras.

Perhaps Vergil's most famous lines of the type *dddd* are IX, 503:

at tuba terribilem sonitum procul aere canoro,

where the meter echoes the sound of the trumpet, and VIII, 596:

quadripedante putrem sonitu quatit ungula campum,

where the horses gallop across the plain; XI, 875 *(ddsd),* is similar:

quadripedumque putrem cursu quatit ungula campum.[10]

The order of the patterns as listed above bears no relation to the frequency of their appearance. If the sixteen patterns were used to the same extent, the frequency of each would be 6.25 per cent, but this happens neither in Greek nor in Latin poetry. The favorite pattern may occur from ten to thirty per cent of the total verses, the first four from forty to seventy, and the first eight from sixty-five to ninety and occasionally higher, especially in the late Greek poetry. This means, of course, that some of the sixteen patterns appear very rarely, if at all; an extreme instance is provided by the *Hero and Leander* of Musaeus, a poem of 341 verses, where six patterns *(dsss, ddss, sdss, ssss, ssds,* and *sssd)* never occur, and three others *(sdds, sdsd,* and *ssdd)* total eight lines only; in other words, Musaeus practically composes his poem with only seven patterns of the possible sixteen.

The percentages of the favorite pattern, the first four, and especially the first eight, are extremely significant in that they help to establish the metrical "fingerprints" of the various poets. Each writer has his individual predilections and idiosyncrasies, and his attitude toward variety and repetition is shown to a marked degree, particularly in the case of the Latin poets, by the fluctuations in these percentages. The variation among several different poets may be seen as follows:

	% first pattern	% first four	% first eight
Homer	21.36	59.90	85.42[11]
Callimachus, *Hymns:*	28.95	71.74	93.14
Quintus of Smyrna:	38.75	81.77	96.15
Musaeus:	36.07	82.99	98.83
Cicero, *Aratea:*	17.95	59.08	82.88
Lucretius:	20.20	54.34	79.81
Catullus LXIV:	27.59	67.90	90.98
Vergil, *Eclogues:*	13.09	41.45	69.09
Georgics:	15.81	48.99	73.42
Aeneid:	14.39	46.95	72.78
Horace, *Satires:*	13.44	43.78	69.99
Epistles:	11.85	40.42	66.76
Ovid, *Metamorphoses:*	13.08	48.37	81.62
Valerius Flaccus:	22.65	54.36	83.35
Silius Italicus:	13.04	43.90	72.64
Ausonius, *Mosella:*	9.38	36.04	62.50
Claudian I:	18.27	55.0	82.21
Claudian II:	18.93	57.07	84.06[12]

With the exception of Catullus LXIV the percentages given above are consistently lower in Latin poetry than in Greek. We find, moreover, an amazing decrease in the concentration on the same patterns when we pass from the Republican poets to Vergil and Horace.

The differences between individual poets in the later periods are also striking, e.g., Valerius Flaccus and Silius Italicus, Ausonius and Claudian. It is important to note that the variation from book to book in the longer epics is very slight; this is clear from the frequency percentages of the first eight patterns:

Lucretius: 79.81; range from 78.19 (II) to 82.99 (V)
Vergil, *Aeneid:* 72.78; range from 71.09 (II) to 77.09 (XII)
Ovid, *Metamorphoses:* 81.62; range from 78.80 (VI) to 84.92 (XIV)
Valerius Flaccus: 83.35; range from 81.27 (I) to 85.77 (V, VI)
Silius Italicus: 72.64; range from 70.93 (XIV) to 76.99 (V)

The metrical pattern which appears most frequently is also a kind of "signpost" to distinguish the works of many Latin poets. It has much less value in the case of the Greek writers, most of whom favor *dddd* (e.g., Homer, Aratus, Apollonius of Rhodes, Quintus of Smyrna, Nonnus, and Musaeus). Beginning with Cicero, the pattern usually preferred by Republican and Augustan poets is *dsss*; these include Lucretius, Catullus LXIV, Vergil's *Georgics* and *Aeneid*,[13] Horace, Germanicus Caesar, and Manilius. Ovid, more interested in dactyls, favored *ddss*, and his imitators in the Silver Age and Late Empire shifted to *dsds*, among them Calpurnius Siculus, Valerius Flaccus, Statius, Claudian, and Sidonius. But in these same periods, *dsss* was preferred by many, including Lucan, Persius, Silius Italicus, Juvenal, and several Christian poets, such as Juvencus, Prosper, Marius Victor, and Avitus.

Another interesting point about the favorite pattern is the consistency with which it occurs in the individual books of most long works:

> Lucretius: *dsss* first in all six books
> Vergil, *Georgics:* *dsss* first in all four books
> > *Aeneid:* *dsss* first in ten books (*ddss* first in V and VII)
> Horace: *dsss* first in *Satires* I and II, *Epistles* I and II
> Manilius: *dsss* first in all five books
> Valerius Flaccus: *dsds* first in all eight books
> Statius, *Thebaid:* *dsds* first in all twelve books[14]

In some long poems we find a greater fluctuation; *dsss* is first in Silius Italicus and likewise first in twelve books; in the other five (V, VIII, IX, XII, XIV) the favorite pattern is *sdss*. In Lucan *dsss*, the favorite pattern, is first in only three books (IV, VI, X) and is tied for first place with *dsds* in two (II, III); in the other five books *dsds* is first. In the *Metamorphoses* of Ovid the favorite pattern is *ddss*, but it is first in only seven of the fifteen books; it is tied with *dssd* in XI, and in the other seven books *dsss* is first in I, III, V, VIII, and IX, *dssd* is first in IV, and *ddsd* in X. But such variation as appears in the *Metamorphoses* is most unusual.[15]

The patterns preferred by the various poets determine the number of spondees and dactyls which appear in the first four feet of the eight most frequent patterns. Of the thirty-two feet in these eight patterns, we find in Homer, and in most Greek poets, ten spondees and twenty-two dactyls. The picture is very different among the Roman poets, and Ennius, the founder of the Latin hexameter, has the exact opposite of Homer (as far as we can ascertain on the basis of the extant fragments): twenty-two spondees and ten dactyls. The most dactylic of the major Latin poets is Ovid, whose *Metamorphoses* has twelve spondees and twenty dactyls. The distribution in Vergil's *Georgics* and *Aeneid* is twenty spondees and twelve dactyls, a proportion which begins with Cicero and is preferred by many later poets, with the exception of those influenced by Ovid, e.g., Calpurnius Siculus, twelve (or eleven) spondees, twenty (or twenty-one) dactyls; Valerius Flaccus and Statius (both *Thebaid* and *Silvae*), fifteen spondees and seventeen dactyls. Many poets favor a proportion of eighteen spondees and fourteen dactyls, among them Lucretius, Lucan, Persius, and, in the late period, Claudian, Sidonius, and Sedulius.

Again we find little variation in the individual books of the longer works:

> Lucretius: 18 *s*, 14 *d;* range from 16 *s*, 16 *d* to 19 *s*, 13 *d*
> Verg., *Georg.:* 20 *s*, 12 *d;* range from 18 *s*, 14 *d* to 21 *s*, 11 *d*
> Verg., *Aen.:* 20 *s*, 12 *d;* range from 18 *s*, 14 *d* to 20 *s*, 12 *d*
> Ovid, *Metam.:* 12 *s*, 20 *d;* range from 12 *s*, 20 *d* to 15 *s*, 17 *d*[16]
> Manilius: 20 *s*, 12 *d;* range from 18 *s*, 14 *d* to 20 *s*, 12 *d*
> Lucan: 18 *s*, 14 *d;* range from 17 *s*, 15 *d* to 21 *s*, 11 *d*
> Valerius Fl.: 15 *s*, 17 *d;* range from 12 *s*, 20 *d* to 15 *s*, 17 *d*
> Stat., *Theb.:* 15 *s*, 17 *d;* range from 12 *s*, 20 *d* to 17 *s*, 15 *d*
> Silius Ital.: 20 *s*, 12 *d;* range from 20 *s*, 12 *d* to 22 *s*, 10 *d*

Vergil has been praised for his perfect control of the dactylic hexameter. A typical statement concerning his metrical artistry is that of Dimsdale:[17]

> Virgil's mastery over the hexameter is unapproached. In his hands it acquired a flow,
> a melody, and a variety of tone which it had never shown before and, despite imitation, was never to show again.

I shall, therefore, use the *Aeneid* of Vergil as the norm, as a standard by which to compare and contrast the other Latin hexameter poets. My procedure seems all the more justified since, as we shall see below, he departed from the earlier poets of the Republic in several important respects, e.g., less concentration on the same metrical patterns, a striking decrease in the frequency of fourth-foot homodyne, and the introduction of greater variety in repeated patterns by a shift in fourth-foot texture. Vergil's innovations were accepted and imitated by many poets, both pagan and Christian, during the course of the Roman Empire.

In both text and Tables I shall henceforth list the sixteen metrical patterns in the order of their frequency in the *Aeneid;* this order is as follows, illustrated with verses from the beginning of Book IV:

dsss (2): vulnus alit venis et caeco carpitur igni
ddss (5): verbaque, nec placidam membris dat cura quietem
dsds (3): multa viri virtus animo multusque recursat
sdss (1): at regina gravi iamdudum saucia cura
ssss (14): iactatus fatis! quae bella exhausta canebat!
ddds (20): Anna, fatebor enim, miseri post fata Sychaei
ssds (7): umentemque Aurora polo dimoverat umbram
sdds (30): sic effata sinum lacrimis implevit obortis

dssd (22): solus hic inflexit sensus animumque labantem
ddsd (58): legiferae Cereri Phoeboque patrique Lyaeo
sdsd (37): ductoresque alii, quos Africa terra triumphis
dsdd (12): credo equidem, nec vana fides, genus esse deorum
sssd (16): ne cui me vinclo vellem sociare iugali
ssdd (40): hinc Gaetulae urbes, genus insuperabile bello
dddd (13): degeneres animos timor arguit. heu, quibus ille
sddd (8): cum sic unanimam adloquitur male sana sororem

One important feature of Vergil's order of patterns in the *Aeneid* is this: each of the first eight patterns has a spondee in the fourth foot; this marks the end of one aspect of his metrical development, for the *Eclogues* have six spondees and two dactyls in the fourth foot of the first eight patterns, the *Georgics* seven spondees and one dactyl. Very few of the other Roman poets have fourth-foot spondees in their first eight patterns; they are Cicero, Manilius, Silius Italicus, Nemesianus in his *Cynegetica,* Cyprian of Gaul, and the anonymous *De providentia Dei.*

Notes to Chapter 1

1. The total of 250,000 verses given above applies only to the hexameter poetry and does not include the longer line of the elegiac couplet. The statistics in this volume are based on my scansion of over 143,000 verses. For the period from Ennius through the Silver Age (and including Nemesianus and Serenus) the complete works of each poet have been utilized, but I have been highly selective in the case of the Greek poets (less than one-tenth of the total verses) and I have examined about one-third of the Latin poetry of the Late Empire; see the Bibliography for the works of the Greek and late Latin poets which I have used and for my verse totals of each.

2. See Cooper, *Introduction to the Latin Hexameter,* pp. 18-19, who applies the term "spondaic hexameter" to a verse of this type.

3. This figure is based on my scansion of 1,920 verses, 960 each from the *Iliad* and the *Odyssey.* La Roche, *WS* 20 (1898), pp. 1-69, gives 1,378 spondaic verses for the *Iliad* and the *Odyssey* as a whole, one every 20.2 lines.

4. There are no spondaic verses in either Nonnus or Musaeus.

5. Knapp, *The Aeneid of Vergil,* p. 75.

6. For definitions of "inner metric" and "outer metric," see O'Neill, *TAPhA* 71 (1940), page 336, note 3; cf. Getty, *Lustrum* 8 (1963), p. 120.

7. *BSGL* 20 (1868), pp. 18-19; cf. Winbolt, *Latin Hexameter Verse,* pp. 113-115.

8. For example, *dddd* is the "opposite" of *ssss, ddds* of *sssd, ddsd* of *ssds,* etc. Bushnell, *TAPhA* 33 (1902), p. lvii, uses the term "reverse" to define "the result obtained by substituting for every dactyl a spondee, and *vice versa,*" but "opposite" seems more accurate. I apply the term "reverse" to the patterns which present the sequence of dactyls and spondees in truly reverse order, e.g., *sssd* and *dsss, sddd* and *ddds; sssd* is thus both the "opposite" of *ddds* and the "reverse" of *dsss;* see below, Chapter 5.

9. Drobisch, *BSGL* 18 (1866), p. 76, had originally favored a similar arrangement in five groups, beginning with *ssss,* but his listing of the patterns did not permit the diagonal lines given above.

10. Wilkinson, *Golden Latin Artistry,* p. 132, says: "the French Alexandrine ... has not the variety of the Virgilian hexameter; it cannot gallop." For a thorough analysis of the effectiveness of lines composed of *ssss* and *dddd,* see Maxa, *WS*
19 (1897), pp. 78-116; cf. also Winbolt, *Latin Hexameter Verse,* pp. 118-125; Cooper, *Introduction to the Latin Hexameter,* pp. 28-31.

11. These percentages are based on my own scansion of 1,920 verses. They are slightly higher than those in Duckworth, *TAPhA* 95 (1964), pp. 14 f., where I derived my percentages from the totals for the entire *Iliad* and *Odyssey* as given by La Roche, *WS* 20 (1898), pp. 1-69. La Roche's statistics are far from trustworthy. On the many inaccuracies in his totals for the *Aeneid,* as given in *WS* 23 (1901), pp. 121-142, see Duckworth, *TAPhA* 95 (1964), pp. 53-56. On La Roche's scansions of Homer, see Jones, *TAPhA* 97 (1966), p. 275.

12. Claudian II = *De raptu Proserpinae,* a mythological epic; for the invectives and panegyrics included in Claudian I, see the Bibliography.

13. Vergil's *Eclogues,* influenced by the *Idylls* of Theocritus, are more dactylic; the favorite pattern is *ddss.*

14. In the *Silvae* of Statius *dsds* is likewise the favorite pattern; of the twenty-six hexameter poems it is first in fifteen and tied for first place in four others.

15. Lee, *Metamorphoseon, Liber I,* p. 33, on the basis of Book I where *dsss* is the most frequent pattern, wrongly believed that *dsss* was also first in the poem as a whole; see Duckworth, *TAPhA* 95 (1964), p. 24, note 31; 97 (1966), p. 81. Lee's assumption on the basis of the first book would have been correct if he had been speaking of Lucretius, Vergil's *Georgics* and *Aeneid,* Horace, Manilius, Valerius Flaccus, or the *Thebaid* of Statius.

16. The distribution of twelve spondees and twenty dactyls appears in thirteen of the fifteen books of the *Metamorphoses;* in Book V, where *sdss* and *dddd* are tied for eighth place, we have twelve spondees and twenty dactyls, or fifteen spondees and seventeen dactyls; the latter proportion occurs also in Book II. The *Halieutica,* ascribed to Ovid, has a most non-Ovidian distribution of nineteen to twenty-one spondees and thirteen to eleven dactyls (*ssds, dssd,* and *ddsd* tied for seventh place); this is a strong argument against the authenticity of the poem; see below, Chapter 9.

17. *History of Latin Literature,* p. 265; cf. Bailey, "Virgil" in *OCD,* p. 951: "In the *Aeneid* Virgil reaches the full command of Latin poetic diction and of the hexameter as its vehicle."

Chapter 2

VARIETY IN SIXTEEN-LINE UNITS

The study of the outer metric of hexameter verse has in the past been far too mechanical. About thirty years ago, O'Neill wrote as follows:[1]

> When we have determined statistically the frequencies of dactyls and spondees in each of the first five feet and the frequencies of various combinations of dactyls and spondees in these feet, we know all that there is to know about the outer metric of the hexameter.

I disagree, for I am convinced that new criteria of value concerning variety and repetition can be established to elucidate the metrical procedures of Vergil and the other Latin poets[2] and to provide additional information about poetic development, literary indebtedness, and the authenticity of works of uncertain authorship.

The important thing in any discussion of outer metric is not *what* patterns appear, but *how* they are used; it is not merely a question of frequency, but a matter of spacing. Do we find monotonous repetition of the same patterns in several lines in succession, or do Vergil and the other poets attempt to avoid repeated patterns in adjacent verses?

In the case of Vergil's *Aeneid,* we have seen that his favorite pattern *(dsss)* occurs in about one-seventh of the total verses, the first four almost one-half, and the first eight almost three-quarters. Although these frequencies are much lower than those given above for Catullus LXIV, Valerius Flaccus, and many others, they still may be sufficiently high to preclude a satisfying variety in the different combinations of dactyls and spondees. If the same pattern appears frequently two or three times in succession, a dangerous monotony may result unless precautions are taken, either deliberately or unconsciously, to vary the lines by other means.

Before discussing in detail the repetition of patterns, I wish to examine one aspect of variety — the number of different patterns (out of a possible sixteen) which appears in units of sixteen lines each (disregarding spondaic verses, interpolations, and, for the *Aeneid,* all incomplete verses). Even in the *Aeneid,* with one fourth of the patterns appearing in almost half of the verses, one might expect this number to be relatively low, but such is not the case. Only nine such sixteen-line units have fewer than seven patterns,[3] whereas eleven units have as many as thirteen patterns in each, as, for example, I, 189-204, which contains no repeated pattern until we reach 202, the fourteenth line of the unit:

189 *(sssd):* ductoresque ipsos primum capita alta ferentis
190 *(ddss):* cornibus arboreis sternit, tum vulgus et omnem
191 *(dsds):* miscet agens telis nemora inter frondea turbam;
192 *(dsss):* nec prius absistit quam septem ingentia victor
193 *(ddds):* corpora fundat humi et numerum cum navibus aequet.
194 *(sdds):* hinc portum petit et socios partitur in omnis.
195 *(dsdd):* vina bonus quae deinde cadis onerarat Acestes
196 *(dddd):* litore Trinacrio dederatque abeuntibus heros
197 *(dssd):* dividit, et dictis maerentia pectora mulcet:
198 *(ddsd):* "O socii (neque enim ignari sumus ante malorum),
199 *(sddd):* o passi graviora, dabit deus his quoque finem.
200 *(ssdd):* vos et Scyllaeam rabiem penitusque sonantis
201 *(sdss):* accestis scopulos, vos et Cyclopia saxa
(202-204 repeat 194, 198, 192, respectively.)

The average number of patterns per sixteen-line unit gives a clear picture of one aspect of variety in hexameter poetry. The averages are high in Vergil's works: *Eclogues,* 9.7;[4] *Georgics,* 9.3; and *Aeneid,* 9.4. Since I use the *Aeneid* as a norm, I shall give the averages in several other poets in order to show the extent to which they differ from Vergil:

Homer:	8.0
Callimachus:	6.6
Nonnus:	5.5
Lucretius:	8.6
Catullus LXIV:	7.0
Horace:	9.5
Ovid, *Metamorphoses:*	8.9
Lucan:	8.9
Valerius Flaccus:	8.4
Statius, *Thebaid:*	9.2
Silius Italicus:	9.5
Juvenal:	9.6
Serenus:	9.3
Claudian I:	8.3
Cyprian of Gaul:	7.6

Of the poets listed above, only Horace, Statius, Silius Italicus, Juvenal, and Serenus have totals closely resembling that in the *Aeneid*. With the exception of Catullus LXIV and Cyprian, all Latin poets have an average per unit of eight or more patterns, but many, and especially those who imitate Vergil, have a range from nine to ten; e.g., among the late Christian poets, Juvencus, 9.0; Paulinus of Nola, 9.4; Prosper of Aquitaine, 9.4; *De providentia Dei*, 10.0; Paulinus of Pella, 9.7.

Again, in the case of long poems, the consistency from book to book is remarkable:

Lucretius:	8.6; range, 8.3 (V, VI) to 8.9 (I, II)
Vergil, *Aen.:*	9.4; range, 9.0 (IV) to 9.8 (II, IX)
Ovid, *Metam.:*	8.9; range, 8.6 (XIV) to 9.1 (VI)
Manilius:	8.8; range, 8.6 (IV) to 8.9 (I, III)
Lucan:	8.9; range, 8.7 (IX) to 9.3 (II)
Valerius Fl.:	8.4; range, 8.1 (VI) to 8.7 (I)
Statius, *Theb.:*	9.2; range, 8.9 (VIII) to 9.4 (IV, VI, XI, XII)
Silius Ital.:	9.5; range, 8.9 (V) to 10.0 (III)

The maximum average number of patterns per unit in any book of Lucretius, Manilius, and Valerius Flaccus thus does not exceed the minimum average number in Vergil, Statius, and Silius Italicus.

Since the Latin poets with very few exceptions average more than eight patterns per sixteen-line unit, it will be of interest also to consider the percentage of units with eight or more patterns. These percentages in Vergil are high: *Eclogues*, 97.87; *Georgics*, 92.59; *Aeneid*, 92.46, and differ much from the corresponding percentages in Greek poetry:

Homer:	68.91
Theocritus:	68.92
Callimachus:	18.87
Quintus of Smyrna:	13.33
Nonnus:	0.

In most Latin poetry at least eighty per cent of the sixteen-line units have eight or more patterns; the exceptions are the following:

Lucretius:	76.10
Catullus LXIV:	30.43
Dirae:	70.0
Valerius Flaccus:	74.86
Claudian I:	74.0
Claudian II:	77.61
Cyprian:	50.62
Avitus:	75.37
Corippus:	77.63

Percentages even higher than that in Vergil's *Aeneid* appear in a number of poets:

Horace, *Epistles:*	97.12
Laus Pisonis:	93.75
Statius, *Achilleid:*	95.65
Silius Italicus:	93.37
Juvenal:	93.45
Nemesianus, *Eclogues:*	94.44
Nemesianus, *Cynegetica:*	95.0
Avienus, *Aratea:*	95.65
Prudentius:	94.83
Sidonius	97.14
De providentia Dei	100.0[5]

The percentage range from book to book in Vergil's *Aeneid* is from 86.44 (XII) to 100.0 (VI).[6] Lucretius, with a range from 68.75 (VI) to 85.29 (I), shows a greater fluctuation, and the percentages are highest in the first two books. The opposite is true of Horace, whose percentage in the *Satires* is 85.22 (Book I, 83.64; Book II, 86.67), but in the later *Epistles* it rises to 97.12. The percentage ranges in the other long works reveal no such changing trends:

Ovid, *Metam.:*	86.35; from 77.36 (XIV) to 91.30 (X)
Manilius:	86.52; from 83.33 (III) to 89.29 (I)
Lucan:	87.43; from 81.09 (III) to 98.03 (V)
Valerius Fl.:	74.86; from 65.52 (VIII) to 83.02 (I)
Statius, *Theb.:*	90.20; from 82.98 (V) to 96.08 (XII)
Silius Italicus:	93.37; from 88.24 (XV) to 100.0 (II)

The statistics concerning variety in sixteen-line units are closely related to those dealing with patterns repeated in adjacent and near-adjacent lines. I turn to the repetition of patterns in the next chapter.

Notes to Chapter 2

1. *TAPhA* 71 (1940), p. 336, note 3.

2. Many of the criteria discussed below either are not applicable to the Greek hexameter, or they prove little; there are no such differences among the Greek poets that we find among the Romans.

3. *Aeneid* X-XII, with 28.20 per cent of the sixteen-line units, has five of the nine, or 55.56 per cent. Many other metrical abnormalities appear in these three books; see below, Chapter 7.

4. Five *Eclogues* (I, V, VI, VII, and IX) range from 10.2 to 10.8; *Eclogue* IV is unusual in this as in many other respects, and has an average of only 7.4; the average in the *Eclogues*, excluding IV, is 9.8; see below, Chapter 7.

5. Several short poems also have percentages of 100.0: *Culex, Moretum,* Horace's *Ars Poetica, Halieutica, Einsiedeln Eclogues,* Petronius, Ausonius' *Mosella* and *Cento Nuptialis.*

6. The percentages in Books XII (86.44) and XI (87.72) are the lowest in the *Aeneid;* see above, note 3.

Chapter 3

REPEAT CLUSTERS AND REPEATED PATTERNS

The same pattern may occur in two, three, or more lines in succession; these I term "repeats." Only twice does Vergil use the same pattern five times in adjacent verses, and these appear in his earlier poetry, *Ecl.* X, 36-40 *(sdss)* and *Georg.* I, 46-50 *(dsss)*. Elsewhere he allows himself a maximum of four repeated patterns in succession, and these very rarely — four times in the *Georgics*, and only seven in the *Aeneid*.[1] The frequencies for the same pattern occurring in four or more verses together are thus as follows:

Eclogues:	once in 825.0 lines
Georgics:	one every 436.4 lines
Aeneid:	one every 1,400.7 lines

The repetition of the same pattern four or more times in succession occurs nineteen times in Lucretius, or once every 386.1 lines; there are two instances in Catullus LXIV, or once every 188.5 lines, and in one of these we find *sdss* in six lines (99-104), a fivefold repetition. The poets after Vergil tend to avoid the concentration on the same pattern in adjacent lines, with the exception of Manilius (once every 464.2 lines) and Valerius Flaccus (once every 558.5 lines). Horace has only one instance in the 4,080 verses of the *Satires* and *Epistles* (*sdss* five times in succession in *Sat.* II, 5, 96-100). The frequencies in other poets are as follows:

Ovid, *Metamorphoses:*	one every 1,084.8 lines
Lucan:	one every 2,005.3 lines
Statius, *Thebaid:*	one every 1,617.2 lines[2]
Silius Italicus:	one every 1,355.2 lines
Juvenal:	one every 1,892.5 lines

In the Late Empire the use of the same pattern four times in succession is very rare, and we almost never find the same pattern in five adjacent lines.[3]

Often the same pattern may occur frequently but separated by one or two verses; I call these repetitions "near repeats" and when they appear, as often happens, in the vicinity of the repeats, they form what may be termed "repeat clusters." In *Aen.* V, 632-647, we have the repetition of *dsss* as follows:

632: o patria et rapti nequiquam ex hoste penates,
633: nullane iam Troiae dicentur moenia? nusquam
635: quin agite et mecum infaustas exurite puppis.
636: nam mihi Cassandrae per somnum vatis imago
638: hic domus est" inquit "vobis." iam tempus agi res
641: haec memorans prima infensum vi corripit ignem
644: Iliadum. hic una e multis, quae maxima natu,
646: "Non Beroe vobis, non haec Rhoeteia, matres,
647: est Dorycli coniunx; divini signa decoris

In this passage the same pattern appears nine times in sixteen lines, with three repeats (632-633, 635-636, 646-647) and five near repeats (633 and 635, 636 and 638, 638 and 641, 641 and 644, 644 and 646). I have, somewhat arbitrarily, limited the "repeat clusters" to those passages in which *six or more* instances of the same pattern are found in *sixteen or fewer* lines.

The frequency of these clusters in Vergil is as follows:

Eclogues:	3 clusters, one every 275.0 lines
Georgics:	15 clusters, one every 145.5 lines
Aeneid:	49 clusters, one every 200.1 lines[4]

12

The extent to which Vergil departed from his predecessors in his avoidance of repeat clusters is truly amazing:

Cicero, *Aratea:*   one every 59.6 lines
Lucretius: one every 49.2 lines
Catullus LXIV: one every 29.0 lines

The frequencies among the later poets are in general higher than in the *Aeneid*, for example:

Horace: one every 156.9 lines
Ovid, *Metamorphoses:*   one every 112.5 lines
Manilius: one every 83.6 lines
Lucan: one every 82.7 lines
Valerius Flaccus: one every 44.7 lines
Statius, *Thebaid:*   one every 101.1 lines
Silius Italicus: one every 187.6 lines

In the Silver Age only Valerius Flaccus has a frequency (44.7) resembling that of the Republican poets. Among the later poets repeat clusters are unusually rare in Serenus (once every 275.3 verses), Ausonius (one instance in the 480 verses of the *Mosella*), and Prudentius (once every 311.0 lines); they are much more numerous in many other late poets:

Claudian I: one every 67.8 lines
Claudian II: one every 78.9 lines
Avitus: one every 65.3 lines
Dracontius: one every 78.1 lines
Cyprian: one every 54.0 lines
Arator: one every 67.2 lines
Corippus: one every 51.2 lines[5]

I return now to the repeats (the same pattern two or more times in adjacent lines = R) and the near repeats (the same pattern separated by one or two lines = NR). For instance, in *Aen.* IX, 381-389, where *dsss* occurs six times in nine lines, the distribution is as follows: 381, 382, 383, 386, 387, 389; for my calculations I consider that we have here three adjacent repeats (381-382, 382-383, 386-387) and two near repeats (383 and 386, with two lines between; 387 and 389, with one line intervening).

The frequencies of the repeats in Vergil are as follows:

Eclogues: 63 R, one every 13.1 lines
Georgics: 177 R, one every 12.3 lines
Aeneid: 789 R, one every 12.4 lines[6]

Vergil's desire to avoid excessive repetition again becomes apparent when we examine the corresponding frequencies in earlier Greek and Latin hexameter poetry — one repeat every *x* lines, as follows: Homer (1,920 verses), 8.8; Theocritus, 8.2; Callimachus, 5.4; Apollonius of Rhodes, 7.7; Lucretius, 8.8; Catullus LXIV, 7.0. Only Cicero in the *Aratea*, one repeat every 11.4 lines, approaches Vergil. Among the later poets, by far the majority ranges from one every eight lines (cf. Valerius Flaccus, 8.6) to one every eleven lines (cf. Ovid, *Metamorphoses*, 10.7). The frequencies closely resembling that of the *Aeneid* are those in Statius, *Thebaid*, 12.1, and *Silvae*, 12.2; Silius Italicus, 11.8; Juvenal, 12.0, and Serenus, 12.1.[7] A few poets use repeated passages more sparingly than Vergil, e.g., Horace, one every 13.0 lines; Grattius, 16.3; Nemesianus, *Cynegetica*, 14.8, and *Eclogues*, 15.2; Sidonius, 16.1.

The figures for the repeats plus the near repeats (as defined above) are the following in Vergil:

Eclogues: 161 R + NR, one every 5.1 lines
Georgics: 482 R + NR, one every 4.5 lines
Aeneid: 2,112 R + NR, one every 4.6 lines

Frequencies considerably higher than those of Vergil appear in several poets:

Cicero, *Aratea:*	one R + NR every 3.9 lines
Lucretius:	one R + NR every 3.6 lines
Catullus LXIV:	one R + NR every 3.0 lines
Persius:	one R + NR every 3.9 lines
Valerius Flaccus:	one R + NR every 3.5 lines
Claudian I:	one R + NR every 3.6 lines
Cyprian of Gaul:	one R + NR every 3.2 lines[8]

In many works the frequency of the repeats plus the near repeats resembles that in the *Aeneid,* or is even lower; for instance:

Horace:	one R + NR every 4.8 lines
Grattius:	one R + NR every 4.9 lines
Germanicus, *Aratea:*	one R + NR every 4.5 lines
Silius Italicus:	one R + NR every 4.6 lines
Juvenal:	one R + NR every 4.8 lines
Nemesianus, *Cyng.*:	one R + NR every 5.2 lines
Nemesianus, *Ecl.*:	one R + NR every 4.6 lines
Avienus, *Aratea:*	one R + NR every 5.1 lines
Ausonius, *Mosella:*	one R + NR every 5.3 lines
Paulinus of Pella:	one R + NR every 5.6 lines

By far the majority of the repeats and the near repeats occurs in the patterns appearing most frequently; e.g., in the *Georgics* of Vergil *dsss* occurs in 15.81 per cent of the total verses, but the *dsss* repeats comprise 29.38 per cent of the total number of repeats and, if we include the near repeats, the percentage rises slightly to 31.33. In the *Aeneid,* where the *dsss* frequency is 14.39 per cent, we find 175 *dsss* repeats, or 22.18 per cent of the total repeats and, with the near repeats added, 23.15 per cent. The proportion of the *dsss* repeats to the total occurrences of *dsss* in the *Georgics* is 15.07 per cent, and it rises to 43.77 per cent when we include the near repeats. The corresponding percentages in the *Aeneid* are 12.40 and 34.66. I shall show in the following tabulation how Vergil's percentages for his favorite pattern compare with those of other poets, both earlier and later (R = repeats, R + NR = repeats plus near repeats, as above):

		I	II	III	IV	V
	Pattern with most R	% total verses	R, % total R	R, % total pattern	R + NR, % total R + NR	R + NR, % total pattern
Cicero, *Arat.*:	*dsss*	17.95	40.48	19.77	24.39	34.88
Lucretius:	*dsss*	20.20	37.60	21.20	36.30	50.17
Catullus LXIV:	*dsss*	27.59	44.44	23.08	41.60	50.0
Verg., *Georg.*:	*dsss*	15.81	29.38	15.07	31.33	43.77
Verg., *Aen.*:	*dsss*	14.39	22.18	12.40	23.15	34.66
Horace:	*dsss*	12.67	20.06	12.19	21.21	34.62
Ovid, *Metam.*:	*dsss*[9]	12.74	18.08	13.47	17.21	33.60
Manilius:	*dsss*	17.33	32.67	18.09	31.25	44.20
Lucan:	*dsss*	15.40	26.74	15.30	25.26	39.11
Valerius Fl.:	*dsds*	22.65	46.37	23.72	42.86	53.36
Statius, *Theb.*:	*dsds*	16.24	30.88	15.67	27.75	39.72
Statius, *Silv.*:	*dsds*	16.47	33.21	16.48	28.08	39.19
Silius Ital.:	*dsss*	13.04	19.71	12.82	19.30	32.37
Juvenal:	*dsss*	13.66	26.67	16.25	22.66	34.24
Claudian I:	*dsds*	18.27	36.63	19.59	31.10	47.30
Claudian II:	*dsds*	18.93	35.45	18.66	32.37	43.06[10]

The lower the ratio of the most frequent repeats (and repeats plus near repeats) to the total repeats (and total repeats plus near repeats) or to the total of the pattern, the less monotonous the meter becomes in any particular poem. It will be evident from the lists as given above that Vergil's

Georgics in this respect provide a transition from the higher percentages of the Republican poets to the low and more satisfying percentages of the *Aeneid*, Horace, Ovid's *Metamorphoses,* and Silius Italicus.[11] These four poets take the greatest pains to avoid excessive repetition of one particular pattern. In the Empire a high concentration on the most repeated pattern appears again in Manilius, Valerius Flaccus, and Claudian, with Lucan, Statius, and Juvenal midway between the two extremes.[12]

The percentages from column to column are remarkably consistent, whether on a high level (e.g., Catullus LXIV, Valerius Flaccus) or on a low level (e.g., Vergil's *Aeneid*, Silius Italicus). The repeats of the favorite pattern, *dsss* or *dsds,* comprise in each instance a percentage of the total repeats (Column II) which regularly is about one and one-half to two times the frequency of the pattern (Column I), and this latter percentage is approximately the same as the ratio of the *dsss* or *dsds* repeats to the total pattern (Column III). The ratio of the *dsss* or *dsds* repeats plus near repeats to the total repeats plus near repeats (Column IV) is in most instances close to that of the *dsss* or *dsds* repeats to the total repeats (Column II).[13] The ratio of the *dsss* or *dsds* repeats plus near repeats to the total pattern (Column V) is usually from two to two and one-half times that of the repeats to the total pattern (Column III).

In other words, the percentages in Columns I and III have a close correlation, as do those in Columns II and IV, but those in Columns II and IV are almost twice those in Columns I and III, and those in Column V are more than twice those in Columns I and III.[14]

These statistical distinctions may seem to involve wearisome minutiae, but later in the volume they will provide helpful criteria in matters of disputed dating or authenticity. On occasion, the details concerning the second most repeated pattern (e.g., *ddss* in Lucretius, Vergil's *Aeneid*, Ovid's *Metamorphoses,* and Valerius Flaccus; *dsds* in Vergil's *Georgics*, Horace, and Lucan; *sdss* in Silius Italicus and Juvenal; *dsss* in Statius' *Thebaid* and *Silvae,* and in Claudian) may also furnish corroborative evidence of value.

Notes to Chapter 3

1. La Roche, *WS* 23 (1901), p. 135, adds an eighth instance, *ddss* in *Aen.* XI, 507-510, but he reads *supera* in 510 with Ribbeck, not *supra,* as in Hirtzel and other editions.

2. In the *Silvae* of Statius the frequency is over twice as high, one instance every 663.2 lines.

3. The exact opposite is true of late Greek hexameter poetry, where fourfold and fivefold repetition becomes increasingly common: Quintus of Smyrna, one instance every 73.8 lines; Nonnus, 96.0; Musaeus, 85.3. In Quintus' *Posthomerica,* I, 112-119, *dddd* appears *eight* times in succession.

4. In *Aeneid* I-IX we find one cluster every 271.0 lines; in X-XII they appear more than twice as often, once every 119.9 lines; this is another of the many features which indicate that the last three books of the epic did not receive a final metrical revision; see below, Chapter 7.

5. Cf., however, the excessive use of repeat clusters in the late Greek poets: Quintus of Smyrna, one every 18.5 lines; Nonnus, 15.7; Musaeus, 17.1.

6. The large number of repeat clusters in *Aeneid* X-XII (see above, note 4) would of course indicate that these books contain a higher number of repeats, one every 11.4 lines, than we find in the other nine books, one every 12.9 lines.

7. There is considerable variation from book to book in the longer works, but each poet stays in his approximate range: e.g., Vergil, *Aeneid* (average, one every 12.4 lines), from 10.4 (VIII) to 15.4 (V); Ovid, *Metamorphoses* (average, 10.7), from 9.1 (III) to 12.7 (I); Lucan (average, 11.4), from 10.2 (II) to 13.6 (X); Valerius Flaccus (average, 8.6), from 7.6 (VIII) to 9.8 (II); Silius Italicus (average, 11.8), from 9.5 (VIII) to 14.9 (XVII).

8. The frequencies of repeats plus near repeats are high throughout Greek hexameter poetry; e.g., Homer, one instance every 3.5 lines; Theocritus, 3.1; Callimachus, 2.7; Quintus of Smyrna, 2.2.

9. Ovid's favorite pattern is *ddss,* 13.08 per cent of the total verses, but *dsss* has the most repeats.

10. The percentages are practically identical in Claudian I, selected invectives and panegyrics, and in Claudian II, his mythological epic *De raptu Proserpinae.* Differences in literary genres and in subject matter have almost no effect on the metrical procedures of most poets; cf. above the percentages in Statius' *Thebaid,* a long epic, with those in his *Silvae,* short occasional poems.

11. Cicero's percentages are high in the case of the *dsss* repeats (Columns II and III), but those dealing with *dsss* repeats plus near repeats (Columns IV and V) resemble those in Vergil's *Aeneid* and Horace.

12. In the case of the repeats plus near repeats, Juvenal's percentages, like those of Cicero, fall to the level of those in the *Aeneid* and Horace; see Columns IV and V.

13. The most striking exception in the lists given above is Cicero's *Aratea: dsss* repeats, 40.48 per cent of the total repeats; *dsss* repeats plus total repeats, 24.39 per cent of the total repeats plus near repeats; see above, note 11.

14. I omit detailed statistics such as these for the most repeated pattern in Greek hexameter poetry, usually *dddd,* where the percentage of total repeats ranges from 25.96 in Hesiod and 41.28 in Homer to 66.50 in Quintus of Smyrna and 71.43 in Musaeus. These percentages are likewise about one and one-half to two times the normal frequency of the pattern (Hesiod, 18.23; Homer, 21.36; Quintus of Smyrna, 38.75; Musaeus, 36.07).

Chapter 4

VARIETY IN REPEATED PATTERNS: FOURTH-FOOT TEXTURE

I wish now to examine various aspects of variety to be found in the same pattern repeated in adjacent lines ("repeats") or separated by one or two verses ("near repeats"). Even when the identical pattern appears in two or more lines in succession, and occasionally in "repeat clusters" (the same pattern six or more times in sixteen or fewer lines), Vergil and other poets are able to vary the effect of the repeated patterns by one or more of several devices. I propose to list the three more obvious devices briefly and to concentrate on the fourth, which, to the best of my knowledge, has not hitherto been applied to the problem of metrical variety. Unless otherwise noted, all verses cited below are taken from *Aeneid* IV.

1. The metrical pattern is the same, but there is a definite variation in the sound effects produced by the vowels and consonants, especially alliteration and assonance.

90 *(dsss):* Quam simul ac tali persensit peste teneri
91 *(dsss):* cara Iovis coniunx nec famam obstare furori (*s, t, p*, and *e* sounds in 90; *c, a, o*, and *f* in 91)

186 *(dsss):* luce sedet custos aut summi culmine tecti
187 *(dsss):* turribus aut altis, et magnas territat urbes (*s* and *c* consonants followed by *t* and *r; u* and *e* shifting to *u* and *a*)

482 *(dsss):* axem umero torquet stellis ardentibus aptum:
483 *(dsss):* hinc mihi Massylae gentis monstrata sacerdos (alliteration: *a* in 482, *m* in 483)

526 *(dsds):* quaeque lacus late liquidos quaeque aspera dumis
527 *(dsds):* rura tenent, somno positae sub nocte silenti. (repetition of *quaeque* and alliteration of *l* in 526; *t, n, s*, and *o* sounds stressed in 527)

554 *(ssss):* Aeneas celsa in puppi iam certus eundi
555 *(ssss):* carpebat somnos rebus iam rite paratis (intricate interweaving of *c, p*, and *r* consonants; vowels mostly *a* and *e*)

2. The metrical pattern is the same, but the variation results from the different position of the sense-pauses (both primary and secondary).[1]

62 *(sdsd):* aut ante ora deum // pinguis spatiatur ad aras,
63 *(sdsd):* instauratque diem donis, // pecudumque reclusis

155 *(ddds):* pulverulenta fuga glomerant // montisque relinquunt.
156 *(ddds):* at puer Ascanius // mediis in vallibus acri

163 *(ddds):* Dardaniusque nepos Veneris // diversa per agros
164 *(ddds):* tecta metu petiere; // ruunt de montibus amnes.

223 *(ddds):* "vade age, // nate, voca Zephyros // et labere pennis
224 *(ddds):* Dardaniumque ducem, // Tyria Karthagine qui nunc

283 *(dsss):* heu quid agat? // quo nunc reginam ambire furentem
284 *(dsss):* audeat adfatu? // quae prima exordia sumat?

381 *(ddsd):* i, sequere Italiam ventis, // pete regna per undas.
382 *(ddsd):* spero equidem mediis, // si quid pia numina possunt,

383 *(dsds):* supplicia hausurum scopulis // et nomine Dido
384 *(dsds):* saepe vocaturum. // sequar atris ignibus absens

450 *(ssss):* Tum vero infelix // fatis exterrita Dido
451 *(ssss):* mortem orat; // taedet caeli // convexa tueri.

3. The metrical pattern is the same, but the variation results from the different types of dactyls and spondees; these determine (or, more probably, are determined by) the arrangement of caesuras and diaereses in each line. I list the structure of the dactyls and spondees in parallel columns:[2]

Dactyls	Spondees
1. one word alone	a. one word alone
2. two complete words, mono-syllable and dissyllable	b. two complete words
3. two complete words, dissyl-lable and monosyllable	
4. monosyllable and part of next word	c. monosyllable and part of next word
5. elided dissyllable and part of next word	
6. dissyllable and part of next word	
7. long = part of one word; 2 shorts = one word	
8. first two syllables = part of one word; 2nd short = mono-syllable	d. part of one word and monosyl-lable
9. long = part of one word; 2 shorts part of another	e. parts of two words
10. 1st two syllables = part of one word; 2nd short part of an-other	
11. from first part of a polysyl-labic word	f. first two syllables of a polysyl-labic word
12. from second part of a poly-syllabic word	g. last two syllables of a polysyl-labic word
13. two whole words and part of a third	
14. long = part of one word; 1st short = monosyllable; 2nd short = part of next word	
15. three words (monosyllables or elided dissyllables)	

I list below several repeated patterns from *Aeneid* IV, indicating the nature of each dactyl and spondee by the appropriate number and letter as given in the lists above:

               6   d   c   e   12   a
9 *(dsss):* "Anna soror, quae me suspensam insomnia terrent!
             2   c   e   g   l   a
10 *(dsss):* quis novus hic nostris successit sedibus hospes,

            b   f   9   e   10   g
18 *(ssds):* si non pertaesum thalami taedaeque fuisset,
           c   e   9   e   12   a
19 *(ssds):* huic uni forsan potui succumbere culpae

          11   10   9   e   10   g
155 *(ddds):* pulverulenta fuga glomerant montisque relinquunt.
          2   11   9   d   l   a
156 *(ddds):* at puer Ascanius mediis in vallibus acri

          11   10   9   e   8   a
163 *(ddds):* Dardaniusque nepos Veneris diversa per agros

6 9 10 d 1 a
164 *(ddds):* tecta metu petiere; ruunt de montibus amnes.

2 6 9 d 1 a
223 *(ddds):* "vade age, nate, voca Zephyros et labere pennis
11 10 9 e 12 b
224 *(ddds):* Dardaniumque ducem, Tyria Karthagine qui nunc

6 9 e e 10 g
205 *(ddss):* multa Iovem manibus supplex orasse supinis:
1 11 d c 12 a
206 *(ddss):* "Iuppiter omnipotens cui nunc Maurusia pictis
4 10 e g 6 g
207 *(ddss):* gens epulata toris Lenaeum libat honorem,

An examination of the numbers and letters placed over each foot in the passages given above reveals clearly how different is the structure of both dactyls and spondees in the repeated metrical patterns.

4. The metrical pattern is the same, but we find a variation in the fourth-foot texture; that is, the fourth foot shifts from heterodyne (clash of word accent and metrical ictus) to homodyne (coincidence of accent and ictus), or from homodyne to heterodyne.

The importance of fourth-foot texture has been stressed by Jackson Knight, who points out the different effects achieved by heterodyne (resistance, difficulty, effort, weariness, pathos) and homodyne (rapidity, smoothness, freedom from restraint and tension) and shows that Vergil, unlike most Latin hexameter poets (both earlier and later), reduced the amount of fourth-foot homodyne from 50 or 60 per cent to about 35 per cent.[3] His percentages are these: *Eclogues,* 37.27; *Georgics,* 33.45; and *Aeneid,* 35.95. I am not now concerned with the simple, compound, and complex patterns which Jackson Knight finds in fourth-foot texture, nor with the correlation between his various symmetrical patterns and the mathematical proportions which appear in the same passages.[4] The important thing here is to examine the many repeated metrical patterns and to discover the extent to which fourth-foot texture provides effective variety in such repetitions. For this purpose I have had to recheck Vergil's hexameters for homodyned and heterodyned verses, and my percentages are slightly higher than those of Jackson Knight, as follows: *Eclogues,* 39.73; *Georgics,* 36.08; and *Aeneid,* 37.78.[5]

I have followed, as closely as possible, Jackson Knight's procedure, but I have changed certain verses: e.g., Jackson Knight lists *Aen.* IV, 165 *(ssss),* as heterodyne: *speluncam Dido dux et Troianus eandem,*[6] but there seems no clash here in the fourth foot, and this verse I believe to be homodyne. On the other hand, *Aen.* VII, 136-137 *(ddds, ssds):*

implicat et geniumque loci primamque deorum
Tellurem Nymphasque et adhuc ignota precatur

two verses which Jackson Knight lists as homodyne[7] seem clearly examples of heterodyne. These two verses would be considered by Woodward to belong to a separate category: spondaic fourth feet in which there is no accented syllable.[8] But fourth feet such as *lo/cí pri/mamque* and *ad/húc ig/nota* are certainly not homodyned, and I include them among non-homodyned feet (= heterodyned).

Also, I accent two-syllable words on the first syllable. Townend has recently argued for an oxytone accent for many two-syllable words, under certain conditions: (1) parts of *ille* and *iste* and their derivative adverbs, (2) *ergo,* (3) parts of *quantus* and *qualis* and of their demonstratives, (4) compound words such as *quamvis, postquam, quare,* (5) *inter* and a few other disyllabic prepositions, (6) *donec, contra, primum, verum,* (7) *quorum* and *quarum,* (8) parts of *ipse* and *idem,* (9) *eheu* and *euhoe,* (10) *exim* and *olim,* (11) *princeps, praeceps, felix.*[9]

Getty says:[10]

> Townend's work has been strangely ignored, perhaps because its startling departures from the law of the penultimate may seem unaccountably heretical.... But, unless he is systematically refuted, particularly by orthodox upholders of the ictus-accent theory, he continues to suggest awkward questions.

I do not attempt a systematic refutation, but the fact that so many of these same dissyllables occur in the sixth foot, where the paroxytone accent is necessary, argues against Townend.   Ashcroft says:[11]

> Vergil's rule, therefore, is not simply that "the fifth foot shall be a dactyl," but also
> that *in the two final feet of the line scansion and pronunciation must coincide.*

In other words, the first syllable in the sixth foot bears the accent.[12]

I give merely a few of the words in Townend's lists which appear in the sixth foot, with the accent on the first syllable:

> *illuc* (*Aen.* IV, 285; VIII, 20, 229; X, 680);
> *ergo* (*Aen.* VI, 456, 670);
> *tandem* (*Aen.* III, 205; VII, 297);
> *numquam* (*Aen.* VIII, 470; XII, 921);
> *umquam* (*Ecl.* VIII, 7; *Aen.* VIII, 569);
> *nusquam* (*Aen.* II, 438; V, 633);
> *usquam* (four times);[13]
> *donec* (*Aen.* XI, 201);
> *contra* (twelve times);[14]
> *primum* (six times);[15]
> *olim* (eight times);[16]
> *praeceps* (*Aen.* III, 598).

These, I trust, will give me added support for my accenting of dissyllables as paroxytone.

Townend believes that many lines which Jackson Knight counts as homodyne should be heterodyne, and "much more often lines which he counts as heterodyne will become homodyne."[17] He says of *Aen.* I, 1:

> arma virumque cano, Troiae qui primus ab oris

"the oxytone accent makes the fourth foot homodyne."[18] But I agree with Jackson Knight[19] that the fourth foot *(Tro/iae qui)* is heterodyned; Wilkinson says:[20]

> Virgil was at pains to make ictus and accent conflict in the fourth foot where there
> was a choice: thus he wrote *Tro/iae qui / primus* for *qui / Troiae / primus.*

Vergil's repeated patterns may have the same fourth-foot texture, either homodyne *(m)* or heterodyne *(t)*,[21] as, for example, in *Aeneid* IV:

9 *(dsss)*:	"Anna soror, quae me suspensam insomnia terrent!	*(m)*
10 *(dsss)*:	quis novus hic nostris successit sedibus hospes,	*(m)*
18 *(ssds)*:	si non pertaesum thalami taedaeque fuisset,	*(t)*
19 *(ssds)*:	huic uni forsan potui succumbere culpae.	*(t)*

Or the texture may shift either from heterodyne to homodyne, as in:

68 *(dsss)*:	uritur infelix Dido totaque vagatur	*(t)*
69 *(dsss)*:	urbe furens, qualis coniecta cerva sagitta	*(m)*

or from homodyne to heterodyne, e.g.:

348 *(sdss)*:	Phoenissam Libycaeque aspectus detinet urbis	*(m)*
349 *(sdss)*:	quae tandem Ausonia Teucros considere terra	*(t)*

When the same metrical pattern occurs in three verses in succession, we often find a double shift; that is, one kind of texture is enclosed by the other:

75 *(dsds)*:	Sidoniasque ostentat opes urbemque paratam	*(t)*
76 *(dsds)*:	incipit effari mediaque in voce resistit;	*(m)*
77 *(dsds)*:	nunc eadem labente die convivia quaerit,	*(t)*
584 *(sdss)*:	Et iam prima novo spargebat lumine terras	*(m)*
585 *(sdss)*:	Tithoni croceum linquens Aurora cubile.	*(t)*
586 *(sdss)*:	regina e speculis ut primam albescere lucem	*(m)*

The second illustration is the more unusual, in view of the fact that fourth-foot heterodyne appears in Vergil in more than 60 per cent of the verses, fourth-foot homodyne in less than 40 per cent; in passages such as this, the ratio of homodyne to heterodyne is two to one.[22]

The shifting of fourth-foot texture to vary the effect in passages where the same metrical pattern occurs is true also of near repeats; cf., e.g., the repeat cluster in *Aen.* III, 709-718, where *dsss* appears seven times in ten lines, at the very end of the book:

> 709: heu, genitorem, omnis curae casusque levamen *(t)*
> 711: deseris, heu, tantis nequiquam erepte periclis! *(m)*
> 713: hos mihi praedixit luctus, non dira Celaeno. *(t)*
> 714: hic labor extremus, longarum haec meta viarum. *(m)*
> 716: Sic pater Aeneas intentis omnibus unus *(m)*
> 717: fata renarrabat divum cursusque docebat. *(t)*
> 718: conticuit tandem factoque hic fine quievit. *(m)*

The ratio of homodyne to heterodyne is here four to three, and the change from one texture to the other occurs five times out of a possible six. This shift in fourth-foot texture helps to relieve the monotony which would otherwise result from the excessive repetition of *dsss* in this passage.[23]

I give below the percentages of the change in fourth-foot texture for the repeated patterns in the *Eclogues, Georgics,* and *Aeneid* and the relation of these percentages to the percentages of fourth-foot homodyne, and I provide the same information for the pattern in each work which is repeated most frequently:

	Eclogues	*Georgics*	*Aeneid*
% of 4th-foot homodyne:	39.73	36.08	37.78
Total R, % of change:	49.21	43.50	44.49
Differs from homodyne %:	+9.48	+7.42	+6.71[24]
Total R + NR, % of change:	44.10	47.10	45.83
Differs from homodyne %:	+4.37	+11.02	+8.05
Favorite repeat	*ddss*	*dsss*	*dsss*
R, % of change:	45.0	50.0	45.14
Differs from homodyne %:	+5.27	+13.92	+7.36
R + NR, % of change:	46.15	45.70	49.28
Differs from homodyne %:	+6.42	+9.62	+11.50

Since these percentages of change in fourth-foot texture consistently run higher than the percentages of fourth-foot homodyne, we have here an indication that Vergil uses this shift from homodyne to heterodyne and *vice versa* as an additional means to provide variety and to counteract the effect of the monotony inherent in the repetition of the same metrical patterns. That Vergil does this deliberately is implied by the fact that comparable increases over the fourth-foot homodyne percentage are found in so few other Latin poets. When variation from the homodyne percentage occurs, it is all too often on the minus side, and this indicates that most poets had far less regard than Vergil for variety in repeated patterns. In the following tabulation of the major poets, I shall omit the percentages of change and give only the variation, plus or minus, from the percentages of fourth-foot homodyne; Column I gives the fourth-foot homodyne percentage; Columns II and III the variation in total repeats and total R + NR; Columns V and VI give the same information for the pattern most frequently repeated, which is listed in Column IV:

	I	II	III	IV	V	VI
Cicero, *Arat.:*	44.79	+5.21	+0.74	*dsss*	+14.03	+5.21
Lucretius:	47.66	+2.16	+0.41	*dsss*	+1.70	+0.52
Catullus LXIV:	60.44	-25.25	-26.84	*dsss*	-22.94	-25.82
Horace:	48.54	-1.09	+0.63	*dsss*	-2.51	+4.53
Ovid, *Metam.:*	50.0	-3.09	-3.81	*dsss*	+1.49	+2.28
German., *Arat.:*	35.83	+8.29	+5.23	*dsss*	+32.92	+11.67
Manilius:	39.33	+10.05	+6.67	*dsss*	+14.87	+7.86

	I	II	III	IV	V	VI
Calpurnius S.:	61.08	-19.75	-23.30	ddsd	-14.02	-30.78
Lucan:	37.08	+2.01	-1.52	dsss	+11.07	+7.23
Valerius Fl.:	31.70	-0.79	+0.50	dsds	-16.37	-14.37
Statius, *Theb.*:	40.18	+0.45	-0.29	dsds	-15.08	-12.02
Statius, *Silv.*:	38.41	-5.94	-3.37	dsds	-25.08	-19.62
Silius Ital.:	42.95	+3.14	+3.17	dsss	+1.66	+1.52
Juvenal:	48.93	-8.29	-5.65	dsss	-1.31	-5.43
Claudian I:	33.96	-6.80	-4.35	dsds	-20.17	-20.56
Claudian II:	31.86	+4.50	+1.23	dsds	-8.78	-15.19
Cyprian	34.16	-12.21	-11.23	ssds	-31.53	-31.94

Of the poets listed above, Germanicus Caesar, Manilius, and Statius have low percentages of fourth-foot homodyne which resemble those of Vergil; Valerius Flaccus, Claudian, and Cyprian of Gaul are even lower. In only a very few poets do we find percentages of change which show such increases over the homodyne percentages as appear in the three works of Vergil: these include Cicero (especially the most repeated pattern), Germanicus, Manilius, and Lucan (most repeated pattern only); Valerius Flaccus, Claudian,[25] and Cyprian, who have unusually low percentages of fourth-foot homodyne, are heavily on the minus side. I have added Cyprian to the list given above, not because I consider him a "major poet," but in order to illustrate the almost complete failure to change fourth-foot texture in the pattern most frequently repeated *(ssds):* the percentage of change in the *ssds* repeats is 2.63; in the *ssds* repeats plus near repeats it is 2.22!

If several verses have the same metrical pattern, the same word structure (= the same pattern of caesura and diaeresis), the same sense pauses, and the same fourth-foot texture, we may speak of them as having "rhythmical identity."[26] To illustrate from the *Aeneid*, I cite the following:

> I, 226: constitit et Libyae // defixit lumina regnis.
> 265: tertia dum Latio // regnantem viderit aestas,
> 291: aspera tum positis // mitescent saecula bellis;

These verses are identical, all *ddss*, all with the same sense pauses (penthemimeral), the same word structure, the same fourth-foot texture (homodyne). But when verses which are rhythmically identical are separated by twenty-five or thirty verses, as here, they are not objectionable. On the other hand, when repeat clusters contain a number of verses identical or almost identical in all these respects, we have a monotonous type of poetic composition which *is* most objectionable. We shall see later[27] that Valerius Flaccus is especially culpable in this regard, but I cite here *Argon.* I, 546-555, where the same pattern occurs seven times in ten lines:

> 546: perque hiemes, // Bellona, tibi. // nec vellera tantum
> 548: ille dolor, // sed (nulla magis // sententia menti
> 550: qui gemitus // irasque pares // et mutua Grais
> 551: dona ferat. // quae classe dehinc // effusa procorum
> 553: quot proceres // natosque deum, // quae robora cernes
> 554: oppetere et // magnis Asiam // concedere fatis!
> 555: hinc Danaum // de fine sedet // gentesque fovebo

All seven verses contain the metrical pattern *dsds*, all have almost the same sequence of caesuras and diaereses, and, as a result almost the same word-imposition pattern (546, 550, and 553 are identical, and 548 and 551 practically so); in addition, all seven have the same sense pauses in the second and fourth feet, and all have fourth-foot heterodyne. Fortunately, Vergil and most Latin poets avoid the monotony which results from the rhythmical identity occurring in repeat clusters of this type.

Notes to Chapter 4

1. I avoid the term "caesura" here, which I used in this same context in *TAPhA* 95 (1964), p. 40. Cooper, *Introduction to the Latin Hexameter,* p. 21, defines caesura as "no more and no less than the ending of a word within a foot.... Caesura (in the Classical sense) is to be thought of, not as a break, but as a bond. Its principal service in poetry is to link foot with foot, so keeping the line from falling apart."

2. For the following analysis I am indebted to Bolaños, *Estudios Virgilianos,* pp. 85-97. He lists the first thirteen kinds of dactyls (with illustrations from *Georg.* II, 358-408) and the seven kinds of spondees (as seen in *Aen.* II, 281, 296), and comments on their importance in producing effective variations. He does not, however, apply this material to a study of repeated metrical patterns. Also, he omits Nos. 14 and 15 from his list of dactyls. I am indebted to Professor Gilbert Highet of Columbia University for calling to my attention dactyls composed of three syllables, e.g., *Aen.* VI, 791: *hic vir, hic,* and I discuss this type of dactyl (three monosyllables or elided dissyllables) below in Appendix B.

3. Jackson Knight, *Accentual Symmetry in Vergil,* esp. pp. 36-43; cf. also his *Vergil's Troy,* pp. 17-54 [= *Vergil: Epic and Anthropology,* pp. 31-59]; *Roman Vergil,* pp. 292-296 (rev. edition). See Wilkinson, *Golden Latin Artistry,* pp. 120-132; Wilkinson prefers the term "Pulse-Accent theory" to "Ictus-Accent theory."

4. See Duckworth, *Structural Patterns,* pp. 111-117.

5. The percentages of Brown, *Numeri Vergiliani,* p. 63, note 1, are also higher for the individual *Eclogues* than those of Jackson Knight. Brown does not give a total for the *Eclogues* as a whole. In my percentages for fourth-foot homodyne I ignore all corrupt and interpolated lines but include spondaic verses.

6. *Accentual Symmetry,* p. 57.

7. *Ibid.,* p. 47.

8. Woodward, *PhQ* 15 (1936), pp. 126-135; see Jackson Knight, *Accentual Symmetry,* pp. 95-98. Sandbach, *CR* 47 (1933), p. 74, objects to viewing *Aen.* I, 6: *inferretque deos Latio — genus unde Latinum* as fourth-foot heterodyne; but how can *Lati/o genus /* be homodyned (ictus on last syllable of *Latio,* accent on first syllable of *genus*)?

9. Townend, *AJPh* 71 (1950), pp. 22-39, 365-378. The list given above appears on page 365, but on page 33 Townend gives (in addition to *quamvis, postquam,* and *quare*) such compounds as *mecum, tecum, secum, quocum, etsi, tandem, quamquam, (n)umquam, (n)usquam, nondum, necdum, vixdum,* etc.

10. *Lustrum* 8 (1963), pp. 123-124.

11. *G & R* 20 (1951), p. 98. The italics are those of Ashcroft.

12. Verses with a final monosyllable, e.g., *Aen.* IV, 132 *(odora canum vis)* and 314 *(dextramque tuam te),* are exceptions and designed for special effects; see Marouzeau, *Traité de stylistique latine,* pp. 313-316; Austin, *Aeneidos Liber Quartus,* on IV, 132; Hellegouarc'h, *Le monosyllable dans l'hexamètre latin,* pp. 50-69.

13. *Aen.* II, 142; VII, 311; VIII, 568; IX, 420; *usquam* occurs in the *Aeneid* eight times, and four occurrences are in the sixth foot.

14. *Aen.* III, 552; V, 27; IX, 136, 377, 509, 795; X, 16, 285, 343, 359; XI, 374, 873.

15. *Ecl.* IV, 8; *Georg.* I, 61; *Aen.* III, 209; VIII, 408; IX, 253, 603.

16. *Ecl.* II, 37; *Georg.* IV, 433; *Aen.* I, 653; V, 125, 264, 536; IX, 360; X, 12.

17. *AJPh* 71 (1950), p. 374, note 11.

18. *Ibid.,* p. 371; cf. pp. 29-30.

19. *Accentual Symmetry,* p. 49.

20. *CQ* 34 (1940), p. 33; Cf. Wilkinson, *Golden Latin Artistry,* pp. 232-233.

21. In *Structural Patterns,* pp. 111-117, I used "a" to denote fourth-foot heterodyne, "b" to denote fourth-foot homodyne; this was also the procedure of Naughtin, *CQ* 2 (1952), pp. 152-167. I now prefer, as less confusing, the letter "t" for heterodyne, "m" for homodyne.

22. For other examples of heterodyne framed by homodyne, see (in addition to *Aen.* III, 716-718, discussed below) *Ecl.* VI, 61-63 *(ddss)*; IX, 16-18 *(dssd)*; *Georg.* I, 466-468 *(dsds)*; *Aen.* VIII, 230-232 *(dsss),* 265-267 *(ddss),* 706-708 *(dsss)*; XI, 507-509 *(ddss)*; XII, 113-115 *(dsss).*

23. Note also that the three heterodyned lines have a hephthemimeral caesura; those homodyned have a penthemimeral caesura. On the interdependence of hephthemimeral caesura and fourth-foot heterodyne, see Skutsch, *CR* 54 (1940), pp. 93-95, who equates the two and says (page 95) that the speed in *impius haec tam culta novalia miles habebit (Ecl.* I, 70) "is due not to the absence of heterodyne, but to the absence of caesura or pause both from the third and fourth feet." Naughtin, *CQ* 2 (1952), p. 153, comments: "I do not agree that the whole effect of the homodyned line there quoted is explained by the absence of caesura or pause; there is a positive effect of reinforcement of the ictus by coincidence with the stress accent." Furthermore, hephthemimeral caesura does not necessarily produce heterodyne;

cf. *Aen.* IV, 98: *sed quis erit modus, aut quo nunc certamine tanto?* (hephthemimeral caesura but homodyne).

24. *Aeneid* X-XII differ strikingly from the other nine books in their shift of fourth-foot texture in repeated patterns: I-IX, percentage of change, 48.72, an increase of 10.50 over the homodyne percentage; X-XII, percentage of change, 34.85, a decrease of 1.79. The greatest decrease appears in Book XI: percentage of fourth-foot homodyne, 38.55; percentage of change, 33.33, or -5.22.

25. It is interesting to note that Claudian in his mythological epic *De raptu Proserpinae* (= Claudian II) has somewhat more regard for this type of variety than in his invectives and panegyrics (= Claudian I).

26. I am indebted for this phrase to Professor Bernard Peebles of the Catholic University of America. In a letter of February 13, 1968, he cited as examples of such "rhythmical identity" the three verses from *Aeneid* I which I quote in the text.

27. In Chapter 13.

Chapter 5

OPPOSITE AND REVERSE COMBINATIONS

Of the sixteen metrical patterns, eight are the "opposites" of the other eight; *sddd* is the opposite of *dsss*, *ssdd* of *ddss*, *sdsd* of *dsds*, etc. In addition to the eight possible opposite combinations, there are four combinations which I term "reverses," those in which the sequence of dactyls and spondees appears in reverse order, i.e., *dsss* and *sssd*, *sdss* and *ssds*, *ddds* and *sddd*, *ddsd* and *dsdd*.[1]

If we list the patterns in the order of their frequency in the *Aeneid*, it is immediately apparent that, as a general rule, the opposites of the patterns used most often occur most seldom; in other words, the more frequent a pattern, the less frequent its opposite:

	PATTERNS	OPPOSITES
1.	*dsss*	*sddd*
2.	*ddss*	*ssdd*
3.	*dsds*	*sdsd*
4.	*sdss*	*dsdd*
5.	*ssss*	*dddd*
6.	*ddds*	*sssd*
7.	*ssds*	*ddsd*
8.	*sdds*	*dssd*
9.	*dssd*	*sdds*
10.	*ddsd*	*ssds*
11.	*sdsd*	*dsds*
12.	*dsdd*	*sdss*
13.	*sssd*	*ddds*
14.	*ssdd*	*ddss*
15.	*dddd*	*ssss*
16.	*sddd*	*dsss*

The opposite of *dsss* (most frequent) is *sddd* (16th); that of *ddss* (2nd) is *ssdd* (14th); that of *sdss* (4th) is *dsdd* (12th); the opposites of Nos. 7 and 8 are 10 and 9 respectively.

Vergil's first eight patterns all have a fourth-foot spondee and a distribution of twenty spondees and twelve dactyls in the first four feet; Ovid is very different: in the *Metamorphoses* the first eight patterns all have a first-foot dactyl and a distribution of twelve spondees and twenty dactyls, the exact opposite of Vergil's procedure in the *Aeneid*. The arrangement of Ovid's patterns in their order of frequency, and of the corresponding opposites, is on page 26. This is somewhat less symmetrical than in the case of the *Aeneid* but again the opposite of the first pattern *(ddss)* is the sixteenth *(ssdd)*; the opposites of Nos. 5, 6, and 8 are also at the bottom of the list, Nos. 13, 14, and 15 respectively.

In the case of several Latin poets, the pattern used most seldom is not the opposite of the most frequent pattern; e.g., in Lucretius, Persius, and Juvenal, where the first pattern is *dsss*, *ssdd* is sixteenth, with *sddd*, the opposite of *dsss*, No. 15 in Lucretius and Persius, No. 14 in Juvenal; in Horace, Lucan, and Silius Italicus, the first pattern is likewise *dsss*, and its opposite *sddd* is again No. 15, with *dddd* the least frequent pattern. In the case of Valerius Flaccus, Statius, and Claudian, where *dsds* is the first pattern, the sixteenth is regularly *sssd*, with *sdsd*, the opposite of *dsds*, ranging from ninth to twelfth place. These variations, however, do not invalidate the general rule given above: the more frequent a pattern, the less frequent its opposite.[2]

One of the most interesting facts about the use of opposite patterns is this: there is a strong tendency for two opposites to appear in adjacent lines, sometimes with a pattern framed by its opposite; e.g., in *Aeneid* IV:

PATTERNS   OPPOSITES

1.	*ddss*	*ssdd*	
2.	*dsss*	*sddd*	
3.	*dssd*	*sdds*	
4.	*dsds*	*sdsd*	
5.	*ddsd*	*ssds*	
6.	*ddds*	*sssd*	
7.	*dsdd*	*sdss*	
8.	*dddd*	*ssss*	
9.	*sdss*	*dsdd*	
10.	*sdsd*	*dsds*	
11.	*sdds*	*dssd*	
12.	*sddd*	*dsss*	
13.	*ssds*	*ddsd*	
14.	*sssd*	*ddds*	
15.	*ssss*	*dddd*	
16.	*ssdd*	*ddss*	

---

8 *(sddd)*: cum sic unanimam adloquitur male sana sororem:
9 *(dsss)*: "Anna soror, quae me suspensam insomnia terrent!

13 *(dddd)*: degeneres animos timor arguit. heu, quibus ille
14 *(ssss)*: iactatus fatis! quae bella exhausta canebat!

51 *(sdss)*: indulge hospitio causasque innecte morandi,
52 *(dsdd)*: dum pelago desaevit hiems et aquosus Orion,
53 *(sdss)*: quassataeque rates, dum non tractabile caelum."

697 *(ddds)*: sed misera ante diem subitoque accensa furore,
698 *(sssd)*: nondum illi flavum Proserpina vertice crinem
699 *(ddds)*: abstulerat Stygioque caput damnaverat Orco.

In 51-53 and 697-699 the pattern framed by its opposite is the one appearing less often. But, surprisingly enough, in many instances, it is the more frequent pattern which is enclosed by its opposite, e.g., in *Aeneid* III:

393 *(dddd)*: is locus urbis erit, requies ea certa laborum.
394 *(ssss)*: nec tu mensarum morsus horresce futuros:
395 *(dddd)*: fata viam invenient aderitque vocatus Apollo.[3]

In Vergil's works opposites appear in adjacent lines with considerably frequency:

Eclogues: 42 times, averaging once every 19.6 lines
Georgics: 106 times, averaging once every 20.9 lines
Aeneid: 424 times, averaging once every 23.1 lines[4]

We find here a much greater interest in opposite combinations than in the earlier hexameter poets:

Cicero, *Aratea:*   once every 79.8 lines
Lucretius: once every 30.8 lines
Catullus LXIV: once every 37.7 lines

We may therefore assert that this increased emphasis on opposite combinations is another of Vergil's metrical innovations. The frequency in Horace's hexameter poems as a whole is close to those of Vergil, one instance every 21.4 lines, but there is a steady increase from his earlier to his later works, as follows: *Satires* I, 32.1; *Satires* II, 20.8; *Epistles* I, 21.0; *Epistles* II, 16.3. It seems not unreasonable to attribute this change to the influence of Vergil, especially as so many of the later poets, including those who imitate Vergil in other respects, have frequencies resembling closely those of Vergil, e.g., Lucan, one every 22.0 lines; Statius, *Thebaid*, 21.8, and *Silvae*, 20.0; Silius Italicus, 22.3; Juvenal, 22.5; Claudian I, 21.7, and Claudian II, 20.4. Opposite combinations occur in Ovid's *Metamorphoses* and Manilius' *Astronomica* once every 29.3 and 29.0 lines respectively, and these two poets are thus closer to Lucretius (30.8) than to Vergil and Horace. Several poets of the Late Empire have unusually high frequencies, e.g., Avienus, *Aratea*, 15.4; Ausonius, *Mosella*, 17.8; Sidonius, 16.5; *De providentia Dei*, 16.8, and Arator, 16.5.[5]

Vergil's favorite opposite combination is *sdsd-dsds* and this comprises a percentage of the total opposites in each work as follows: *Eclogues*, 19.05; *Georgics*, 23.58; *Aeneid*, 16.04. The fact that Vergil has reduced the percentage from 23.58 in the *Georgics* to 16.04 in the *Aeneid* is not without significance; perhaps he realized that, however useful opposite combinations may be to counteract the effect of numerous repeats and near repeats, too large a proportion of the same opposite combination might itself become monotonous.

Many other poets also prefer *sdsd-dsds;* these include Lucretius, Ovid, Manilius, Lucan, Valerius Flaccus, Statius, Silius Italicus, and Claudian; Catullus LXIV and Horace favor *dsdd-sdss*, and in Juvenal *dsdd-sdss* and *sdsd-dsds* are tied for first place. In most poets the favorite combination has a higher percentage of the total opposites; Horace is near Vergil's procedure in the *Aeneid* with 18.32 per cent,[6] but usually the percentage runs with a surprising consistency between 20 and 25; e.g., Lucretius, 22.69; Ovid, *Metamorphoses*, 22.11; Manilius, 22.92; Lucan, 26.92; Statius, *Thebaid*, 20.40, and *Silvae*, 24.70; Silius Italicus, 21.90; and Juvenal, 21.43 for each of the combinations tied for first place. The percentages are much higher in Catullus LXIV, 33.33; Valerius Flaccus, 33.01; Claudian I, 33.01, and Claudian II, 40.75. These are the same poets in which we find high frequencies of repeats and near repeats. The monotonous repetition of the same patterns and an excessive use of the same opposite combination thus go hand in hand.

Vergil combines certain opposites in adjacent lines more often than others. Although *sdsd-dsds* is the most frequent combination in the *Aeneid* (16.04 of the total opposites), only 18.28 per cent of the total *sdsd* patterns are preceded or followed by *dsds*, whereas the percentage of *sddd*, the least frequent pattern, preceded or followed by its opposite *dsss* is 29.38, and that of *ssdd* combined with *ddss* is 20.0. I give below the percentages in Vergil for the eight patterns used least often (Nos. 9-16), arranged in the order of increasing frequency:

		Eclogues	*Georgics*	*Aeneid*
16. *sddd,*	with *dsss:*	5.0	35.71	29.38
15. *dddd,*	with *ssss:*	5.88	12.24	13.94
14. *ssdd,*	with *ddss:*	26.92	26.92	20.0
13. *sssd,*	with *ddds:*	19.05	10.71	15.54
12. *dsdd,*	with *sdss:*	13.95	20.0	18.41
11. *sdsd,*	with *dsds:*	20.59	29.41	18.28
10. *ddsd,*	with *ssds:*	10.45	12.26	12.28
9. *dssd,*	with *sdds:*	10.45	8.44	10.18

I stated above a general rule concerning opposites: the more frequent a pattern, the less frequent its opposite. We may now formulate a second law: the less frequent a pattern, the more often it will be preceded or followed by its opposite; this is particularly true of *sddd* with *dsss*, *ssdd* with *ddss*, *dsdd* with *sdss*, and *sdsd* with *dsds*. I give the percentages for these four combinations as they appear in a number of other Latin poets:

	sddd with *dsss*	*ssdd* with *ddss*	*dsdd* with *sdss*	*sdsd* with *dsds*
Lucretius:	35.63	25.64	18.75	23.88
Horace:	25.0	21.43	20.0	17.80
Ovid, *Metamorphoses:*[7]	27.73	30.14	14.97	20.09
Germanicus, *Aratea:*	55.55	6.67	15.63	10.0
Manilius:	40.63	24.29	11.32	20.76
Lucan:	37.0	23.35	19.33	32.78
Valerius Flaccus:	23.53	22.41	12.25	46.62
Statius, *Thebaid:*	19.52	29.11	12.19	30.54

	sddd with *dsss*	*ssdd* with *ddss*	*dsdd* with *sdss*	*sdsd* with *dsds*
Statius, *Silvae:*	30.0	20.88	12.89	29.92
Silius Italicus:	27.12	17.68	18.86	20.87
Juvenal:	21.11	17.95	22.64	17.39
Claudian I:	29.45	16.28	19.80	33.01
Claudian II:	61.54	42.86	25.0	38.60

The percentages in Lucretius and the *Georgics* are similar, as are those in the *Aeneid,* Horace,[8] and Silius Italicus. The highest percentages among those given above are in Germanicus, 55.55 per cent of *sddd* with *dsss;* Valerius Flaccus, 46.62 per cent of *sdsd* with *dsds,* and in Claudian II, 61.54 per cent of *sddd* with *dsss,* 42.86 per cent of *ssdd* with *ddss;* these two percentages in Claudian I are much lower (29.45 and 16.28).

Not only do opposites attract each other to a surprising degree (especially *sddd* and *dsss, sdsd* and *dsds*), but the same is true of the four possible reverse combinations; these also appear frequently in adjacent lines, e.g., in *Aeneid* IV:

> 17 *(sdss):* postquam primus amor deceptam morte fefellit;
> 18 *(ssds):* si non pertaesum thalami taedaeque fuisset,
>
> 89 *(sssd):* murorum ingentes aequataque machina caelo.
> 90 *(dsss):* Quam simul ac tali persensit peste teneri

Sometimes one pattern is framed by its reverse, as in *Aeneid* II:

> 385 *(dsss):* sternimus. aspirat primo Fortuna labori.
> 386 *(sssd):* atque hic successu exsultans animisque Coroebus
> 387 *(dsss):* "o socii, qua prima" inquit "fortuna salutis[9]

In *Aeneid* V we find *dsss* framed by *sssd,* one of the striking instances where the more frequent pattern is enclosed by the one which occurs so rarely:

> 382 *(sssd):* tum laeva taurum cornu tenet atque ita fatur:
> 383 *(dsss):* "nate dea, si nemo audet se credere pugnae,
> 384 *(sssd):* quae finis standi? quo me decet usque teneri?

We find in *Aeneid* III two pairs of reverse combinations in chiastic order:

> 114 *(dsss):* ergo agite et divum ducunt qua iussa sequamur:
> 115 *(sssd):* placemus ventos et Gnosia regna petamus.
> 116 *(sssd):* nec longo distant cursu: modo Iuppiter adsit,
> 117 *(dsss):* tertia lux classem Cretaeis sistet in oris. "

Reverse combinations appear in Vergil's three works as follows:

> *Eclogues:*   15 times, once every 55.0 lines
> *Georgics:*   47 times, once every 46.4 lines
> *Aeneid:*   252 times, once every 38.9 lines

Vergil thus increases the use of adjacent reverse patterns from the *Eclogues* through the *Georgics* to the *Aeneid* to a decided degree. This is very unlike the frequencies of his opposite combinations, which, as we have seen, remain fairly constant (*Eclogues,* one every 19.6 lines; *Georgics,* 20.9; *Aeneid,* 23.1).

The frequency of reverse combinations in Lucretius (one every 51.3 lines) and in Catullus LXIV (one every 53.9 lines) resembles that in Vergil's *Eclogues* (55.0); Cicero in his *Aratea* is unique among Vergil's predecessors in that his adjacent reverse patterns occur more than twice as often, one every 24.0 lines, considerably more frequently than in the *Aeneid* (38.9). We find also in Horace and Silius Italicus a greater emphasis on reverse combinations than in the *Aeneid,* one every 29.4 and 29.0 lines respectively, but most later poets are in the *Georgics-Aeneid* area; e.g., Ovid, *Metamorphoses,* one every 39.3 lines; Manilius, 45.9; Lucan, 40.7; Valerius Flaccus, 48.6; Statius,

Thebaid, 46.9, and *Silvae,* 41.5; in Claudian I and II we have somewhat higher frequencies, one every 34.7 and 34.5 lines respectively.

I pointed out above that there is little fluctuation among the favorite opposite combinations (usually *sdsd-dsds* or *dsdd-sdss*) out of the eight possibilities, and that, with a few exceptions, the favorite seldom comprises more than 30 per cent of the total opposites. But, in the case of the four reverse combinations, there is far more variation, and the ratio of the most frequent reverse to the total reverses is often surprisingly high. I turn first to Vergil, where, in each work, a different combination is favored:

> *Eclogues:* *dsdd-ddsd;* 46.67 per cent of the total reverses
> *Georgics:* *sssd-dsss;* 38.30 per cent of the total reverses
> *Aeneid:* *ssds-sdss;* 40.08 per cent of the total reverses

Vergil's choice of *dsdd-ddsd* in the more dactylic *Eclogues* is also that of Ovid, Calpurnius Siculus, Valerius Flaccus, and Statius in his *Silvae* (in the *Thebaid,* the combination is *dsdd-dsdd,* *ddsd* being the less frequent of the two patterns). The combination *sssd-dsss,* preferred by Vergil in the *Georgics,* is the favorite of many didactic poets — Lucretius, the three translators of Aratus (Cicero, Germanicus Caesar, and Avienus), and Serenus in his *Liber Medicinalis.* More poets, however, prefer the reverse combination *ssds-sdss,* Vergil's first choice in the *Aeneid;* these include Catullus LXIV, Horace, Grattius, Manilius, Lucan, Silius Italicus, Juvenal, Claudian (both I and II), Sidonius, Corippus, and many Christian poets, such as Juvencus, Prudentius, Marius Victor, Paulinus of Périgueux, and Avitus. In the *Aeneid,* the favorite reverse combination comprises 40.08 per cent of the total reverses; with very few exceptions (e.g., Lucretius, 39.86; Germanicus, 38.10; Statius, *Thebaid,* 38.16, and *Silvae,* 33.75; Avienus, *Aratea,* 37.93; Paulinus of Nola, 36.0) the other poets have much higher percentages: e.g., Cicero, *Aratea,* 55.0; Horace, 46.04; Manilius, 56.04; Valerius Flaccus, 60.0; Silius Italicus, 55.71; Juvenal, 51.49; Ausonius, *Mosella,* 54.55; Corippus, 52.0.[10]

The emphasis on one reverse combination almost to the exclusion of the other three introduces a monotony almost as great as that resulting from an excessive number of repeats and near repeats. The following percentages are abnormally high: Catullus LXIV, 71.43; Ovid, *Metamorphoses,* 71.05; Grattius, 71.43; Lucan, 70.05; Claudian I, 74.29, Claudian II, 81.25. The highest percentage of all appears in Cyprian of Gaul, where the combination *sdss-ssds* provides 95.74 per cent of the total reverses.[11]

Just as *sddd* is so often preceded or followed by its opposite *dsss,* so *sssd* likewise appears frequently with *dsss,* its reverse; e.g., in *Aeneid* III, *sssd* occurs thirty-four times and is adjacent to *dsss* fifteen times (44.12 per cent); in *Aeneid* VII, we have twenty-three instances of *sssd,* twelve with *dsss* (52.17 per cent). For the *Aeneid* as a whole, the respective numbers are 296 occurrences, 87 with *dsss,* for a percentage of 29.56.[12] The percentage of *sssd* with *dsss* in the *Eclogues* is 14.29, that in the *Georgics* 32.14.

Many poets have a lower percentage of *sssd* with *dsss* than we find in the *Georgics* and the *Aeneid,* e.g., Horace, 23.68; Ovid, 24.85; Lucan, 26.67; Valerius Flaccus, 18.18 (but his percentage of *sddd* with *ddds* is 35.29); Statius, *Thebaid,* 21.19; Silius Italicus, 24.86; Juvenal, 26.72; and Claudian I, 18.18. Other percentages are much higher, e.g., Cicero, *Aratea,* 64.71; Lucretius, 40.14; Catullus LXIV, 40.0; Statius, *Silvae,* 40.0; Claudian II, 50.0;[13] Avitus, 42.86; Cyprian, 50.0; Arator, 50.0; and Corippus, 50.0.

I return now to the *Aeneid.* Of the patterns which appear least frequently, *sddd* and *sssd* deserve especial comment for their use in adjacent lines with *both* opposite and reverse patterns:

	Opposite	Per Cent	Reverse	Per Cent	Total
sddd:	*dsss*	29.38	*ddds*	14.95	44.33
sssd:	*ddds*	15.54	*dsss*	29.56	45.10

In other words, of the sixteen possible patterns which could precede or follow *sddd* and *sssd,* we find in each case either the opposite or the reverse in over 44 per cent of the total occurrences. We have almost the same situation in Vergil's *Georgics:* total percentage of *sddd* with opposite and reverse patterns, 45.23; *sssd* with opposite and reverse patterns, 42.85. The similarity of the *sddd* and *sssd* totals suggests the formulation of a general rule concerning these two patterns:

the combined percentages of *sddd* with its opposite *dsss* and its reverse *ddds* are approximately the same in good hexameter poetry (such as the *Georgics* and the *Aeneid*) as the combined percentages of *sssd* with its opposite *ddds* and its reverse *dsss*. I list below a number of other poets in whose verses we find this same approximate correlation, but sometimes with total percentages which are considerably higher:

	Total %, *sddd* with *dsss* and *ddds*	Total %, *sssd* with *ddds* and *dsss*
Lucretius:	57.47	54.93
Horace:	33.0	30.52
Ovid, *Metamorphoses:*	42.20	42.43
Germanicus, *Aratea:*	40.0	41.66
Statius, *Silvae:*	54.29	57.78[14]
Silius Italicus:	35.17	34.05
Juvencus:	33.33	33.81
Claudian II:	69.23	75.0
Avitus:	50.0	50.0
Corippus:	47.05	50.0

It is interesting to note that Horace, Silius Italicus, and Juvencus have the least concentration on the *sddd* and *sssd* opposite and reverse combinations.

The figures in the *Aeneid* for the other two patterns with both opposites and reverses are as follows:

	Opposite	Per Cent	Reverse	Per Cent	Total
ssds:	*ddsd*	12.28[15]	*sdss*	17.21	29.49
dsdd:	*sdss*	18.41	*ddsd*	9.92	28.33

Here again the totals of the two patterns are almost identical. The rule given above for the similarity of the *sddd* percentages with opposite and reverse patterns and the *sssd* percentages with opposite and reverse patterns seems thus to apply to these two patterns also. But perhaps only to the *Aeneid!* We do not find it in the *Georgics*,[16] and in only a few of the other poets, as follows:

	Total %, *ddsd* with *ssds* (or *ssds* with *ddsd*), *ssds* with *sdss*	Total %, *dsdd* with *sdss* and *ddsd*
Horace:	37.40	32.57
Germanicus, *Aratea:*	33.01	28.66
Statius, *Thebaid:*	25.32	25.20
Statius, *Achilleid:*	30.35	27.46
Statius, *Silvae:*	22.55	24.94
Juvenal:	31.34	31.45
Serenus:	27.45	30.25
Juvencus:	35.71	36.84
Avienus, *Aratea:*	33.80	32.17
Claudian II:	38.97	37.50

Only Horace, Germanicus, Statius *(Silvae)*, Juvencus, and Claudian II appear on both lists; in this particular respect they seem much closer to the Vergilian norm than do the other Latin poets.

Another aspect of the opposite and reverse combinations is this: at times a pattern may be preceded by its opposite or reverse and followed by its reverse or opposite; e.g., in *Aeneid* IV:

52 *(dsdd)*: dum pelago desaevit hiems et aquosus Orion,
53 *(sdss)*: quassataeque rates, dum non tractabile caelum. "
54 *(ssds)*: His dictis impenso animum flammavit amore

Here the opposite precedes and the reverse follows,[17] but often the reverse precedes and the opposite follows, e.g., in *Aeneid* IV:

116 *(dsss)*: confieri possit, paucis (adverte) docebo.
117 *(sssd)*: venatum Aeneas unaque miserrima Dido
118 *(ddds)*: in nemus ire parant, ubi primos crastinus ortus[18]

The frequent appearance of opposite and reverse patterns in adjacent lines serves to counteract the monotony which sometimes results from the many instances of repeated patterns in two or three lines in succession (unless, as I have mentioned above, there is too much concentration on the same opposite or reverse combination). Also, and more significant, the frequency and nature of the opposite and reverse combinations (and of the repeated patterns as well) may be used to determine the metrical likes and dislikes of each poet — his metrical idiosyncrasies, so to speak. The various hexameter poets prefer to combine a high percentage of some patterns with opposites and/or reverses, while the proportion in other combinations is relatively low.[19] I give first some likes and dislikes in Vergil's three works, and I then add those for a few other poets:

	Opposites		Reverses	
	favors	but not	favors	but not
Vergil, *Ecl.*:	*ssdd-ddss*	*sddd-dsss*	*dsdd-ddsd*	*sddd-ddds*
Vergil, *Georg.*:	*sddd-dsss*	*dssd-sdds*	*sssd-dsss*	*sddd-ddds*
Vergil, *Aen.*:	*sddd-dsss*	*dssd-sdds*	*sssd-dsss*	*dsdd-ddsd*
Lucretius:	*sddd-dsss*	*dddd-ssss*	*sssd-dsss*	*dsdd-ddsd*
Horace:	*sddd-dsss*	*sssd-ddds*	*ssds-sdss*	*sddd-ddds*
Ovid, *Metam.*:	*ssdd-ddss*	*dddd-ssss*	*dsdd-ddsd*	*ssds-sdss*
Lucan:	*sddd-dsss*	*dddd-ssss*	*sssd-dsss*	*dsdd-ddsd*
Valerius Fl.:	*sdsd-dsds*	*sdss-dsdd*	*sddd-ddds*	*ssds-sdss*
Statius, *Theb.*:	*sdsd-dsds*	*ssss-dddd*	*sssd-dsss*	*ssds-sdss*
Silius Ital.:	*sddd-dsss*	*sssd-ddds*	*sssd-dsss*	*sddd-ddds*
Juvenal:	*dsdd-sdss*	*dddd-ssss*	*sssd-dsss*	*sddd-ddds*
Claudian I:[20]	*sdsd-dsds*	*(ssss-dddd)*	*ssds-sdss*	*sddd-ddds*
Claudian II:	*sddd-dsss*	*(ssss-dddd)*	*sssd-dsss*	*sddd-ddds*

These distinctions, e.g., between Vergil's *Aeneid* and Ovid's *Metamorphoses*, will be of value later when, in Part II, I discuss the authenticity of poems of disputed authorship, such as the hexameter poems of the *Appendix Vergiliana*.

I close this chapter with an analysis of *Aen.* IV, 1-19, in order to illustrate in one short passage Vergil's use, not only of opposite and reverse combinations, but also of patterns repeated in adjacent and near adjacent lines (as described above in Chapter 3). We have below in one short passage two repeats, one of which *(dsss)* has also three near repeats,[21] three opposites and one reverse. Also, in spite of five instances of *dsss* in the first ten lines, there are ten different patterns in the first sixteen-line unit. The frequency of the repeats, opposites, and reverses is here well above Vergil's normal average, as the following reveals:

	Ecl.	*Georg.*	*Aen.*	IV, 1-19
Patterns per 16-line unit:	9.7	9.3	9.4	10.0
Repeats, one every *x* lines:	13.1	12.3	12.4	9.5
R + NR, one every *x* lines:	5.1	4.5	4.6	3.8
Opposites, one every *x* lines:	19.6	20.9	23.1	6.3
Reverses, one every *x* lines:	55.5	46.4	38.9	19.0

1. *sdss*
2. *dsss* ---------------------------------
3. *dsds*
4. *dsss* ---------------------------------   Near repeats
5. *ddss*
6. *dsss* ---------------------------------
7. *ssds*
8. *sddd* ───────────────────────────
9. *dsss* ───────────────────────────   Opposite
10. *dsss* ───────────────────────────   Repeat
11. *sdss* ───────────────────────────
12. *dsdd* ───────────────────────────   Opposite
13. *dddd* ───────────────────────────
14. *ssss* ───────────────────────────   Opposite
15. *ddss*
16. *sssd*
17. *sdss* ───────────────────────────
18. *ssds* ───────────────────────────   Reverse
19. *ssds* ───────────────────────────   Repeat

1. The patterns *ssss, dddd, sdds,* and *dssd* have no reverse; in the case of *ssdd, ddss, sdsd,* and *dsds*, the reverse is the same as the opposite.

2. Homer, on the basis of 1,920 verses, has an almost perfect concentric arrangement of patterns and opposites: *dddd* (1) and *ssss* (16), *dsdd* (2) and *sdss* (15), *sddd* (3) and *dsss* (14), *dsds* (6) and *sdsd* (11), *sdds* (7) and *dssd* (10), *ddsd*(8) and *ssds* (9); the opposites of Nos. 4 and 5 are 12 and 13 respectively.

3. For *dsds* enclosed by *sdsd*, see *Georg.* IV, 241-243; *Aen.* VI, 787-789; X, 110-112; for *sdss* enclosed by *dsdd*, see *Aen.* I, 380-382; for *ssds* enclosed by *ddsd*, see *Aen.* IV, 626-628; for *ddds* enclosed by *sssd*, see *Aen.* V, 672-674; VIII, 227-229; for *sdds* enclosed by *dssd*, see *Aen.* XII, 528-530. In *Aen.* VIII, 58-61, the opposites are interlocked *(ssds, ddsd, ssds, ddsd)*.

4. Vergil's average in *Aeneid* I-IX is very close to that in the *Eclogues* and the *Georgics:* 324 times, once every 21.8 lines; in X-XII he combines opposites with considerable less frequency than elsewhere in his poetry: 100 times, once every 27.6 lines.

5. Just the reverse is true of the late Greek poets. Opposite combinations were always rare among the Greek poets; cf. the following (one every *x* lines): Homer, 50.5; Hesiod, 53.3; Aratus, 70.4; Theocritus, 58.9; Callimachus, 174.8; Apollonius of Rhodes, 87.3. But in the late Greek poets, who omit many of the sixteen patterns, we find Quintus of Smyrna with three opposite combinations in 960 verses (one every 320); Nonnus with one instance in 960 verses; Musaeus, one in 341 verses.

6. Horace, however, unlike Vergil, changes his most frequent combination from *dsdd-sdss* in the *Satires* (20.24 per cent; *sdsd-dsds* second with 16.67) to *sdsd-dsds* in the *Epistles* (18.69 per cent; *dsdd-sdss* second with 16.82).

7. In the case of the more dactylic Ovid and his imitators Valerius Flaccus and Statius, *sdss* is less frequent than *dsdd,* and the percentage is that of the *sdss* patterns preceded or followed by *dsdd.*

8. The greatest variation in Horace is the percentage of *dddd* with *ssss,* from 6.67 in *Satires* I to 35.71 in *Epistles* II. In Vergil the variation of *dddd* with *ssss* is from 5.88 in the *Eclogues* to 13.94 in the *Aeneid.*

9. For *sssd* framed by *dsss,* see also *Georg.* I, 96-98; *Aen.* III, 709-711, 714-716; VII, 647-649.

10. Cf. also, among the late Christian poets, Juvencus, 51.92; Prudentius, 48.33; Sedulius, 50.0; Marius Victor, 58.06; Avitus, 65.0; Arator, 51.72.

11. Reverse combinations are much more frequent in Greek poetry than are opposite patterns in adjacent lines (see above, note 5), e.g., Homer one in every 27.0 lines; Callimachus, 23.6; Apollonius of Rhodes, 18.1; Nonnus, 20.9. As in the case of many Latin poets, they are often heavily concentrated in one of the four possible combinations. The favorite reverse is usually *ddds-sddd* (but *ddsd-dsdd* in Aratus, Theocritus, and Callimachus). Percentages of the total reverses range from 52.17 in Hesiod and 57.75 in Homer to 73.91 in Nonnus and 87.50 in Musaeus.

12. The percentage in *Aeneid* I-IX is 30.36; in X-XII, 26.39; this decrease is surprising in view of the unusually high frequency of *dsss* in X and XII. We find a greater decrease in the case of *sddd* and *ddds:* I-IX, 16.67; X-XII, 10.0; but cf. *ssds* and *sdss;* I-IX, 15.66; X-XII, 20.93.

13. Claudian shows a striking fluctuation in the percentage of *sssd* with *dsss:* I, 18.18; II, 50.0. His percentages of *ssds* with *sdss,* however, are practically identical: I, 24.76; II, 25.24; likewise the *dsdd-ddsd* percentages: I, 11.83; II, 12.50.

14. In the *Thebaid* the corresponding percentages are 34.76 and 41.06; there is an even greater variation in the unfinished *Achilleid,* 56.25 and 25.0.

15. This percentage is that of the *ddsd* patterns preceded or followed by *ssds;* except in the more dactylic poets, the frequency of *ddsd* is lower than that of *ssds; ssds* almost always has a lower frequency than its reverse *sdss.*

16. The percentages in the *Georgics* are as follows: *ddsd-ssds,* 12.26; *ssds-sdss,* 10.92; total, 23.18; and *dsdd-sdss,* 20.0; *dsdd-ddsd,* 18.46; total, 38.46. Cf., however, the *Eclogues:* percentage of *ssds* with both opposites and reverses, 34.0; of *dsdd* with opposites and reverses, 30.23.

17. Cf. also *Ecl.* I, 31-33 *(ddsd, ssds, sdss); Georg.* III, 495-497 *(sdss, dsdd, ddsd),* IV, 441-443 *(dsss, sddd, ddds); Aen.* II, 794-796 *(dsdd, sdss, ssds),* VIII, 214-216 *(dsdd, ssds, sdss),* 228-230 and IX, 75-77, 285-287 *(ddds, sssd, dsss),* etc.

18. Cf. *dsss, sssd, ddds (Aen.* II, 129-131, 565-567; III, 337-339; VI, 662-664; XI, 307-309); *ddsd, dsdd, sdss (Georg.* II, 429-431; *Aen.* VII, 24-26, 339-341; XII, 665-667); *sdss, ssds, ddsd (Aen.* IV, 648-650; V, 440-442); *ddds, sddd, dsss (Aen.* II, 352-354).

19. The "likes" of a particular poet as listed below are not necessarily what I have earlier called the "favorite" opposite or reverse; e.g., in Vergil's *Aeneid,* the opposite combination *sdsd-dsds* occurs more often than does *sddd-dsss,* but the percentage of *sdsd* patterns preceded or

followed by *dsds* is only 18.28; that of *sddd* with
dsss is 29.38. Likewise, Vergil's most frequent
reverse combination in the *Aeneid* is *ssds-sdss,*
but the percentage of *ssds* with *sdss* is 17.21,
while that of *sssd* with *dsss* is 29.56.

20. There are no examples of the opposite combination *ssss-dddd* in either Claudian I or Claudian II.

21. Five instances of *dsss* in ten lines almost form
a "repeat cluster," but I arbitrarily limit such
clusters to six or more instances of the same
pattern in sixteen or fewer lines; see above,
Chapter 3.

PART II

FACTS AND FINDINGS:
FROM ENNIUS TO THE AGE OF JUSTINIAN

Chapter 6

THE REPUBLICAN POETS

I presented in Part I of this work several different types of variety and repetition, with numerous illustrations from Vergil's *Aeneid,* and I gave on occasion comparative statistics for many other works, especially longer poems such as the *De Rerum Natura* of Lucretius, the *Satires* and *Epistles* of Horace, the *Metamorphoses* of Ovid, and the Silver Latin epics of Lucan, Valerius Flaccus, Statius, and Silius Italicus.

Much more remains to be said about these poems and many shorter works hitherto unmentioned. The various criteria analyzed above — the use of different metrical patterns and especially the eight most commonly favored, the variety which appears in sixteen-line units, the frequencies of repeat clusters, repeats, and near repeats, the shift in fourth-foot texture in repeated patterns, and the numerous opposite and reverse combinations — will all throw new light on many aspects of Latin hexameter poetry and will establish clearly the metrical "fingerprints" of many different poets. We shall at times be able to point out significant changes from the earlier to the later work of a particular writer; we shall be able to see more clearly the metrical indebtedness of many poets of the Silver Age and Late Empire to their predecessors in the late Republic and the Augustan Age; and it will perhaps be possible to determine the authenticity, or lack of authenticity, of several works of disputed authorship. I shall also include some discussion of Greek hexameter poetry to see whether, in spite of the obvious basic differences between the Greek and the Latin hexameter (pointed out in Part I), the Greek poets influenced in any way the Romans as they developed the same literary genres.

The number of Latin poets treated in Part II exceeds forty, in addition to the works of uncertain authorship. I shall present the most significant facts and findings concerning these many poets, but it seems inadvisable to give all the statistical details to support my conclusions; additional percentages and frequencies may be found in the two synoptic Tables at the end of this volume and in my published articles.[1]

Ennius and Homer

I begin with Ennius, the first to introduce the quantitative hexameter into Latin poetry. His *Annales* has survived in almost too fragmentary a form to yield satisfactory results; it is of course impossible to discuss the use of repeated patterns or of opposite and reverse combinations when we are dealing with fragments which so often consist of only one line. I base my statistics on 404 verses,[2] a total which gives an approximate idea, at least, of the metrical patterns which Ennius preferred and the frequency with which they were used; these 404 verses prove conclusively that the Latin hexameter from its beginning was the very opposite of the Greek.

Homer's favorite pattern in the *Iliad* and the *Odyssey* is *dddd,* which occurs in approximately one-fifth of the total verses, or 21.36 per cent.[3] The percentages for the first four and the first eight patterns are 59.90 and 85.42 respectively, and the other eight patterns thus comprise less than fifteen per cent of the verses. The pattern with the lowest frequency is *ssss* (0.42 per cent), the opposite of *dddd.* Homer is predominately dactylic; in the eight patterns which occur over four-fifths of the time, we have in the first four feet a total of twenty-two dactyls and ten spondees.

The situation with Ennius is very different. The lack of articles and particles in the Latin language made the hexameter at the outset far more spondaic. The pattern most frequent in the fragments of Ennius is *ssss,* with a percentage of 15.35; this is the very pattern used least by Homer. The percentages of the first four and the first eight patterns are 41.34 and 65.35, and these likewise differ much from the corresponding percentages in Homer (59.90 and 85.42). From the very beginning of Latin hexameter poetry far greater variety was possible than had been the case in Homer and the other Greek poets. The pattern appearing least frequently in Ennius is *ssdd* (2.72 per cent); in Homer the same pattern is fourth (9.01 per cent).

The dactylic patterns favored by Homer may be compared with the more spondaic patterns of Ennius as follows (I give the first eight patterns only):[4]

	1	2	3	4	5	6	7	8
Homer:	dddd	dsdd	sddd	ssdd	ddds	dsds	sdds	ddsd
Ennius:	ssss	dsss	ssds	ddss	dssd	dsds		
		sdss		sssd				

Only *dsds* appears among the eight most frequent patterns of both poets. The first eight of Ennius contain in the first four feet twenty-two spondees and ten dactyls, the exact opposite of Homer's distribution of twenty-two dactyls and ten spondees. Also, Ennius favors a spondee in the fourth foot (6 *s* to 2 *d*), whereas in Homer the dactylic fourth foot is more frequent (5 *d* to 3 *s*).

No two hexameter poets could thus be more different than Homer and Ennius. Winbolt says of the latter: "He over-emphasises the contrast with Greek, in the manner of pioneers."[5] No other Latin poet has *ssss* as the most frequent pattern, and such a low percentage for the first eight patterns (65.35) is surpassed only by Ausonius in his *Mosella* (62.50). Likewise, no other Latin poet has, for his work as a whole, Ennius' distribution of twenty-two spondees and ten dactyls in the first eight patterns. In the case of Silius Italicus, the most spondaic of the later poets, we find this same distribution in five of the seventeen books of the *Punica*, but he has twenty spondees and twelve dactyls in the poem as a whole.

Lucilius

When we turn to the satires of Lucilius, we have the same problem as in the case of Ennius; the hexameter fragments total 605 (excluding two spondaic verses), but most are short, often only one or two lines, and again we are unable to work with sixteen-line units, repeated patterns, or opposite and reverse combinations.

The percentages of the first, first four, and first eight patterns are 16.86, 47.60, and 74.21 respectively, all higher than the corresponding percentages in the fragments of Ennius. Lucilius is also heavily spondaic, with twenty-one spondees and eleven dactyls in his first eight patterns. This distribution is rare in the whole history of the Latin hexameter; we find it in *Satires* I and *Epistles* I and II of Horace, in the *Aratea* of Germanicus, the *Aetna*, the *Bellum Civile* of Petronius, the *Satires* of Juvenal, and the religious hexameters of Juvencus, Paulinus of Périgueux, and Avitus.[6]

In spite of the spondaic nature of his verse, *ssss*, in first place in Ennius, is now in third position; Lucilius' choice of *sdss* as his favorite pattern is most unusual; *sdss* elsewhere is first only in two short poems of disputed authorship, the *Dirae* in the *Appendix Vergiliana*, and the *Halieutica* ascribed to Ovid. Even in second place *sdss* appears very seldom. Both Horace (*Satires* and *Epistles*) and Juvenal use *sdss* as their second pattern, and this is possibly an indication that the two later satirists were both influenced in this respect by Lucilius (or perhaps Juvenal was following Horace). The only other instances of *sdss* in second place are the following: Ennius (tied with *dsss*), Catullus LXIV, the *Aetna*, Silius Italicus, Paulinus of Pella, and Avitus.

If we had the complete hexameter poems of Lucilius instead of short fragments, it seems highly probable that *sdss* would still be his most frequent pattern; the percentage of the second pattern, *dsss*, is only 10.41, 6.45 per cent below the 16.86 of *sdss*. It is almost amazing that we have the same percentage drop in the case of Ennius: first pattern *(ssss)*, 15.35; second choice (*sdss* tied with *dsss*), 8.91, a difference of 6.44. Ennius' preference for *ssss* would undoubtedly remain unchanged, even if more of the *Annales* were extant.

Cicero, Forerunner of Vergil and Horace

We are fortunately able to compare the patterns and percentages in Cicero's fragments (265 lines) with those of his *Aratea* (479 lines); the results are almost identical: *dsss* is the favorite pattern; the first eight patterns are the same (except that *dssd* is tied with *ssds* for eighth place in the fragments), but in slightly different order, e.g., *ddss*, third in the *Aratea*, second in the fragments; *sdss*, fourth in the *Aratea*, third in the fragments. The frequency percentages are approximately the same, as follows:

	Aratea	Fragments	Total
First pattern:	17.95	18.87	18.28
First four:	59.09	55.47	57.39
First eight:	82.88	81.13	82.26

There are two points of interest here: these percentages are considerably higher than those of Ennius and Lucilius, and the similarity of the percentages in the fragments to those in the *Aratea* provides added validity for the statistics given above for Ennius and Lucilius, which are based on short fragments only.

Ennius had preferred *ssss*, Lucilius *sdss*. Beginning with Cicero, *dsss* emerges as the first pattern and continues as the favorite not only of Lucretius and Catullus LXIV but also of Vergil (both *Georgics* and *Aeneid*), Horace, and many later poets. The second pattern in Cicero's *Aratea* is *ssss* (the influence of Ennius?) and this is in second place in no other Latin poet.[7] The distribution of spondees and dactyls in the first eight patterns moves from twenty-two and ten in Ennius to twenty-one and eleven in Lucilius to twenty and twelve in Cicero; this determines the distribution in many later poets, e.g., Catullus LXIV, Vergil's *Georgics* and *Aeneid*, Horace, Germanicus, Manilius, and Silius Italicus.

Even more significant is the fact that Cicero's first eight patterns are identical with those in Vergil's *Aeneid* (but in slightly different order); each of the eight patterns has a spondee in the fourth foot (Ennius had six fourth-foot spondees, Lucilius seven). Cicero thus anticipates Vergil's procedure in the *Aeneid*; this indicates that Cicero was perhaps more influential on the later poets and especially Vergil than is usually realized, and supports the statement of Ewbank:[8]

> This unconsciously close correspondence, therefore, which exists between the two
> poets goes to prove that Cicero's feeling for rhythm and arrangement was very
> closely allied to that of Virgil. . . . Hence, in this matter of the 'spondaic fourth'
> Cicero, with unerring instinct, pointed the way to his great successor.

This similarity between Cicero and Vergil is all the more impressive, when we realize how few Latin poets have spondaic fourth feet in all first eight patterns; they are, as I stated in Chapter 1, only Manilius, Silius Italicus, Nemesianus in the *Cynegetica*, the anonymous *De providentia Dei*, and Cyprian of Gaul.

The importance of Cicero as a forerunner of Vergil and Horace will be seen more clearly when we compare his patterns and percentages with those of Lucretius and Catullus LXIV. Also, I shall combine Cicero's treatment of repeated patterns and of opposite and reverse combinations with that of Lucretius and Catullus.

Repetition in Lucretius and Catullus

In the six books of Lucretius' *De Rerum Natura* and in Catullus' epyllion about Peleus and Thetis (LXIV), *dsss* is likewise in first place; Lucretius' distribution of spondees and dactyls in the first eight patterns is eighteen and fourteen, with six fourth-foot spondees, whereas Catullus has twenty spondees and twelve dactyls, and seven spondees in the fourth foot.

The percentages of the first pattern in the Republican poets shows a steady increase: Ennius, 15.35; Lucilius, 16.86; Cicero, *Aratea*, 17.95; Lucretius, 20.20;[9] Catullus, 27.59. Such a heavy concentration on one metrical pattern as appears in Lucretius and Catullus was obviously distasteful to the Augustan poets, and we shall find an amazing decrease in the first-pattern percentages in Vergil, Horace, and Ovid.

The percentages of the first eight patterns likewise increase from Ennius, 65.35, to Catullus, 90.98.[10] Catullus' heavy concentration on eight patterns results in a repetitious monotony unparalleled in the Republican poets. A musician with sixteen notes at his disposal would not be making the most of his instrument if he used half of the notes only nine per cent of the time.[11]

The steady increase in various types of repetition from Cicero to Catullus will be apparent also from the following tabulation:

	Cicero	Lucretius	Catullus
Patterns per 16-line unit:	8.5	8.6	7.0
% of units with 8 or more:	82.76	76.10	30.43
Same pattern 4 or more times, 1 every x lines:	479.0	386.1	188.5
Repeat clusters, 1 every x lines:	59.6	49.2	29.0
Repeats, 1 every x lines:	11.4	8.8	7.0
R + NR, 1 every x lines:	3.9	3.6	3.0
Two most repeated patterns:	*dsss*	*dsss*	*dsss*
	ddss	*ddss*	*sdss*
Combined R, % total R:	57.15	59.64	68.51
Combined R + NR, % total N + NR:	47.15	57.65	65.60

In each of these categories, we find Catullus in an extreme position, an indication of the excessive monotony of his hexameter verse. This trend in the late Republic toward repetition will be reversed by the Augustan poets Vergil and Horace, who not only imitate Cicero in some respects, but go far beyond him in other aspects of variety.

One means of introducing variety into repeats and near repeats is to change the fourth-foot texture from homodyne to heterodyne, or from heterodyne to homodyne. The percentage differences in both the repeats and the repeats plus the near repeats are as follows:

	Cicero	Lucretius	Catullus
% fourth-foot homodyne:	44.79	47.66	60.44
R, differs from homodyne %:	+5.21	+2.16	-25.25
R + NR, differs from homodyne %:	+0.74	+0.41	-26.84

Again the extent to which Catullus is out of line is apparent: unusually high percentage of fourth-foot homodyne and almost no desire to change the fourth-foot texture in repeats and near repeats. Cicero has the lowest homodyne percentage of the three Republican poets listed above,[12] about three per cent less than that of Lucretius.[13]

In the case of opposite and reverse patterns in adjacent lines (e.g., *sddd* with its opposite *dsss*, or with its reverse *ddds*), we find the following variations:

	Cicero	Lucretius	Catullus
Opposites, one every x lines:	79.8	30.8	37.7
Reverses, one every x lines:	24.0	51.3	53.9

Cicero shows little desire to have a pattern preceded or followed by its opposite; in the *Aratea* opposites occur once every 79.8 lines, but he apparently introduced them considerably more often in his later poetry. Statistics based on patterns in adjacent lines can be very misleading in the case of fragments and tend to give too low a frequency; even so, the average for the fragments is higher than that in the *Aratea,* one every 53.0 verses (total for Cicero, one every 67.6 verses). We should expect to have almost no opposite combinations in Catullus, since the opposites of his eight most frequent patterns can appear only 9.02 per cent of the time; surprisingly enough, however, we find one opposite combination every 37.7 lines. Three of the seven occurrences of *dsdd* are with its opposite *sdss; sddd* appears only twice (152, 231) and each time it is preceded by *dsss*. In Lucretius the percentage of *sddd* with *dsss* is 35.63, that of *ssdd* with *ddss* 25.64. The opposite combinations which occur most often are the following: Cicero, *sssd-ddds* tied with *ddsd-ssds*, 33.33 per cent each of the total opposites; Lucretius, *sdsd-dsds*, 22.69 per cent, and Catullus, *dsdd-sdss*, 33.33 per cent.

The desire to introduce metrical variety by means of opposites in adjacent lines apparently begins with Lucretius, one instance every 30.8 lines (with a range from 23.3 in Book I to 42.5 in

Book V). With very few exceptions, the later poets, from the time of Augustus to the age of Justinian, all use opposite combinations considerably more often, from once every 15 to once every 25 lines.

Although opposite combinations are rare in Cicero, we find an unusual fondness for reverse combinations; they are more than twice as frequent as in the other two Republican poets, and in this respect Cicero seems to have had little influence on either Lucretius or Catullus. In all three poets the pattern which appears most frequently with its reverse is *sssd;* the percentages of *sssd* with *dsss* are: Cicero, 64.71; Lucretius, 40.14; Catullus, 40.0. This combination in Cicero comprises 55.0 per cent of the total reverses and in Lucretius 39.86 per cent; in Catullus, *ssds-sdss* provides 71.43 per cent of the total reverses. Cicero's frequency of reverse combinations, one every 24.0 lines, is higher than appears elsewhere in Latin poetry; the closest approach to Cicero in this respect is Horace, *Ars Poetica,* one every 25.0 lines; Nemesianus, *Eclogues,* one every 24.4 lines; and Avitus, one every 26.1 lines.

The Chronology of the Books of Lucretius

The distribution of spondees and dactyls in the first eight patterns of the *De rerum natura* is eighteen and fourteen, but there is considerable variation among the individual books: I (nineteen spondees, thirteen dactyls), II, and V (eighteen spondees, fourteen dactyls each) form a more spondaic group, and the remaining books have a larger proportion of dactyls: III and IV (sixteen spondees and sixteen dactyls each), VI (seventeen spondees, fifteen dactyls). On the basis of enjambement Büchner argues that Books I, II, and V were earlier than III, IV, and VI.[14] Bailey accepts Büchner's conclusions and says: "The study provides an almost unique opportunity of tracing the gradual development of Lucretius' conscious art."[15] Bailey gives other arguments (e.g., Memmius is mentioned eleven times in I, II, and V, but his name does not occur in III, IV, and VI) which also indicate that I, II, and V are closely connected and were written first.[16] It is significant that the distribution of spondees and dactyls in the individual books gives added support to the grouping favored by Büchner and Bailey.

If Lucretius in his earlier books is more spondaic (and this would be natural, considering the emphasis on spondees displayed by his predecessors Ennius, Lucilius, and Cicero), he also evinces in these same books a greater interest in variety, especially in I and II, with V forming a transition to the other three books;[17] the following categories illustrate important differences:

	I-II-V	III-IV-VI
% 16-line units with 8 or more patterns:	79.57	72.57
Repeats, one every *x* lines:	9.1	8.5
4th-foot homodyne %:	48.63	46.66
dsss R, % of change:	52.56	46.20
Differs from homodyne %:	+3.93	-0.46
dsss R + NR, % of change:	50.40	45.99
Differs from homodyne %:	+1.77	-0.67
Opposites, % *ssdd* with *ddss:*	28.57	23.26
Reverses, one every *x* lines:	40.7	69.8
% *dsdd* with *ddsd:*	18.52	9.09

We thus find fewer repeated patterns and a greater shift in fourth-foot texture in I, II, and V than in the other three books. Also, the frequency of reverse combinations is far higher in I, II, and V than in the other books; perhaps this too is the influence of Cicero who has in the *Aratea* one reverse every 24.0 lines, the highest frequency in Latin hexameter poetry. The percentage of *dsdd* preceded or followed by *ddsd* in the three earlier books is twice that in the others.

Two more striking differences may be pointed out between the two groups of books. (1) Books I, II, and V, with a greater proportion of spondees in the first eight patterns, also have a higher frequency of spondaic verses, one every 180.3 lines; in the more dactylic III, IV, and VI, the spondaic verses occur once every 280.1 lines. (2) I shall discuss below (in Appendix B) a rare type of first-foot dactyl, one composed of three monosyllables or elided dissyllables; these dactyls are more frequent in Lucretius than in most Latin poets, e.g., *aut quod in* (IV, 1137), *et quod ab* (V, 685), and *fit quoqu(e) ut* (eight instances in Book VI). The frequency of these three-word dactyls in the *De rerum natura* as a whole is one every 210.5 lines, but they are relatively few in I, II, and V, one every 465.8 lines; in the other three books they occur more than three times as often, once every 134.9 lines, and in Book VI the frequency is once every 71.1 lines. Perhaps Lucretius was hurried or careless in the composition of his final book, or he may have developed a fondness for "formulaic" expressions such as *fit quoqu(e) ut*.

As a result of the various types of evidence adduced above, there seems no doubt that Büchner and Bailey are correct in their belief that Books I, II, and V are earlier than III, IV, and VI.

Catullus and Callimachus

Catullus is by far the most distinguished of the *novi poetae*, the Latin poets of the late Republic who brought to Rome the themes and techniques of the Greek poets of Alexandria and especially their leader Callimachus. Catullus' best work is the least Alexandrian, and consists of the lyrics, elegies, and epigrams which have made him (and his beloved Lesbia) deservedly famous.

His epyllion on the marriage of Peleus and Thetis, which encloses the tragic story of Ariadne (LXIV), has been praised for passages of astonishing beauty and at the same time criticized for its monotony.[18] The monotony results largely from the poet's handling of the hexameter patterns. His metrical procedures differ not only from those of the other Republican poets, as we have seen, but are in most respects quite unlike those of any other Latin poet, with the possible exception of one or two writers of the Late Empire, especially the Christian poet Cyprian of Gaul. For example, Catullus' high percentage of the first eight patterns, 90.98, is surpassed by Cyprian with 91.06; only 30.63 per cent of Catullus' sixteen-line units have the usual eight or more patterns, and Cyprian is next with 50.62 per cent. Catullus has the highest frequency of repeats, one every 7.0 lines (Cyprian, 7.9), and of repeats plus near repeats, one every 3.0 lines (Cyprian, 3.2).[19]

How are these and the many other abnormalities in Catullus to be explained? Are they possibly the result of his devotion to Alexandrian poetry, of a desire to imitate Callimachus?[20] Catullus has far more spondaic verses than any other Latin poet, one every 13.6 lines, or 7.37 per cent. Callimachus in his five hexameter *Hymns* has one spondaic verse every 15.1 lines, or 6.62 per cent. This striking similarity suggests a comparison of Catullus and Callimachus in several of the categories of variety and repetition.

The Greek hexameter, from Homer to Musaeus, differs greatly from the Latin hexameter, from Ennius to Corippus. The first pattern in Greek poetry is usually *dddd*, but *sddd* in Theocritus and *dsdd* in Hesiod and Callimachus, and the distribution in the first eight patterns is almost always ten spondees and twenty-two dactyls. Since most Roman poets preferred more spondees, the favorite patterns of Callimachus and Catullus will therefore be very different. But the percentages of the patterns and the frequencies of the repeats may indicate that Catullus has followed Callimachus in several respects:

	Catullus	Callimachus
Percentage, first pattern:	27.59	28.95
Percentage, first four:	67.90	71.74
Percentage, first eight:	90.98	93.14
Patterns per 16-line unit:	7.0	6.6
% of units with 8 or more:	30.43	18.87
Repeat clusters, 1 every *x* lines:	29.0	23.0
Repeats, 1 every *x* lines:	7.0	5.4
R + NR, 1 every *x* lines	3.0	2.7
Favorite R, % total R:	44.44	45.34
Favorite R, % total pattern:	23.08	28.85
Favorite R + NR, % total R + NR:	41.60	46.46
Favorite R + NR, % total pattern:	50.0	59.68

The results of this tabulation seem amazing. In their excessive concentration on eight patterns, with the resulting lack of variety and high frequencies of the repeated patterns, no two poets could be more similar.[21] It is important to note also that the percentages and frequencies of Callimachus as listed above are higher than in the other Alexandrian poets,[22] just as those of Catullus are much higher than in the other Latin poets; this is perhaps another significant indication of Catullus' indebtedness to his Greek predecessor. At any rate, we have here convincing proof that the abnormal metrical technique of Catullus in LXIV is to be explained by his close imitation of Callimachus.

Summary

In both Ennius and Lucilius we find a heavy concentration on spondees in the first eight patterns, and relatively low percentages for the first, first four, and first eight patterns. Beginning with Cicero, repetition of the same patterns, with correspondingly higher percentages, increases through Lucretius, especially in the later books (III, IV, and VI), and culminates in the monotonous emphasis in Catullus LXIV on eight patterns only (90.98 per cent); this and many other unusual features of Catullus' metrical technique are to be explained by his imitation of Callimachus.

Cicero was the first to make *dsss* the favorite pattern; not only did the Republican poets follow him in this respect, but Vergil and Horace as well (and many later poets, influenced by Vergil's *Georgics* or *Aeneid*). Cicero also established the distribution of twenty spondees and twelve dactyls for the first eight patterns, and was the only poet before Vergil (in the *Aeneid*) to have a fourth-foot spondee in each of these same patterns. The frequencies and percentages of Vergil and Horace are in general much closer to those of Cicero and mark a definite trend away from the metrical procedures of Lucretius and especially Catullus; this is seen in their avoidance of repeats and near repeats, in the higher percentages of change in fourth-foot texture, and in the steadily increasing use of reverse patterns in adjacent lines.

Büchner states correctly that Cicero is an important bridge to the Augustans.[23] Recently, the same view has been expressed in more detail by Townend:[24]

> Altogether Cicero, even in his earliest work, stands relatively close to Virgil. Lucretius, writing appreciably later, demonstrates the dangers of assuming that verse-technique advances in a straight line from one poet to another.... He is scarcely influenced by the advances already achieved by Cicero, if not before. Catullus, again, occupies a special position as a member of a school of deliberate innovators who copied the Greek Alexandrines.... Such evidence as there is supports the conclusion that Cicero's ear for the cadences and rhythms of words was largely responsible for some at least of these advances which the Augustans were to appropriate to their own use.

Cicero is thus a kind of milestone from which Lucretius and Catullus move in one direction, the easier road toward greater repetition and monotony, whereas Vergil and Horace advance in the opposite direction toward greater variety of every kind — the more uncharted route. The important conclusions to be drawn are that there is no straight development in metrical technique from the Republican to the Augustan poets, and that Cicero as a metrician is *the* important predecessor of Vergil and Horace.

1. See Duckworth, *TAPhA* 95 (1964), pp. 9-65; 96 (1965), pp. 73-95; 97 (1966), pp. 67-113; 98 (1967), pp. 77-150. For the numerical totals of the sixteen patterns in the various poets, see the Tables at the end of each article.

2. My figures are based on Warmington's text. Both Drobisch, *BSGL* 18 (1866), pp. 92-94, 20 (1868), p. 40, and Cordier, *Les débuts de l'hexamètre latin*, p. 66, give totals which differ slightly from mine; they use Vahlen's edition and include several verses listed by Warmington as spurious. The percentages based on their totals, however, are close to those which I give below; e.g., for the first eight patterns my percentage is 65.35; that of Drobisch is 66.18; that of Cordier 64.99.

3. My percentages are based on 1,920 verses (960 from each epic). The totals of La Roche, *WS* 20 (1898), pp. 3, 9, produce a *dddd* percentage for both epics of 19.93, as given in Duckworth, *TAPhA* 95 (1964), pp. 14-15. Also, La Roche, p. 10, lists *dddddss* as the most frequent pattern among the 1,378 spondaic verses, with 285 occurrences; we thus have a percentage of 20.68, very close to the *dddddds* percentage.

4. In Ennius, *dsss* and *sdss* are tied for second place, *ddss* and *sssd* for fifth place.

5. *Latin Hexameter Verse*, p. 114. On the spondaic nature of Ennius' verse, see also Cordier, *Les débuts de l'hexamètre latin*, pp. 65-69.

6. This same distribution appears in Vergil, *Georgics* IV; Lucan, Book III; Silius Italicus, Books II, III, IV, IX, XII, and XIII; Juvenal, *Satires* VIII, XII, XIV, and XVI.

7. If we include the fragments, *ssss* moves to fourth place, not fifth, as stated by Ewbank, *The Poems of Cicero*, p. 47. For this and other inaccuracies in Ewbank's calculations, see Duckworth, *TAPhA* 96 (1965), p. 75, note 9.

8. *The Poems of Cicero*, p. 48.

9. The percentage range in the individual books of the *De rerum natura* is from 17.88 (Book I) to 23.10 (Book V). Merrill, *UCPPh* 5 (1922-23), pp. 253-334, gives approximately the same percentages for each book, with the exception of Book II, where "nearly 11 per cent" (p. 282) is obviously an error for "nearly 19 per cent"; Merrill's totals produce a percentage of 18.57.

10. Lucretius (79.81 per cent) is slightly lower than Cicero (*Aratea*, 82.88; total 82.26).

11. Catullus' *Epithalamium* (LXII), also in hexameters, has an even higher percentage for the first eight patterns, 92.54, although that of *dsss*, the most frequent pattern, is only 20.89 (27.59 in LXIV). Usually *sddd* (the opposite of *dsss*) is one of the least frequent patterns; in this poem it has second place, as it provides the oft-repeated refrain: *Hymen o Hymenaee, Hymen ades o Hymenaee*. Townend, in Dorey (ed.), *Cicero*, p. 124, apparently overlooks LXII when he refers to Catullus as "represented by a single poem in hexameters, 'The Marriage of Peleus and Thetis' (64), in some 400 verses."

12. If we include the fragments of Cicero, the percentage of fourth-foot homodyne is 46.17, still slightly lower than that in Lucretius. On the basis of fragments only, the percentages of fourth-foot homodyne in Ennius and Lucilius are 43.56 and 46.79 respectively.

13. The range for fourth-foot homodyne in the individual books of Lucretius is from 44.72 (IV) to 49.59 (III). On homodyne and heterodyne in Lucretius, see Naughtin, *CQ* 2 (1952), pp. 152-167.

14. *Beobachtungen*, pp. 63-66. Cf. Mewaldt, *RE* 13.2 (1927), col. 1669.

15. *Titi Lucreti Cari... Libri Sex*, Vol. I, p. 123.

16. *Ibid.*, pp. 32-37.

17. One exception appears in the percentages of the first, first four, and first eight patterns, where Book V is slightly higher than VI; these same percentages are consistently low in both I and II; see Duckworth, *TAPhA* 97 (1966), p. 110.

18. See Dimsdale, *History of Latin Literature*, p. 156. Wilkinson, *Golden Latin Artistry*, p. 129, points out that a molossus word (— — —) occurs after the strong caesura in 146 out of the 408 lines, and says: "The rhythmic monotony is intolerable."

19. As a result of his unusually high percentage of fourth-foot homodyne and almost no interest in change of fourth-foot texture in repeated patterns, Catullus' percentage of change is consistently far below the homodyne percentage: R, -25.25 (surpassed only by Petronius, -27.07); R + NR, -26.84 (next is Calpurnius Siculus with -23.30). Catullus is similarly below the homodyne percentage in the case of the most repeated pattern: R, -22.94; R + NR, -25.82, but a number of later poets have differences even greater, e.g., Petronius, Avienus, *Aratea*, Paulinus of Périgueux, Cyprian, and Arator.

20. On the indebtedness of Catullus to Callimachus and the other Alexandrian poets, see Granarolo, *L'Oeuvre de Catulle*, pp. 284-286, 375-377, and the bibliography there cited.

21. Although I criticize both Callimachus and Catullus for excessive concentration on eight patterns

and for their resultant lack of metrical variety,
I must in all fairness point out that their use of
so many spondaic verses provides in a sense an
additional, if different, type of variety. On the
other hand, Aratus has even more spondaic
verses, one every 6.9 lines, or 11.41 per cent
(almost twice as frequent as in Callimachus), but
his percentage of the first eight patterns of the
non-spondaic verses is much lower, 83.96. This
resembles that of other Greek poets (Homer,
Hesiod, and Theocritus), and many Roman poets
as well (Cicero, Ovid in the *Metamorphoses,*
Valerius Flaccus, Claudian, and Avitus).

22. This is especially true of the percentage of
sixteen-line units with eight or more patterns:
Aratus, 60.66; Theocritus, 68.92; Apollonius of
Rhodes, 56.67; but Callimachus an astounding
18.87 per cent.

23. Büchner, *RE* 7A.1 (1939), col. 1266: "Nimmt
man alles zusammen so wird C. zu einer
wichtigen Brücke zu den Augusteern"; see also
col. 1260.

24. In Dorey (ed.), *Cicero,* pp. 126-128.

Chapter 7

VERGIL

When we turn to the hexameters of Vergil, we are in a different metrical world. In the *Eclogues*, the earliest of his three authentic works, we find that Vergil's percentages and frequencies differ most strikingly from those of his Republican predecessors, in many instances more so than do those of the *Georgics* and *Aeneid*. Hardie correctly says: "The versification of the Eclogues might almost be regarded as a revolt, a protest or reaction against the rhythm of the preceding generation."[1]

I shall illustrate, at the very beginning of my chapter on Vergil's hexameter technique, the nature of this "protest or reaction" by means of an analysis of one sixteen-line unit each from Cicero, Lucretius, Catullus, and Vergil. In order to avoid the danger of using passages which might twist the evidence, I select arbitrarily the first sixteen lines from Cicero's *Aratea* (excluding 3, a spondaic verse),[2] from Book I of the *De rerum natura*, from Catullus LXIV (excluding three spondaic verses, 3, 11, and 15), and from *Eclogue* II, by general agreement the earliest of the pastorals.

Cicero, *Aratea*, 1-17

(dsss)	E quibus hunc subter possis cognoscere fultum;	*(t)*
(sdsd)	nam caeli mediam partem terit, ut prius illae	*(t)*
(ddss)	Et prope conspicies paruum, sub pectore clarae	*(t)*
(dsss)	Andromedae, signum, Deltoton dicere Grai	*(m)*
(ddds)	quod soliti, simili quia forma littera claret	*(m)*
(dsdd)	huic spatio ductum simili latus extat utrumque	*(t)*
(sdds)	at non tertia pars lateris; namque est minor illis,	*(t)*
(ssss)	sed stellis longe densis praeclara relucet.	*(t)*
(dsds)	Inferior paulo est Aries et flamen ad Austri	*(t)*
(sddd)	inclinatior atque etiam uehementius illi	*(t)*
(ssss)	Pisces, quorum alter paulo praelabitur ante	*(t)*
(ddds)	et magis horrisonis Aquilonis tangitur alis;	*(m)*
(ssdd)	atque horum e caudis duplices velut aere catenae	*(t)*
(ssss)	discedunt, quae diuersae per lumina serpunt	*(t)*
(sdss)	atque una tamen in stella communiter haerent,	*(t)*
(ddss)	quem ueteres soliti Caelestem dicere Nodum.	*(m)*

Lucretius, I, 1-16

(ddds)	Aeneadum genetrix, hominum divumque voluptas,	*(t)*
(dsss)	alma Venus, caeli subter labentia signa	*(t)*
(ddss)	quae mare navigerum, quae terras frugiferentis	*(m)*
(dsdd)	concelebras, per te quoniam genus omne animantum	*(t)*
(dsss)	concipitur visitque exortum lumina solis:	*(m)*
(ddss)	te, dea, te fugiunt venti, te nubila caeli	*(t)*
(sdds)	adventumque tuum, tibi suavis daedala tellus	*(m)*
(ssds)	summittit flores, tibi rident aequora ponti	*(m)*
(sdss)	placatumque nitet diffuso lumine caelum.	*(m)*
(ddds)	nam simul ac species patefactast verna diei	*(m)*
(dddd)	et reserata viget genitabilis aura favoni,	*(m)*
(dsds)	aëriae primum volucres te, diva, tuumque	*(t)*
(ddss)	significant initum perculsae corda tua vi.	*(m)*
(ddss)	inde ferae pecudes persultant pabula laeta	*(m)*
(dssd)	et rapidos tranant amnis: ita capta lepore	*(t)*
(ddss)	te sequitur cupide quo quamque inducere pergis.	*(m)*

Catullus LXIV, 1-19

(dsss)	Peliaco quondam prognatae uertice pinus	*(m)*
(sdss)	dicuntur liquidas Neptuni nasse per undas	*(m)*
(sdss)	cum lecti iuuenes, Argiuae robora pubis,	*(m)*
(ssss)	auratam optantes Colchis auertere pellem	*(t)*
(sdds)	ausi sunt uada salsa cita decurrere puppi,	*(t)*
(dsss)	caerula uerrentes abiegnis aequora palmis.	*(m)*
(ddss)	diua quibus retinens in summis urbibus arces	*(m)*
(dsds)	ipsa leui fecit uolitantem flamine currum,	*(m)*
(dsss)	pinea coniungens inflexae texta carinae.	*(m)*
(dsss)	quae simul ac rostro uentosum proscidit aequor	*(m)*
(ddss)	tortaque remigio spumis incanuit unda,	*(t)*
(sdss)	emersere freti candenti e gurgite uultus	*(m)*
(sdss)	illa, atque haud alia, uiderunt luce marinas	*(m)*
(sdss)	mortales oculis nudato corpore Nymphas	*(m)*
(sdss)	nutricum tenus exstantes e gurgite cano.	*(t)*
(dsss)	tum Thetidis Peleus incensus fertur amore,	*(m)*

Vergil, *Ecl.* II, 1-16

(ssds)	Formosum pastor Corydon ardebat Alexim,	*(t)*
(ddss)	delicias domini; nec quid speraret habebat.	*(m)*
(sssd)	tantum inter densas, umbrosa cacumina, fagos	*(m)*
(ddds)	adsidue veniebat. ibi haec incondita solus	*(m)*
(dsds)	montibus et silvis studio iactabat inani:	*(t)*
(sddd)	'O crudelis Alexi, nihil mea carmina curas?	*(t)*
(sdds)	nil nostri miserere? mori me denique cogis?	*(t)*
(ddss)	nunc etiam pecudes umbras et frigora captant;	*(t)*
(ddss)	nunc viridis etiam occultant spineta lacertos,	*(t)*
(ddss)	Thestylis et rapido fessis messoribus aestu	*(t)*
(dsss)	alia serpyllumque herbas contundit olentis	*(t)*
(ssds)	at mecum raucis, tua dum vestigia lustro,	*(m)*
(dsds)	sole sub ardenti resonant arbusta cicadis.	*(t)*
(ddsd)	nonne fuit satius tristis Amaryllidis iras	*(t)*
(ddsd)	atque superba pati fastidia? nonne Menalcan?	*(m)*
(sdss)	quamvis ille niger, quamvis tu candidus esses?	*(t)*

Vergil, in the first sixteen-line unit of *Eclogue* II, differs from both Lucretius and Catullus, but resembles Cicero, in two important respects: (1) greater variety, with ten different patterns in sixteen lines; Lucretius nine, Catullus six, but Cicero eleven;[3] (2) a striking reduction in fourth-foot homodyne, five instances only; Lucretius ten, Catullus twelve, but only four in Cicero. One short passage perhaps proves little, but we have here *in parvo* two important Vergilian innovations, to be discussed below, and also strong evidence that Vergil's "protest" was against the technique of Lucretius and Catullus, not that of Cicero, who in this particular sixteen-line unit has even more variety and a higher percentage of heterodyne than Vergil.

Also, the Vergilian lines have a lightness and a delicacy lacking in his predecessors, and especially Catullus; note the heavy molossus-word (— — —) in the third and fourth feet, after the penthemimeral caesura: in Lucretius, *exortum* (5), *diffuso* (9), *perculsae* (13), *persultant* (14); in Catullus, *prognatae* (1), *Neptuni* (2), *Argiuae* (4), *abiegnis* (7), *inflexae* (10), *uentosum* (12), *uiderunt* (16), *nudato* (17), *incensus* (19). We have, in sixteen lines, four instances in Lucretius and nine in Catullus,[4] but only two in Cicero, both proper names (*Deltoton* in 5, *Caelestem* in 17), and in Vergil not a single instance; this distinction perhaps shows clearly what Vergil (and Cicero before him) accomplished by his reduction of fourth-foot homodyne and his avoidance in homodyned lines of molossi of this type.

I disagree, therefore, with Williams, at least in part, when he says:[5]

Within the framework of the Greek pastoral genre Virgil uses the flexible and languorous cadences of the Latin hexameter which he had inherited from Catullus, and
himself developed with a delicacy which makes the metrical movement of these
poems *sui generis.*

There is little that is flexible and languorous in the cadences of Catullus, and it is the Catullan type
of hexameter that Vergil seeks to avoid above all.[6]

Vergil's Metrical Art: His Innovations

I gave, under the various categories in Part I, the relevant statistics for Vergil's three works,
and many of these I shall not repeat. Some will be necessary, however, to show his radical departure from the procedures of Lucretius and Catullus, the extent to which he is influenced by Cicero,
and the development of his own metrical art from the *Eclogues* through the *Georgics* to the *Aeneid.*
Vergil's metrical innovations may be listed under four main categories:

1. Far less concentration on the patterns occurring most frequently, and, as a result, a striking decrease in the frequencies of repeat clusters and repeated patterns. Vergil's percentages of
his favorite pattern are lower than those of the Republican poets, even of Ennius, with the exception
of the *Georgics* (15.81; Ennius, 15.35), and those of the first eight patterns are likewise lower,
again with the exception of Ennius. Nothing like Ennius' percentage of 65.35 had appeared prior to
that in the *Eclogues,* 69.09. The highest average number of patterns per sixteen-line unit had been
that in Lucretius, 8.6, but with the *Eclogues* we jump to 9.7 (*Georgics,* 9.3; *Aeneid,* 9.4), and the
percentage of units with eight or more patterns goes from 82.76 in Cicero to 97.37 in the *Eclogues*
(*Georgics,* 92.59; *Aeneid,* 92.46). Repeat clusters had appeared with less frequency in Cicero than
in Lucretius and Catullus, once every 59.6 lines. Here perhaps Vergil's "revolt" is seen in its
most startling form: repeat clusters occur in the *Eclogues* once every 275.0 lines (*Georgics,*
145.5; *Aeneid,* 200.1). Cicero had used repeats and near repeats far less often than Lucretius and
Catullus, but his frequencies (R, one every 11.4 lines; R + NR, one every 3.9 lines) still seem high
when we find the corresponding numbers in the *Eclogues* to be 13.1 and 5.1; in the *Georgics* and
Aeneid the frequencies are practically identical, but slightly higher than in the *Eclogues* (12.3 and
4.5, 12.4 and 4.6 respectively).

2. An amazing decrease in the percentage of fourth-foot homodyne. This percentage had increased from 44.79 in Cicero to 60.44 in Catullus; Vergil definitely avoided the coincidence of ictus
and accent in the fourth foot and gave more power and conflict to his verse, especially in the *Georgics* (36.08) and the *Aeneid* (37.78); the percentage in the *Eclogues* is a bit higher (39.73), but still
appreciably lower than that in Cicero.

3. The shift from fourth-foot heterodyne to homodyne, or from homodyne to heterodyne, to
give variety to repeated patterns. Vergil's percentages of change both in repeats and in repeats
plus near repeats, in relation to the homodyne percentages, are consistently higher than those of
the earlier poets, and, in the case of repeats, highest in the *Eclogues,* +9.48 (*Georgics,* +7.42,
Aeneid, +6.71); the difference in Cicero is +5.21. When we turn to the pattern most often repeated,
we see an even greater desire to introduce variety, e.g., *Georgics,* R, +13.92, and here Cicero
seems to point the way with +14.03; *Aeneid,* R + NR, +11.50 (Cicero, +5.21). We find no such increases over the fourth-foot percentages in Lucretius, and in Catullus the decreases range from
-22.94 to -26.84.

4. A consistent use of opposite patterns in adjacent lines as an additional type of variety. The
frequency in Vergil per *x* lines is as follows: *Eclogues,* 19.6; *Georgics,* 20.9; *Aeneid,* 23.1. Nothing like this had appeared earlier in Latin poetry; the closest frequency is that of Lucretius, one
every 30.8 lines.

These four categories best illustrate Vergil's "revolt" and help to explain his "metrical mastery."[7]
I did not include above as one of Vergil's innovations the emphasis on dactyls in the *Eclogues,*
with *ddss* the favorite pattern and a distribution in the first eight patterns of sixteen spondees and
sixteen dactyls. This differs strikingly from the stress on spondees in the Republican poets (with

the exception of Books III and IV of Lucretius), but is not typical of Vergil.[8] In both the *Georgics* and the *Aeneid,* Vergil shifts to *dsss* as his most frequent pattern and favors a distribution of twenty spondees and twelve dactyls (both first preferred by Cicero).

The *Georgics* has been praised for "its perfection of finish" and considered "an example of artistic excellence of the highest degree."[9] Vergil here develops a metrical uniformity lacking in the *Eclogues* and establishes norms which determine his metrical technique also in the *Aeneid.* In certain respects, however, the *Georgics* lacks the metrical perfection of the *Aeneid;* the percentages of the first, first four, and first eight patterns are slightly higher, and repeat clusters are more numerous. In two respects the *Georgics* marks an intermediate stage between the *Eclogues* and the *Aeneid.*

1. In the first eight patterns a fourth-foot spondee occurs six times in the *Eclogues,* seven in the *Georgics,* and eight in the *Aeneid;* in his final work, Vergil thus returns to the practice of Cicero, one of the few other poets in the entire history of the Latin hexameter to have a spondaic fourth foot in all first eight patterns.

2. Vergil develops an increasing fondness for reverse combinations in adjacent lines; in the *Eclogues* they occur every 55.0 lines, about the same frequency as in Lucretius and Catullus; in the *Georgics,* once every 46.4 lines; in the *Aeneid,* once every 38.9 lines. Reverse combinations appear even more often in Horace but they do not attain the frequency in Cicero (one every 24.0 lines), who is thus not only the pioneer in the use of reverse combinations but employs them more frequently than any other Latin poet.

The *Eclogues:* Vergil and Theocritus

The *Eclogues* are much more dactylic than either the *Georgics* or the *Aeneid.* The two refrains in *Eclogue* VIII (*ddsd* and *dddd*),[10] based on the refrains in Theocritus, *Idylls* I (*ddsd*) and II (*sddd* and *dddd*) give the poem and the collection as a whole a dactylic tone that is lacking in Vergil's two later works.[11] Yet the basic emphasis on spondees is unmistakable, and this is especially noticeable in the first eight patterns, six of which have a spondaic fourth foot.

I said above that the *Eclogues* lack the metrical uniformity which appears in the *Georgics* and the *Aeneid.* This is perhaps best seen in the most frequent pattern: *ddss* is first in the collection as a whole (13.09 per cent), but there is a wide variation in the individual poems, e.g., *sdss* in I (13.25 per cent), *dssd* in III (15.32 per cent), *dsds* in V (14.61 per cent), *ddsd* in VIII (17.59 per cent, one result of the refrains mentioned above, with *dddd* 11.11 per cent), and *dsss* in X (14.29 per cent). In only two pastorals is *ddss* in first place, II (20.55 per cent) and IV (an abnormally high 24.19).

The emergence of *dsss* as the first pattern in X, by general agreement the latest of the *Eclogues,* is of particular interest, since this is Vergil's favorite pattern in the *Georgics* (also in each of the four books) and the *Aeneid* (also in ten books, all but V and VII). In *Eclogues* VI and VII *dsss* is tied for first place, and it is second in IV and VIII; these four poems are among Vergil's later pastorals. There seems to be a definite relation between Vergil's use of *dsss* and the dating of the individual poems. In *Eclogue* II, accepted by all as the earliest, *dsss* is in fifteenth place,[12] and it is tied (with *sdss* and *ddds*) for fourth place in III, considered the second pastoral in order of composition.[13]

In the case of Catullus and Callimachus, the favorite patterns are very different but the percentages and frequencies are almost identical. When we turn from the *Eclogues* of Vergil to the *Idylls* of Theocritus, to which they are so indebted for language and subject matter, the percentages and frequencies are necessarily very different, since Theocritus has the typically high percentages of Greek hexameter poetry: first pattern, 18.43; first four, 63.51; first eight, 84.35.[14] These are very different from the low percentages of the *Eclogues.* One might expect, however, that Vergil in his more dactylic pastorals would imitate Theocritus' patterns in general, just as the refrains in *Eclogue* VIII (*ddsd* and *dddd*) echo those of *Idylls* I and II, but this is not the case. The first eight patterns of each poet are as follows (with *dssd* and *ddsd* tied for fourth place in the *Eclogues*). Only two patterns, *dssd* and *ddsd,* appear on both lists; in other words, the differences are almost as great as those in the first eight patterns of Ennius and Homer. The distribution of spondees and

	1	2	3	4	5	6	7	8
Eclogues:	ddss	dsss	dsds	dssd		sdss	ddds	sdds
				ddsd				
Idylls:	sddd	dsdd	dddd	ssdd	ddsd	dssd	sdsd	ssds

dactyls in the first eight patterns is sixteen and sixteen in Vergil, twelve and twenty in Theocritus,[15] but fourth-foot spondees are six in Vergil and only one in Theocritus. Vergil's first eight patterns, with a percentage of 69.09, occur in Theocritus a total of 24.33 per cent.

Vergil imitates Theocritus most closely in his earliest pastoral. *Eclogue* II is the most Theocritean, since the first eight patterns contain twelve spondees and twenty dactyls. *Eclogue* VIII is similar; *sdss* and *sdds* are tied for eighth place; depending upon which is included, the spondees in the first eight patterns total twelve or thirteen, the dactyls twenty or nineteen; this is, of course, partly the result of the two dactylic (and Theocritean) refrains, *ddsd* and *dddd*. But the fact that II and VIII are the most dactylic of the pastorals may also be connected with Vergil's arrangement of the corresponding poems (I and IX, II and VIII, III and VII, IV and VI) around V as the central poem.[16] *Eclogues* II and VIII thus go together in their distribution of spondees and dactyls as in many other respects.[17] *Eclogues* III and VII, considered by Otis the two other "fully Theocritean poems,"[18] have a more spondaic distribution, eighteen and fourteen, and seventeen and fifteen respectively.

Bolaños likewise points out that the high dactylic count of *Eclogues* II and VIII is to be explained by the fact that they are close imitations of Theocritus, and he says that IV is the most independent and the most Vergilian of the *Eclogues*.[19] Bolaños is misleading here; IV is Vergilian in that it is the most spondaic of the collection (nineteen spondees and thirteen dactyls in the first eight patterns), but in most respects it is the least Vergilian of the ten poems, and especially in its metrical technique. I turn to the problem of *Eclogue* IV in the following section.

Eclogue IV: Vergil and Catullus

Vergil in his famous Messianic poem prophesies the birth of a child who will inaugurate a new Golden Age. Williams has an excellent summary of the eclogue:[20]

> The poem is still partly pastoral — the golden age is Arcadian, the goats will come home of their own accord — but it is elevated and eulogistic in tone, like a birthday hymn or a marriage song, and its prophetic phrases are religious and mystic, in some ways very like Isaiah. Through the Sibylline oracles it seems to have affinities with Eastern thought: it has been widely regarded since the time of Lactantius as a prophecy of Christ. The scholarly discussion on this poem is greater in bulk than for any other short poem in antiquity.

Eclogue IV is not only unique among the pastorals for its theme, style, and subject matter, but it is equally unusual in its metrical structure, and the full extent to which it differs from the other nine poems has not hitherto been observed. I mentioned above that *ddss*, the most frequent pattern, occurs 24.19 per cent; this is higher than for any of the other *Eclogues* and almost twice as high as the percentage for the most frequent pattern in the collection as a whole (13.09). But the first four patterns in IV *(ddss, dsss, dsds, sdds)* total 72.58 per cent, as against 41.45 per cent for all ten *Eclogues*; and the first eight patterns add to an amazing 91.93 per cent, leaving only about eight per cent for the other eight patterns. The metrical situation in IV is thus very unlike that in the other *Eclogues*.

If we analyze the other nine pastorals apart from *Eclogue* IV, the differences are even more striking, as the percentages in the tabulation on page 51 indicate. Why should the frequency of the first eight patterns in *Eclogue* IV be almost 92 per cent, when the average frequency for the first eight patterns in the other nine *Eclogues* is 68.28, a total less than the percentage in IV of the *first four* patterns (72.58)? Why should the most frequent pattern in IV occur 24.19 per cent, when the average of the patterns appearing most often in the other nine poems is only 12.09, almost exactly half?

The high percentages of the patterns in *Eclogue* IV suggest a comparison with Theocritus:

Patterns	*Ecl.* I-X	*Ecl.* IV	*Ecl.* I-III, V-X
Most frequent:	13.09	24.19	12.09
First four:	41.45	72.58	39.71
First eight:	69.09	91.93	68.28
Spondees:	16	19	15
Dactyls:	16	13	17

first, 18.43; first four, 63.51; first eight, 84.35. Although these percentages in *Idylls* I-XIII are much higher than those of *Eclogues* I-X, they are, curiously enough, much lower than those of *Eclogue* IV. Even if we eliminate *Idylls* VIII and IX, often considered spurious,[21] the percentages for the other eleven *Idylls* are still considerably lower: 18.96, 65.03, 85.36 respectively.

Eclogue IV, totaling 63 lines, is composed of heptads: 3 + 7 + 7 + 28 + 7 + 7 + 4;[22] Préaux, in a recent discussion of the structure of the poem, explains the choice of 63 verses as appropriate for a birthday poem, 63 being considered a critical age.[23] But perhaps Vergil in this respect *was* influenced by Theocritus; the fourth *Idyll* also contains 63 verses and the numbers seven and fourteen are found in the metrical patterns: the most frequent pattern *(ssdd)* occurs fourteen times, and three other patterns *(dsdd, dddd,* and *sssd)* each appear seven times. Also, the percentage for the most frequent pattern in *Eclogue* IV is 24.19, in *Idyll* IV, 22.22; that for the first eight patterns in *Eclogue* IV is 91.93, in *Idyll* IV 90.48; these are not very dissimilar.

I do not, however, believe that *Eclogue* IV, so Roman and metrically so spondaic, is to be explained primarily by Vergil's imitation of *Idyll* IV. There is no similarity in the subject matter of the two poems, and the source of the metrical peculiarities of the eclogue must be sought elsewhere.

We turn now to Catullus LXIV, the Peleus and Thetis-Ariadne poem. The influence of this work upon *Eclogue* IV is recognized by all. As Wilkinson says, "Virgil was certainly impressed by the *Peleus and Thetis:* he echoes it a number of times, and his *Pollio* is largely a response to it."[24] The frequency percentages for the two poems are as follows, with those for Vergil's other nine pastorals listed to point up the comparison:

	Ecl. I-III, V-X	*Ecl.* IV	Catullus
First pattern:	12.09	24.19	27.59
First four:	39.71	72.58	67.90
First eight:	68.28	91.93	90.98
Spondees:	15	19	20
Dactyls:	17	13	12
4th-foot spondee:	5	6	7

The unusually high percentages in *Eclogue* IV thus resemble closely the procedure of Catullus, as does the distribution of spondees and dactyls in the first four feet, and the high proportion of fourth-foot spondees.

When we examine the more important categories of variety and repetition, we find that the Fourth *Eclogue* likewise differs from the other nine poems and that, with one striking exception, the percentages and frequencies are almost identical with those of Catullus.

	Ecl. I-III, V-X	*Ecl.* IV	Catullus
Patterns per 16-line unit:	9.8	7.4	7.0
R, one every *x* lines:	13.4	10.3	7.0
R + NR, one every *x* lines:	5.3	3.9	3.0
% of 4th-foot homodyne:	40.65	28.57	60.44
R, percentage of change:	50.88	33.33	35.19
differs from homodyne %:	+10.23	+4.76	-25.25
R + NR, percentage of change:	45.52	31.25	33.60
differs from homodyne %:	+4.87	+2.68	-26.84

	Ecl. I-III, V-X	*Ecl.* IV	Catullus
Favorite repeat,			
% of total repeats:	29.82	50.0	44.44
% of total pattern:	18.28	20.0	23.08
% of change:	52.94	0.0	37.50
differs from homodyne %:	+12.29	-28.57	-22.94
Favorite R + NR,			
% of total R + NR:	22.07	43.75	41.60
% of total pattern:	34.41	46.67	50.0
% of change:	62.50	28.57	34.62
differs from homodyne %:	+21.85	0.0	-25.82
Opposites, one every x lines:	19.1	31.0	37.7

The tabulation given above proves again that *Eclogue* IV obviously bears almost no relation to the other nine pastorals and displays the same lack of variety and the same concentration on repeated patterns as does Catullus, especially in the high percentages of the pattern most frequently repeated. The outstanding difference between the Fourth *Eclogue* and Catullus LXIV lies in the percentage of fourth-foot homodyne: Catullus, an abnormally high 60.44, and Vergil with an equally abnormal 28.57, the lowest of the *Eclogues*.[25] This striking variation affects materially the difference between the percentage of fourth-foot texture change and the percentage of fourth-foot homodyne. With the exception of the favorite repeat, the percentage of change itself in *Eclogue* IV resembles that in Catullus.

Also, in spite of the low homodyne percentage in *Eclogue* IV, we find many lines with a molossus after the penthemimeral caesura, such as line 5:

> magnus ab integro saeclorum nascitur ordo

Three instances appear in succession in 28-30 and there are six in nine lines in 42-50. In the frequent use of the molossus, *Eclogue* IV likewise resembles Catullus LXIV.

Metrically, then, as in so many other respects, Vergil seems deliberately to imitate Catullus in this famous poem, which is so different from his other pastorals. The many similarities between the two poems give added support to the statement of Jackson Knight:[26]

> The Fourth *Eclogue,* perhaps the most Catullan of Vergil's certain poems, recalls
> the hexameters of Catullus in phrases, in the unity of single lines, in schematization
> of balanced word order, and in the quality of the verse groups.

The *Georgics:* Hesiod and Aratus

Klingner states that the *Georgics* has no model with which it can be compared, in the sense that the *Eclogues* can be compared with the *Idylls* of Theocritus, or the *Aeneid* can be compared with Homer's *Iliad* and *Odyssey* and with the *Argonautica* of Apollonius of Rhodes.[27] If this were entirely true, it would perhaps be another indication of the greatness of Vergil's achievement in didactic poetry. But there are of course Greek models; the poem is partially indebted to the *Phaenomena* of Aratus and to the *Georgika* and *Alexipharmaka* of Nicander,[28] and even more so to the *Works and Days* of Hesiod, but it is less a didactic treatise in the Hesiodic and Hellenistic sense than a true work of poetic art. I wrote some years ago:[29]

> In the development of the poet's art, the *Georgics* stands between his more youthful
> and Alexandrian pastorals and the more severe and lofty style of national epic, but
> in content and significance much nearer the latter. It is in itself an epic dealing with
> all aspects of life — political and social, religious and philosophical — and its com-
> prehensive nature is seen in the endings of the four books on the themes of War,
> Peace, Death, and Rebirth.

Since the comparison of Catullus and Callimachus bore fruitful results and explained the unique features of Catullus' hexameter technique, I examined the *Idylls* of Theocritus in relation to Vergil's

Eclogues, but with less success. There are far fewer metrical similarities than one might antici-
pate in this collection of ten bucolic poems which *in toto* are far more dactylic than any previous
Latin poetry. The influence of Theocritus is seen most clearly in II, the earliest of the *Eclogues,*
and in VIII, the corresponding poem, with its Theocritean refrains.

In the *Georgics,* as we have seen, Vergil achieves his metrical maturity (except for the intermediate position of the fourth-foot spondee and the frequency of reverse combinations), and we
should not expect him to be influenced by the patterns and percentages of the Greek didactic poets.
My examination of Hesiod and Aratus proves that the frequencies of the patterns are slightly lower
in Hesiod than in Homer, and that those in Aratus are likewise lower than in Theocritus, Callimachus, and Apollonius, but they still bear no relation to the percentages in the *Georgics.* Also, Hesiod and Aratus have fewer repeats than the other Greek poets, one every 9.2 and 9.5 lines respectively, and these frequencies are also lower than those in Lucretius and Catullus, 8.8 and 7.0. But
if Vergil in this respect is influenced by anyone, it is Cicero (11.4), and he goes well beyond him
(*Eclogues,* 13.1; *Georgics,* 12.3; *Aeneid,* 12.4).

The Problem of *Aeneid* X-XII

My analysis of the metrical patterns in Vergil's *Aeneid* and especially of the variety and repetition to be found therein has had certain surprising and unexpected results. In instance after instance my findings for *Aeneid* X-XII differ from those concerning the other nine books; in other
words, Vergil in these three books seems to depart from his normal procedure elsewhere in the
Aeneid and likewise in the *Georgics.* I commented briefly in Part I on several of these discrepancies and anomalies,[30] and shall now present the evidence as fully as possible:

1. Books X and XII have the highest percentages of *dsss,* 15.90 and 16.30 respectively;[31] the
   frequency of *dsss* in X-XII is 15.34 per cent, as against 14.02 in I-IX. There is a similar
   variation in the case of *dsds:* 12.15 per cent in X-XII; 10.76 in I-IX.

2. Only nine sixteen-line units in the *Aeneid* contain less than seven metrical patterns. Five
   of these (55.56 per cent) are in Books X-XII. The percentages of units with eight or more
   patterns likewise indicates a greater variety in the first nine books: I-IX, 93.27; X-XII,
   90.12 (XI-XII, 87.07).

3. Vergil very rarely uses the same metrical pattern four times in succession — only seven
   times in the *Aeneid,* but three of these triple repetitions (42.86 per cent) occur in X-XII.
   In other words, the frequency is once every 1,761.8 lines in I-IX, but once every 919.3
   lines in X-XII.

4. Even more significant is the evidence from repeat clusters, six or more occurrences of
   the same pattern in sixteen or fewer verses. The *Aeneid* contains 49 such clusters, an
   average of one every 200.1 lines. But 23 of these clusters (46.94 per cent) appear in X-
   XII; the frequency is thus one every 271.0 lines in I-IX, but one every 119.9 lines in X-XII,
   more than twice as often.

5. We find in I-IX 548 repeats, an average of one every 12.9 lines; X-XII has 241, an average
   of one every 11.4 lines. The larger number of repeats (and near repeats) and the unusually high percentage of repeat clusters naturally go together, and the next point is likewise
   related.

6. The percentage of repeats in the first four patterns likewise varies: *Aeneid* as a whole,
   68.31; I-IX, 66.42; X-XII, 72.61. The variation is greatest in the percentages for *dsss* and
   dsds repeats; *dsss:* I-IX, 20.99; X-XII, 24.90; *dsds:* I-IX, 17.15; X-XII, 22.41.[32]

7. These same patterns, *dsss* and *dsds,* show in X-XII a higher percentage of repeats in relation to the total occurrences of the two patterns; *dsss:* I-IX, 11.64; X-XII, 14.18; *dsds:* I-
   IX, 12.40; X-XII, 16.12; if we include the *dsds* near repeats, the percentage difference is
   even greater: I-IX, 28.40; X-XII, 34.63.

8. Opposite patterns appear in adjacent lines with the same approximate frequency, *until* we reach *Aeneid* X-XII: *Eclogues*, once every 19.6 lines; *Georgics*, once every 20.9 lines; *Aeneid* I-IX, once every 21.8 lines; but X-XII, once every 27.6 lines.

9. There is considerable variation in the percentages of the different opposites; *sddd* is preceded or followed by *dsss* 28.47 per cent of the occurrences in I-IX, but 32.0 in X-XII; this is not surprising because the frequency of *dsss* is highest in X and XII. In the case of *ssdd* preceded or followed by *ddss*, the percentages change strikingly in the opposite direction: I-IX, 22.78; X-XII, 13.89. Apparently Vergil in X-XII lost interest in having *ssdd* and *ddss* in adjacent lines; this is true to a lesser degree of *sssd* and *ddds*: I-IX, 16.52; X-XII, 12.50.

10. The total statistics for reverse patterns reveal little variation; one reverse pattern every 38.3 lines in I-IX; one every 40.6 lines in X-XII. The percentages for the individual reverse patterns differ, however; *sssd* is preceded or followed by *dsss* 30.36 per cent of the time in I-IX, but only 26.39 per cent in X-XII. This change is just the opposite of what the high frequency of *dsss* in X and XII would lead us to expect. The percentages for *sddd* preceded or followed by *ddds* show a greater variation: 16.67 in I-IX; 10.0 in X-XII. But for *ssds* adjacent to *sdss* X-XII has the higher percentage, 20.93, with 15.66 in I-IX. The most frequent combination in I-IX *(sssd-dsss)* comprises 36.96 per cent of the total reverses; that in X-XII *(ssds-sdss)* 52.94, a much higher percentage of the total.

11. Perhaps the most significant statistical abnormality appears in the shift from fourth-foot heterodyne to homodyne (or the reverse) in repeated patterns. The percentage of repeats containing such a change in fourth-foot texture runs consistently higher in Vergil's poetry than the normal fourth-foot homodyne percentages, *until* we come to *Aeneid* X-XII: *Eclogues*, 49.21, +9.48; *Georgics*, 43.50, +7.42; *Aeneid* I-IX, 48.72, + 10.50, but X-XII, 34.85, -1.79. The greatest discrepancy appears in Book XI, 33.33, -5.22. This sudden change in the treatment of fourth-foot texture in repeated passages in X-XII is most striking and can hardly be attributed to coincidence.

12. If we examine the four most frequent patterns, containing 68.31 per cent of the total repeats, we find that the percentage of change in fourth-foot texture remains about the same in the case of *dsss* repeats: I-IX, 45.22, +7.0; X-XII, 45.0, +8.36. The two repeats where Vergil's procedure in X-XII is so very different are *ddss*: I-IX, 56.52, +18.30; X-XII, 27.27, -9.37; and *dsds*: I-IX, 39.36, +1.14; X-XII, 14.81, -21.83; the X-XII percentage in each case is less than half, and far below the percentage of fourth-foot homodyne. Curiously enough, *sdss*, the fourth pattern in frequency, also varies, but in the opposite direction: I-IX, 44.44, +6.22; X-XII, 53.57, +16.93.

Many of the statistical variations listed above might individually seem inconclusive, but their cumulative effect is overwhelming and indicates without question that, in his choice and treatment of metrical patterns, in the relative frequency of repeated, opposite, and reverse patterns, and especially in his handling of fourth-foot texture in repeated patterns, Vergil displays in *Aeneid* X-XII a metrical technique very unlike his normal procedure.

How are these many metrical peculiarities and abnormalities in X-XII to be explained? We cannot assume that these three books were written first and that Vergil then changed his metrical practices (the many close similarities between the *Georgics* and *Aeneid* I-IX would also argue against this possibility) nor can we believe that the three books were composed last and that the poet, after relatively uniform procedure in the four books of the *Georgics* and in nine books of the *Aeneid*, suddenly changed his treatment of metrical patterns in so many respects, either deliberately or subconsciously. The theory of either early or late composition is made most unlikely by our knowledge of Vergil's method of composition, as we have it from the Donatus-Suetonius *Life* (23):

> Aeneida prosa prius oratione formatam digestamque in XII libros particulatim componere instituit, prout liberet quidque, et nihil in ordinem arripiens.

There seems no good reason to doubt this statement, for, as Otis says:[33]

> ...it is hard, in any event, to imagine Vergil writing in any other way. He planned the poem *as a whole* and then wrote it piecemeal. Obviously this made for some inconsistencies and inequalities...Most of these difficulties are accounted for (it is a great excess of zeal to argue them all away as some would do) if we assume that much of 3 and 5 was written quite late (i.e. after 1, 6, 7, 8) and that the necessary retouches in the other books (to bring them into accord with the later ideas) had been left to the uncompleted revision.

Otis is of course speaking of the much discussed inconsistencies and discrepancies in plot and character, especially those between Book III and certain other books.

I cannot, therefore, accept as an explanation for the many metrical abnormalities in *Aeneid* X-XII either early or late composition of the three books in question. Nor am I willing to accept as a possible theory the view that these three books just happen to be different metrically from Vergil's usual procedure. There are too many factors involved, all indicating that the metrical variety (or rather, the lack of it) and the use of adjacent patterns (repeated, opposite, reverse) are in X-XII very unlike what we find elsewhere in Vergil's poetry.

Is it not best to assume that, in addition to the other revisions intended by Vergil, the elimination of excessive metrical repetition and the introduction of additional variety was on the agenda? Let us go a step farther and suppose that he had already made the changes which he desired in Books I-IX. The Donatus-Suetonius *Life* (32) states that he read II, IV, and VI to Augustus and Octavia *multo post perfectaque demum materia*. Why was the metrical *materia* in X-XII not perfected? The most obvious and satisfactory answer seems to be this: by 19 B.C. the necessary metrical revisions had progressed through Book IX; X-XII contain so many curious and unusual features of a metrical sort simply because Vergil's death left these three books unrevised.

DSSS and the Subjective Style

Vergil's favorite pattern is *dsss;* its frequency increases in his later *Eclogues* (tied for first place in both VI and VII, and first in X, the final poem), and it is first in both the *Georgics* (and in each of the four books) and the *Aeneid* (and in each book but V and VII). The hexameter line beginning with *dsss* has dactyls in the first and fifth feet only; the six feet thus form a tripartite pattern, with *ds* at the beginning and the end enclosing two spondees:

$$d \; s \; / \; s \; s \; / \; d \; s$$

As Cooper points out, we have here a "subtle symmetry," quite different from the simple alteration of *dsdsds*.[34] Also, the sequence of three spondees, found elsewhere only in *ssss* and *sssd* (the reverse of *dsss*) gives to the line a tone of majesty and solemnity which is perhaps more suitable for certain themes than for others.

My most significant discovery concerning Vergil's use of *dsss* emerged only when I had compared my metrical analyses with those passages which, according to Otis, best illustrate Vergil's subjective style.[35] By "subjective style" Otis means the manner in which Vergil shares the emotions of his characters (empathy) and presents his own personal reaction to their emotions (sympathy). This "empathetic-sympathetic style" is new to epic poetry, and, as Otis shows by many detailed comparisons, differs strikingly from the more objective, narrative style of Homer and Apollonius; he says: "Virgil not only reads the minds of his characters; he constantly communicates to us his own reactions to them and to their behavior."[36]

The "subjective" passages in the *Aeneid* are those of a more emotional and dramatic nature. The narrative, more Homeric, passages are objective. I now find an amazing correlation of subject matter and meter everywhere in the epic; the metrical patterns occurring most frequently in the emotional and subjective speeches and episodes are not the same as those in the narrative and objective passages. Although the percentage of *dsss* in the *Aeneid* as a whole is 14.39, there are many episodes and speeches where Vergil employs this pattern very sparingly, from three to five per cent; in other passages the percentage rises to 25 or 30 per cent. This is a surprisingly wide fluctuation!

It is well known how skillfully the poet adapts his metrical patterns to the sense of individual verses[37] or to that in groups of verses.[38] He likewise alters his patterns in larger units to suit his subject matter and style. But in what type of passage does he favor a high percentage of *dsss*, and why is the same pattern used so sparingly on other occasions?

I first noticed this correlation of meter and style in the second half of *Georgics* IV, where we have a story within a story: the tragic tale of Orpheus and Eurydice framed by the story of Aristaeus. Otis says: "the style of the *Orpheus* is utterly subjective in contrast to the objectivity of Homeric epic or the *Aristaeus*."[39] The pattern *dsss* is first in the *Aristaeus* (14.88 per cent) as in the book as a whole (15.63 per cent), but in the Orpheus and Eurydice story *dsss* drops sharply to 5.41 per cent and is tied for sixth place with three other patterns.[40] The more dactylic *ddss*, second in the *Aristaeus* with a percentage of 12.50, rises in the *Orpheus* to first position and 18.92 per cent; similarly, *dsds* is 11.90 per cent in the *Aristaeus*, but 16.22 in the *Orpheus*.

Otis also discusses *Eclogues* VIII, 17-61, and II as embryonic examples of Vergil's new subjective style.[41] In the pastorals as a whole, the percentages of *dsss* and *ddss* are, respectively, 10.67 and 13.09; in the first song of VIII they are as follows: *dsss*, 11.11; *ddss*, 20.0, and in II the differences are even greater: *dsss*, 2.74; *ddss*, 20.55. This would indicate that from the beginning Vergil considered *dsss* less suitable than *ddss* for his subjective style.

In *Georgics* IV, *dsss* is unusually low where we have subjective style, in this case the emotional and dramatic story of Orpheus and Eurydice;[42] on the other hand, for the more objective style of the *Aristaeus*, the percentage is still lower than that in Book IV as a whole. Under what circumstances does Vergil increase *dsss* to 25 or 30 per cent? To answer this question we turn again to the *Aeneid*, and I shall illustrate the wide range in the *dsss* percentages by analyzing one or more subdivisions from each book of the epic.[43] The percentages in parentheses between the book number and the lines give the *dsss* percentages for the particular book as a whole.

I	(13.88)	1a-80	Prologue. Juno and Aeolus	17.86
		81-156	The storm and Neptune	6.58
		157-222	Aeneas and the Trojans in Africa	7.58
		223-296	Venus and Jupiter	17.57
		418-519	Carthage and Dido	19.42
	BUT	418-452	Aeneas sees Carthage	5.71
		453-493	Scenes of the Trojan war	29.27
		520-656	The Trojans welcomed	12.78
	BUT	520-560	Speech of Ilioneus	7.69

At the beginning of the book, with its emphasis on Rome, Carthage, and Juno, *dsss* is well above average;[44] it is low during the storm and the arrival in Africa (and Aeneas' laments), and again high in the Venus-Jupiter scene, which stresses the future greatness of Rome and Augustus. Aeneas' emotions at the sight of Carthage produce a low *dsss* percentage, but it rises immediately to 29.27 when the scenes of the Trojan War are described. When Ilioneus makes his appeal to Dido and describes the hardships endured by the Trojans, *dsss* is again low.

II	(14.52)	57-194	Sinon	13.33
	BUT	57-144	First two speeches	8.24
		145-194	Third speech	22.0
		559-633	Aeneas-Venus episode	20.55
		634-729	Aeneas at home	11.70
		730-804	Departure and loss of Creusa	9.59

Sinon's first two speeches are emotional and therefore have a lower *dsss* frequency than the third which is more logical and convinces the Trojans by explaining the reason for the Trojan Horse. The *dsss* percentage in the Aeneas-Venus scene is almost twice as high as in the two concluding and more emotional episodes. The presence here of divinity (Venus and the vision of the gods destroying Troy) is probably the reason for the high percentage in 559-633.[45] We have seen that the Juno-Aeolus and Jupiter-Venus episodes in Book I are also well above normal.

III	(14.73)	274-293	Actium	20.0
		294-505	Buthrotum	12.38

BUT 463-505 Gifts and farewell	7.14	
588-718 Rescue of Achaemenides	16.28	
BUT 612-654 Speech of Achaemenides	4.76	

The Actium episode, the central portion of the second main division, strikes a Roman note and hence has a high proportion of *dsss* patterns. The frequency of *dsss* in the long episode of Andromache and Helenus at Buthrotum is more normal, but the percentage drops decidedly in the more emotional farewell scene. Also, we find a low *dsss* frequency in the emotional appeal of Achaemenides in the final subdivision of the book.

IV (13.47)	90-128 Juno-Venus scene	20.51	
	296-330 Speech of Dido	11.43]	
	331-361 Speech of Aeneas	3.33]	8.33
	362-392 Speech of Dido	9.68]	
	Framing narrative (279-295, 393-415)	23.08	
	584-629 Dido's curses	13.04	
	BUT 584-606 (personal and emotional)	4.35	
	607-629 (Aeneas, Rome, Carthage)	21.74	
	630-705 Suicide and Anna's lament	6.58	

In the Juno-Venus scene, the *dsss* percentage is again high, as seems usual in passages concerning divinities. Equally important is the fact that the highly emotional speeches of Dido and Aeneas in the central portion of the second main division differ to a striking degree in their use of *dsss* from the narrative framework (8.33 per cent as against 23.08). Also, *dsss* occurs only once in Aeneas' central speech (331-361), a percentage of 3.33; perhaps this is an indication of the depth of his emotion.[46] Another surprising variation occurs within Dido's curse; in the first part, more personal and emotional (584-606), the *dsss* percentage is 4.35; in the second half (607-629), foreshadowing Aeneas' later fate and the undying hostility between Rome and Carthage, the percentage rises sharply to 21.74. In the final scene (Dido's suicide, Anna's lament, and the release of Dido's spirit), *dsss* falls to half its normal frequency. These variations in Book IV seem especially significant and help to reveal Vergil's metrical practice — his avoidance of *dsss* in the more dramatic and emotional passages.

V (12.40)	114-285 Boatrace	9.30
	BUT 162-182 (Subjective style)	4.76
	286-361 Footrace	10.96
	BUT 315-342 (Subjective style)	3.85
	604-663 Iris and the Trojan women	27.12
	827-871 Death of Palinurus	8.89

For Book V, one of the two books of the *Aeneid* in which *dsss* is not in first place but is slightly outnumbered by *ddss* (the other is VII), I give the percentages not only for the boatrace and the footrace, but also for the passages in each which Otis cites as excellent illustrations of Vergil's subjective style, his "empathetic-sympathetic" method.[47] As in the Orpheus story in *Georgics* IV, the *dsss* percentage in each case is amazingly low. The comparison with the appearance of Iris to the Trojan women (objective epic narrative) is striking (27.12 per cent). The note of tragedy at the end of the book (Palinurus' death) appropriately has a *dsss* frequency well below normal.

VI (14.03)	212-235 Burial of Misenus	8.33
	236-267 Sacrifices	22.58
	450-476 Meeting with Dido	22.22
	756-807 Julian line	15.38
	BUT 756-787 Alban kings, Romulus	12.50
	788-807 Augustus	20.0

Scenes of death, e.g., the burial of Misenus, have a low *dsss* percentage (emotions involved), but the solemnity of the same pattern is appropriate for the sacrifices to the various divinities in 236-267. And what about the high proportion of *dsss* in 450-476 (22.22 per cent)? Does this sound the death knell to Dido's love for Aeneas, "all passion spent" (cf. the low *dsss* percentages in the speeches of Dido and Aeneas in Book IV)? The high frequency of *dsss* in 788-807 (20 per cent) is consistent with Vergil's treatment of Augustus elsewhere, both in Book I and in VIII, 675-728, where the percentage is even higher (24.53).

VII	(13.47)	107-169	Eating of tables. Embassy	17.74
	BUT	107-147	Eating of tables	10.0
		148-169	Embassy	31.82
		170-285	Reception of Embassy. Speeches	13.04
	BUT	212-248	Speech of Ilioneus	19.44
		286-322	Speech of Juno	8.33

The sending of the envoys to Latinus in 148-169 is pure objective narrative, hence the very high *dsss* percentage. The frequency is high in the speech of Ilioneus where he talks about the Trojan War and the future home of Aeneas and his followers in Italy.[48] On the other hand, the percentage is low in Juno's speech because of its emotional content.[49]

VIII	(14.01)	102-183	Welcome by Evander	9.88
	BUT	152-174	Evander's speech	4.55
		184-305	Festival of Hercules	13.93
	BUT	225-261	Hercules-Cacus fight	21.62
		306-369	The Site of Rome	17.74
	BUT	306-336	Speech of Evander	9.68
		337-369	The walk through Rome	25.48
		626-728	Description of the shield	19.61
	BUT	626-674	Early history of Rome	14.29
		675-728	Augustus	24.53

Evander's offer of friendship (152-174) has a low *dsss* frequency. The high percentages appear here in the description of Rome (337-369) and in the scenes of combat, the victory of Hercules over Cacus and of Octavian over Antony.[50] When we view the *Aeneid* as a trilogy (I-IV, V-VIII, IX-XII),[51] the victory and triumphs of Augustus as described on the shield in 675-728 form the climax of the central third of the poem. The *dsss* percentage in the shield as a whole is high since it deals with scenes of Roman history, but it is significant that the percentage is even higher in the passage concerning Augustus, and likewise higher than in the references to Augustus in Books I and VI.[52]

IX	(15.80)	367-449	Departure and death	19.28
	BUT	367-421	Attempt to escape	29.09
		422-449	Deaths of the youths	0.
		450-589	Fighting	18.25
	BUT	450-502	Grief of Euryalus' mother	11.54
		503-589	Battle	22.35

The high *dsss* percentage in the attempt of Nisus and Euryalus to escape is in striking contrast to the *zero* per cent in the description of their deaths. This is perhaps the most amazing fluctuation of the pattern in the entire *Aeneid*. The relatively low percentage in the lament of Euryalus' mother seems appropriate as does the higher percentage in the renewal of the battle.

X	(15.90)	256-361	Landing and battle	21.15
		362-478	Aristeia of Pallas	17.95
		479-509	Death of Pallas	3.33
		510-605	Renewal of fighting	22.11
		689-746	Aristeia of Lausus	15.79
		747-832	Death of Lausus	10.47

In the central portion of the book scenes of fighting, with high *dsss* percentages, frame the tragic death of Pallas, where the frequency of the same pattern is unusually low. The percentage in the description of Lausus' death is well below normal, but perhaps not as low as one might have anticipated.

XI	(13.72)	1-99	Mourning for Pallas	15.31
	BUT	29-58	Aeneas' speech	3.45
		59-99	Preparations for trip	24.39

139-224	Grief of Evander. Burial of dead	16.28
BUT 139-181	Lament of Evander	20.93
182-224	Burial of dead	11.63
376-444	Turnus' speech. Renewed attack	14.29
BUT 376-444	Speech of Turnus	11.76
445-467	Renewed attack	21.74
532-596	Diana's speech about Camilla	4.62

The low *dsss* percentage is appropriate for Aeneas' expression of grief over the body of Pallas, as is the high percentage for the descriptive passage which follows in 59-99. But Evander's lament for Pallas in 139-181 seems abnormal, as does the description of Camilla's youth and training in 532-596; the former should have a low percentage, and the latter, more objective and less emotional, would seem to demand a much higher proportion of *dsss* patterns. However, as I mentioned above, *Aeneid* X-XII have many other unusual metrical features which perhaps indicate that the final three books of the poem did not receive the same careful metrical revision that Vergil had given to the other nine books. The difference between the frequency in Turnus' emotional outburst against Drances (376-444) and the higher percentage in the renewal of the fighting immediately afterwards seems more normal.

XII	(16.30)	10-53 Turnus and Latinus	6.82
		54-80 Turnus and Amata	0.
		289-553 Turnus in battle. Aristeias	19.25
		593-611 Death of Amata	10.53
		697-790 First encounter	22.34
		791-842 Jupiter and Juno	19.23
		843-952 Death of Turnus	11.93

The emotional scenes at the beginning (10-53, 54-80) have a low proportion of *dsss* patterns. The fighting in 289-553 and the preliminary encounter of Aeneas and Turnus in 697-790 have high percentages, as does the reconciliation of Jupiter and Juno, which ends with a glorification of the future Romans. In the final encounter and death of Turnus the *dsss* percentage drops well below the average for the book, but, in the light of Vergil's procedure in the earlier books, one might expect even lower percentages both here and in the description of the death of Amata (593-611); do we have again, as perhaps in XI, an indication of lack of metrical revision?

To summarize, although *dsss* is Vergil's favorite pattern in the *Aeneid*, with an overall percentage of 14.39 and a range in the individual books from 12.40 (V, where *dsss* is in second place) to 16.30 (XII), it shows a surprising variation according to style and subject matter, from zero to 5 or 6 per cent in many passages, from 20 to 30 per cent or higher in others. The *dsss* pattern has a low frequency in episodes and speeches which are dramatic, psychological, and emotional, where the style is subjective or "empathetic-sympathetic," and especially in scenes of death and laments for the dead. On the other hand, *dsss* appears with an abnormally high frequency in certain types of episodes: those in a more objective style, particularly scenes of mass fighting and individual combat; those in which divinities (Jupiter, Juno, Venus, etc.) appear and speak; those dealing with Rome and Augustus. This last is true of the *Georgics* also, where *dsss* has an average percentage of 15.81. Unusually high percentages are the following: 27.27 in I, 5b-42 (the gods and Octavian); 17.65 in I, 463b-514 (omens, civil war, need for Octavian as a savior); 26.83 in II, 136-176 (praise of Italy); 20.83 in III, I-48 (a temple of song for Octavian).[53]

Vergil's metrical patterns, at least in the case of *dsss*, are thus fitted to his subject matter and to his style. As in individual lines, where the words do not determine the meter but are subordinated to the metrical patterns which the poet so often adapts to the sense, so in his larger units the patterns are not determined by the words. Subject matter, style, and meter go hand in hand. The words are written to the music, not the music to the words. Jackson Knight expressed this clearly some years ago, when he said:[54]

> Rhythm and metre are just as likely to suggest words as words are likely to enforce a certain metrical or rhythmical form. There is no doubt of this. Vergil's imagination to a large extent worked by ear; that is, what he said often depended at least partly on the sounds, and not merely on the thoughts, which he remembered.

Notes to Chapter 7

1. *JPh* 30 (1907), p. 272.

2. *Aratea* 1-17 = lines 229-245 in Traglia' edition.

3. Vergil's greater variety is seen also in the following: 33 spondees in the first four feet out of a possible 64 (37 in Cicero, 31 in Lucretius, and 45 in Catullus), and twelve spondees in the fourth foot (Cicero, twelve; Lucretius, thirteen; Catullus, all sixteen).

4. If I include a homodyned molossic combination, e.g., *in summis* (8), the total in Catullus is eleven (and in Lucretius five); see Wilkinson, *Golden Latin Artistry,* p. 129. *Eclogue* II has in 1-16 two molossic combinations, both heterodyne (*umbras et* in line 8, *quamvis tu* in 16).

5. *Virgil,* p. 7.

6. The one exception is *Eclogue* IV, to be discussed below.

7. Williams, *Virgil,* p. 42, says: "Virgil's metrical mastery may be illustrated by a brief consideration of three aspects of it"; he then mentions briefly (1) variety, (2) the conflict introduced by Vergil's greater emphasis on fourth-foot heterodyne, and (3) the adaptation of the metrical movement to the tone and sense of various passages. New material on this third aspect will be presented below when I discuss *dsss* and the subjective style.

8. This particular distribution (sixteen spondees, sixteen dactyls) is rare; it appears also in the *Culex* and the *Moretum,* and in a few later poets, especially Statius: Books I and VI of the *Thebaid,* Book I of the *Achilleid,* and in about half of the individual poems of the *Silvae.*

9. Williams, *Virgil,* p. 14; see also Duckworth, *AJPh* 80 (1959), p. 237.

10. I follow Forbiger, Jahn, and Perret in rejecting the refrain in VIII, 76; see Duckworth, *AJPh* 83 (1962), pp. 446-447, and note 11. The omission of 76 automatically removes the reason for adding 28a.

11. Drobisch, *BSGL* 20 (1868), p. 28, excluded the two refrains of *Eclogue* VIII from his calculations, but wrongly so, since the refrains, in Vergil as in Theocritus, are an essential and effective part of the poetry. My statistics for the *Eclogues* are therefore necessarily more dactylic than those of Drobisch.

12. The unusually low frequency of *dsss* in II may result in part from the emotional content of the poem; see below on *dsss* and the subjective style.

13. On the chronology of the *Eclogues,* see Duckworth *CW* 51 (1957-58), p. 123; Otis, *Virgil,* pp. 131-133.

14. My statistics are based on the first thirteen *Idylls,* the more bucolic of Theocritus' poems. *Idylls* VIII-XI seem out of line in their percentages for both the first four and the first eight patterns. If we exclude these four poems, the percentage range for the remaining nine is as follows: first four: 63.49 (IV) to 77.78 (XII); first eight: 88.41 (II) to 96.30 (III). The corresponding range for VIII-XI is: first four: 44.44 (IX) to 56.41 (XI); first eight: 77.77 (IX) to 83.33 (XI). Both IX, with the lowest percentages, and VIII have been considered spurious by several scholars; see Gow, *Theocritus,* II, pp. 170-171, 185, and the low percentages of VIII and IX support the rejection of these two poems. The frequency percentages of X and XI are also low, but these are accepted as genuine; they differ, however, from the ordinary bucolics of Theocritus in that X is agricultural and XI presents a grotesque treatment of Polyphemus.

15. In this respect Theocritus is slightly less dactylic than the other Greek poets, where we find ten spondees and twenty-two dactyls (Hesiod, eleven and twenty-one).

16. See Maury, *Lettres d'Humanité* 3 (1944), pp. 71-147, and especially 99-109; Duckworth, *AJPh* 75 (1954), pp. 3-4, *Structural Patterns,* pp. 3-4; Otis, *Virgil,* pp. 128-143.

17. Otis points out also that Vergil's "subjective style" first appears in both VIII and II in a rudimentary form; see his *Virgil,* pp. 105-124, for his analyses of the two poems.

18. *Virgil,* p. 128.

19. *Estudios Virgilianos,* pp. 94-95.

20. *Virgil,* pp. 10-11.

21. See above, note 14.

22. See Duckworth, *Structural Patterns,* pp. 21-22.

23. *RBPh* 41 (1963), pp. 63-79. On the importance of the number 63 in *Eclogue* IV and elsewhere in Vergil, see Savage, *TAPhA* 93 (1962), pp. 420-434; 94 (1963), p. 258, note 15, where he also points out Aeschylus' use of 63 in oracular passages in both the *Agamemnon* and the *Eumenides.*

24. *Golden Latin Artistry,* p. 194; see Rand, *The Magical Art of Virgil,* pp. 110-111; Westendorp Boerma, *Acta Classica* 1 (1958), p. 55 (and bibliography there cited); Berg, *Vergil's Bucolic Hero,* pp. 150-161.

25. The percentage range in the other pastorals is from 32.22 in V to an unusually high 53.49 in VI. It is interesting to note that IV and VI thus mark the two extremes of fourth-foot homodyne in the

Eclogues, although these two poems (like I and IX, II and VIII, III and VII) are part of the concentric structure framing V, the important pastoral on the death and resurrection of the bucolic hero Daphnis. Brown, *Numeri Vergiliani,* p. 63, note 1, says that *Eclogue* IV "stands forth as the most intensely heterodyned not only of all the *Eclogues* but of all Vergilian works (one mark more of the care lavished on that many-faceted jewel). Equally, *Eclogue* VI remains the most richly (and deliberately) homodyned."

26. Jackson Knight, *Roman Vergil,* p. 330.

27. *Römische Geisteswelt,* p. 233.

28. Brown, *Numeri Vergiliani,* p. 109, agrees with other scholars that Vergil derived the title of his *Georgics* from the *Georgika* of Nicander. On a surprising acrostic indebtedness to Aratus, see Brown, pp. 96-114.

29. *AJPh* 80 (1959), p. 237.

30. See Chapter 2, note 3; Chapter 3, notes 4, 6; Chapter 4, note 24; Chapter 5, notes 4, 12.

31. These *dsss* percentages are exceeded elsewhere in Vergil only in the unique *Eclogue* IV (20.97, in second place) and in *Georgics* I (16.16) and II (17.38). But *dsss* in the *Georgics* as a whole comprises 15.81 per cent, as against 14.39 in the *Aeneid.* The fact that X and XII contain so many battle scenes may account in part for the higher frequency of *dsss,* since this pattern is low in emotional and dramatic scenes and high in descriptive passages, those written in a more objective style. I discuss this aspect of Vergil's metrical art in the following section of this chapter.

32. There is a similar, if less striking, variation in the percentages if we include the near repeats: *dsss:* I-IX, 22.36; X-XII, 25.12; *dsds:* I-IX, 14.27; X-XII, 19.17.

33. *Virgil,* p. 417.

34. *Introduction to the Latin Hexameter,* p. 31.

35. *Virgil,* pp. 41-96.

36. *Ibid.,* p. 88.

37. See above, Chapter 1, on *ssss* and *dddd* patterns.

38. See Wilkinson, *Golden Latin Artistry,* pp. 74-83.

39. *Virgil,* p. 200; cf. p. 197, where Otis says: "the Homeric atmosphere is maintained in the *Aristaeus* as it is in no other portion of Virgil's poetry."

40. These are *ddds, sdsd,* and *dddd;* in the *Aristaeus dddd* is tied for last place with *ssdd.* In the *Georgics* as a whole and also in the *Aeneid, dddd* has fifteenth place, and *sddd* is sixteenth and last.

41. *Virgil,* pp. 105-124.

42. The Aristaeus and Orpheus stories have often been compared to the Peleus-Thetis and Ariadne stories in Catullus LXIV; cf., e.g., Duckworth, *AJPh* 80 (1959), p. 233, and note 19; Otis, *Virgil,* p. 193. There is no such metrical change in Catullus; the most frequent pattern is *dsss,* with a high percentage of 27.59; in the Peleus-Thetis section the percentage is 24.74, but in the central Ariadne story it rises to 30.48. This is very different from Vergil's procedure in *Georgics* IV, where the *Orpheus* differs from the *Aristaeus* not only stylistically but also metrically, as a result of the suppression of *dsss.*

43. For my analyses of the individual books I follow as closely as possible the divisions and subdivisions of each book as published in my tripartite outline of the *Aeneid* some years ago; see *Vergilius* 7 (1961), pp. 2-11; *Structural Patterns,* pp. 25-33. Otis' structural analyses of the individual books differ in many details; see Duckworth, *AJPh* 86 (1965), p. 419, and note 27.

44. Juno's speech in I, 34-49, has a *dsss* percentage of 31.25; this high frequency results from the presence of *dsss* in four successive lines (46-49), in which she asserts her majesty: *ast ego, quae divum incedo regina Iovisque / et soror et coniunx,...*; in the remainder of her speech *dsss* occurs only once (8.33 per cent).

45. It cannot be argued that the possibly unfinished state of the Aeneas-Helen episode (567-588) is in any way responsible for this high percentage; the frequency of *dsss* in 567-588 is 13.64 per cent, that is, slightly under the average for the book, whereas the percentage for the remainder of the subdivision is 23.63. On the Aeneas-Helen episode, see Duckworth, *TAPhA* 91 (1960), p. 215, and bibliography cited in note 57; *Structural Patterns,* pp. 85-86, and note 46; Otis, *Virgil,* p. 243, note 1.

46. It is significant also that Aeneas' speech is at the very center of *Aeneid* IV; see Duckworth, *TAPhA* 91 (1960), p. 189; *Structural Patterns,* p. 24.

47. *Virgil,* pp. 53-59 (on 162-182); pp. 41-51 (on 315-342). In 162-182, *ddss, dssd,* and *sddd* (Vergil's least frequent pattern) all have percentages of 14.29, indicating the strongly dactylic nature of the passage.

48. Cf. *dsss* in Ilioneus' account of the Trojans' sufferings in I, 520-560 (7.69 per cent); the frequency in Ilioneus' speech in VII is naturally above average because of its different content.

49. The percentage of *dsss* in Juno's lament in VII (8.33) is identical with that in her speech in I, 34-49, if we exclude the last four verses (all *dsss*); see above, note 44.

50. On Hercules and Cacus as symbolic of Octavian and Antony, see Schnepf, *Gymnasium* 66 (1959),

pp. 250-268; Bellen, *RhM* 106 (1963), pp. 23-30; Galinsky, *AJPh* 87 (1966), pp. 18-51.

51. See Duckworth, *TAPhA* 88 (1957), pp. 1-10; *Structural Patterns*, pp. 11-13; Wigodsky, *C & M* 26 (1965), pp. 192-197; Galinsky, *AJPh* 89 (1968), pp. 165-183.

52. This seems an additional indication that Book VIII marks the climax and conclusion of the central, more Roman and Augustan portion of the epic. Otis, *Virgil*, pp. 274, note 1, 344-345, 419, following Camps, adds IX to the second section and favors an unbalanced trilogy as follows: I-IV, V-IX, X-XII; as a result, the Nisus-Euryalus episode in IX, 176-449, looks backward instead of preparing for Vergil's portrayal of character in the final books of the poem; see Duckworth, *AJPh* 88 (1967), pp. 141-150.

53. Ovid's use of *dsss* in the *Metamorphoses* is of interest in this connection; unlike Vergil, Ovid varies the frequency of the pattern from book to book, with a range from first to fifth place. In Book XV as a whole, *dsss* ranks fifth (after *ddss*, *dsds*, *ddsd*, and *dssd*), with a percentage of 10.77; likewise in lines 1-744 it has fifth place (10.03 per cent), but at the end of the book where Julius Caesar and Augustus are praised (745-870) *dsss* moves into first place (15.08 per cent). Similarly, in XIV, where *dsss* is second with a percentage of 14.13, the pattern rises to 16.25 in 772-851, the early history of Rome; this provides an effective contrast with the *dsss* percentage of 8.05 in 623-771, the story of Vertumnus and Pomona.

54. *Accentual Symmetry*, p. 37.

Chapter 8

HORACE

In the *Georgics* Vergil develops a metrical uniformity lacking in the *Eclogues* and establishes norms which determine also his metrical procedures in the *Aeneid*.[1] This consistency in the metrical patterns and percentages is all the more surprising when we realize that the composition of these two works extends over a period of almost twenty years.

The hexameter poetry of Horace has an even greater chronological spread; between the earliest satires of Book I and his latest epistles there is an interval of at least twenty-five years, and perhaps thirty, if the *Ars Poetica* was composed near the end of his life, some years after the Letter to Augustus (II, 1). Is Horace equally consistent in his hexameter technique over this period, or do his metrical procedures change with the passing years?

Horace was devoted to Vergil and referred to him on several occasions. The strongest expression of his friendship is that in *Odes* I, 3, 8: *animae dimidium meae,* "the half of my soul." There are numerous similarities in the works of the two Augustan poets: e.g., *Eclogue* IV and *Epode* XVI; *Odes* I, 2, and *Georg.* I, 463-514; *Odes* I, 12, III, 1-6, and *Aen.* VI, 756-886. After Vergil's death in 19 B.C. Horace refers again and again to the *Aeneid* in his *Carmen Saeculare* and Book IV of his *Odes*.[2]

The close friendship of the two poets and the many similarities of theme and attitude in their verse (in spite of the difference in literary genres) suggest that their metrical practices may also be related. My analysis of Horace's hexameter poetry, therefore, has two aims: (1) to compare his patterns and percentages with those of Vergil; and (2) to discover if his metrical technique changed over the years in his four hexameter collections, from *Satires* I[3] to *Epistles* II. In the following section I include the *Ars Poetica* with the two long epistles of Book II.

The Development of Horace's Hexameter Art

Horace's favorite pattern, in each of the collections, is *dsss*. This also appears most often in Cicero, Lucretius, Catullus LXIV, and in Vergil's *Georgics* and *Aeneid*. But Horace's frequencies are lower than those of Vergil; his overall percentage is 12.67 (lower even than in the *Eclogues*, 13.09), with a range from 14.03 (*Satires* II) down to 10.82 (*Epistles* II). Vergil's percentages are higher in the *Georgics* and *Aeneid* (15.81 and 14.39), but still much lower than in the Republican poets.

The second most frequent pattern in Horace is *sdss* (also in each of the four collections; in *Epistles* II, *sdss* is tied for second place with *dsds*). In the *Georgics*, *dsds* is second; in the *Aeneid*, *ddss*. The second pattern in Catullus LXIV is also *sdss*, but Horace's predilection for *sdss* is probably to be explained by Lucilius' use of *sdss* as his most frequent pattern. The percentages of Horace's second pattern, like those of his first, are lower in his later poetry: *Satires* I, 11.36; *Satires* II, 10.71; *Epistles* I, 10.74; *Epistles* II, 9.89.

The first four patterns (*dsss, sdss, dsds,* and *ddss*) have in Horace a frequency of 42.16 per cent, with a range from 43.95 (*Satires* II) to 39.96 (*Epistles* II); these percentages are again low when compared with those of Vergil's *Georgics* (48.99) and *Aeneid* (46.95), but resemble those of the *Eclogues* (41.45). Horace thus concentrates on four favorite patterns considerably less than does Vergil, and this is true also of the first eight patterns: Horace, 67.97 per cent, with a range from 71.16 (*Satires* I) to 66.30 (*Epistles* I); Vergil, *Eclogues*, 69.09; *Georgics*, 73.42, and *Aeneid*, 72.78. In their use of the eight most frequent patterns, both Vergil and Horace are very different from the poets of the late Republic, where we have a range from 79.81 in Lucretius to 90.98 in Catullus LXIV. However indebted Vergil was to Cicero, he took the important step of reducing the earlier emphasis on eight patterns and thus, beginning with the *Eclogues*, eliminated monotonous repetition to a considerable degree. Horace carries this innovation even farther and his works in chronological order reveal a surprising decrease in the percentages of the first, first four, and first eight patterns:[4] the statistics for the four hexameter books are as follows:

	Satires		Epistles		Total
	I	II	I	II	
First pattern:	12.82	14.03	12.82	10.82	12.67
First four:	43.59	43.95	40.85	39.96	42.16
First eight:	71.16	69.81	66.30	67.22	67.97

The low percentages of the *Epistles* do not appear again in the whole history of Latin hexameter poetry (to the middle of the sixth century), with the notable exception of Ausonius in his *Mosella:* 9.38, 36.04, and 62.50 respectively.

We find in Horace's first eight patterns a distribution in the first four feet of twenty spondees and twelve dactyls, the same as in Vergil's *Georgics* and *Aeneid* (also in Cicero and Catullus); in the individual collections, except for *Satires* II, the distribution is twenty-one spondees and eleven dactyls, identical with that in the fragments of Lucilius, and undoubtedly another indication of Horace's indebtedness to the originator of Roman satire. In the first eight patterns, Horace has seven fourth-foot spondees in the *Satires,* but only six in the *Epistles;* Vergil, on the contrary, shows a steady increase: *Eclogues,* six; *Georgics,* seven; *Aeneid,* eight.

The average number of patterns per sixteen-line unit again shows Horace's greater desire for metrical variety over the years. The figures for Vergil are approximately the same: 9.7 *(Eclogues),* 9.3 *(Georgics),* 9.4 *(Aeneid).* In the case of Horace, we find a definite increase from his earlier to his later poetry: 9.0 *(Satires* I), 9.6 *(Satires* II), 9.7 *(Epistles* I), 9.9 *(Epistles* II). The percentages of sixteen-line units with eight or more patterns likewise indicate more variety in the *Epistles: Satires* I, 83.64; *Satires* II, 86.67; *Epistles* I, 97.67; *Epistles* II, 96.72.

I have defined repeat clusters as passages in which the same pattern appears six or more times in sixteen or fewer lines. Such clusters were very frequent in Republican poetry, even in Cicero (one every 59.6 lines). Vergil deliberately avoided them, the occurrences per *x* lines being: *Eclogues,* 275.0; *Georgics,* 145.5; *Aeneid,* 200.1. Horace, in his hexameter poetry as a whole, has one cluster every 156.9 lines (close to Vergil's procedure in the *Georgics*), but they are slightly more frequent in the *Satires* (one every 150.7 lines) than in the *Epistles* (one every 163.9 lines). But, unlike Vergil, who has fewer clusters in his final work than in the *Georgics,* Horace in *Epistles* II shows a greater concentration of clusters (one every 137.1 lines) than in *Epistles* I (one every 201.2 lines, about the same as in the *Aeneid*).

The frequency of repeats and of repeats plus near repeats in Horace's hexameter poetry as a whole (once every 13.0 and 4.8 lines respectively) is about the same as in Vergil's three works (12.5 and 4.7). However, in Vergil's early *Eclogues* repeats and near repeats occur less often than in his more mature compositions; the opposite is true of Horace, with the highest frequencies in *Satires* I; repeats and repeats plus near repeats once every 11.2 and 4.2 lines; the corresponding frequencies in *Epistles* II are: one repeat every 13.9 lines (but 15.5 in *Satires* II); repeats plus near repeats once every 5.1 lines (but 5.3 in *Epistles* I). Both Vergil and Horace differ from the Republican poets in their avoidance of repeats and near repeats, but Horace in his later *Epistles* uses them even less than Vergil.

Two of Vergil's important innovations in hexameter technique were described above; (1) a striking reduction in the percentages of fourth-foot homodyne, and (2), in his repeats and repeats plus near repeats, percentages of change in fourth-foot texture which show a definite increase over the homodyne percentages; in this manner he introduces an added element of variety into his repeated patterns.

Neither of these innovations seems to have appealed to Horace. The percentage of fourth-foot homodyne in his poetry as a whole is 48.54, with a range from 43.77 *(Satires* II) to 52.49 *(Epistles* II); these are much higher than in Vergil, from 36.08 *(Georgics)* to 39.73 *(Eclogues).* Also, Horace in his repeated patterns displays no particular desire to raise the percentages of change in fourth-foot texture above the homodyne percentages. The statistics are on page 65. The lack of change in the repeats of *Epistles* II is striking (-9.01 below the percentage of fourth-foot homodyne); even more unusual is the fact that the *Ars Poetica,* with -12.38, differs so much from the two Epistles of Book II, -4.12. This is one of several important features where the *Ars Poetica* is unlike the Letters to Florus and Augustus, and we perhaps have here new criteria for the much-discussed

	Satires		Epistles		Total
	I	II	I	II	
4th-foot homodyne, %:	46.80	43.77	51.69	52.49	48.54
Repeats, % of change:	46.74	45.71	53.01	43.48	47.45
Differs from homodyne %:	-0.06	+1.94	+1.32	-9.01	-1.09
Repeats and near repeats, % of change:	49.79	47.56	48.42	51.08	49.17
Differs from homodyne %:	+2.99	+3.79	-3.27	-1.41	+0.63

problem of the date of its composition. I shall return to this topic in the final section of this chapter.

In his higher percentages of fourth-foot homodyne and in his failure to increase the fourth-foot texture change in repeated patterns, Horace thus stands closer to the Republican poets than to Vergil. There are two extenuating circumstances, however: (1) Horace's percentages of change in fourth-foot texture are actually about the same as those of Vergil: in the case of the repeats, the range in Horace is from 43.48 (*Epistles* II) to 53.01 (*Epistles* I); in Vergil from 43.50 *(Georgics)* to 49.21 *(Eclogues)*. Vergil's percentages of change show a definite increase over the fourth-foot homodyne percentages merely because Vergil reduced the latter to such an extent, and Horace failed to follow him in this respect. (2) Horace in his repeats concentrates less on one pattern than Vergil does. In the case of *dsss*, the most frequent pattern, the repeats are 29.38 per cent of the total repeats in the *Georgics*, 22.18 of those in the *Aeneid;* Horace is somewhat lower: the *dsss* repeats account for 20.06 per cent of his total repeats. The difference in the *dsds* repeats is even greater: percentage of total repeats, *Georgics*, 15.25; *Aeneid*, 18.76; but Horace, 11.15 (*Satires*, 14.20; *Epistles*, 7.89).[5]

Opposite patterns in adjacent lines appear in Vergil's works with a remarkable consistency (but slightly less often in the *Aeneid*): *Eclogues*, one every 19.6 lines; *Georgics*, 20.9; *Aeneid*, 23.1 (but only 21.8 in Books I-IX). The average for Horace's hexameter poetry is similar (one every 21.4 lines), but his procedure is quite different. In the earliest collection (*Satires* I) opposite combinations are much less frequent than in Vergil, one every 32.1 lines; in *Satires* II and *Epistles* I (20.8 and 21.0 respectively) we have the same frequency as in the *Georgics*, but in *Epistles* II they occur once every 16.3 lines.

The intensive use of opposites in adjacent lines to provide variety is apparently an Augustan innovation, first introduced by Vergil in his *Eclogues*. Horace shows the greatest interest in these combinations in his final collection, where they appear almost twice as often as in *Satires* I.

I have examined the eight least frequent patterns to discover which pattern is preceded or followed most often by its opposite. The percentage of *sddd* with *dsss* is highest both in Vergil's *Georgics* (35.71) and in his *Aeneid* (29.38); in Horace it is 25.0, but in *Satires* II it reaches a high of 31.25. The percentages of the eight patterns with their opposites range in Vergil's *Aeneid* from 29.38 *(sddd-dsss)* to 10.18 *(dssd-sdds)*. The corresponding range in Horace is from 25.0 *(sddd-dsss)* to 6.84 *(sssd-ddds)*. The percentage of *dddd* preceded or followed by *ssss* is 13.10 (cf. Vergil's *Georgics*, 12.24; *Aeneid*, 13.94), but in *Epistles* II it is 37.71 (*Ars Poetica*, 40.0). In *Satires* II Horace favors the use of *sddd* with *dsss* in adjacent lines, but in the final collection (even though *dsss* is still the most frequent pattern) he prefers to combine *dddd* with *ssss*.

Neither in Horace nor in Vergil, however, do the *sddd-dsss* opposites comprise the highest percentage of the total number of opposites. The most frequent combination in Horace is *dsdd-sdss*, 18.32 per cent of the total (*sddd-dsss*, 13.09 per cent), and in Vergil it is consistently *sdsd-dsds*: *Eclogues*, 19.05; *Georgics*, 23.58; *Aeneid*, 16.04. But Horace, unlike Vergil, changes his most frequent combination from *dsdd-sdss* in the *Satires* (20.24 per cent; *sdsd-dsds* second with 16.67) to *sdsd-dsds* in the *Epistles* (18.69 per cent; *dsdd-sdss* second with 16.82).

Reverse patterns in adjacent lines occur in Horace much more frequently (total, one every 29.4 lines) than in Vergil, where we have a steady increase in their use: *Eclogues*, one every 55.0 lines; *Georgics*, 46.4; *Aeneid*, 38.9. Horace shows no such changing trend; the frequencies for the four hexameter books, one every *x* lines, are as follows: *Satires* I, 34.3; *Satires* II, 25.8; *Epistles* I, 27.9; *Epistles* II, 31.0. We thus have here another interesting difference in the metrical procedure of the two poets: Vergil uses opposites without much change from his earlier to his later poetry, but increases the frequency of his reverses; Horace, on the contrary, from *Satires* I through *Epistles* II, increases the frequency of his opposites, but not that of his reverses. Horace, however, goes beyond Vergil in his use of reverse combinations. His average of one every 29.4 lines is exceeded only by that in Cicero's *Aratea* (one every 24.0 lines) among the earlier poets.

Horace's percentage of *ssds* patterns preceded or followed by *sdss* is 24.90, but in *Satires* II it rises to 33.33 (cf. Vergil's *Georgics*, 10.92; *Aeneid*, 17.21). In *Epistles* II 23.33 per cent of *ssds* appears with *sdss*, but this is still a higher frequency than that of the other three reverse combinations in the book. In other words, Horace prefers *ssds* with *sdss* (24.90 per cent), but the *sssd* patterns with *dsss* are a close second (23.68). The percentage of *sddd* with *ddds* is lowest, 8.0. Vergil in the *Aeneid* favors *sssd* with *dsss* (29.56), and *dsdd* with *ddsd* is lowest (9.92). Horace's preference for *ssds*-*sdss* is seen also by the fact that this combination comprises 46.04 per cent of the total number of reverses, and *sssd*-*dsss* is second, with 32.37 per cent; cf. Vergil's *Aeneid*: *ssds*-*sdss*, 40.08 per cent; *sssd*-*dsss*, 34.52 per cent.

In summary, we have two important aspects of Horace's hexameter technique:

1. He goes beyond Vergil in his low percentages of the first, first four, and first eight patterns, with a resultant greater variety of patterns in the sixteen-line units and a lower frequency of repeated patterns. He also uses reverse combinations to a greater extent than does Vergil, but he differs from his friend in returning to higher percentages of fourth-foot homodyne, and he likewise fails to increase the percentages of fourth-foot texture change over the homodyne percentages.

2. Horace's hexameter works in chronological order reveal a steady increase in variety from *Satires* I to *Epistles* II. This is very unlike the practice of Vergil and most Latin poets, where, from first to last, we find an amazing consistency in percentages and frequencies, with the exception of Lucretius, whose latest books (III, IV, and VI) move in the opposite direction, toward greater repetition, and display, in addition, a greater interest in more dactylic patterns. Horace also has a striking increase in the frequency of opposite combinations, which are twice as numerous in *Epistles* II as in *Satires* I.

I have thus far included the *Ars Poetica* with the two *Epistles* of Book II. But where, actually, does this treatise on literary composition stand amid these changing trends from Horace's earliest hexameter collection to his latest? It seems very probable that the various criteria described above may be used to determine more exactly the date of the poem.

The Dating of the *Ars Poetica*

One of the most discussed problems in connection with the *Ars Poetica* is that of the time of its composition. Suggested dates range over a period of twenty years. The various possibilities, with selected sponsors,[6] are the following:

1. 28-27 B.C., between *Satires* II and *Odes* I-III.[7]
2. 23-20 B.C., between *Odes* I-III and *Epistles* I.[8]
3. 20-19 B.C., between *Epistles* I and the Letter to Florus (*Epistles* II, 2).[9]
4. About 18 B.C., between the Letter to Florus (*Epistles* II, 2) and the *Carmen Saeculare*.[10]
5. 17-16 B.C., after the *Carmen Saeculare*, but before the composition of *Odes* IV.[11]
6. About 15 B.C., before the Letter to Augustus (*Epistles* II, 1) of 14 or 13 B.C.[12]
7. Between 12 and 8 B.C. According to this view, the *Ars Poetica* is after both Book IV of the *Odes* and the Letter to Augustus and is thus Horace's latest work, probably composed near the end of his life.[13]

I shall not discuss again the various arguments based on external evidence; these have been set forth recently in admirable fashion by both Dilke and Brink. The latter believes that only two periods are possible for the composition of the *Ars Poetica*: the *intervallum lyricum* from 23 to about 18 B.C., and the period between the publication of *Odes* IV and the end of Horace's life; he says: "I see no unexceptionable proof on external criteria that one of the two periods must be preferred to the other.... The argument must then turn to the internal evidence."[14] It is the internal evidence, especially the mature and comprehensive nature of the criticism in the *Ars Poetica*, which leads Brink to favor a date after 14-13 B.C.

Metrical considerations have been introduced by several scholars but have proved somewhat inconclusive. It is of course true, as Wickham maintains, that arguments based on meter must be used with caution, especially if the numbers involved are too small to be meaningful.[15] Metrical arguments can perhaps give additional support to a theory rather than establish absolute proof. I am convinced, however, that the metrical analyses given above, based on the frequency percentages of the favorite patterns, on the variety in sixteen-line units, and on Horace's use of repeated, oppo- site, and reverse patterns in adjacent lines, provide new evidence of considerable significance which supports the late dating of the *Ars Poetica,* as favored in recent years by Dilke, Perret, and Brink. I shall itemize the various points where the poem differs not only from the two *Epistles* of Book II but seems to mark the end of a trend or progression from Horace's earliest hexameter poetry to his latest (i.e., the *Ars Poetica*). Since the Letter to Florus (II, 2) is usually dated in 19 B.C. and that to Augustus (II, 1) about 13 B.C., I list them in this order in the few tables which follow, and place the *Ars Poetica* in the final column.

1. In Horace's use of the first three patterns, the hexameter collections reveal a more or less steady decrease in frequency, with the *Ars Poetica* marking the end of a progression in each in- stance, an apparent indication of lateness of date:

	Satires			*Epistles*		
	I	II	I	II, 2	II, 1	*A. P.*
First:[16]	12.82	14.03	12.82	13.89	11.85	10.32
Second:	11.36	10.71	10.74	11.11	11.11	9.68
Third:	10.10	9.60	9.24	11.11	9.26	8.62

The *Ars Poetica,* therefore, not only is unlike the Letter to Florus (II, 2) but goes beyond the Let- ter to Augustus (II, 1) in its decreasing use of the first three patterns. In each case we have the end of a progression toward greater variety and less concentration.

2. The percentages for the first four patterns, the second four, and the first eight are as follows:

	Satires			*Epistles*		
	I	II	I	II, 2	II, 1	*A. P.*
First four:	43.59	43.95	40.85	44.91	41.48	36.84
Second four:	27.57	25.85	25.45	25.93	27.79	29.05
First eight:	71.16	69.81	66.30	70.83	69.26	65.89

Just as the first four patterns in the *Ars Poetica* have a much lower percentage than elsewhere in Horace, so that for the second four is higher. The percentage for the first eight is likewise lower than in the other works. In each instance we find a steady progression from II, 2, to II, 1, to the *Ars Poetica*. Since approximately a six-year interval exists between the Letter to Florus and that to Augustus, and since the *Ars Poetica* in percentage totals differs even more from II, 1, than II, 1, differs from the earlier II, 2, we have here, I believe, a decisive argument for assigning the *Ars* to a date several years later than the Letter to Augustus, i.e., to a period very shortly before Hor- ace's death.

3. In the first eight patterns the totals of the spondees and the dactyls in the first four feet likewise change over the years:

	Satires			*Epistles*		
	I	II	I	II, 2	II, 1	*A. P.*
Spondees:	21	20	21	21	17	18
Dactyls:	11	12	11	11	15	14

The higher proportion of dactyls in the first four feet argues against a dating of the *Ars Poetica* in the *intervallum lyricum* from 23 to about 18 B.C., in which case, as Brink points out, it must be later than 14 B.C. [17] The similarity here of the *Ars Poetica* to the Letter to Augustus is striking.

4. When we examine the variety of metrical patterns in units of sixteen lines, again we find that the *Ars Poetica* and the Letter to Augustus mark the end of a trend, both in the numerical average per unit and in the percentage of units with eight or more different patterns:

	Satires		*Epistles*			
	I	II	I	II, 2	II, 1	*A. P.*
Average patterns per unit:	9.0	9.6	9.7	9.5	10.3	10.1
% of units with eight or more:	83.64	86.67	97.67	84.62	100.0	100.0

5. Horace's use of repeat clusters in the *Ars Poetica* is unique. Since, as we have seen, this poem shows the lowest percentage for the eight patterns appearing most frequently, we should expect that repeat clusters would be rarer here than in his earlier poetry; the opposite is the case, for we find five, an average of one every 95 lines. The two long Letters of Book II have one each, and the range in the earlier collections is from one every 147.1 lines (*Satires* I) to one every 201.2 lines (*Epistles* I). Perhaps Horace had reduced the concentration on the first four and the first eight patterns to such an extent (36.84 and 65.89 per cent respectively) that he no longer objected to the more frequent appearance of repeat clusters.

6. Horace is far less consistent in his use of fourth-foot homodyne than is Vergil; the percentages for the *Satires* are considerably lower than those for the *Epistles*.[18] The Letter to Florus has the highest amount of fourth-foot homodyne, with a steady decrease through the Letter to Augustus to the *Ars Poetica*, as follows:

Satires		*Epistles*			
I	II	I	II, 2	II, 1	*A. P.*
46.80	43.77	51.69	56.48	52.22	50.84

7. Repeats occur in the *Ars Poetica* at about the same rate (one every 12.2 lines) as in *Satires* I (one every 11.2 lines) and *Epistles* I (one every 12.1 lines). The figures for the other works are: *Satires* II, one every 15.5 lines; *Epistles* II, 2, one every 15.4; and *Epistles* II, 1, one every 16.9. The evidence from repeats is thus inconclusive, but the high frequency of repeats in the *Ars Poetica* results in part from the large number of repeat clusters; they appear more than twice as often in the *Ars* as in *Epistles* II, 2, and II, 1. The *Ars* is unlike the other works and almost unique in the extent to which Horace fails to vary the repeats and (to a lesser degree) the repeats plus near repeats by a shift in fourth-foot texture from homodyne to heterodyne, or from heterodyne to homodyne. The statistics for *Epistles* II, 2, II, 1, and the *Ars* are as follows:

	II, 2	II, 1	*A. P.*
% of change in repeats:	50.0	50.0	38.46
Differs from homodyne %:	-6.48	-2.22	-12.38
% of change in R + NR:	57.14	52.08	47.92
Differs from homodyne %:	+0.66	-0.14	-2.92

Horace is perhaps less interested in change in fourth-foot texture in the *Ars* because the percentages of the first four and the first eight patterns are so much lower than elsewhere in his hexameter poetry.[19]

8. The *Ars Poetica* differs somewhat from the other works in its treatment of *dsss* and *dsds* repeats: the *dsss* repeats show a high percentage of the total *dsss* patterns, but in the case of *dsds* the repeats plus near repeats have a low percentage both of the total repeats plus near repeats, and also of the total *dsds* patterns; here again the *Ars* resembles *Epistles* II, 1, more closely than II, 2. The relevant statistics are as follows (and it must be realized that the numbers included in this category are small, and the results therefore less conclusive than in the categories given above):

	Satires		Epistles			
	I	II	I	II, 2	II, 1	A. P.
dsss R, % of dsss:	10.61	11.84	12.40	10.0	16.0	16.33
dsds R + NR,						
% of dsds:	35.58	25.96	23.66	33.33	16.0	21.74
% of total R + NR:	15.59	12.0	11.58	18.60	8.51	10.42

9. Horace shows a steadily increasing use of opposite combinations, ranging from one every 32.1 lines in *Satires* I to one every 15.0 lines in *Epistles* II, 1. The *Ars Poetica* resembles the Letter to Augustus in this respect, not the Letter to Florus, which has the same frequency as *Satires* II and *Epistles* I:

Satires		Epistles			
I	II	I	II, 2	II, 1	A. P.
32.1	20.8	21.0	21.6	15.0	15.3

10. In the case of the individual combinations, the totals are almost too small to yield significant results. But the percentages of *sddd* occurring with *dsss*, of *ddsd* with *ssds*, and of *dddd* with *ssss* are of interest:

	Satires		Epistles			
	I	II	I	II, 2	II, 1	A. P.
sddd-dsss:	23.08	31.25	22.73	12.50	50.0	11.76
ddsd-ssds:	10.81	9.09	9.26	11.76	25.0	28.57
dddd-ssss:	6.67	11.76	8.70	0.	33.33	40.0

In each instance the percentage for the *Ars Poetica* marks the end of a progression — decreasing in the case of *sddd-dsss* and increasing with *ddsd-ssds* and *dddd-ssss*.[20]

11. Reverse combinations appear in the *Ars Poetica* more often than elsewhere in Horace's poetry, one instance every 25.0 lines; the closest frequency to this is in *Satires* II, one every 25.8 lines, and reverses are less numerous in *Epistles* II, 2, and II, 1 (once every 30.9 and 54.0 lines respectively). The totals of the individual reverse patterns in adjacent lines are again too small to be of much significance. The percentage of *ssds* with *sdss* in the *Ars* (29.41) is higher than elsewhere in Horace's hexameters, with the exception of *Satires* II (33.33); the percentage of *sssd* with *dsss* (18.75) is the lowest, with the exception of the Letter to Augustus (11.11).

To summarize, of the eleven categories listed above, some have far more significance than others. Those dealing with large totals (Nos. 1-4 and 6) — the frequency percentages of the first four and the first eight patterns, the distribution of the spondees and dactyls in the first eight patterns, variety in sixteen-line units, and percentages of fourth-foot homodyne — are the most decisive; they show a steady trend toward less concentration and greater variety, with the *Ars Poetica* at the end of the progressions and thus the latest of Horace's works. The remaining categories (Nos. 5 and 7-11) indicate in general that the unusual features of the *Ars Poetica* link it far more closely to the Letter to Augustus than to either *Epistles* I or the Letter to Florus,[21] and likewise support the view that 12-8 B.C. is definitely to be preferred to the *intervallum lyricum* of 23-18 B.C. Dilke, Perret, and Brink, therefore, seem correct in their dating of the *Ars Poetica*.

Notes to Chapter 8

1. There are, however, numerous metrical irregularities and abnormalities in *Aeneid* X-XII; these are best explained, as I said above, by the hypothesis that Vergil did not live long enough to give to the final three books the same careful metrical revision which the other books had received.

2. See Duckworth, *TAPhA* 87 (1956), pp. 281-316.

3. In my statistics for the first book of the *Satires*, I exclude X, 1a-8a, rejected by all editors as spurious. Several scholars, however, have favored the authenticity of these eight verses, e.g., Hendrickson, *CPh* 11 (1916), pp. 249-269; Rothstein, *Hermes* 68 (1933), pp. 70-83; D'Anna, *Maia* 7 (1955), pp. 26-42; Pennisi, *Helikon* 2 (1962), pp. 112-130.

4. The minor exceptions are the increases in the percentages of the first and the first four patterns from *Satires* I to *Satires* II, and also the slight increase in the percentages of the first eight patterns from *Epistles* I to *Epistles* II.

5. If we include the near repeats, Horace continues to show less emphasis on one particular pattern: the *dsss* R + NR comprise 31.33 per cent of the total R + NR in the *Georgics*, 23.15 in the *Aeneid*, but 21.21 in Horace; the corresponding percentages for the *dsds* R + NR are: *Georgics*, 16.60; *Aeneid*, 15.67, but Horace, 12.80 (*Satires*, 13.68; *Epistles*, 11.70).

6. I give, under each of the suggested dates, at least one Horatian scholar favoring that particular date; for others, see Duckworth, *TAPhA* 96 (1965), pp. 84-85, notes 28-33.

7. See Elmore, *CPh* 30 (1935), pp. 1-9; this early dating is rejected unanimously by other scholars.

8. See Nettleship, *JPh* 12 (1883), pp. 43-61. The year 22 B.C. is now favored by Newman, *Augustus and the New Poetry*, pp. 361-362; *The Concept of Vates*, pp. 127-130.

9. See Wilkins, *Epistles*, pp. 330-332.

10. See Becker, *Das Spätwerk des Horaz*, p. 111.

11. See Kiessling-Heinze, *Briefe*, p. 288.

12. See Wili, *Horaz*, p. 309 (published in 15 B.C., but written earlier, true to the principle stated in *Ars Poet.* 388: *nonumque prematur in annum*).

13. See Dilke, *BICS* 5 (1958), pp. 49-57; Perret, *Horace*, p. 190 (Eng. trans., pp. 151-152); Brink, *Horace on Poetry*, p. 217; cf. pp. 239-243.

14. *Horace on Poetry*, pp. 242-243.

15. *The Works of Horace*, Vol. II, pp. 333-334.

16. The most frequent pattern in each of Horace's four hexameter collections is *dsss*, but *sdss* is first in *Epistles* II, 1. Also, *sdss* is consistently in second place in the earlier works, but *ddss* holds this position in *Epistles* II, 1, and *dsds* is second in the *Ars Poetica*.

17. *Horace on Poetry*, p. 242.

18. This could possibly result from the influence of Lucilius on the *Satires*; the fragments of Lucilius yield a fourth-foot homodyne percentage of 46.79 (cf. Cicero, *Aratea*, 44.79; Lucretius, 47.66). It is surprising that Vergil's low homodyne percentages (from 36.08 in the *Georgics* to 39.73 in the *Eclogues*) seem to have had no effect on Horace's *Epistles*, where the percentages are considerably higher than in the *Satires*.

19. Or is it possible that the strange discrepancy here between the *Ars Poetica* and the other hexameter works indicates that the poem was written so near Horace's death that it was not completely revised? The same striking lack of shift in fourth-foot texture in *Aeneid* X-XII is one of many irregularities which imply that Vergil did not live to complete the revision of his epic.

20. It is perhaps worth noting that, since *dddd* is Horace's least frequent pattern, the *dddd-ssss* combination appears only eleven times in all his hexameter poetry; four of the eleven occurrences are in the *Ars Poetica*, once every 118.8 lines, as against once every 515.0 lines in his other poems. Next in frequency is the Letter to Augustus, one instance in 270 lines.

21. This is especially true of Nos. 8, 9, 10 (% of *ddsd* with *ssds* and of *dddd* with *ssss*), and 11 (% of *sssd* with *dsss*).

70

Chapter 9

OVID, MASTER OF DACTYLIC RHYTHM

Ovid's use of hexameter patterns in the *Metamorphoses* is very unlike what we find in Vergil and Horace and in fact differs strikingly also from the metrical practices of the Republican poets. Ovid has been described as "the greatest artist in verse that Rome produced, the supreme master both in the elegy and in the epos."[1] Other classical writers give a very different impression of Ovid's hexameter technique; Otis refers to "the un-Virgilian character of Ovid's metric" in the *Metamorphoses* and says:[2]

> He sacrificed most of the weight, gravity, and *ethos* of Virgil's hexameter to rapid and unbroken movement. . . . Ovid puts in everything (dactyls, regular pauses, coincidence of ictus and accent, rhyme, alliteration, grammatical simplicity and concision) that will speed up and lighten; leaves out everything (elision, spondees, grammatical complexity, clash of ictus and accent, overrunning of metrical by sense units) that will slow down and encumber his verse.

Similarly, Jackson Knight stresses the dactylic nature of Ovid's hexameter verse:[3]

> Ovid's verse-technique uses the well-known resources of dactylic metre, but uses them with a lavish freedom unknown and perhaps unsought before. Economy is not wanted. Ovid seems to like almost as many dactyls as he can get, and often, except in the middle of the verse, almost as many coincidences of word-accent and metrical ictus as can easily be contrived.

I said above that, when we turn from the Republican poets to Vergil, we are in a different metrical world, one with far less concentration on the same metrical patterns and with much lower percentages of fourth-foot homodyne; also I gave a sixteen-line unit from the beginning of Cicero, Lucretius, Catullus LXIV, and Vergil's Second *Eclogue* (the earliest of the pastorals), in order to illustrate the innovations introduced by Vergil.

Likewise, when we turn from Vergil and Horace to the hexameters of Ovid in his *Metamorphoses,* we are again in a different metrical world, this time with the emphasis on dactyls rather than spondees, and far less interest in variety in the first eight patterns. Again I shall quote as a preliminary illustration three sixteen-line units, this time from the conclusions of their three hexameter works: the end of Book XII of Vergil's *Aeneid,* that of the *Ars Poetica* (excluding line 467, a spondaic verse),[4] and that of Book XV of the *Metamorphoses.*

Vergil, *Aen.* XII, 937-952

(dsds)	Ausonii videre; tua est Lavinia coniunx,	*(t)*
(dsdd)	ulterius ne tende odiis.' stetit acer in armis	*(t)*
(ssds)	Aeneas volvens oculos dextramque repressit.[5]	*(t)*
(sdss)	Et iam iamque magis cunctantem flectere sermo	*(m)*
(dsds)	coeperat, infelix umero cum apparuit alto	*(t)*
(dsss)	balteus et notis fulserunt cingula bullis	*(m)*
(sdss)	Pallantis pueri, victum quem vulnere Turnus	*(t)*
(ddds)	straverat atque umeris inimicum insigne gerebat.	*(m)*
(dssd)	ille, oculis postquam saevi monimenta doloris	*(t)*
(dsds)	exuviasque hausit, furiis accensus et ira	*(t)*
(dsds)	terribilis: 'tune hinc spoliis indute meorum	*(t)*
(ddss)	eripiare mihi? Pallas te hoc vulnere, Pallas	*(t)*
(dsds)	immolat et poenam scelerato ex sanguine sumit.'	*(m)*
(ssss)	hoc dicens ferrum adverso sub pectore condit	*(t)*

(dsss) fervidus. ast illi solvuntur frigore membra   *(m)*
(ddds) vitaque cum gemitu fugit indignata sub umbras.   *(m)*

Horace, *Ars Poet.* 460-476

(dsss) clamet 'io cives!' non sit qui tollere curet.   *(m)*
(sdss) si curet quis opem ferre et demittere funem   *(m)*
(ssss) 'qui scis an prudens huc se deiecerit atque   *(m)*
(sssd) servari nolit?' dicam, Siculique poetae   *(t)*
(sdds) narrabo interitum. deus immortalis haberi   *(m)*
(ddss) dum cupit Empedocles, ardentem frigidus Aetnam   *(m)*
(dsdd) insiluit. sit ius liceatque perire poetis.   *(m)*
(dsss) nec semel hoc fecit, nec si retractus erit iam   *(m)*
(dsss) fiet homo et ponet famosae mortis amorem.   *(m)*
(dsss) nec satis apparet cur versus factitet, utrum   *(m)*
(ddds) minxerit in patrios cineres, an triste bidental   *(t)*
(dssd) moverit incestus: certe furit, ac velut ursus,   *(t)*
(sdds) obiectos caveae valuit si frangere clathros,   *(t)*
(ssdd) indoctum doctumque fugat recitator acerbus;   *(t)*
(sdds) quem vero arripuit, tenet occiditque legendo,   *(m)*
(sddd) non missura cutem nisi plena cruoris hirudo.   *(m)*

Ovid, *Metam,* XV, 864-879

(ddss) Vestaque Caesareos inter sacrata penates,   *(t)*
(sdsd) et cum Caesarea tu, Phoebe domestice, Vesta,   *(m)*
(dsss) quique tenes altus Tarpeias Iuppiter arces,   *(m)*
(dsss) quosque alios vati fas appellare piumque est: *(m)*
(ddss) tarda sit illa dies et nostro serior aevo,   *(m)*
(dssd) qua caput Augustum, quem temperat, orbe relicto   *(m)*
(ssdd) accedat caelo faveatque precantibus absens!   *(m)*
(dssd)   Iamque opus exegi, quod nec Iovis ira nec ignis   *(m)*
(dsdd) nec poterit ferrum nec edax abolere vetustas.   *(t)*
(ddsd) cum volet, illa dies, quae nil nisi corporis huius   *(m)*
(dsdd) ius habet, incerti spatium mihi finiat aevi: *(t)*
(dddd) parte tamen meliore mei super alta perennis   *(t)*
(dsds) astra ferar, nomenque erit indelebile nostrum,   *(m)*
(ddsd) quaque patet domitis Romana potentia terris,   *(m)*
(ddsd) ore legar populi, perque omnia saecula fama,   *(m)*
(dsss) siquid habent veri vatum praesagia, vivam.   *(t)*

The number of different patterns in these sixteen-line units is as follows: nine in Vergil and Ovid, eleven in Horace, one more indication of Horace's desire for greater variety. The number of dactyls in the first four feet (out of a possible sixty-four) is: Vergil, twenty-eight; Horace, twenty-seven; but Ovid, thirty-six. Even more significant is the number of fourth-foot dactyls in the sixteen lines: Vergil, two; Horace, five; but Ovid, ten. Ovid's use in this sixteen-line unit of *dsdd* (twice) and *ddsd* (thrice) is especially noteworthy, since neither of these patterns is favored by Vergil or Horace, i.e., neither appears among their eight most frequent patterns. Only six of the sixteen lines in Vergil have fourth-foot homodyne (a normal 37.50 per cent), but both Horace and Ovid have homodyne in eleven lines (68.75 per cent, higher than average for these two poets).

Ovid's Hexameter Technique

The metrical pattern appearing in the *Metamorphoses* with the greatest frequency is not *dsss* as Lee wrongly implies on the basis of Book I, where *dsss* is first with a percentage of 13.97; Lee states:[6]

There would probably be alterations of emphasis if the count were extended to include all fifteen books of the poem, but I do not believe they would be big enough to upset the broad conclusions drawn from an examination of only one book.

Unfortunately, Lee is in error here. Ovid's procedure in I does *not* give a true picture, for in the poem as a whole *ddss* is first (13.08 per cent) and *dsss* is second (12.57 per cent). It is interesting that the percentage of the first pattern is almost identical with that in the *Eclogues* (13.09) and much lower than any of the first-pattern percentages in the Republican poets.

When we recall how consistently the poets from Cicero through Vergil and Horace prefer *dsss* as their favorite pattern, the procedure of Ovid in this respect is most unusual, to say the least; he varies the position of *dsss* from book to book as follows: first in I, III, V, VIII, IX; second in II, IV, XII, XIII, XIV; third in XI and tied for third place (with *ddss*) in X; fourth in VI; and fifth in both VII and XV (where the respective percentages are 10.47 and 10.77). No such variation in the use of *dsss* had appeared in the earlier poets,[7] where *dsss* is first in each book of the *De rerum natura* and the *Georgics,* in ten of the twelve books of the *Aeneid,* and in each of Horace's hexameter collections.

The eight most frequent patterns in the *Aeneid* and the *Metamorphoses* are as follows:

	1	2	3	4	5	6	7	8
Aen.:	*dsss*	*ddss*	*dsds*	*sdss*	*ssss*	*ddds*	*ssds*	*sdds*
Metam.:	*ddss*	*dsss*	*dssd*	*dsds*	*ddsd*	*ddds*	*dsdd*	*dddd*

We find here an amazing difference between Vergil and Ovid in their preference for the eight most frequent patterns; *sdss* and *ssss*, fourth and fifth in the *Aeneid,* move to ninth and fifteenth position, while *dddd*, fifteenth in the *Aeneid,* is now eighth. Ovid's fondness for *dssd, ddsd,* and *dsdd* is especially evident: these three patterns were ninth, tenth, and twelfth in the *Aeneid,* but in the *Metamorphoses* they are in third, fifth, and seventh position.

Ovid's use of *dssd* and *ddsd* seems of particular significance. Radford refers (in italics) to *"the unusually high ratio of DSSD and of DDSD, which is as a rule the true distinguishing mark of Ovid's works, mature and juvenile alike."*[8]

Although in this book I do not normally include the hexameter lines of elegiac poetry, a recent examination of all the hexameters in Ovid's numerous works[9] now makes it possible to compare the poet's use of *dssd* and *ddsd* throughout his career. With the exception of the *Medicamina* (50 hexameters only), the two patterns vary from first to fifth place, i.e., *dssd* is first in the *Heroides* XVI-XXI, *Fasti,* and *Tristia,* second in the *Heroides* I-XV, and *Ibis,* third (as in the *Metamorphoses*) in the *Amores, Ars Amatoria* III, *Remedium,* and *Epistulae ex Ponto,* and fifth in *Ars Amatoria* I-II (the only instance where *dssd* is below third place); *ddsd* is first in the *Heroides* I-XV, and *Ibis,* third in the *Ars Amatoria* I-II, fourth in the *Amores, Ars Amatoria* III, *Heroides* XVI-XXI, *Tristia,* and *Epistulae ex Ponto,* and fifth in the *Fasti* (as in the *Metamorphoses*). This analysis shows clearly the constant emphasis which Ovid, unlike Vergil and the other earlier poets,[10] has placed on *dssd* and *ddsd;* the frequencies of these two patterns, however, are consistently higher in his elegiac poetry than in the *Metamorphoses.*

The percentage of Ovid's first eight patterns in the *Metamorphoses* is 81.62 (with a range from 78.80 in Book VI to 84.92 in XIV) and this is much higher than that in the *Aeneid,* 72.78 (cf. Horace, *Satires,* 69.99; *Epistles,* 66.76) and marks a return to the higher frequencies of Cicero and Lucretius.

The most striking difference between Ovid and Vergil is in the distribution of spondees and dactyls in the first four feet of the eight most frequent patterns: *Aeneid,* twenty spondees and twelve dactyls; *Metamorphoses,* twelve spondees and twenty dactyls, the exact opposite of what we find in the *Aeneid,* and unlike anything that we have seen in earlier Latin hexameter poetry. Ovid's distribution is close to that which we have in most Greek poetry from Homer to Musaeus, ten spondees and twenty-two dactyls (eleven and twenty-one in Hesiod, twelve and twenty in Theocritus). Metrically, therefore, Ovid is far more Greek than any previous Roman poet, far more "Homeric" than Vergil, and almost as "Homeric" as Homer himself. I say "Homeric" rather than "Hellenistic" advisedly, because the percentage of the first eight patterns in Homer, though higher than Ovid's, is considerably lower than those of Callimachus and Apollonius of Rhodes.[11]

One easy way to distinguish the first eight patterns of Ovid from those of Vergil is this: in the *Aeneid* the fourth foot is always a spondee; in the *Metamorphoses* the first foot is always a dactyl.

When we examine the eight most frequent hexameter patterns in Ovid's elegiac poetry, we find also that, again with the exception of the *Medicamina,* all the poems, from the earliest to the latest, exhibit the same characteristics: high percentages, from 78.84 *(Amores)* to 89.27 *(Fasti),*[12] and the same distribution of twelve spondees and twenty dactyls, with the first foot always a dactyl. These facts should be kept in mind when scholars assign to Ovid works of uncertain authorship, e.g., the hexameter poems of the *Appendix Vergiliana,* where the percentages are lower and there is no such predominance of dactyls.

Additional statistics for the *Metamorphoses* are the following: the number of patterns per sixteen-line unit averages 8.9 (with a range from 8.6 in Book XIV to 9.1 in VI); this is higher than in the Republican poets but lower than in Vergil and Horace. The percentage of units with eight or more patterns is 86.35 (ranging from 77.36 in XIV to 91.30 in X), again higher than in the Republican poets (and Horace's *Satires*) but lower than in Vergil and Horace's *Epistles.* Repeat clusters occur on an average once every 112.5 lines (range from one every 80.0 lines in IV to one every 208.0 lines in XII) and in this respect Ovid stands closer to Vergil and Horace than to Cicero, Lucretius, and Catullus. Repeats average one every 10.7 lines (range from 9.1 in III to 12.7 in I) and repeats plus near repeats one every 4.1 lines (range from 3.6 in IV to 4.7 in VI), somewhat more frequent than in Vergil and Horace, but considerably less so than in Lucretius and Catullus. The two most frequently repeated patterns in the *Metamorphoses* are *dsss* (202 repeats, 504 repeats plus near repeats) and *ddss* (173 repeats, 496 repeats plus near repeats). The combined repeats of these two patterns comprise 33.57 per cent of the total repeats, and the combined repeats plus near repeats are 34.14 of the total repeats plus near repeats. These percentages are surprisingly low, very unlike those in the Republican poets,[13] even lower than those in Vergil, and resemble the corresponding percentages in Horace's *Satires* (33.95 and 35.47 respectively).

In his frequency of fourth-foot homodyne Ovid reverts to the practice of the Republican poets (as had Horace); actually, the percentage of fourth-foot homodyne in the *Metamorphoses,* 50.0 (with a range from 45.28 in VIII to 53.29 in XIV) is considerably higher than that in Cicero's *Aratea* (44.79) and Lucretius (47.66) and is surpassed, among the earlier poets, only by that in Catullus (60.44) and in Horace's *Epistles* (52.08).[14] Ovid's percentage of change in fourth-foot texture is 46.91 for repeats and 46.19 for repeats plus near repeats; this is higher than in Vergil (except in the *Georgics,* where the percentage of change for repeats plus near repeats is 47.10), but with a fourth-foot homodyne percentage of 50.0 we have a difference of -3.09 for repeats and -3.81 for repeats plus near repeats. In all the earlier poets so far discussed we find a percentage of shift in texture higher than that of fourth-foot homodyne, with the exception of Catullus (-25.25 and -26.84) and Horace's *Epistles* (-3.40 and -2.29).

The *Metamorphoses* contains a total of 407 patterns preceded or followed by its opposite, an average of one every 29.3 lines; this frequency resembles that of Lucretius (one every 30.8 lines) and is considerably lower than that of Vergil and Horace. Ovid's most frequent opposite combination is *sdsd-dsds,* which comprises 22.11 per cent of the total opposites. Again this is similar to Lucretius (*sdsd-dsds,* 22.69 per cent) and also to Vergil's *Georgics* (*sdsd-dsds,* 23.58 per cent); this same combination is also the favorite in Vergil's *Aeneid* and Horace's *Epistles,* but the percentages are much lower (16.04 and 18.69 respectively).

The percentage of *ssdd* patterns (sixteenth in order, with a total of 146) preceded or followed by *ddss* (first, with a total of 1,561) is 30.14; this is a higher proportion than appears earlier in hexameter poetry (cf. Lucretius, 25.64 per cent; Vergil, *Georgics,* 26.92 per cent).[15] The percentage of *sddd* with *dsss* is 27.73, close to that in the *Aeneid,* 29.38, and in Horace, *Satires,* 28.89; Lucretius is higher (35.63) as is Vergil in the *Georgics* (35.71). The percentage of *sssd* with *ddds* is 17.58; this likewise is closer to the *Aeneid* (15.54) than to the other poets (cf. Horace, 6.84).

In regard to reverse patterns in adjacent lines, we find in the *Metamorphoses* 304 instances, one every 39.3 lines, about the same as in the *Aeneid,* one every 38.9 lines. The most frequent reverse combination is *dsdd-ddsd,* which in earlier poetry is first only in Vergil's *Eclogues* (and there only seven occurrences); in Cicero's *Aratea* and Catullus LXIV there are no instances of *dsdd-ddsd.*[16] In both the earlier and the later poets the favorite reverse is usually *ssds-sdss.* Ovid has 216 instances of *dsdd-ddsd,* 71.05 per cent of the total reverse combinations, a high proportion paralleled by only a few poets in all Latin hexameter verse.[17] The percentage of *dsdd* preceded or followed by *ddsd* is 24.0; no such percentage for this particular reverse had appeared among the earlier poets,[18] nor was it to occur again in the history of the Latin hexameter; Ovid's emphasis on these two patterns accounts for the unusually high percentage. His percentage of *sssd* with *dsss* is 24.85, about the same as in Horace (*Satires,* 24.76; *Epistles,* 22.35). In the earlier poets, the corresponding percentages are much higher (with a steady decrease from 64.71 in Cicero's *Aratea* to 29.56 in the *Aeneid*).

To summarize these various aspects of Ovid's procedure as a hexameter poet, I shall list the salient points mentioned above under four headings:

1. Ovid resembles the Republican poets in the following respects: high percentage of the first eight patterns and high percentage of fourth-foot homodyne; the frequency of opposite patterns in adjacent lines is similar to that in Lucretius; the most frequent opposite in both *(sdsd-dsds)* comprises almost the same percentage of the total opposites.

2. Ovid stands between the Republican poets and Vergil: number of patterns per sixteen-line unit; percentage of units with eight or more patterns; frequency of repeat clusters; frequency of repeated patterns in adjacent lines, and also of repeats plus near repeats.

3. Ovid's practice is that of Vergil and/or Horace: low percentage of the most frequent pattern; relation of the most frequent repeat plus near repeats to the total repeats plus near repeats; percentages of *sddd* preceded or followed by *dsss,* and of *sssd* preceded or followed by *ddds.* Ovid's frequency of reverse patterns in adjacent lines is similar to that in the *Aeneid;* his percentage of *sssd* with *dsss* resembles that in Horace.

4. Ovid's *Metamorphoses* is unlike all earlier Latin poetry (excluding, of course, his own previous works) in many important respects: the unusual treatment of *dsss,* from first to fifth position in the different books; the (almost Homeric) distribution of twelve spondees and twenty dactyls in the first four feet of the first eight patterns; the low percentage of change in fourth-foot texture of repeated patterns in relation to the fourth-foot homodyne percentage; the high percentage of *ssdd* preceded or followed by *ddss;* the choice of *dsdd-ddsd* as the most frequent reverse combination, with an abnormally high percentage of *dsdd* preceded or followed by *ddsd.* These differences between Ovid and the earlier poets, especially in the distribution of spondees and dactyls in the first eight patterns, are so great that it seems foolhardy to assign poems of uncertain authorship to Ovid if these same poems resemble Lucretius or Vergil more closely in their metrical structure.

Ovid's metrical technique is thus in many respects the exact opposite of what I have described above as the "Vergilian norm." We shall see, when we turn later to the Silver Age and Late Empire, that many poets (whom I term "post-Ovidian") follow Ovid in their emphasis on dactylic patterns, but that an equal or larger number (including in general the best of the later poets) are far more Vergilian, especially in the manner in which they avoid an excessive use of dactyls and too heavy a concentration on the same metrical patterns. First, however, we have to consider many short poems of the late Republic and a number of didactic works of the early Empire, including the *Halieutica,* believed to be a late composition by Ovid.

The Non-Ovidian Nature of the *Halieutica*

Of the *Halieutica,* a short poem on sea-fishing, Duff says: "It is only in this fragment, outside his *Metamorphoses,* that we have continuous hexameters from his hand."[19] In the handbooks of Latin literature and in most scholarly articles on Ovid, the *Halieutica* is accepted as the work of Ovid at the end of his life. A typical statement is that of Owen:[20]

> It cannot be questioned that the *Halieutica* is the genuine work of Ovid, a trifle with the composition of which the exiled poet amused himself at the close of his life. The precise references to and citations from the poem as we have it which are found in Pliny (*N. H.* XXXII. 11-13 and 152-153) preclude any doubt as to its authenticity. The opinions that have been advanced to the contrary, that it is the work of a later poet which Pliny mistook for that of Ovid, or that it is a forgery made up from Pliny's quotations, cannot be seriously maintained. It is incredible that Pliny could have mistaken the work of another for that of Ovid, and no forger could have been ingenious enough to have forged this poem.

Fraenkel has words of high praise for the poem: "We find that the style is surprisingly fresh and brilliant and the presentation pleasantly animated in the best Ovidian manner."[21]

On the other hand, several scholars over the years have rejected Ovidian authorship for reasons of prosody, non-Ovidian vocabulary, use of connectives in catalogues, and repetitions; these include Birt,[22] Housman,[23] Axelson,[24] Wilkinson, and Richmond. The arguments of Birt and Axelson are summarized by Koltowski,[25] but he accepts the poem as authentic on the testimony of Pliny. Wilkinson, however, rejects the evidence of Pliny and says:[26]

> That Pliny thought Ovid wrote it signifies little ... the un-Ovidian traits in the metre are too many. . . . It is not impossible that the author of the *Medicamina Faciei* whiled away his tedious hours by composing a didactic poem on this subject; but if he did, it is unlikely to have been the one we have.

Richmond in the Foreword to his edition of the poem states clearly his belief that "Ovid was not the author."[27] Lee criticizes Richmond for not discussing the problem of authenticity in greater detail, and says: "it still seems a pity that he did not include at least a summary of the arguments *pro* and *con* in this edition."[28] But Richmond does list many points against Ovidian authorship in his commentary,[29] and in an article published earlier he had given a number of arguments to support his position, as follows:[30]

> The *Halieutica* ascribed to Ovid departs from his practice because:
>
> 1) it imitates a lost Greek original slavishly,
> 2) it imitates Ovid's Latin predecessors ineptly, and
> 3) its general texture does not seem to have as much Ovidian diction as one might expect. The emphasis seems rather to be on imitation of other authors.
>
> It seems that it cannot have been written by Ovid because:
>
> 1) a verse of the *Ibis* has, apparently, been misunderstood, and
> 2) there is plausibile <sic> evidence that the author knew the works of Lucan and Seneca.
>
> This would mean a dating *post* 65 A.D., more or less.

I have spoken above of Ovid's preference for *dssd* and *ddsd*, the high percentage of the first eight patterns, and the unusual distribution in the first eight patterns of twelve spondees and twenty dactyls, not only in the *Metamorphoses* but also in his various elegiac works. How does the *Halieutica* compare with the other poems in these respects? I give below the first eight patterns of the *Metamorphoses* and the *Halieutica* and I also repeat those of the *Aeneid*, since Richmond says, in discussing the diction of the *Halieutica*, that "the influence of Vergil is very marked."[31] Perhaps the metrical patterns also show the influence of Vergil.

	1	2	3	4	5	6	7	8
Aeneid:	dsss	ddss	dsds	sdss	ssss	ddds	ssds	sdds
Metam.:	ddss	dsss	dssd	dsds	ddsd	ddds	dsdd	dddd
Hal.:	sdss	dsds	ssss		sdds	dsss	ssds	
			ddss				dssd	
							ddsd	

The differences between the *Halieutica* and the *Metamorphoses* are almost as great as those between the *Metamorphoses* and the *Aeneid*. The distribution of spondees and dactyls in the first eight patterns of the *Halieutica* is nineteen to twenty-one spondees, thirteen to eleven dactyls; this is Vergilian (twenty and twelve), definitely not Ovidian (twelve and twenty). Also, the percentage of the first eight patterns in the *Halieutica* (73.23) is close to that in the *Georgics* (73.42) and the *Aeneid* (72.78) and very unlike that in the *Metamorphoses* (81.62, with a range from 78.80 in Book I to 84.92 in XIV). It seems scarcely possible that a poet who stressed the use of dactyls to the extent which we find in the *Metamorphoses* would shift to spondees and lower percentages even in a short fragment written at the end of his poetic career.

The metrical patterns of the *Halieutica* likewise are most unusual, especially if we wish to ascribe the fragment to Ovid.

1. The appearance of *sdss* in first place is almost unique; elsewhere in Latin poetry it appears in this position only in Lucilius, Horace, *Epistles* II, 1 (second in Horace's hexameters as a whole, probably the influence of Lucilius), and in the *Dirae (Lydia)*, one of the hexameter poems of the *Appendix Vergiliana*. In the *Metamorphoses sdss* is in ninth position.

2. In the *Halieutica ssss* is tied for third place with *ddss*; in the *Metamorphoses ssss* is in fifteenth position, but fifth in the *Aeneid*.

3. The pattern *sdds*, in fifth place in the *Halieutica*, is eleventh in the *Metamorphoses*, eighth in the *Aeneid*.

4. Three patterns are tied for seventh position in the *Halieutica*: *ssds, dssd,* and *ddsd*; in the *Metamorphoses dssd* and *ddsd* are third and fifth respectively, with *ssds* in thirteenth place; in the *Aeneid ssds* is also in seventh position.

5. In the *Halieutica dsss* is in sixth position; this also is most unusual, for in all Latin hexameter poetry the range of *dsss* is always from first to third place, with the following exceptions: fourth in Ausonius *(Mosella)*, Prudentius, Sedulius, and Dracontius, all of the Late Empire; sixth in the *Halieutica;* eighth in Calpurnius Siculus, and tied for eighth in Arator. In his use of *dsss* the author of the *Halieutica* thus differs from both Vergil and Ovid.

In other respects also, the *Halieutica* is metrically very unlike the *Metamorphoses* and actually resembles more closely the didactic poetry of the first century A.D., which in turn is indebted to Vergil's *Georgics*.[32] In the statistics which follow I list, in addition to the *Metamorphoses* and the *Halieutica*, both the *Georgics* and the *Aratea* of Germanicus Caesar, one of the most Vergilian of the later didactic poets:

	Metam.	*Hal.*	*Georg.*	*Arat.*
Patterns per 16-line unit:	8.9	9.1	9.3	9.2
% units with 8 or more:	86.35	100.0	92.59	90.48
% of 4th-foot homodyne:	50.0	36.22	36.08	35.83
Repeats, one every *x* lines:	10.7	12.2	12.3	10.0
% shift in 4th-foot texture:	46.91	45.45	43.50	44.12
Differs from homodyne %:	-3.09	+9.23	+7.42	+8.29
R + NR, one every *x* lines:	4.1	5.0	4.5	4.5
% shift in 4th-foot texture:	46.19	55.56	47.10	41.06
Differs from homodyne %:	-3.81	+19.34	+11.02	+5.23
Opposites, one every *x* lines:	29.3	15.9	20.9	24.2
Reverses, one every *x* lines:	39.3	127.0	46.4	32.2

These figures likewise prove that Ovid is not the author of the *Halieutica*; it differs from the *Metamorphoses* in every respect, not only in its percentage of fourth-foot homodyne, but in the introduction of greater variety in repeated patterns by shifting from homodyne to heterodyne, or the reverse, and in the frequency of the opposite and reverse combinations. The poem belongs to an entirely different hexameter tradition, that of didactic poetry.

But what about the other works of Ovid? What additional light, if any, do they throw on the unique metrical features of the *Halieutica*? I referred above to the patterns and percentages of the elegiac poems, as given by Costa, and I stressed the fact that the distribution of spondees and dactyls in the first eight patterns is always twelve and twenty respectively, identical with that in the *Metamorphoses*, with the sole exception of the very short *Medicamina* (where we find fifteen spondees and seventeen dactyls). In other words, not a single authentic work of Ovid has the emphasis on spondees which appears in the *Halieutica*.

Also, I pointed out that the percentage of the first eight patterns is uniformly high in all the elegiac works, from 78.84 in the *Amores* to 89.27 in the *Fasti*, and it is important to note that the percentages are unusually high in the poems of his later years: *Tristia*, 86.87; *Ibis*, 83.86; and *Epistulae ex Ponto*, 85.85. But the *Halieutica*, supposedly written at the end of his life, has a percentage of only 73.23! Costa himself realizes the extent to which the *Halieutica* differs metrically from the other poems, but he fails to draw the proper conclusion and says merely: "the authenticity of the fragment can no longer be placed in doubt."[33]

And what of the more spondaic patterns, each with an initial spondee, which appear so frequently among the first eight patterns of the *Halieutica: sdss* (first), *ssss* (tied for third), *sdds* (fifth), *ssds* (tied for seventh)? In the authentic works of Ovid the position of each is as follows:[34] *sdss* ranges from ninth to eleventh place (except for the *Medicamina*, seventh), *ssss* from eleventh to sixteenth, *sdds* from ninth to thirteenth, and *ssds* from twelfth to fifteenth. Owen believes that lack of revision accounts for the metrical and other blemishes which have caused the genuineness of the *Halieutica* to be impugned unnecessarily.[35] But is it conceivable that, even in a hastily written and obviously unfinished poem, Ovid would so depart from his normal metrical procedure as to move *sdss* to first place, a pattern which (except in the *Medicamina*) always ranks from ninth to eleventh position? Or that *ssss* could be tied for third place, when elsewhere in his poetry it ranges from eleventh to sixteenth? These are not metrical blemishes, but an entirely different way of writing hexameter poetry. Likewise, is it possible that Pliny could read the extant *Halieutica* and accept these patterns and frequencies as Ovidian? The authenticity of the poem has been questioned for reasons of prosody, vocabulary, and style; on the basis of metrical patterns and frequencies alone we are fully justified in concluding that Ovid did *not* compose the extant *Halieutica*.

The many proponents of Ovidian authorship may object to this conclusion for two reasons:

1. The many names of fish occurring throughout the poem may have compelled Ovid to use metrical patterns different from those which he usually favored.

The lines giving the names of fish are forty-three in number, roughly one third of the total. I have examined the first nine patterns in both groups of verses, and I find no evidence that the frequency of the patterns with initial spondees results in any way from the presence of such fish-names. The percentage of *sdss* in the lines without these names is only slightly lower (16.67 to 18.14) and that of *ssss* is actually higher (9.52 to 6.98). The author of the poem favored these patterns over *dsss*, in sixth place (but always first to third in the authentic works of Ovid), although the proportion of *dsss* in the lines naming fish is almost twice as high as in the other verses (9.30 per cent to 4.76). Among the patterns with initial spondees, the percentage in the lines with the fish-names is appreciably higher only in the case of *sdds* (11.63 to 4.76).

2. Another objection which might be raised is that in Ovid's authentic works we are dealing with percentages based on hundreds and thousands of verses, whereas the *Halieutica* is too short a fragment to produce decisive results. A poem of 127 verses[36] could not be expected to conform to Ovid's normal metrical practice.

To meet this objection I have examined the first 130 hexameters in each of Ovid's poems, again following the chronological order as given by Costa,[37] but adding *Metamorphoses* II and XV to Book I, and since the *Halieutica* is dated at the end of Ovid's life, I give statistics for the beginning of *Tristia* V as well as for that of Book I, and also for *Epistulae* IV in addition to Book I. I include the percentages of fourth-foot homodyne for each of these 130-line sections. Finally, since the *Nux* (91 hexameters) and the *Consolatio ad Liviam* (237 hexameters) are usually considered spurious,[38] I compare these also with the *Halieutica* and Ovid's authentic poems.[39]

The 130-hexameter sections from the beginning of Ovid's poems show little deviation from the statistics based on the entire works. In almost every case the first eight patterns begin with dactyls and produce the usual distribution of twelve spondees and twenty dactyls.[40] The fact that the *Halieutica* is a short fragment therefore does not explain its unusual metrical features. Furthermore, Ovid in his latest poetry shows no sign of departing from his normal technique. There is no desire to increase the use of such patterns as *sdss, ssss,* and *sdds* which are so frequent in the *Halieutica;* in the 130-hexameter sections of his latest poetry (*Tristia* I and V, *Ibis, Epistulae ex Ponto* I and IV), *sdss* ranges from ninth to fifteenth place, *ssss* from tenth to fifteenth, *sdds* from ninth to fourteenth. It should be noted also that the frequency of the first eight patterns moves from 81.54 per cent in Book I of the *Tristia* to 90.77 in Book V, from 83.08 in Book I of the *Epistulae ex Ponto* to 93.08 in Book IV. This increasing lack of interest in metrical variety at the end of Ovid's career contrasts sharply with the percentage of 73.23 for the first eight patterns in the *Halieutica,* supposedly composed by Ovid in the same period. The homodyne percentages in the 130-hexameter sections are, with the exception of *Ars Amatoria* I and III, markedly higher than in the *Halieutica.*

Both the *Nux* and the *Consolatio ad Liviam,* usually considered spurious, seem far more Ovidian than the *Halieutica;* in the *Nux ssss* is tied for eighth place with *dddd,* and *sdss* is eighth in the

Consolatio; otherwise the distribution of dactyls and spondees seems close to Ovid's normal procedure.[41]

In summary, the metrical patterns and frequencies of the *Halieutica* and the resultant distribution of spondees and dactyls argue strongly for the non-Ovidian nature of the poem and support the views of Birt, Housman, Axelson, Wilkinson, and Richmond that the extant poem could not be the work of Ovid, and also (as Housman maintained) that it could not have been ascribed to Ovid by Pliny.[42]

Notes to Chapter 9

1. Radford, *TAPhA* 51 (1920), p. 149.

2. *Ovid as an Epic Poet*, pp. 74, 76.

3. "Ovid's Metre and Rhythm," p. 111.

4. This is the only spondaic verse in all four hexameter collections (a total of 4,081 lines); on the other hand, we find four such verses in the few hexameters in his lyric meters (*Epodes*, XIII, 9; XVI, 17 and 29; and *Odes* I, 28, 21).

5. Hirtzel in his Oxford text agrees with other modern editors in placing a semi-colon at the end of line 939. I prefer the full stop which appears in practically every edition of Vergil prior to that of Heyne in 1775; see Duckworth, *TAPhA* 91 (1960), p. 202, note 34.

6. *Metamorphoseon, Liber I*, p. 33.

7. With the exception of Vergil's more dactylic *Eclogues*, where, as I pointed out above, *dsss* has a low frequency in the earlier poems but becomes much more prominent in the latest.

8. *AJPh* 44 (1923), p. 299.

9. See Tr. Costa, "Formele Hexametrului," pp. 236-275. I follow Costa's chronological order, placing *Ars Amatoria* III after the *Medicamina*, and *Heroides* XVI-XXI after the *Remedium*. Since I exclude spondaic verses, my percentages differ slightly from those of Costa.

10. In Cicero's *Aratea*, *dssd* and *ddsd* are in twelfth and eleventh place respectively; in most earlier works *dssd* is among the eight most frequent patterns, but not *ddsd*; the two patterns are sixth and eighth in Lucretius, sixth and eleventh in Catullus and Horace, fifth and tenth in the *Georgics*. Again the *Eclogues* are an exception, with *dssd* and *ddsd* tied for fourth place; see below, Chapter 10 (on the *Culex*).

11. The percentage of the first eight patterns in Hesiod (81.56) resembles that of Ovid (81.62) most closely.

12. For the percentages of the first, first four, and first eight patterns in the elegiac poems, see Appendix A.

13. The percentage range is from 57.15 and 47.15 in Cicero's *Aratea* to 68.51 and 65.60 in Catullus LXIV.

14. The percentage for Horace's hexameter poems as a whole is 48.54, that for the *Satires* only 45.24. Later poets with high percentages of fourth-foot homodyne include Calpurnius Siculus (61.08), *Laus Pisonis* (54.02), Petronius (52.07), Persius (58.0), and Avienus, *Aratea* (56.15).

15. The percentage in Catullus is 33.33, but this hardly counts, as there are only three instances of *ssdd*, one with *ddss;* in the *Ciris*, also earlier, we find seven instances of *ssdd*, four with *ddss* (57.14 per cent). Several later poets have high percentages of *ssdd* with *ddss*, e.g., Persius, 40.0; Corippus, 42.11; Claudian II, 42.86; Dracontius, 46.94; and Proba, 63.64.

16. In later hexameter poetry *dsdd-ddsd* appears very rarely as the most frequent reverse combination, and only in those poets who emphasize dactyls in the manner of Ovid, e.g., Calpurnius Siculus, Columella X, Valerius Flaccus, Statius, Paulinus of Nola, and Arator.

17. In Catullus the *ssds-sdss* combination comprises 71.43 per cent of the total reverses (only seven, five of which are *ssds-sdss*). Other high *ssds-sdss* percentages are 71.43 in Grattius, 70.05 in Lucan, 74.29 in Claudian I, 81.25 in Claudian II; in Cyprian, where *ssds* is the most frequent pattern, the percentage of *sdss-ssds* is 95.74.

18. The highest percentage previously was in Vergil's *Georgics*, 18.46; cf. Lucretius, 12.92; Vergil, *Eclogues*, 16.28; *Aeneid*, 9.92; Horace, *Satires*, 7.41; *Epistles*, 17.02 (total Horace, 12.57).

19. *Literary History of Rome . . . Golden Age*, p. 428.

20. *CQ* 8 (1914), p. 267. Cf. Schanz-Hosius, *Geschichte*, II, p. 251: "ein Zweifel an ihrer Echtheit ist ausgeschlossen." See also Mozley, *Ovid. The Art of Love*, p. xi; Owen, "Ovid," in *OCD*, p. 632.

21. *Ovid*, p. 161.

22. *De Halieuticis;* but cf. Vollmer, *RhM* 55 (1900), p. 528: "namque Ovidi esse halieutica Plinius potius quam Birtius audiendus est."

23. *CQ* 1 (1907), pp. 275-278, on the false quantities in the poem; cf. p. 277, on *ănthĭās* (line 46): "to Pliny therefore the hexameter *anthias his, tergo quae non videt, utitur armis* would have been a scarce less wondrous spectacle than the eruption of Vesuvius." Against Housman, see Owen in *CQ* 8 (1914) pp. 267-269, who explains the false quantities as the result of vulgar Greek pronunciation.

24. *Eranos* 43 (1945), pp. 23-35; the arguments against authenticity are based on "Prosodie, Versbau, Sprache, Stil" (p. 33).

25. *Eos* 51 (1961), pp. 109-118.

26. *Ovid Recalled*, p. 363.

27. *Halieutica*, p. vii.

28. *CR* 13 (1963), p. 295.

29. See on line 11 (p. 32), 46 (*anthias;* see Appendix 6, p. 110), 58 (p. 54), 64 (*tergore*, p. 57), 65 (*sine fine*, p. 58), 73 and 74 (Vergilian imitations, pp. 63, 65), 100 (*ratium* indicates that Ovid was not the author, p. 76), 103 (*cantharus:* the author misinterpreted *Ibis* 308, p. 78).

30. "On Imitation," p. 39.

31. *Ibid.*, p. 24.

32. I discuss the *Aetna* and other didactic poems below in Chapter 11.

33. "Formele Hexametrului," p. 275: "Autenticitatea fragmentului nu mai poate fi pusă la îndoială." I am indebted to Professor Herbert S. Long of Hamilton College for assistance in reading Rumanian.

34. See Appendix A for the position of these four patterns in the individual poems.

35. "Ovid," in *OCD*, p. 632.

36. The corrupt or missing verses in Richmond's edition are 2, 10, 25, 44, 127-129; 52 is bracketed, but inserted as 65a.

37. See above, note 9.

38. See Duff, *Literary History of Rome...Golden Age,* p. 428; Mozley, *Ovid. The Art of Love,* pp. xi-xii; Wilkinson, *Ovid Recalled,* p. 364. In *OCD,* p. 632, Owen accepts the *Nux* as genuine.

39. The statistics appear in Appendix A.

40. The only exceptions are *sdds* in eighth place in the *Ars Amatoria* I and *Metamorphoses* I, *sdss* eighth in *Ars Amatoria* III, *sdsd* eighth in *Tristia* V and tied for eighth place (with *dddd*) in *Epistulae ex Ponto* IV.

41. The *Nux* seems more Ovidian than the *Consolatio;* in the latter poem the percentage of fourth-foot homodyne is abnormally high (56.54) and the frequency of the first eight patterns (75.95) is lower than in Ovid's authentic works and approaches that in the *Halieutica* (73.23).

42. Pliny, *N.H.* XXXII, 11-13, refers to fish mentioned by Ovid in his *Halieutica: scarus, lupus, murena, polypus, mugil, (lupus, murena), anthias.* These names appear in the same order in *Halieutica* 9-48: *scarus* (9), *lupus* (23), *murena* (27), *polypus* (32), *mugil* (38), [*lupus* (39), *murena* (43),] *anthias* (46), with one exception: *sepia* (19) is omitted by Pliny. In 152-153 Pliny lists various other fish which occur in *Halieutica* 94-134 in approximately the same order. If Pliny did not read the extant *Halieutica,* the poem which we now have must have followed closely the original work by Ovid known to Pliny. Or is it possible that Pliny had so little understanding of Ovidian meter that he wrongly ascribed the extant poem to Ovid?

Chapter 10

THE *APPENDIX VERGILIANA*

I turn now to the hexameter poems of the *Appendix Vergiliana* — the *Culex*, the *Moretum*, the *Ciris*, the *Dirae (Lydia)*, and the *Aetna*. I shall make no attempt to repeat or even summarize the many different arguments already advanced for and against the authenticity of these poems. At the end of the nineteenth century they were considered spurious by most scholars; forty years ago they were accepted as the youthful work of Vergil by several writers, including such distinguished Americans as E. K. Rand and Tenney Frank,[1] who used them as a source of biographical material, creating in a sense a new Vergil for twentieth-century readers; in recent years they have again been rejected, and of the entire *Appendix* only a few of the *Catalepton* are accepted as genuine.[2] The various verbal and metrical tests applied to the poems have failed to produce conclusive results. It is my hope that an examination of variety and repetition in the hexameter poems of the *Appendix* may throw new light on their metrical structure and indicate which of the poems might be by Vergil and which almost certainly are not authentic.[3]

Although, as I shall attempt to prove below, these poems with the exception of the *Aetna* all seem to date from the late Republic and thus from the time of Vergil's youth, I have purposely postponed my analyses until after the chapters on Vergil and Ovid. Many scholars consider the *Culex* and the *Ciris*, at least, to be post-Vergilian, and several have assigned one or more of these poems to Ovid. Radford, perhaps the most extreme in this respect, believes that the *Culex*, *Ciris*, and *Aetna* formed part of Ovid's *carmina iuvenalia*, written in an early, more spondaic, period before he developed the dactylic style of his mature works,[4] and in a later article he assigns the *Dirae* and the *Moretum* also to Ovid's early years;[5] he is convinced that Ovid "first composed in spondees" and adds: "Latin being a highly spondaic language, it seems just about as possible for a youthful poet to lisp in Chinese or in Choctaw as in Latin dactyls."[6]

Others, although they do not postulate an early spondaic period (for which there is no evidence in the extant works of Ovid), do find a metrical similarity between the poems of the *Appendix* and those of Ovid; e.g., Plésent says: "en particulier, les formes de l'hexamètre du *Culex* sont à peu près celles d'Ovide,"[7] but he is definitely in error here. As I have already stated, the authentic works of Ovid, from the *Heroides* and the *Amores* to the *Tristia* and the *Epistulae ex Ponto*, all have the same characteristics: high percentages for the first eight patterns (all 80.0 or more with the exception of the *Amores*, 78.84); also (with the exception of the short *Medicamina*), a distribution of twelve spondees and twenty dactyls in these same eight patterns, and a first-foot dactyl in each. Neither the *Culex* nor the other hexameter poems of the *Appendix* resemble the poetry of Ovid in these respects. A distribution of sixteen spondees and sixteen dactyls in the first eight patterns, as in the *Culex* and the *Moretum*, is certainly not Ovidian, and even less so is that of eighteen spondees and fourteen dactyls, as in the *Ciris* and the *Dirae*, while the *Aetna*, with twenty-one spondees and eleven dactyls, is more spondaic in this respect than any of the poets so far considered, with the exception of the fragmentary Ennius and Lucilius, and Horace in *Satires* I and *Epistles* I and II. The high percentages of the first eight patterns in Ovid are paralleled only by those of the *Dirae*, 82.02; cf. *Culex*, 77.45; *Moretum*, 77.50; *Ciris*, 77.12; *Aetna*, 72.01.

The statistics for the hexameter poems of the *Appendix* — patterns and percentages, variety in sixteen line units, repeated patterns, change in fourth-foot texture, and opposite and reverse combinations — appear in synoptic Tables I and II. I turn now to the individual poems and discuss the implications of these statistics for the authenticity of each.

The *Culex* and the *Moretum:* Vergilian?

I begin with the *Culex*, since the external evidence from antiquity argues strongly for the existence of a *Culex* composed by Vergil, and since themes such as praise of country life, description of a serpent, and the portrayal of mythological and Roman heroes in the Underworld could reveal

Vergil's youthful interest in the same topics which he later developed with far greater success in the *Georgics* and the *Aeneid*. Many modern scholars view the presence of these topics in the *Culex* as proof that the poem is a deliberate forgery which echoes in an awkward fashion the themes which had appeared in Vergil's published works.

Radford, who assigns the *Culex* to Ovid, stresses the fact that *dssd* and *ddsd*, so prominent in Ovid's poetry (from first to fifth place), appear in the *Culex* in third and eighth position respectively. But there is no argument here for Ovidian authorship. These same two patterns are tied for fourth place in Vergil's *Eclogues*.[8]

Actually, the first eight patterns of the *Culex* are those of the *Eclogues* in slightly different order; I list below the order of the patterns as they appear in the two works:

	dsss	*ddss*	*dsds*	*sdss*	*ddds*	*sdds*	*dssd*	*ddsd*
Culex:	2	1	5	7	4	6	3	8
Eclogues:	2	1	3	6	7	8	4-5	4-5

This identity of patterns does not necessarily imply Vergilian authorship (the percentages of the first, first four, and first eight patterns are higher: *Culex*, 15.69, 46.08, 77.45; *Eclogues*, 13.09, 41.45, 69.09 respectively), but it could well be an argument for dating the composition of the *Culex* in the middle of the first century B.C. If a later poet attempted to imitate the patterns and frequencies of the *Eclogues*, it seems strange that he did not include lower percentages in the first eight patterns, especially since these percentages in the *Eclogues* mark so sharp a departure from the higher frequencies of Cicero, Lucretius, and Catullus.

Numerous other similarities between the *Culex* and the *Eclogues* are apparent, and I give in parentheses the corresponding frequencies and percentages for the *Metamorphoses* (abbreviated as *M*) to prove how very different Ovid's procedure is in almost every respect: the distribution of spondees and dactyls in the first eight patterns in both the *Culex* and the *Eclogues* is sixteen and sixteen (*M*, twelve spondees and twenty dactyls).[9] The average number of patterns per sixteen-line unit is high, 9.6; *Eclogues*, 9.7 (*M*, 8.9); with 100 per cent of the units containing eight or more patterns; *Eclogues*, 97.87 per cent (*M*, 86.35). The percentage of fourth-foot homodyne is low, 36.76; *Eclogues*, 39.73 (*M*, 50.0); with a marked increase in the percentage of change in fourth-foot texture, +8.69; *Eclogues*, +9.48 (*M*, -3.09). Repeat clusters appear once every 204.0 lines; *Eclogues*, once every 275.0 lines (*M*, once every 112.5 lines); and repeated patterns in adjacent lines once every 18.5 lines; *Eclogues*, 13.1 (*M*, 10.7).[10] The *dsss* repeats plus near repeats comprise 15.38 per cent of the total repeats plus near repeats; *Eclogues*, 15.53 per cent (*M*, 17.21); and they comprise 29.17 per cent of the total occurrences of *dsss*; *Eclogues*, 28.41 (*M*, 33.60). The combined total of repeats plus near repeats of the two most frequently repeated patterns (*ddss* and *dsss*) provide 38.46 per cent of the total repeats plus near repeats; *Eclogues*, 39.75 (*M*, 34.14). Opposites occur on an average once every 18.4 lines; *Eclogues*, once every 19.6 (*M*, once every 29.3); and *ssdd* is preceded or followed by *ddss* 28.57 per cent of the time; *Eclogues*, 26.92 per cent (*M*, 30.14 per cent).

In all these respects the *Culex* reveals a metrical technique amazingly similar to that of the *Eclogues*[11] and very unlike that of the *Metamorphoses*. Only in the frequency of reverse patterns in adjacent lines do we find a major divergence: *Culex*, one every 29.1 lines; *Eclogues*, one every 55.0 (*M*, one every 39.3);[12] the percentage of *dsdd* preceded or followed by *ddsd* is similar: *Culex*, 14.29; *Eclogues*, 16.28 (*M*, 24.0).

Columella wrote his *Res Rustica* in the age of Nero and composed Book X in hexameters as an avowed imitation and continuation of Vergil's *Georgics*.[13] The fact that Columella knew and used passages in the *Culex*[14] has been taken as evidence that he too, as well as Statius and Martial, viewed the poem as authentic.[15]

The many metrical similarities between the *Culex* and the *Eclogues* indicate that Vergil could have composed the epyllion. Is he the author? Two factors here seem especially important: the higher percentages in the first eight patterns, and the low percentage of fourth-foot homodyne; if a later poet attempted to compose a poem such as Vergil might have written in his youthful days,[16] why did he imitate Vergil's low homodyne and not his low frequencies? On the other hand, no poet before Vergil has such a low homodyne percentage; are we to believe that Vergil in this respect followed an unknown minor poet? It seems preferable to assume that the *Culex* is by Vergil, written earlier than the *Eclogues* and displaying his fondness for fourth-foot heterodyne, but before he decided to introduce greater variety and avoid excessive repetition in the eight most frequent patterns.[17]

Statistics based on short poems such as the *Moretum* (122 verses) and the *Dirae* (183 verses) are naturally less conclusive than those derived from longer works containing several hundreds or thousands of verses. On the other hand, as I showed above in discussing the non-Ovidian nature of the *Halieutica*, the 130-hexameter sections from Ovid's authentic works display the same basic characteristics in regard to patterns and percentages as do the poems as a whole. We seem justified, therefore, in applying the various criteria of variety and repetition to these short poems also.

In the case of the *Moretum*, we find a number of striking resemblances to the *Culex* and the *Eclogues* which might favor Vergilian authorship.

Although in different order (*dsss* is first; *ddss*, *dsds*, and *ddds* are tied for second place), the eight most frequent patterns in the *Moretum* are the same as in the *Eclogues* and the *Culex*, with one exception: *dsdd* (tied with *dssd* for seventh place) appears instead of *ddsd* (tied with *dssd* for fourth in the *Eclogues*, eighth in the *Culex*); the percentage of the most frequent pattern is 15.83, *Culex*, 15.69; and that of the first eight patterns is 77.50; *Culex*, 77.45. The distribution of spondees and dactyls in the first eight patterns is sixteen and sixteen, identical with that in the *Culex* and the *Eclogues*. This seems particularly significant, for, with the exception of Books III and IV of the *De rerum natura*, the distribution of sixteen spondees and sixteen dactyls does not appear elsewhere in Republican or Augustan hexameter poetry.

The *Moretum* averages 9.3 patterns per sixteen-line unit (*Culex*, 9.6; *Eclogues*, 9.7), and the percentage of units with eight or more patterns is 100.0 (*Culex*, 100.0; *Eclogues*, 97.87). The percentage of fourth-foot homodyne is low, 33.33 (*Culex*, 36.76; *Eclogues*, 39.73), and this too argues for Vergilian authorship.[18] The frequency of repeats plus near repeats is one every 4.8 lines, midway between the *Culex* (4.5) and the *Eclogues* (5.1). The *dsss* repeats plus near repeats in the *Moretum* comprise 31.58 per cent of the total occurrences of *dsss*: *Culex*, 29.17; *Eclogues*, 28.41.[19] Opposite combinations appear once every 15.0 lines; *Culex*, 18.4, and *Eclogues*, 19.6; in the case of reverses: *Moretum*, one every 60.0 lines; *Culex*, 29.1, but *Eclogues*, 55.0.

In all these instances the technique of the *Moretum* resembles that of the *Culex*, or the *Eclogues*, or both. There are also differences: repeat clusters are relatively more frequent: *Moretum*, one instance, or one every 120.0 lines; *Culex*, two, or one every 204.0 lines; *Eclogues*, three, or one every 275.0 lines. Repeats are likewise more frequent, one in every 9.4 lines (*Culex*, 18.5; *Eclogues*, 13.1), and we find in the *Moretum* little interest in shifting the fourth-foot texture in repeated patterns; the percentage of change in relation to the percentage of fourth-foot homodyne is -10.25; cf. *Culex*, +8.69; *Eclogues*, +9.48. These few discrepancies in so short a poem, however, seem hardly sufficient to overweigh the importance of the many similarities pointed out above.

Another factor to consider is this: Columella concludes Book X of his *Res Rustica* as follows (433-436):

> hactenus hortorum cultus, Silvine, docebam
> siderei vatis referens praecepta Maronis,
> qui primus veteres ausus recludere fontes
> Ascraeum cecinit Romana per oppida carmen.

The phrase "praecepta Maronis" is of interest here, when we realize that Columella imitated the authentic works of Vergil, the *Culex*, and also the *Moretum*, but not the *Ciris*, *Dirae*, or *Aetna*; this implies that Columella accepted both the *Culex* and the *Moretum* as Vergilian, as poems of the "sidereus vates."[20]

The many metrical similarities between the *Culex* and the *Eclogues* favor the conclusion that the *Culex* is the work of Vergil, and, since the *Moretum* resembles so closely both the *Culex* and the *Eclogues*, it too should probably be considered authentic.[21]

The Alexandrian Nature of the *Ciris*

If the *Culex* could be a composition of the youthful Vergil, the same can not be said of the *Ciris*.[22] The very fact that the *Ciris* has fifteen spondaic verses, one every 35.7 lines, indicates that it was written neither by Vergil (*Culex* and *Moretum*, no spondaic verses; *Eclogues*, one every 276.0 lines; *Georgics*, one every 437.4; *Aeneid*, one every 409.5) nor by Ovid (*Metamorphoses*, one every 323.5).[23] In the frequent use of spondaic verses the *Ciris* is apparently indebted to Catullus LXIV, as in other respects.[24] We find in Catullus thirty spondaic verses, or one every 13.6 lines.[25] The high incidence of spondaic verses in both poems is undoubtedly the result of the influence of the Hellenistic poets, especially Callimachus (one spondaic verse every 15.1 lines).

The first pattern of the *Ciris*, *dsss*, has a high percentage of 18.46, unlike the corresponding percentages in Vergil (*Eclogues*, 13.09; *Georgics*, 15.81; *Aeneid*, 14.39), but similar to that in Cicero (*Aratea* and fragments, 18.28).[26] The percentage of the first eight patterns (77.12) resembles that of the *Culex* (77.45), but that of the first four is higher (*Ciris*, 51.92; *Culex*, 46.08); the *Culex* here is in a Vergilian range, and the *Ciris* is not.[27]

In the *Ciris*, the patterns per sixteen-line unit average 9.1, higher than in the Republican poets and Ovid's *Metamorphoses*, but somewhat lower than in Vergil and Horace (and the *Culex*). Repeat clusters occur once every 86.7 lines, considerably less often than in the Republican poets, but two or three times as frequently as in Vergil and Horace (cf. *Culex*, one every 204.0 lines; *Metamorphoses*, one every 112.5 lines). Fourth-foot homodyne is 44.30 per cent, and the difference in the percentage of change in repeated patterns is -2.84; these are most un-Vergilian, and again differ from the *Culex* (36.76, +8.69).

The following table gives comparative percentages for *dsss* repeats and *dsss* repeats plus near repeats:

	dsss repeats		*dsss* R and NR	
	% repeats	% *dsss*	% R + NR	% *dsss*
Ciris:	39.02	16.67	34.17	42.71
Culex	9.09	4.17	15.38	29.17
Eclogues:	15.87	11.36	15.53	28.41
Georgics:	29.38	15.07	31.33	43.77
Aeneid:	22.18	12.40	23.15	34.66
Horace:	20.06	12.19	21.21	34.62
Metamorphoses:	18.08	13.47	17.21	33.60

The differences here between the *Culex* and the *Ciris* are amazing, and in every instance but one (repeat plus near repeat percentage of total *dsss* in the *Georgics*) the percentages in the *Ciris* are higher than those in the three authentic works of Vergil. Also, and this seems especially significant, the percentages in each column show a steady increase from the *Culex* through the *Eclogues* to a high point in the *Georgics*, with a marked falling off in the *Aeneid*.[28] The percentages of Horace and Ovid reveal that the trend away from heavy concentration of *dsss* repeats and *dsss* repeats plus near repeats continues throughout the Augustan poets.[29] We have here additional evidence, I believe, that the *Ciris* was composed neither by Vergil nor by Ovid, and also that metrically it belongs to the middle of the first century B.C., and probably well before the time of the *Culex*.

These same *dsss* percentages of the *Ciris* in relation to those in the Republican poets are as follows:

	dsss repeats		*dsss* R and NR	
	% repeats	% *dsss*	% R + NR	% *dsss*
Ciris:	39.02	16.67	34.17	42.71
Cicero:	40.48	19.77	24.39	34.88
Lucretius:	37.60	21.20	36.30	50.17
Catullus:	44.44	23.08	41.60	50.0

These percentages indicate clearly that the author of the *Ciris*, in his use of *dsss* repeats and near repeats stands far closer to the Republican poets than to Vergil, Horace, and Ovid. Also, the first eight patterns in the *Ciris*, in almost the same order, are identical with the first eight patterns of Lucretius:[30]

	dsss	ddss	dsds	sdss	ddds	dssd	ssss	ddsd
Lucretius:	1	2	3	4	5	6	7	8
Ciris:	1	2	3	5	4	7-8	7-8	6

In his use of opposite and reverse patterns in adjacent lines, the author of the *Ciris* likewise follows the procedures of the Republican poets; the statistics for opposites every x lines are as follows: *Ciris*, 32.5; Lucretius, 30.8; Catullus LXIV, 37.7; but *Moretum*, 15.0; *Culex*, 18.4; *Eclogues*, 19.6; *Georgics*, 20.9; *Aeneid*, 23.1.[31] In the case of reverse combinations we have every x lines: *Ciris*, 65.0, and then, in order of increasing frequency, *Moretum*, 60.0; *Eclogues*, 55.0, Catullus, 53.9; Lucretius, 51.3; *Georgics*, 46.4; *Dirae*, 44.5, *Aeneid*, 38.9; *Culex*, 29.1, and Cicero, *Aratea*, 24.0. Reverse combinations thus appear less frequently in the *Ciris* than in any other work in Republican and Augustan poetry.

We thus have strong evidence of non-Vergilian authorship and every indication that the *Ciris* is to be dated in the late Republic; it should not be considered post-Vergilian.[32] Those who argue from the many so-called Vergilian echoes that the *Ciris* is to be dated later must face certain questions. Why are there so many spondaic verses? Why in so many respects are the metrical procedures in the *Ciris* identical with those of the late Republic, especially in the treatment of *dsss* repeats and near repeats? Would a poet of the early Empire be so oblivious to the greater variety which Vergil and Horace had introduced into hexameter verse? This is possible, but seems hardly probable. Perhaps we have here an added argument to support Skutsch' theory that the author of the *Ciris* was none other than Cornelius Gallus and that it was Vergil who borrowed phrases and lines from the work of his friend.[33] It has also been suggested that Vergil cooperated with Gallus in writing the *Ciris* and contributed a number of lines to it; in this case he would have had no scruple about using again lines which he himself had written or helped to write.[34]

The Problem of the *Dirae*

When we turn to this short poem, we have not only the problem of Vergilian authorship but also that of unity. Is the so-called *Lydia* (104-183) the conclusion of the *Dirae* or an independent poem? Arguments and conclusions differ widely; Steele favors two poems, both by Vergil;[35] Van der Graaf says that "the *Dirae* is one and indivisible," and views it "as one of Vergil's juvenile poems";[36] Büchner considers the *Lydia* a separate work and denies Vergilian authorship to both poems.[37]

In the statistics on the *Appendix* given in Tables I and II, I list the *Dirae (Lydia)* as a unit. I now discuss the patterns and percentages for the *Dirae* 1-103 (abbreviated D) and the *Lydia* (abbreviated L) in an attempt to throw new light on the problem of unity as well as on the authenticity of the poem (or poems).[38]

1. The favorite metrical pattern in D is *sdss*, with a percentage of 16.67, and in L it is likewise *sdss*, with a percentage of 17.11. The percentages here are similar, but higher than in the *Culex*, the *Moretum*, and the three authentic works of Vergil. The presence of *sdss* as the first pattern is most unusual, for in all Republican and Augustan hexameter poetry *sdss* is first only in Lucilius (based on fragments), in Horace, *Epistles* II, 1, and in the *Halieutica*, wrongly ascribed to Ovid. In all later poetry, both Silver Age and Late Empire, *sdss* never again appears in first place.[39] We have here a very strong argument both for unity and against Vergilian authorship.[40]

2. In D, *dssd* is tied for second place with *dsss* (13.73 per cent); in L, *dssd* is second (15.79 per cent) and *dsss* is third (14.47 per cent). Nowhere else in Republican or Augustan hexameter poetry does *dssd* rank second until we come to Ovid.[41] This position of *dssd* in D and L also argues for unity of authorship, but does not necessarily disprove composition by Vergil (cf. *Eclogues*, *dssd* tied for fourth place; *Culex*, third place).

3. The first eight patterns are the same, except for *ddsd*, fifth place in D but not among the first eight in L; *sdds*, sixth place in L but no occurrences in D; *sdsd*, tied for eighth place in L but tied for tenth place in D. The percentages of the first four and the first eight patterns are, respectively: D, 53.92, 83.33; L, 59.21, 84.21; these percentages are most un-Vergilian and far higher than in any other hexameter poem of the *Appendix*, higher even than in the Republican poets, with the exception of Catullus. This too implies the same poet for D and L.

4. The distribution of spondees and dactyls in the first eight patterns in *D* is eighteen and fourteen; in *L*, nineteen and thirteen; total, eighteen and fourteen; cf. the *Ciris* and Lucretius, both eighteen and fourteen.

5. In *D* we find no spondaic verses, but *L* has three (136, 150, 170); this has been cited as a strong argument against unity. In Catullus LXIV, however, the spondaic verses (thirty in number) appear only at the beginning and the end of the poem; there are none between lines 119 and 252, a section including the lament of Ariadne and Aegeus' farewell speech to Theseus. It seems entirely possible that one poem could likewise have three spondaic verses with all three in the latter part of the poem. The frequency of the spondaic verses, one every 60.3 lines, though less than that in the *Ciris* (one every 35.7 lines) argues against Vergilian authorship.

6. The average number of metrical patterns per sixteen-line unit is: *D*, 8.8; *L*, 8.3; these are lower than in Vergil or in any of the other poems of the *Appendix*, and resemble the averages in Cicero and Lucretius. The percentage of units with eight or more patterns is 66.67 for *D*, 75.0 for *L* (= 70.0 for *D* and *L* combined). Such low percentages appear neither in Vergil nor elsewhere in the *Appendix*, and are surpassed only by the abnormal 30.43 in Catullus LXIV; the percentage in Lucretius is 76.10, with a range from 68.75 in Book VI to 85.29 in Book I. Here again we can see the hand of one poet in *D* and *L* and additional evidence that the *Dirae* is to be dated in the late Republic, but is not the work of Vergil.

7. Repeat clusters occur once every 102.0 lines in *D*, once every 76.0 lines in *L* (total, once every 89.0 lines). This is less frequent than in the Republican poets, but more so than in the other poems of the *Appendix*, with the exception of the *Ciris* (once every 86.7 lines) and of course bears no relation to Vergil's procedure. We have here no argument against unity of authorship.

8. Büchner points out that coincidence of ictus and accent in the fourth foot (i.e., fourth-foot homodyne) in *D* is 46.6 per cent, which he considers "unvergilisch," and in *L* only 25 per cent.[42] This would indicate that *D* and *L* were written by two different poets. Büchner here follows the percentages given by Jackson Knight,[43] which are wrong, especially for *L*, as Van der Graaf has pointed out.[44] There are twenty-five instances of homodyne in *L*, i.e., not 25.0 per cent, but 31.65, and the percentage for *D* is 46.08, or 39.78 for *D* and *L* combined. If we disregard the homodyned Battarus refrain which appears seven times, the percentage for the remainder of *D* is 39.22, which brings it also into a Vergilian range, and makes the difference between *D* and *L* even less significant. I do not find here a strong argument against the unity of the poem, but I do not believe that the low homodyne percentage necessitates ascribing the poem to Vergil. Too many other factors speak against Vergilian authorship, and all we can conclude is that the fourth-foot homodyne percentage perhaps shows the influence of the *Moretum*, the *Culex*, and possibly the *Eclogues*.

9. Repeats average in *D* one every 10.2 lines, in *L* one every 12.7 lines; in *D* and *L* together one every 11.1 lines, about the same as in Cicero *(Aratea)* and much less frequent than in Lucretius and Catullus LXIV. *L* is in the Vergilian area, *D* is not; however, when we turn to repeats plus near repeats, *D* and *L* are very similar: *D*, one every 3.6 lines, *L* one every 3.8 lines; these are similar to Cicero (3.9) and Lucretius (3.6), but very different from Vergil (*Eclogues*, 5.1; *Georgics*, 4.5; *Aeneid*, 4.6). Again we have an argument against Vergilian authorship, and nothing to disprove unity or a dating in the late period of the Roman Republic.

10. The percentages of fourth-foot texture change in repeats are: *D*, 40.0 and *L*, 50.0 (combined *D* and *L*, 43.75); in repeats and near repeats, *D*, 42.86 and *L*, 45.0 (combined *D* and *L*, again 43.75); these are sufficiently close to indicate unity of authorship, but the variation in the fourth-foot homodyne percentages creates a difference from the homodyne percentages as follows: repeats, *D*, -6.08; *L*, +18.35 (combined *D* and *L*, +3.97); repeats and near repeats, *D*, -3.22; *L*, +13.35 (combined *D* and *L*, again +3.97). Since this point is closely related to item 8 above, it should not be used as a separate argument against unity of authorship.

11. The opposite and reverse patterns in adjacent lines are too few to provide evidence either for or against unity of authorship: opposites, one each in *D* and *L*; reverses, four in *D*, none in *L*. The favorite reverse in *D* is *sssd-dsss* (surprising, since *dsss* is not the most frequent pattern), comprising three of the four reverses; since *sssd* occurs only three times in *D*, it is preceded or followed by *dsss* 100 per cent of the time.

Of the items listed above, Nos. 1 through 7 and 9 are by far the most conclusive and provide strong evidence for the unity of the *Dirae* and the *Lydia*. On all counts, Vergilian authorship is impossible, but the time of composition seems to be that of the late Republic.

I summarize briefly my conclusions for the hexameter poems of the *Appendix Vergiliana,* with the exception of the *Aetna* (to be discussed in the next chapter):

1. The *Culex,* with its striking metrical similarities to the *Eclogues,* could be and probably is a youthful work of Vergil; there are also differences which are difficult to explain if the *Culex* is the work of a later forger imitating Vergil's technique.

2. The *Moretum* resembles both the *Culex* and the *Eclogues* and is probably by Vergil. It seems significant that Columella borrowed not only from Vergil's authentic works but also from both the *Culex* and the *Moretum.*

3. The *Ciris* is definitely not by Vergil but dates from the first century B.C. The theory of Skutsch that Vergil borrowed phrases and lines from his friend Cornelius Gallus still seems attractive.

4. The *Dirae (Lydia)* can not possibly be the work of Vergil, but the evidence favors the view that it is one poem rather than two and that it is to be dated in the late Republic.[45]

Notes to Chapter 10

1. Rand, *HSPh* 30 (1919), pp. 103-185; Frank, *Vergil, A Biography.*

2. See Duckworth, *Structural Patterns,* pp. 93-94. For brief summaries of recent work on the *Appendix,* see Duckworth, *CW* 51 (1957-58), pp. 92, 116-117; 57 (1963-64), pp. 195-197.

3. The metrical structure of the various poems is treated by Büchner, *P. Vergilius Maro,* cols. 68-157 *passim* [= "Vergilius" in *RE* 8A. 1, cols. 1088-1177]. My statistics are based on the new OCT edition of the *Appendix* and therefore differ slightly from earlier analyses, e.g., those of Lederer, "Ist Vergil der Verfasser...?" pp. 14-30; Plésent, *Le Culex,* p. 431; Eldridge, *Num Culex et Ciris...quaeritur,* pp. 6-12.

4. *TAPhA* 51 (1920), pp. 160-163.

5. *TAPhA* 52 (1921), pp. 156-161.

6. *TAPhA* 51 (1920), p. 151. Radford also ascribes to this hypothetical early period much of the Tibullan corpus (the Lygdamus elegies, the Sulpicia elegies and letters, the Cornutus and Messalinus elegies, and the hexameter *Panegyric to Messalla.* He accepts the *Halieutica* as genuine (p. 163), but likewise assigns it to the imaginary early spondaic period.

7. *Le Culex,* p. 33, note 3. Plésent, however, does not accept Ovidian authorship, but (pp. 497-500) favors the view that the *Culex* was written by one of the *poetae minores* in the circle of Asinius Pollio shortly after Vergil's death.

8. Radford, *Philologus* 86 (1930-31), pp. 102-104, ignores the *Eclogues* and argues for the similarity of the *Culex*-patterns to those in Ovid.

9. The distribution of sixteen spondees and sixteen dactyls in the *Culex* and the *Eclogues* is thus midway between that of twenty and twelve in Cicero, Catullus, Vergil's *Georgics* and *Aeneid,* and Horace on the one hand, and that of twelve and twenty in the works of Ovid on the other.

10. The frequency of repeats plus near repeats every *x* lines is 4.5; this is somewhat closer to the *Metamorphoses* (4.1) than to the *Eclogues* (5.1); but compare the *Georgics* (4.5).

11. Plésent, *Le Culex,* pp. 483-485, comments on the many similarities in the versification of the *Culex* and the *Eclogues,* but he attributes these, at least in part, to the influence of Alexandrian models on the two poets.

12. The high frequency of reverse combinations in the *Culex* may reveal an indebtedness to Cicero; cf. *Aratea,* one reverse every 24.0 lines; *Aratea* and fragments, one every 27.6 lines.

13. Columella says in **X**, praef. 3, that his friend Silvinus had urged "ut poeticis numeris explerem Georgici carminis omissas partes, quas tamen et ipse Vergilius significaverat posteris se memorandas relinquere"; see Vergil, *Georg.* IV, 116-119, 147-148. It is surprising to find that Columella's hexameters are Ovidian rather than Vergilian; see below, Chapter 11.

14. See Weinold, *Die Dichterischen Quelle,* pp. 41-44.

15. *Ibid.,* pp. 57-59.

16. This is the view of Fraenkel, *JRS* 42 (1952), pp. 1-9.

17. On the basis of mathematical symmetry, the *Culex* seems more Vergilian than do the other poems in the *Appendix;* see Duckworth, *Structural Patterns,* pp. 94-96.

18. Büchner, *P. Vergilius Maro,* cols. 151-152, wrongly gives the homodyne percentage as a very low 26.0 and uses this as one of his arguments to prove that the *Moretum* is metrically non-Vergilian.

19. The similarity in the case of repeats and of repeats plus near repeats is even more striking
if we compare the most frequently repeated
patterns, *dsss* in the *Moretum*, *ddss* in the
Culex and the *Eclogues*, as follows:

	Repeats (*dsss* or *ddss*)		R+NR (*dsss* or *ddss*)	
	% repeats	% pattern	% R+NR	% pattern
Moretum:	23.08	15.79	24.0	31.58
Culex:	22.73	7.81	23.08	32.81
Eclogues:	31.75	18.52	24.22	36.11

20. See Douglas, *A Study of the Moretum*, pp. 74-99;
cf. Weinold, *Die Dichterischen Quellen*, p. 49:
"Bei keinem Stück der Appendix lässt sich die
Nachahmung durch Columella so überzeugend
herausarbeiten wie beim Moretum."

21. Cf. Steele, *TAPhA* 61 (1930), p. 216: "The
characters Simylus and Scybale are unique, and
Vergil is the only one whose experience, so far
as we know, might have brought him in contact
with them."

22. Cf. Eldridge, *Num Culex et Ciris ... quaeritur*,
p. 66; Büchner, *P. Vergilius Maro*, col. 98: "Die
Verstechnik der Ciris ist *toto coelo* von der des
Culex verschieden." See Lederer, "Ist Vergil
der Verfasser...?" pp. 26, 29; on the basis of
metrical arguments he considers the *Culex* by
Vergil, the *Ciris* not.

23. The frequency of spondaic verses in the other
works of Ovid is as follows: *Heroides* I-XV, one
every 238.4 lines; *Amores*, one every 613.0
lines; *Ars Amatoria* III, one every 406.0 lines;
Fasti, one every 245.2 lines; there are no spondaic verses in *Ars Amatoria* I-II, *Remedia*,
Heroides XVI-XXI, *Tristia*, *Ibis*, or *Epistulae ex
Ponto*. I use here the statistics compiled by
Costa, "Formele Hexametrului," pp. 236-275.

24. Granarolo, *L'Oeuvre de Catulle*, p. 324, says
that the *Ciris* is "fortement tributaire de Catulle
sous bien des rapports."

25. Schuster, "Valerius," *RE* 7A.2 (1948), col. 2393,
wrongly gives the number of spondaic verses in
Catullus LXIV as twenty-seven, as does Townend,
in Dorey (ed.), *Cicero*, p. 126.

26. In Ovid's *Metamorphoses* as a whole the first
pattern is 13.08 per cent (almost identical with
that in Vergil's *Eclogues*) and the range is from
11.99 (Book VI) to 15.71 (Book II). In no work of
Ovid does the overall percentage of the first
pattern go beyond 17.50 (*dssd* in the *Tristia*).

27. Cf. Vergil's *Eclogues*, 41.45 per cent (including
the abnormally high 72.58 in *Eclogue* IV, where
Vergil imitates the frequencies of Catullus
LXIV); *Georgics*, 48.99; *Aeneid*, 46.95.

28. We must, of course, remember that in both the
Culex and the *Eclogues* the most frequent pattern
is not *dsss* but *ddss*, and that in both works *ddss*
has more repeats and near repeats than does

dsss. The four corresponding *ddss* percentages
for the *Culex* are 22.73, 7.81, 23.08, 32.81; for
the *Eclogues*, 31.75, 18.52, 24.22, 36.11. These
are still much lower than the *Ciris* percentages
(with one exception; *Eclogues: ddss* repeats
comprise 18.52 per cent of the total occurrence
of *ddss*; *Ciris: dsss* repeats are 16.67 per cent
of the total *dsss*). In Ovid's *Metamorphoses* the
dsss repeats and near repeats are more numerous (202 R, 504 R + NR) than those of *ddss* (173
R, 496 R + NR), even though *ddss* is the most
frequent pattern.

29. The *dsss* percentages in Horace are approximately the same for the *Satires* and the *Epistles*.
This suggests that Vergil, in changing to lower
percentages in the *Aeneid*, may have been influenced by Horace's procedure in the *Satires*.

30. See Steele, *Authorship of the Culex*, pp. 40-41.
Steele, however, reverses the order of *ddds* and
sdss in the *Ciris*, also that of *dssd* and *ddsd*,
thus making the similarity of the patterns in the
Ciris and the *De rerum natura* appear greater
than it actually is.

31. The percentage of *ssdd* preceded or followed by
ddss is 57.14. There is nothing like this among
the other poets; the closest approach is in Catullus LXIV, 33.33 per cent, and in the *Metamorphoses*, 30.14; cf. Lucretius 25.64; *Moretum*,
25.0; *Culex*, 28.57; *Eclogues* and *Georgics*, each
26.92; *Aeneid*, 20.0; Horace, 21.43. For later
poets with high percentages of *ssdd* with *ddss*,
see Chapter 9, note 15.

32. The pseudo-Tibullan *Panegyricus Messallae* in
212 hexameters, usually dated between 31 and
27 B.C., resembles the *Ciris* in several respects: the percentage of the first eight patterns
is 76.88, close to the 77.12 percentage in the
Ciris; the distribution in the first eight patterns
is eighteen spondees and fourteen dactyls, as in
the *Ciris* (and Lucretius); the average number of
patterns per sixteen-line unit is 9.1, as in the
Ciris; the *dsss* repeats and near repeats comprise 34.67 per cent of the total repeats and near
repeats, and in the *Ciris* the percentage is 34.17;
the frequency of opposites is one every 26.5 lines,
in the *Ciris* one every 32.5 lines. There are differences as well: *sdds* and *sdsd* appear in the
first eight patterns in place of *sdss* and *ddsd;*
repeat clusters are less frequent, one in 212.0
lines (*Ciris*, one every 86.7 lines). The percentage of fourth-foot homodyne is an unusually low
32.08 (the influence of Vergil?), but 44.30 in the
Ciris; reverses one every 26.5 lines (cf. Cicero,
one every 24.0 lines) but in the *Ciris*, one every
65.0 lines.

33. *Aus Vergils Frühzeit* and *II. Gallus und Vergil*,
passim. Duff, *Literary History of Rome ...
Golden Age*, p. 355, considers Skutsch's explanation the "more plausible" one. Additional evi-

dence to support the authorship of Cornelius Gallus is given by Savage, *TAPhA* 93 (1962), pp. 437-442.

34. See Hardie, *JPh* 30 (1907), p. 289.

35. *Authorship of the Dirae and Lydia*, p. 35.

36. *The Dirae*, pp. 134, 145.

37. *P. Vergilius Maro*, cols. 109-116.

38. My method is somewhat similar to that of Van der Graaf, *The Dirae*, pp. 44-122, but he includes many other criteria (e.g., word-forms, caesura, elision) and does not touch upon metrical variety, repeated patterns, or opposite and reverse combinations.

39. With the exception of individual books, as in the case of the *Punica* of Silius Italicus (V, VIII, IX, XII, XIV); *sdss* is first also in Juvenal XV and Nemesianus, *Eclogue* II.

40. Van der Graaf, *The Dirae*, p. 144, admits this: "The result of the metrical schemes on the whole does not favor the authenticity of D" (by D he means the combined *Dirae* and *Lydia*).

41. After Ovid *dssd* is second in the fourth *Satire* of Persius and first in the sixth *Eclogue* of Calpurnius Siculus. It is not prominent again until the late period: second in Avienus (both *Aratea* and *Descriptio orbis terrae*), and first in the *Mosella* of Ausonius. In most poets after Ovid, *dssd*

ranges from fifth to eighth place, and in several it does not appear among the first eight patterns.

42. *P. Vergilius Maro*, col. 113.

43. *Accentual Symmetry*, p. 42; Jackson Knight says: "the figures suggest that it is right to regard them as two separate pieces."

44. *The Dirae*, p. 70.

45. I have not discussed either the *Copa* (19 hexameters) or *Catalepton* IX (32 hexameters), as many of the criteria used above do not apply to elegiac verse. Although these two poems are almost too short to provide conclusions of value, they seem most un-Vergilian, e.g., percentage of first pattern: *Copa*, 21.05; *Catalepton* IX, 25.81; percentage of first eight patterns: *Copa*, 89.47; *Catalepton* IX, 90.32; percentage of fourth-foot homodyne: *Copa*, 42.11; *Catalepton* IX, 59.38. Actually, these two poems resemble Tibullus II, 5 (the Messalinus poem), but have even higher frequencies; the corresponding percentages in Tibullus II, 5, are 22.95, 81.97, 40.98. The *Panegyricus Messalae* (see above, note 32) is not by Vergil, but it is far more Vergilian than either the *Copa* or *Catalepton* IX, with percentages of 16.98, 76.88, 32.08 respectively. The author of *Catalepton* IX imitated the *Panegyricus Messallae*; see Westendorp Boerma, *P. Vergili Maronis...Catalepton*, Pars altera, p. 10.

Chapter 11

THE *AETNA* AND POST-VERGILIAN DIDACTIC POETRY

The Donatus-Suetonius Life of Vergil includes the *Aetna* among the poems of the *Appendix Vergiliana* with the phrase *de qua ambigitur* (18). This expression of doubt concerning its authenticity is shared by most modern scholars,[1] who date the poem (on the basis of language, style, meter, and imitations of other poets) in the first century A.D., probably in the time of Nero or even later, but before the famous eruption of Vesuvius in 79 A.D.[2]

Several didactic poems were composed during the early Empire, from the time of Augustus to the age of Nero: the *Cynegetica* of Grattius, the *Aratea* of Germanicus Caesar, the *Astronomica* of Manilius, and *Res Rustica,* Book X, of Columella. These works are relatively short, with the exception of the *Astronomica* in five books (4,178 lines, exclusive of spondaic and corrupt verses), and the poets, with the exception of Columella, all reveal in varying degrees the strong influence of Vergil's *Georgics.* The possibility, even the probability, that the *Aetna* likewise is to be dated in the first century A.D. suggests that I compare these didactic works as a group, show wherein they resemble the *Georgics,* and determine, if possible, how the metrical technique of the *Aetna* is related to that of the other poems. I include in the following discussion two later works, both of the third century, the *Cynegetica* of Nemesianus and the *Liber Medicinalis* of Serenus.[3]

The Influence of Vergil's *Georgics*

Of the seven poets under consideration, all but two follow the practice of Cicero, Lucretius, Catullus, Vergil, and Horace in preferring *dsss* as their first metrical pattern;[4] Columella favors *ddss,* first pattern in Ovid's *Metamorphoses,* and Nemesianus in his choice of *dsds* imitates the procedure of the Silver Age poets Calpurnius Siculus, Valerius Flaccus, and Statius, whom I term "post-Ovidian." The percentages of the first pattern range from a low 12.99 in Grattius to 17.33 in Manilius. Again with the exception of Columella, the first four patterns are always the same as in the *Georgics,* but in slightly different order, as follows:

Georgics:	*dsss*	*dsds*	*ddss*	*sdss*
Aetna:	*dsss*	*sdss*	*dsds*	*ddss*
Grattius:	*dsss*	*dsds*	*sdss*	*ddss*
Germanicus, Manilius, and Serenus:	*dsss*	*ddss*	*sdss*	*dsds*
Nemesianus:	*dsds*	*dsss*	*sdss*	*ddss*
(Columella:	*ddss*	*dsds*	*dsss*	*dssd*)

The percentages of the first four patterns in most instances are very close to that in the *Georgics,* 48.99, e.g., *Aetna,* 48.58; Grattius, 47.68; Germanicus, 47.86; Serenus, 47.59. Nemesianus is low with 45.23 and Manilius high with 53.59.

The percentages of the first eight patterns likewise resemble that in the *Georgics,* 73.42; cf. *Aetna,* 72.01; Grattius, 73.47; Germanicus, 72.82; Nemesianus, 71.08; the two exceptions are Manilius (77.33) and Columella (81.84). The first eight patterns in Manilius and Nemesianus are the same as in Vergil's *Aeneid;*[5] we have therefore the same distribution of twenty spondees and twelve dactyls in the first eight patterns, with the fourth foot always a spondee. Two poems are even more spondaic, the *Aetna* and Germanicus' *Aratea,* where we find twenty-one spondees and eleven dactyls in the first eight patterns, and these patterns are the same in both poems with one exception — *sdsd* in the *Aratea, sdds* in the *Aetna.*

Columella is unique among the didactic poets; not only is *ddss* the first pattern as in Ovid's *Metamorphoses,* but *dssd* and *ddsd* are fourth and fifth respectively. A high ratio of these two patterns is considered characteristic of Ovid's poetry. The percentage of the first eight patterns in Columella is 81.84 (*Metamorphoses,* 81.62), the distribution of spondees and dactyls is fifteen and seventeen (somewhat more spondaic than Ovid, but less so than any other of the didactic poets), and seven of the first eight patterns have a dactyl in the first foot (Ovid, all eight). Columella states that he is writing a supplement to Vergil's *Georgics*,[6] but he follows the metrical technique of Ovid, not that of Vergil.

And what about the *Aetna* in relation to the *Georgics* and these later poems? The choice of patterns and their frequencies are similar to those in the *Georgics*, but they resemble also those in Grattius' *Cynegetica* (*ddss* and *ssds* in fourth and fifth position in both), and perhaps even more so those in the *Aratea* of Germanicus (percentage of first eight patterns, 72.01 and 72.82 respectively; distribution of spondees and dactyls, an unusual twenty-one and eleven in each). I find nothing here to support Vergilian authorship of the *Aetna* or to disprove a dating of the poem in the first century A.D.

The comparative averages and percentages for variety in sixteen-line units, fourth-foot texture, and repeated, opposite, and reverse patterns provide valuable information not only about the *Aetna* but about post-Vergilian didactic poetry as well. In general we find that the later metrical techniques resemble more or less closely those of the *Georgics*. The average number of patterns per sixteen-line unit is from 9.1 to 9.4 (*Georgics*, 9.3), with the exception of 8.8 in Manilius (cf. Lucretius, 8.6; *Metamorphoses*, 8.9) and 10.0 in Nemesianus. Repeat clusters range from one every 83.6 lines in Manilius to one every 275.3 lines in Serenus (cf. *Georgics*, 145.5; *Aetna*, 212.0). The percentage of fourth-foot homodyne is in the Vergilian range, with the exception of Grattius (50.83), Columella (44.04), and Serenus (42.38); the two lowest percentages are 31.69 in Nemesianus and 33.18 in the *Aetna*. Repeats are more frequent than in the *Georgics* (one every 12.3 lines) with the exception of Nemesianus (one every 14.8) and Grattius (one every 16.3), and the frequency of repeats plus near repeats is either the same as in the *Georgics* (Germanicus) or greater, again with the exception of Nemesianus (one every 5.2 lines) and Grattius (one every 4.9).

The percentage of change in fourth-foot texture both in repeats and in repeats plus near repeats is considerably higher than the percentage of fourth-foot homodyne in the *Aetna* (+9.68 and +4.92 respectively), Germanicus (+8.29 and +5.23), Manilius (+10.05 and +6.67) and Serenus (+11.47 and +5.81); these works thus resemble the *Georgics* (+7.42 and +11.02). The other three poets are all in the minus column, with a range from -1.54 (Columella, repeats) to -5.58 (Columella, repeats plus near repeats). The *dsss* repeats in the *Georgics* comprise 29.38 per cent of the total repeats and 15.07 of the total pattern; in both categories the percentages in the other poems are lower,[7] with the exception of Grattius (36.36 and 17.14) and Manilius (32.67 and 18.09).[8] The percentages of fourth-foot texture change in the *dsss* repeats and repeats plus near repeats (*dsds* in the case of Nemesianus) are consistently higher than the percentage of fourth-foot homodyne in every case (repeats from +7.50 in Grattius to +32.92 in Germanicus; repeats plus near repeats from +7.62 in Serenus to +11.98 in the *Aetna*), with the exception of Columella (repeats, -1.18) and Nemesianus (repeats, -31.69; repeats and near repeats, -26.43). The corresponding increases in the *Georgics* are +13.92 and +9.62. The variation in opposite combinations per *x* lines is from 16.8 in Grattius to 29.0 in Manilius (*Georgics*, 20.9); in reverses, from 31.8 in the *Aetna* to 46.4 in Nemesianus (46.4 likewise in the *Georgics*).

I pointed out above that Columella's metrical patterns and frequencies are those of Ovid and not of Vergil. Columella's high percentage of fourth-foot homodyne (44.04; *Metamorphoses*, 50.0), the relation of shift in fourth-foot texture to the fourth-foot homodyne percentage in repeats (-1.54; *Metamorphoses*, -3.09) and in repeats plus near repeats (-5.58; *Metamorphoses*, -3.81), the low percentage of *dsss* repeats, both in relation to the total repeats (17.50; *Metamorphoses*, 18.08) and to the total occurrences of *dsss* (12.96; *Metamorphoses*, 13.47) — all these factors likewise argue in favor of the Ovidian nature of Columella's hexameters.

In general, the metrical technique which we find in the *Aetna*, Germanicus, Manilius, and the third-century Serenus is far closer to that of Vergil in the *Georgics* than is that of the other three didactic poets, with Columella definitely unlike Vergil, in spite of his avowed imitation of the *Georgics*.

The *Aetna* and the *Aratea* of Germanicus

I return now to the *Aetna*, which, as I have already shown, is similar to the *Aratea* of

Germanicus in the percentages of the first four and first eight patterns and identical in the distribution of twenty-one spondees and eleven dactyls. The resemblances between these two poems are even more amazing when we examine the frequencies and percentages based on variety and repetition which in several instances differ considerably from the corresponding figures in the *Georgics*.

I select (from the statistics in Table II) the following points which seem particularly significant: fourth-foot homodyne percentages: *Aetna*, 33.18; *Aratea*, 35.83 (*Georgics*, 36.08); difference between the percentage of change in fourth-foot texture and the homodyne percentage: repeats, *Aetna*, +9.68; *Aratea*, +8.29 (*Georgics*, +7.42); repeats plus near repeats, *Aetna*, +4.92; *Aratea*, +5.23 (*Georgics*, +11.02); *dsss* repeats plus near repeats, *Aetna*, +11.98; *Aratea*, +11.67 (*Georgics*, +9.62). The *dsss* repeats comprise 23.21 per cent of the total repeats in the *Aetna*; 23.53 per cent in the *Aratea* (29.58 per cent in the *Georgics*); the *dsss* repeats plus near repeats make up 33.70 per cent of the total occurrences of *dsss* in the *Aetna*, 36.70 per cent in the *Aratea* (*Georgics*, 43.77 per cent). Reverse combinations appear once every 31.8 lines in the *Aetna*, once every 32.2 lines in the *Aratea*; these frequencies are higher than in the other didactic poems, and the lowest are in the *Georgics* and in the *Cynegetica* of Nemesianus, both once every 46.4 lines.[9]

Here again we find no evidence for Vergilian authorship of the *Aetna*.[10] In almost every respect the metrical techniques of the *Aetna* as described above resemble very closely those of the *Aratea* of Germanicus. How is this to be explained? There are four possibilities: (1) the similarities are purely coincidental, but this I doubt, for they are too numerous; (2) the *Aetna* was earlier and Germanicus was the imitator; the difficulty here is that Germanicus would certainly have followed the hexameter technique of Vergil in the *Georgics* more closely than that of a minor and inferior poet; (3) Germanicus himself wrote the *Aetna*; this could well explain the many almost exact resemblances, but would create other problems: why is the *Aetna* ascribed to an "incertus auctor," and how was it added to the *Appendix Vergiliana?* (4) the author of the *Aetna* knew and was impressed by the *Aratea* and imitated as faithfully as possible the metrical technique of Germanicus Caesar. This last seems the most satisfactory solution and dates the composition of the *Aetna* in the second quarter of the first century A.D., preferably before the time of Columella and Calpurnius Siculus, when the influence of Ovid's metrical procedures becomes more noticeable.[11]

A Note on Serenus

Serenus, although writing in the third century A.D., has a metrical technique very similar to that of the technical poets of the early first century, more so than does Nemesianus, also of the third century. We have seen that all these poets, with the exception of Columella, show in varying degrees marked resemblances to Vergil's *Georgics*, the most finished and most perfect of all Latin didactic poems.

There are also striking similarities between the metrical procedures of Serenus and those in Vergil's *Aeneid*. Perhaps these are to be explained by Serenus' imitation of the earlier didactic poets, e.g., Germanicus Caesar, who seems the most Vergilian of the group and is probably the model for the later *Aetna*. It seems more likely, however, that Serenus is directly following the technique of Vergil in the *Aeneid*. As Raby says, Serenus "had learned his art in the schools of rhetoric,"[12] and Vergil in antiquity was regarded as a master of oratory, with the *Aeneid* providing examples of every oratorical style. Vergil's metrical technique likewise was imitated by many later poets, those not seduced by the dactylic rhythms of Ovid.

The first five metrical patterns in both Germanicus and Serenus are the same as in the *Aeneid*, with *ssss* in fifth place (*dssd* is fifth in the *Georgics*).[13] The following statistics reveal how closely Serenus follows the technique of the *Aeneid*, and I add Germanicus for purposes of comparison:

	Aeneid	German.	Serenus
% of first pattern:	14.39	16.10	14.99
% of first four:	46.95	47.86	47.59
% of first eight:	72.78	72.82	73.12
Patterns per 16-line unit:	9.4	9.2	9.3
% of units with 8 or more:	92.46	90.48	88.41
Repeats, one every *x* lines:	12.4	10.0	12.1

	Aeneid	German.	Serenus
% of change, differs from *m* %:	+6.71	+8.29	+11.47
R + NR, one every *x* lines:	4.6	4.5	4.4
% of change, differs from *m* %:	+8.05	+5.23	+5.81
Most frequent repeat:	*dsss*	*dsss*	*dsss*
% total repeats:	22.18	23.53	23.08
% total pattern:	12.40	14.68	12.73
% of change, differs from *m* %:	+7.36	+32.92	+19.52
R + NR, % total R + NR:	23.15	26.49	23.29
% total pattern:	34.66	36.70	35.15
% of change, differs from *m* %:	+11.50	+11.67	+7.62
Opposites, one every *x* lines:	23.1	24.2	22.9
% of *dsdd* with *sdss:*	18.41	15.63	18.75
Reverses, one every *x* lines:	38.9	32.2	39.2
% of *sssd* with *dsss:*	29.56	38.10	28.0
% of *ssds* with *sdss:*	17.21	17.07	17.65

Actually, in most of the items listed above, Serenus seems closer to Vergil than to Germanicus; how are such amazing similarities to be explained? This seems a striking illustration of the extent to which Vergil's metrical technique influenced a much later poet working in an entirely different literary genre (if indeed a versified list of medical remedies can be called literature). There can scarcely be a greater diversity in subject matter than between Vergil's *Aeneid* and Serenus' medical treatise, and yet the metrical procedures are practically identical.

Notes to Chapter 11

1. Not, however, by those who, in the first quarter of the twentieth century, accepted the poems of the *Appendix* as authentic and then used them as a source of biographical material for the youthful Vergil; see Rand, *HSPh* 30 (1919), pp. 155-172, who favors the view that *"Aetna* was written before the *Bucolics*, and by the same writer" (p. 169); DeWitt, *Virgil's Biographia Litteraria*, pp. 98-107, who accepts the poem as authentic, but dates it after November, 43 B.C. Frank, *Vergil*, pp. 58-63, is somewhat more cautious and says: "The first fruit of Vergil's studies in evolutionary science at Naples was the *Aetna*, if indeed the poem be his" (p. 58).

2. See, for example, Büchner, *P. Vergilius Maro*, cols. 116-135; Richter, *[Vergil] Aetna*, pp. 1-7; Goodyear, *Incerti Auctoris Aetna*, pp. 56-59. Cf. also Weissengruber, *WS* 78 (1965), pp. 128-138.

3. See Tables I and II for the percentages and frequencies of these poems. The *Halieutica*, which belongs to this same didactic group, was treated in detail in Chapter 9.

4. In the *Astronomica* of Manilius *dsss* is first in the poem as a whole and likewise first in each of the five books. We find surprisingly little variation from book to book; the percentage of the first pattern is 17.33, with a range from 15.91 (IV) to 18.49 (I, III); the percentage of the first eight patterns is 77.33, varying from 75.84 (I) to 79.03 (IV); the average number of patterns per sixteen-line unit is 8.8, from 8.6 (IV) to 8.9 (I, III); the percentage of fourth-foot homodyne is 39.33, ranging from 37.42 (IV) to 41.05 (I). Only in the frequency of reverse combinations do we find a wide divergence; in I, once every 74.8 lines; in the other four books the range is from 48.9 (IV) down to 33.8 (III); once every 45.9 lines in the *Astronomica* as a whole.

5. The second eight patterns in Manilius, from *dssd* (ninth) to *sddd* (sixteenth), are in exactly the same order as the second eight patterns in Vergil's *Aeneid*.

6. See Columella X, praef. 3, and lines 433-436.

7. Although the first pattern in Columella is *ddss*, the pattern with the most numerous repeats and near repeats is *dsss*, in third position. In the case of Nemesianus, the most frequent pattern, *dsds*, also provides the most repeats and near repeats; the *dsds* repeats comprise 27.27 per cent of the total repeats (*dsss*, 22.73 per cent).

8. There is even less variation in the case of the *dsss* repeats plus near repeats; all the poems are lower than the *Georgics*, with the exception of Manilius, where the percentage of total occurrences of *dsss* is 44.20 (*Georgics*, 43.77).

9. Cf. also Manilius, one reverse every 45.9 lines, with a wide range from 33.8 (Book III) to 74.8 (Book I); see above, note 4.

10. Cf. Büchner, *P. Vergilius Maro*, col. 127: "Der Vers des Aetna etwas ganz anderes ist als der lukrezische oder vergilische Vers, und zwar etwa Späteres." My statistics for the *Aetna* (and the other post-Vergilian didactic poems likewise) show, however, a much closer similarity to Vergilian than to Lucretian hexameter techniques.

11. As Columella in didactic poetry, although professing to imitate Vergil's *Georgics*, is Ovidian in his hexameters, so Calpurnius Siculus in pastoral and Valerius Flaccus in epic are likewise metrically far closer to Ovid than to Vergil. On Calpurnius Siculus, see below, Chapter 12; on Valerius Flaccus, see Chapter 13.

12. *Secular Latin Poetry*, Vol. I, p. 43.

13. In both Manilius and Nemesianus *ssss* is likewise in fifth position.

Chapter 12

THE SILVER AGE: PASTORAL

M y discussion of the *Aetna* and other post-Vergilian didactic poems included Nemesianus' work on hunting and Serenus' medical treatise, both of the third century A.D., and this has taken us chronologically ahead of our story. I return now to the Silver Age of Latin literature which extends from the reign of Nero (54-68 A.D.) to that of Hadrian (117-138 A.D.). In this period we have a number of hexameter poets, several of them of major stature, and their works belong primarily to the genres of pastoral, epic, and satire.

The pastoral poetry to be considered includes the *Eclogues* of Calpurnius and Nemesianus, the two short Einsiedeln poems, and the *Laus Pisonis*, which is usually discussed with the others. These poems, as Duff says, "present a bundle of interconnected and, though baffling, still not uninteresting problems."[1] Are the two Einsiedeln pastorals by the same poet and, if so, are they the work of Calpurnius Siculus, Calpurnius Piso, or perhaps Lucan?[2] Are the four *Eclogues* of Nemesianus, originally published with the seven of Calpurnius, to be ascribed to the third century Nemesianus, author of the *Cynegetica*? Did Calpurnius Siculus write the *Laus Pisonis* to praise his patron, or is the poem the work of Lucan?[3] The theory that Calpurnius Siculus was the author has been accepted by many scholars,[4] but opposed by others.[5] It is my hope that the following metrical analyses of the poems may throw additional light on these particular problems.

The Einsiedeln Pastorals

These two poems, found in a tenth century manuscript at Einsiedeln and first published in 1869,[6] are dated in the early years of Nero's reign. They are almost too short (47 and 38 lines respectively) to provide metrical information of value, and this is especially true when we compare the two poems. There are interesting differences between the two, however: in I the first pattern is *dsss*, with a frequency of 19.15 per cent, and *ddss* is second; in II *ddss* is first, 15.79 per cent, and *dsss* is tied with seven other patterns for sixth place. Somewhat more significant are the percentage differences of the first eight patterns: I, 85.11; II, 65.79. This is a far wider range than we find in the *Eclogues* of Calpurnius Siculus, from 70.65 (VI) to 81.65 (IV), or in those of Nemesianus, from 75.86 (I) to 83.56 (IV), and argues against identity of authorship.

The possibility that the two poems are the work of two different writers is strengthened by the evidence from variety and repetition, as follows:

	I	II
Patterns per 16-line unit:	9.2	10.0
% of 4th-foot homodyne:	51.06	31.58
Repeats, one every *x* lines:	9.4	12.7
% of 4th-foot change:	60.0	33.33
Differs from *m* percentage:	+8.94	+1.75
R + NR, one every *x* lines:	5.9	5.4
% of 4th-foot change:	62.50	42.86
Differs from *m* percentage:	+11.44	+11.28
Opposites, one every *x* lines:	15.7	12.6

On the basis of the many differences listed above, the two fragmentary poems are probably not by the same poet; we are dealing with such short works, however, that no certainty is possible.

If the two Einsiedeln eclogues *are* the work of one and the same person, there is no compelling reason to ascribe them to Lucan, as does Verdière;[7] *ddsd* and *dsdd* are tied (with *sdss*) for fifth place in the two pastorals as a whole, but do not appear among the first eight patterns in Lucan.

Even less likely as the author is Calpurnius Siculus, who includes *dssd* and *dddd* among his first eight patterns, and whose first pattern, *dsds*, has an unusually low percentage of 12.80; in the Einsiedeln poems, neither *dssd* nor *dddd* are among the first eight patterns, and the frequency of the first pattern, *ddss*, is 16.47 per cent.

In the statistics derived from variety and repetition, we find additional evidence that the Einsiedeln poems, short as they are, cannot be the work of either Lucan or Calpurnius Siculus. The following points of comparison with Lucan (= *L*) and Calpurnius (= *C*) seem the most significant: fourth-foot homodyne percentages: 42.35; *L*, 37.08; *C*, 61.08; repeats, one every *x* lines: 10.6; *L*, 11.4; *C*, 10.1; percentage of fourth-foot texture change in repeats differs from the homodyne percentage: +7.65; *L*, +2.01; *C*, -19.75; repeats plus near repeats, one every *x* lines: 5.7; *L*, 4.2; *C*, 4.2; percentage of change in repeats plus near repeats differs from the homodyne percentage: +10.98; *L*, -1.52; *C*, -23.30; opposites, one every *x* lines: 14.1; *L*, 22.0; *C*, 23.0; reverses, one every *x* lines: 85.0 (one instance only); *L*, 40.7; *C*, 44.6. Perhaps the most decisive criteria here are the percentages of fourth-foot homodyne and especially the extent to which the percentages of change in fourth-foot texture differs from the fourth-foot homodyne percentages; the metrical technique of Lucan and Calpurnius is entirely different.

Calpurnius Siculus and the *Laus Pisonis*

Dimsdale says of Calpurnius Siculus: "His trifling hexameters, correct in their adherence to the metrical usage of bucolic verse, do not succeed in avoiding monotony."[8] This is a curious statement: what does he mean by "the metrical usage of bucolic verse"? Calpurnius' predecessor in pastoral poetry is Vergil, but he certainly does not follow the metrical technique of Vergil's *Eclogues*; his eight most frequent patterns are those of Ovid's *Metamorphoses*, but in different order,[9] and his distribution of twelve or eleven spondees and twenty or twenty-one dactyls is practically identical with that first introduced into Latin poetry by Ovid; such a high proportion of dactyls appears in no other poet of either the Silver Age or the Late Empire.

I spoke above of the *Laus Pisonis*, a panegyric praising a certain Calpurnius Piso for his eloquence, generosity, and skill in sports and games, the authorship of which is uncertain.

The patterns and percentages in the panegyric are very similar to those in the *Eclogues* of Calpurnius Siculus: *dsds* is first in both, and seven of the first eight patterns are the same,[10] with *ddsd* unusually frequent in both (second in the *Eclogues*, third in the *Laus*); the use of *dddd* is similar (seventh in the *Eclogues*, eighth in the *Laus*) and in both works the two patterns with the lowest frequencies are *ssss* and *sssd*. The percentages of the first four and first eight patterns are remarkably close: *Eclogues*, 44.99 and 75.20; *Laus*, 43.68 and 76.25. Most significant, however, is the distribution of spondees and dactyls in the first eight patterns of the *Laus Pisonis*: thirteen and nineteen respectively, and this is almost identical with the twelve and twenty of Ovid and the twelve or eleven and twenty or twenty-one of Calpurnius. Even Columella, Ovidian as he is, has a distribution of fifteen spondees and seventeen dactyls, as do Valerius Flaccus in the *Argonautica* and Statius in the *Thebaid* and the *Silvae* (the *Achilleid* is closer with fourteen spondees and eighteen dactyls). No such emphasis on dactyls as we find in Calpurnius' *Eclogues* and in the *Laus Pisonis* appears again in the whole range of Latin hexameter poetry; the nearest approach is Arator in the sixth century, fifteen or fourteen spondees, seventeen or eighteen dactyls.

If Calpurnius Siculus is not the author of the *Laus Pisonis*, we must then accept the existence of another poet living at the same time who likewise favored dactyls over spondees in the manner of Ovid to a degree unmatched by any of about twenty-five other hexameter poets in a period of five hundred years. This seems most unlikely. In any case, Lucan is excluded as a possible author; his distribution of spondees and dactyls is eighteen and fourteen, and, with one exception (*dssd* for *ssss*), his eight most frequent patterns are the same as in Vergil's *Aeneid*.

The statistics based on fourth-foot texture and repeated patterns likewise indicate strongly that the *Laus Pisonis* should be assigned to Calpurnius Siculus (and not to Lucan). We have the following additional similarities between the panegyric (= *LP*) and the *Eclogues* (= *CE*), and I add in parentheses the corresponding figures for Lucan (= *L*): unusually high percentages of fourth-foot homodyne: *LP*, 54.02; *CE*, 61.08 (*L*, 37.08); repeats, one every *x* lines: *LP*, 9.7; *CE*, 10.1 (*L*, 11.4); percentage of change in repeats differs from homodyne percentage: *LP*, -16.98; *CE*, -19.75

(L, +2.01); percentage of change in repeats plus near repeats differs from homodyne percentage: LP, -13.28; CE, -23.30 (L, -1.52);[11] favorite repeat, percentage of total repeats: LP, 22.22; CE, 22.67 (L, 26.74); percentage of change in favorite repeat differs from homodyne percentage: LP, -20.69; CE, -14.02 (L, +11.07); percentage of change in the most frequent repeats plus near repeats differs from homodyne percentage: LP, -23.25; CE, -30.78 (L, +7.23).

When we combine the percentages of the two most repeated patterns, we have the following (and I add here the corresponding percentages for Vergil's *Aeneid* and Ovid's *Metamorphoses*):

	LP	CE	L	Aen.	Metam.
Combined R, % total R:	40.74	42.67	51.24	38.02	33.57
Combined R + NR, % total R + NR:	40.38	36.66	50.36	39.67	34.14

These combined percentages of the *Laus Pisonis* and the *Eclogues* of Calpurnius are very similar and quite unlike those of Lucan; surprisingly enough, they resemble the percentages of Vergil rather than those of Ovid.

On the basis of the metrical evidence assembled above, there seems no good reason to doubt that Calpurnius Siculus is the author of the *Laus Pisonis*.

Calpurnius Siculus and Nemesianus

The four pastorals of Nemesianus long went under the name of Calpurnius Siculus, but the evidence for the separation is very strong.[12] Also, however much Nemesianus may have imitated Calpurnius (in addition to Vergil), he is metrically very different. He avoids the emphasis on dactylic patterns so characteristic of Ovid and Calpurnius, and, in fact, with nineteen spondees and thirteen dactyls in his first eight patterns, he is far more spondaic than is Vergil in his *Eclogues* (sixteen spondees, sixteen dactyls) and is close to Vergil's procedure in the *Georgics* and the *Aeneid* (twenty spondees, twelve dactyls). Also, seven of his first eight patterns are identical with those of the *Georgics* and the *Aeneid*. In this respect there is little difference between the *Eclogues* of Nemesianus and his *Cynegetica;* the eight most frequent patterns of the *Cynegetica* are those of Vergil's *Aeneid* and thus have twenty spondees and twelve dactyls. The first pattern in the two works of Nemesianus is *dsds: Eclogues*, 15.05 per cent; *Cynegetica*, 15.38 per cent.

The other differences between the pastorals of Nemesianus (= *NE*) and those of Calpurnius (= *CE*) are likewise very striking: e.g., percentage of fourth-foot homodyne: *NE*, 41.07; *CE*, 61.08; repeats, one every x lines: *NE*, 15.2 (on this, see below); *CE*, 10.1; percentage of fourth-foot change in repeats: *NE*, 57.14; *CE*, 41.33; difference from fourth-foot homodyne percentage: *NE*, +16.07; *CE*, -19.75; change in repeats plus near repeats, difference from fourth-foot homodyne percentage: *NE*, +0.16; *CE*, -23.30; opposites, one every x lines: *NE*, 29.0; *CE*, 23.0; reverses, one every x lines: *NE*, 24.4; *CE*, 44.6; favorite reverse: *NE*, *ssds-sdss*; *CE*, *dsdd-ddsd*.

This difference in the most frequent reverse combination is of especial interest. Calpurnius' preference for *dsdd-ddsd* is typical of Ovid and some Silver Age poets (Columella X, Einsiedeln poems, Valerius Flaccus, Statius' *Thebaid* and *Silvae*), but otherwise this particular reverse combination is almost never a favorite; the exceptions are Vergil's *Eclogues* and, in the late period, Paulinus of Nola and Arator. The reverse *ssds-sdss* of Nemesianus is far more frequent; it is the favorite in Catullus LXIV, Vergil's *Aeneid*, Horace, Grattius, Manilius, the *Aetna*, Lucan, Persius, Silius Italicus, Juvenal, and is preferred by thirteen of the eighteen poets in the late period. The combination *ssds-sdss* often provides a surprisingly high percentage of the total reverses, e.g., Catullus LXIV, 71.43; Grattius, 71.43; Lucan, 70.05; Claudian I, 74.29; Claudian II, 81.25; and Cyprian, an amazing 95.74.

The *Eclogues* of Nemesianus (= *NE*) differ in some respects from the *Cynegetica* (= *NC*), but this is due in part to the fact that the *Cynegetica* is in the tradition of the earlier didactic poets; e.g., opposites, one every x lines: *NE*, 29.0; *NC*, 21.7 (*Georgics*, 20.9; *Aetna*, 22.7); reverses, one every x lines: *NE*, 24.4; *NC*, 46.4 (*Georgics*, 46.4; Manilius, 45.9). The most interesting similarity is the frequency of repeated patterns: *NE*, one every 15.2 lines; *NC*, one every 14.8 lines. Nemesianus has far fewer repeats than most poets; they appear almost twice as often in the early period

(Lucretius, 8.8; Catullus LXIV, 7.0). Vergil (*Eclogues*, 13.1; *Georgics*, 12.3; *Aeneid*, 12.4) and Horace (13.0) lessened the amount of repetition, but Ovid (*Metamorphoses*, 10.7) reversed the trend. The only instances of less frequent repeats than we find in Nemesianus are the following: *Culex*, 18.5; Grattius, 16.3; Ausonius, *Cento*, 18.7;[13] Sidonius, 16.1; and Paulinus of Pella, 15.3. The low frequency of repeated patterns in both *NE* and *NC* gives added support to the theory, now generally accepted, that the *Eclogues* of Nemesianus should be assigned to the author of the *Cynegetica*.

In one respect the *Eclogues* of Nemesianus are almost unique: reverse patterns in adjacent lines are more frequent than opposite combinations. In practically every poet, from the Republican period to the Late Empire, opposites occur much more often than reverses;[14] the following are typical:

	Opposites one every *x* lines	Reverses one every *x* lines
Lucretius:	30.8	51.3
Catullus LXIV:	37.7	53.9
Vergil, *Aeneid:*	23.1	38.9
Ovid, *Metamorphoses:*	29.3	39.3
Grattius:	16.8	38.5
Manilius:	29.0	45.9
Calpurnius, *Eclogues:*	23.0	44.6
Lucan:	22.0	40.7
Silius Italicus:	22.3	29.0
Juvenal:	22.5	37.5
Nemesianus, *Cynegetica:*	21.7	46.4
Claudian I:	21.7	34.7
Claudian II:	20.4	34.5

I have discovered, in the whole range of Latin hexameter poetry, the following instances where reverse combinations are more frequent than opposites:

	Opposites one every *x* lines	Reverses one every *x* lines
Cicero, *Aratea:*	79.8	24.0
Dirae (Appendix Verg.):	89.0	44.5
Nemesianus, *Eclogues:*	29.0	24.4
Paulinus of Périgueux:	39.2	37.8
Avitus:	30.7	26.1
Cyprian:	59.0	27.6

In addition, we find reverses favored over opposites in a few books of longer works, e.g., Ovid, *Metamorphoses* I, IV, VI, XI, and XIV; Silius Italicus, *Punica* VIII and XI; Juvenal, *Satires* IV and XV; Claudian, *In Eutropium* II, and *De raptu Proserpinae* III.

These few isolated instances prove how unusual Nemesianus' procedure is when, in his *Eclogues* as a whole, he prefers reverse combinations to opposites.

Notes to Chapter 12

1. *Minor Latin Poets*, p. 209.

2. See Duff, *Minor Latin Poets*, pp. 319-321; Verdière, *T. Calpurni Siculi ... carmina*, pp. 43-44, who favors Lucan and gives to the poems the title *De laude Caesaris*.

3. Lucan's authorship is supported by Ullman, *CPh* 24 (1929), pp. 109-132. Duff, *Minor Latin Poets*, p. 290, says: "The names of Ovid, Saleius Bassus and Statius have been advocated, of whom the first lived too early and the others too late to write the *Laus Pisonis*."

4. E.g., Haupt, Birt, Trampe, Schenkl, F. Skutsch, Teuffel, Plessis; see Hubaux, *Les thèmes bucoliques*, pp. 184-185.

5. Especially by Ferrara, *Calpurnio Siculo*. See Martin, *Laus Pisonis*, pp. 23-37, who says (p. 27): "The problem as to the author of the *Laus Pisonis* is then to-day as far from solution as ever"; so Duff, "Laus Pisonis" in *OCD*, p. 484: "The authorship is uncertain." But Verdière, *T. Calpurni Siculi...carmina*, pp. 27-31, argues on the basis of style and parallel passages that Calpurnius Siculus is the author.

6. By Hagen in *Philologus* 28 (1869), pp. 338-341.

7. See above, note 2.

8. *History of Latin Literature*, p. 388.

9. E.g., *ddss*, first in Ovid, is third in Calpurnius Siculus; *dsds*, fourth in Ovid, is first in Calpurnius; *dsss*, second in Ovid, is tied in Calpurnius for eighth place with *sdsd*; in Ovid *sdsd* is the tenth pattern.

10. The patterns which differ are *dsdd*, sixth in Calpurnius but not among the first eight in the *Laus*; *sdds*, tied with *ddss* for fourth place in the *Laus* but not among the first eight in the *Eclogues*.

11. In each of the seven *Eclogues* of Calpurnius Siculus the percentage of change in the repeats is lower than the homodyne percentage, from -5.67 (III) to -43.88 (I); likewise, in the case of repeats plus near repeats, from -13.40 (III) to -33.86 (VII). The variation in the ten books of Lucan is as follows: repeats, from -6.21 (IV) to +14.24 (IX); repeats plus near repeats, from -6.04 (III) to +2.94 (VII).

12. See Duff, *Literary History of Rome in the Silver Age*, p. 264.

13. The *Mosella* of Ausonius has one repeat every 14.1 lines.

14. In Greek hexameter poetry, on the other hand, opposites are far less frequent than reverses; see Table III, and cf. above, Chapter 5, note 5.

Chapter 13

THE SILVER AGE: EPIC

In the last two chapters, my arrangement by literary genres (didactic poetry and pastoral) has distorted the chronology; in Chapter 11 I included the *Cynegetica* of Nemesianus and the *Liber Medicinalis* of Serenus, both of the third century A.D., with the *Cynegetica* of Grattius, the *Aratea* of Germanicus Caesar, the *Astronomica* of Manilius, the *Aetna,* and the tenth book of Columella's *Res Rustica,* all of the Julio-Claudian period. Likewise, in Chapter 12, I discussed the *Eclogues* of Nemesianus in relation to those of Calpurnius Siculus; this was of course inevitable, since until 1854 the four poems of Nemesianus were usually published under the name of Calpurnius. Thus for a second time we return from Nemesianus to the Silver Age.

The Four Epic Poets

All four epic poets — Lucan, Valerius Flaccus, Statius, and Silius Italicus — are Vergilian in numerous respects; they imitate the language and thought of Vergil, or they echo his characters and episodes, or they introduce his themes and devices, such as catalogues, underworld scenes, prophecies, and storms.[1] These same poets likewise display in varying degrees a love for rhetorical effects, and in this regard they follow Ovid rather than Vergil. As Dimsdale points out, "Rhetoric was the note of Ovid, and in him the influence of rhetoric on Roman poetry first becomes prominent."[2]

In their use of hexameter patterns Vergil and Ovid are at opposite poles. We have seen above that the first eight patterns of the *Aeneid* (and of the *Georgics* also) have, in their first four feet, a distribution of twenty spondees and twelve dactyls; in the *Metamorphoses* (and in the hexameter lines of Ovid's elegiac poetry as well) we find a distribution of twelve spondees and twenty dactyls. Vergil reduces the percentages both of the eight most frequent patterns and of fourth-foot homodyne, but Ovid reverts to the higher frequencies and percentages of the Republican poets and thereby loses both the variety and dignity of the "Vergilian norm."

In the Silver Age Columella composes *Res Rustica* X in hexameters as a continuation of Vergil's *Georgics,* but his metrical patterns and percentages are those of Ovid, not of Vergil. Calpurnius Siculus continues the pastoral tradition of Vergil's *Eclogues,* but his hexameters are even more Ovidian, with an emphasis on dactyls found in no other Latin poet after Ovid.

Where do the four epic poets, otherwise so Vergilian, stand in this respect? Do they follow the metrical procedures of Vergil, or do they, like Columella and Calpurnius Siculus, prefer a more dactylic form of hexameter? I give below the order of the first eight patterns, the relevant percentages, and the distribution of spondees and dactyls, and I repeat, for purposes of comparison, the corresponding statistics from the *Aeneid* and the *Metamorphoses:*

	Verg.	Ovid	Lucan	Val. Fl.	Stat.	Sil. It.
	Aen.	*Metam.*			*Theb.*	
dsss	1	2	1	3	2	1
ddss	2	1	3	2	3	5
dsds	3	4	2	1	1	4
sdss	4		4	8	8	2
ssss	5	15		15		3
ddds	6	6	6	4	4	8
ssds	7		5			6
sdds	8		8			7
dssd		3	7	5	5	
ddsd		5		6	7	

	Verg. Aen.	Ovid Metam.	Lucan	Val. Fl.	Stat. Theb.	Sil. It.
dsdd		7		7	6	
sssd				16	16	
ssdd		16				
dddd	15	8	16			16
sddd	16		15		15	15
% 1st pattern:	14.39	13.08	15.40	22.65	16.24	13.04
% 1st four:	46.95	48.37	52.28	54.36	48.90	43.90
% 1st eight:	72.78	81.62	78.61	83.35	74.26	72.64
First eight —						
Spondees:	20	12	18	15	15	20
Dactyls:	12	20	14	17	17	12
4th-foot spondee:	8	4	7	5	5	8
1st-foot dactyl:	4	8	5	7	7	4

We are here dealing with long epics: Lucan's *De bello civili* in ten books (8,021 verses), the *Argonautica* of Valerius Flaccus in eight books (5,585 verses), Statius' *Thebaid* in twelve books (9,703 verses), and the *Punica* of Silius Italicus in seventeen books (12,197 verses),[3] and we must keep in mind the fact that the figures listed above give the averages for each of the four poems. There are variations from book to book, but in most instances these are minor, and it is amazing that each poet's procedure is so consistent throughout his work. For example, *dsds* is first in the *Argonautica* with a percentage of 22.65; the same pattern is first in each of the eight books with a range from 21.08 (I) to 25.98 (III). These first pattern percentages are all unusually high, and the average of 22.65 is surpassed, in all Latin hexameter poetry, only by Lucretius, Book V (23.10), Vergil's *Eclogue* IV (24.19), and Catullus LXIV (with a record high of 27.59). Just as the second pattern in Catullus *(sdss)* drops to 15.65, so the second pattern in Valerius Flaccus *(ddss)* falls to 11.39, almost exactly half of the first pattern (22.65).

In Statius' *Thebaid* as a whole, *dsds* is again the first pattern (16.24 per cent) and it is likewise first in each of the twelve books (with a percentage range from 14.16 in VI to 19.06 in VIII).[4] Lucan and Silius Italicus show somewhat greater variation from book to book. In the *De bello civili* as a whole, *dsss* is first with 15.40 per cent, but *dsds* is a close second with 15.37; *dsss* is first in Books IV, VI, X, and tied with *dsds* for first place in II and III, with *dsds* first in the other five books; the first-pattern percentages range from 14.15 (*dsss* in X) to 17.08 (*dsds* in I). In the *Punica, dsss* is first with 13.04 per cent and also first in twelve books; in the other five (V, VIII, IX, XII, XIV) *sdss* is first, and the range of the first-pattern percentages is from 11.78 (*dsss* in XI) to 17.60 (*dsss* in VI). This percentage of 17.60 in Book VI is most unusual, since the next highest is 14.71, in Book XVI. When we compare Silius' percentages with the range of *dsds* in Valerius Flaccus (21.08 to 25.98), it is apparent that Silius Italicus has a concentration on one pattern almost half of what we find in the *Argonautica*, by far the lowest of the four Silver Latin epic poets. In other respects also we shall see that Silius is far more interested in variety than the other three poets.

The fact that *sdss* is first in five books of the *Punica* and second in the poem as a whole is also of considerable interest. We have seen that *sdss* is elsewhere the first pattern only in Lucilius, the *Dirae*, Horace, *Epistles* II, 1, and the *Halieutica*, wrongly ascribed to Ovid. In Ennius *sdss* is tied with *dsss* for second place, and it is second in Catullus LXIV, Horace, the *Aetna*, and in later poetry only Juvenal and (in the fifth century) Paulinus of Pella and Avitus; from Catullus to Avitus, when *sdss* is the second pattern, *dsss* is first, as in the case of Silius Italicus.

The percentages of the first eight patterns have a range of about two points plus or minus the average; I give first the average and then the range in the individual books:

Lucan:	78.61	76.46 (II) to 80.29 (IV)
Valerius Flaccus:	83.35	81.27 (I) to 85.77 (V, VI)
Statius:	74.26	72.32 (VI) to 78.21 (II)
Silius Italicus:	72.64	70.93 (XIV) to 76.99 (V)

As in the case of the first pattern, Valerius Flaccus has much the highest percentages and Silius Italicus the lowest.

When we turn to the eight patterns preferred by the four poets and their distribution of spondees and dactyls, we find that Valerius Flaccus and Statius are definitely Ovidian and that Lucan and Silius Italicus follow the Vergilian norm. The order of the patterns in Valerius Flaccus and Statius is almost identical (*dsds* first, *ddds* fourth, *dssd* fifth, *sdss* eighth) and the emphasis on *ddsd* and *dsdd* (sixth or seventh in both poems) proves the dactylic and Ovidian nature of their hexameters, as does the resultant distribution of fifteen spondees and seventeen dactyls in the first eight patterns.

Summers is therefore wrong when he terms the hexameter technique of Statius "Virgilian rather than Ovidian."[5] Butler, on the other hand, refers to Lucan's "desire to steer clear of the influence of Vergil" and adds: "His affinity to Ovid is greater."[6] This is certainly not true of Lucan's choice of metrical patterns; seven of his first eight are those of Vergil's *Aeneid,* and his distribution of eighteen spondees and fourteen dactyls are much closer to those of Vergil (twenty and twelve) than to those of Ovid (twelve and twenty). Silius' first eight patterns are identical with Vergil's, as is his distribution of twenty spondees and twelve dactyls. This is not surprising, as the influence of Vergil on Silius Italicus was of course paramount; Duff is correct when he says: "Silius owes much more to Virgil's *Aeneid* than to any other source."[7] It is important to note that in no book of the *Punica* is the distribution of spondees and dactyls less than twenty and twelve respectively, in six books (II, III, IV, IX, XII, XIII) it is twenty-one and eleven, and in five (I, VI, VII, X, and XIV) it rises to twenty-two spondees and ten dactyls. Actually, therefore, Silius to this extent is much more spondaic than Vergil,[8] and approaches the practice of Ennius. In other respects also Silius is said to resemble Ennius, and Wallace concludes that "the *Annales* of Ennius served as a model for Silius in the composition of the *Punica,* and possibly as a historical source."[9]

Petronius' Parody of Lucan

Petronius in his *Satyricon* writes a short *Bellum Civile,* a reworking of the theme of Lucan's epic;[10] these verses on the civil war of Caesar and Pompey have been viewed as a criticism or parody of the *De bello civili.*[11] Is Petronius metrically similar to Lucan, or does he subtly criticize his technique by preferring different patterns and percentages?

The order of the first eight patterns in each is as follows:

	1	2	3	4	5	6	7	8
Lucan:	*dsss*	*dsds*	*ddss*	*sdss*	*ssds*	*ddds*	*dssd*	*sdds*
Petronius:	*ddss*	*dsss*	*sdss*	*dssd*		*dsds*	*ssds*	*ssss*
				sdsd				

Petronius (= P) clearly does not follow Lucan (= L) in his choice of metrical patterns; the differences are numerous: first pattern in P, *ddss* (as in Ovid); in L, *dsss,* with *ddss* third; *dsds,* second in L, is sixth in P, and such a low position for *dsds* is most unusual.[12] P favors *sdsd* (tied with *dssd* for fourth place) and *ssss* (eighth), neither of which appears in the first eight patterns of L (*sdsd,* tenth; *ssss,* eleventh). This preference for *sdsd* is unique; *sdsd* is tied for sixth position in Grattius and is seventh in Germanicus Caesar,[13] but nowhere, except in Petronius, does it appear in fourth place.

The percentage of the first pattern in P is 12.11, in L 15.40; again a striking difference, and the percentage in P is lower than what we find in the Republican poets, Vergil, the *Appendix Vergiliana,* Ovid, and the post-Vergilian didactic poets. Prior to Petronius, only Horace has lower first-pattern percentages (*Epistles* II, 10.82; total *Epistles,* 11.85, with *Epist.* II, 1, 11.85 and *Ars Poetica,* 10.32).[14] The percentage of the first eight patterns is 70.93 in P, 78.61 in L, and again P is surprisingly low; among the earlier poets we find lower percentages only as follows: Ennius, 65.35; Vergil, *Eclogues,* 69.09; Horace, 67.97 (*Ars Poetica,* 65.89). The percentage of the first eight patterns in the *Ilias Latina,* to be discussed below, is 69.92. Several of the fourth and fifth century poets are likewise lower.[15]

The distribution of spondees and dactyls in the first four feet of the first eight patterns is twenty-one and eleven in P, eighteen and fourteen in L. This high proportion of spondees in P is most unusual; after Ennius and Lucilius, we find it only in Vergil (*Georgics* IV), Horace (*Satires* I, *Epistles* I and II), Germanicus Caesar, and the *Aetna*, and later only in Silius Italicus (eleven books), Juvenal, Juvencus, Paulinus of Périgueux, and Avitus.

Whether or not Petronius in his parody of Lucan deliberately criticizes him for his metrical practices, one thing is certain: by his own handling of patterns and frequencies, Petronius reveals his own hexameter likes and dislikes; he desires greater variety (this is indicated by his low percentages for the first and the first eight patterns) and also a more spondaic type of hexameter (this is proved by the distribution of twenty-one spondees and eleven dactyls in the first eight patterns).

The statistics based on repeated, opposite, and reverse patterns likewise show that Petronius and Lucan are very unlike in their metrical technique. In several of the categories P again displays a greater interest in variety, e.g., number of patterns per sixteen-line unit: 9.3 in P, 8.9 in L; percentage of sixteen-line units with eight or more patterns: 100.0 in P, 87.43 in L; one repeat cluster every 144.5 lines in P, 82.7 in L; one repeat every 14.5 lines in P, 11.4 in L; repeats plus near repeats, one every 5.2 lines in P, 4.2 in L.[16]

In his treatment of opposite patterns in adjacent lines Petronius is again unique; one opposite every 14.5 lines (L, 22.0), and this high frequency is unparalleled in the whole range of Latin hexameter poetry;[17] on the other hand, reverse combinations are relatively rare, one every 57.8 lines (L 40.7), and in this respect Petronius reverts to the practice of the Republican poets;[18] in all later hexameter poetry, reverse patterns in adjacent lines are more frequent than in Petronius.

The percentage of fourth-foot homodyne in Petronius is unusually high, 52.07 (L, 37.08), and the percentages of fourth-foot texture change are all low, and differ strikingly from the corresponding percentages in Lucan, as follows:

	P	L
R, % of change:	25.0	39.09
Differs from homodyne %:	-27.07	+2.01
R + NR, % of change:	42.86	35.56
Differs from homodyne %:	-9.21	-1.52
Most frequent R:	*ddss*	*dsss*
% of change:	16.67	48.15
Differs from homodyne %:	-35.40	+11.07
R + NR, % of change:	23.08	44.31
Differs from homodyne %:	-28.99	+7.23

Petronius' procedure here makes for far greater monotony, and I much prefer the lower homodyne and the higher percentage of change which we find in Lucan and which are so similar to the corresponding percentages in Vergil's *Aeneid*.

How are these many differences to be explained? Petronius dislikes Lucan's emphasis on rhetoric and his avoidance of divine machinery; perhaps he is also suggesting a better way to write hexameter verse. In some respects his procedure is an improvement (less concentration on the same patterns, and more spondees), in others (high homodyne percentage and low percentage of change in fourth-foot texture) it is definitely inferior. Butler says: "The verse is uninspired, the method is impossible, the remedy is worse than the disease."[19]

Monotonous Repetition in Valerius Flaccus

Many have commented on the Ovidian nature of the meter of Valerius Flaccus; Dimsdale, for instance, says: "In his verse for all his wish to be Virgilian he has fallen under the influence of the smoother and more imitable Ovid, to whom, indeed, in his preference of the dactyl, Valerius approaches more nearly than any other Latin poet."[20] This last is inaccurate; we have already seen that it is Calpurnius Siculus, both in his *Eclogues* and in the *Laus Pisonis*, who is the most Ovidian in his preference for dactyls.

The fact not generally realized is that Valerius goes far beyond Ovid in his repetition of patterns and his complete disregard of variety. I shall illustrate from several of the categories listed in Tables I and II, and compare not only his averages but also the variation in the individual books with the corresponding figures for Ovid and the other three epic poets of the Silver Age. The differences between Valerius and Statius, the other "Ovidian" poet, should be noted, and also the extent to which Silius Italicus reveals a greater interest in many aspects of variety than do the other three.

1. Patterns per sixteen-line unit:

	Average	Range
Ovid:	8.9	8.6 (XIV) to 9.1 (VI)
Lucan:	8.9	8.7 (IX) to 9.3 (II)
Valerius:	8.4	8.1 (VI) to 8.7 (I)
Statius:	9.2	8.9 (VIII) to 9.4 (IV, VI, XI, XII)
Silius:	9.5	8.9 (V) to 10.0 (III)

Valerius' low average of patterns per sixteen-line unit, 8.4, is surpassed only by 7.0 in Catullus LXIV, 7.4 in Vergil's Fourth *Eclogue*, and 8.3 in Lucretius V and VI; in later poetry, only by 8.1 in Claudian, *In Eutropium* I and II, 8.1 in Corippus, *Johannis* I, and 7.6 in Cyprian.

2. One repeat cluster every *x* lines:

	Average	Range
Ovid:	112.5	80.0 (IV) to 208.0 (XII)
Lucan:	82.7	68.5 (I, IV) to 135.5 (V)
Valerius:	44.7	38.9 (III) to 49.9 (I)
Statius:	101.1	69.6 (VIII) to 144.3 (III)
Silius:	187.6	93.9 (IX) to 654.0 (XVII)

Repeat clusters (passages in which the same metrical pattern appears six or more times in sixteen or fewer lines) are abnormally frequent in Valerius, 125 instances, an average of one every 44.7 lines; this is two and one-half times as often as in Ovid's *Metamorphoses*, and is surpassed in all Latin hexameter poetry only by Catullus LXIV, one every 29.0 lines; Lucretius V, 39.1, and III, 43.3;[21] and, in the late period, Avitus, *De mundo initio*, 40.6; and Corippus, *Johannis* I, 34.1. Repeat clusters likewise occur more often in Lucan and Statius than in Ovid, but Silius Italicus reverts to the lower frequency of Vergil (*Aeneid*, one cluster every 200.1 lines, with a range from 86.1 in XII to 804.0 in IX; Book IV contains not a single cluster).

3. Percentage of fourth-foot homodyne:

	Average	Range
Ovid:	50.0	45.28 (VIII) to 53.29 (XIV)
Lucan:	37.08	32.31 (V) to 42.59 (I)
Valerius:	31.70	27.10 (VIII) to 37.27 (VII)
Statius:	40.18	36.27 (II) to 44.43 (VI)
Silius:	42.95	40.58 (XV) to 46.11 (I)

Valerius' average of 31.70 per cent for fourth-foot homodyne is lower than had appeared earlier (cf. the *Culex*, 36.76; the *Moretum*, 33.33; Vergil's *Eclogues*, 39.73, *Georgics*, 36.08, *Aeneid*, 37.78; Germanicus Caesar, 35.83; the *Aetna*, 33.18)[22] and is surpassed by only three later poets: Nemesianus, *Cynegetica*, 31.69; Claudian, *Panegyricus de quarto consulatu Honorii Augusti*, 31.45, *De raptu Proserpinae* I, 29.02, and II, 30.46; Corippus, *Johannis* VIII, 29.74; and *dsds* is likewise the most frequent pattern in these three poets.

Mozley says of Valerius' rhythm that "some lines follow each other with monotonous sameness, and there is a fondness for particular pauses, such as the 2nd and 4th caesura (the latter is a special favourite with the Silver Latin writer)."[23] Fourth-foot heterodyne and hephthemimeral caesura go hand in hand and seem especially characteristic of *dsds;* too much *dsds* combined with heterodyne, as in Valerius, produces a jerky effect,[24] and Statius, whose first pattern is also *dsds* (but 16.24 per cent; Valerius, 22.65), avoids the excessive emphasis on heterodyne which mars the verse of Valerius. Statius is considered "far less monotonous than Ovid, Lucan, or Valerius."[25]

4. One repeat every *x* lines:

	Average	Range
Ovid:	10.7	9.1 (III) to 12.7 (I)
Lucan:	11.4	10.2 (II) to 13.6 (X)
Valerius:	8.6	7.6 (VIII) to 9.8 (II)
Statius:	12.1	10.2 (V) to 14.4 (III, XI)
Silius:	11.8	9.5 (VIII) to 14.9 (XVII)

Again Valerius Flaccus goes to extremes. Such a high frequency of repeated patterns in adjacent lines had not appeared since the Republican period (Lucretius, 8.8;[26] Catullus LXIV, 7.0), and would not be seen again until the late period, in Paulinus of Périgueux, *De vita Martini* I, one every 8.4 lines; Cyprian, one every 7.9 lines; and Corippus, *Johannis* I, one every 7.6 lines. Statius avoids repeats even more than Lucan and Silius, and approaches the frequencies of Vergil (*Georgics,* one every 12.3 lines, *Aeneid,* 12.4).

5. Most frequent repeat, percentage of change in fourth-foot texture:

	Pattern	Average	Range
Ovid:	*dsss*	51.49	31.25 (IX) to 81.82 (VI)
Lucan:	*dsss*	48.15	31.82 (IV) to 75.0 (III)
Valerius:	*dsds*	15.33	9.62 (III) to 22.22 (II)
Statius:	*dsds*	25.10	11.11 (III) to 43.33 (VIII)
Silius:	*dsss*	44.61	15.79 (XIII) to 88.89 (XVII)

When the same pattern occurs in two or more verses in succession, the change in fourth-foot texture (from homodyne to heterodyne, or from heterodyne to homodyne) counteracts the monotony inherent in the repetition of the same metrical patterns. If the percentages of such change consistently run higher than the percentages of fourth-foot homodyne, we have an indication that the poet is deliberately attempting to provide additional variety; this is the case in Vergil's *Aeneid:* repeats, +6.71; repeats plus near repeats, +8.05; most frequent repeat, +7.36; cf. Lucan: repeats, +2.01; favorite repeat, +11.07; Silius: repeats, +3.14; repeats plus near repeats, +3.17; favorite repeat, +1.66. When Valerius Flaccus combines a low fourth-foot homodyne percentage such as 31.70 and a high incidence of *dsds* repeats (46.37 per cent of the total repeats), we should expect some variety in fourth-foot texture, but what do we find? A percentage of change of only 15.33 (as low as 9.62 in Book III), and this is 16.37 per cent below his fourth-foot homodyne percentage. Nothing like this low percentage of shift in fourth-foot texture had appeared earlier.

In Catullus LXIV the percentage of change differs from the homodyne percentage as follows: repeats, -25.25; repeats plus near repeats, -26.84; most frequent repeat, -22.94; most frequent repeats plus near repeats, -25.82. But Catullus has a fourth-foot homodyne of 60.44, the highest in Latin poetry with the exception of Calpurnius Siculus, *Eclogues,* 61.08. The percentage of change in Catullus is therefore as follows: repeats, 35.19; repeats plus near repeats, 33.60; most frequent repeat, 37.50; most frequent repeats plus near repeats, 34.62. These are all higher than the corresponding percentages in Valerius, and Catullus' percentage of change in the most frequent repeat (37.50) is more than twice that in Valerius (15.33).

In the *Thebaid* Statius' percentage of change in his most frequent repeat (likewise *dsds*) is 25.10; this is also low, but higher than that in Valerius. The percentage of change in Statius' *Silvae,* however, is only 13.33. Among the later poets Claudian I has a percentage of change (in the most frequent repeat) of 13.79;[27] Arator, 10.0, and Cyprian an unbelievably low 2.63.

Other categories could be added, but seem unnecessary; the comments given above prove conclusively the excessive monotony of Valerius Flaccus and show how, in most respects, the other "Ovidian" poet, Statius, avoided the same pitfalls. Actually, Valerius is unique among the hexameter poets of his day for the sameness of his verses and his complete lack of regard for the various types of variety which could have counteracted his too great concentration on the same metrical patterns, especially *dsds*. To illustrate again the "rhythmical identity" to which I referred in Chapter 4, I quote the repeat cluster in *Argonautica* IV, 196-203:

taurus aquis // qui primus init // spernitque tumentem	*(dsds)*
pandit iter, // mox omne pecus // formidine pulsa	*(dsds)*
pone subit, // iamque et mediis // praecedit ab undis.	*(dsds)*
At procul e silvis // sese gregibusque ferebat	*(dssd)*
saevus in antra gigans; // quem nec sua turba tuendo	*(ddsd)*
it taciti // secura metus. // mortalia nusquam	*(dsds)*
signa manent; // instar scopuli, // qui montibus altis	*(dsds)*
summus abit // longeque iugo // stat solus ab omni.	*(dsds)*

In this passage *dsds* appears six times in eight verses,[28] with no change in fourth-foot texture (i.e., all heterodyne), with the same sense pauses in the second and fourth feet, and with almost the same word-divisions within the feet (cf. the beginnings: *taurus aquis, pandit iter, pone subit, signa manent, summus abit*). This is typical of Valerius' handling of *dsds*. I said above that repeat clusters are abnormally numerous in the *Argonautica*: 125 instances, an average of one every 44.7 lines; 101 clusters, or 80.80 per cent of the total are *dsds*, and this accounts for the jerkiness and monotony of so much of his hexameter verse.

Statius' Epic Meter and His *Silvae*

My statistics for Statius thus far have been based entirely upon the twelve books of his *Thebaid*. I wish now to examine also the fragmentary *Achilleid* and to compare his hexameter technique in the two epics. And what about his *Silvae*, five books of short poems addressed to friends? Some of these express congratulations or praise or sympathy, and others describe villas or baths or works of art. These are themes usually presented in the elegiac meter, and Statius has made a new departure in using the hexameter for most of the poems (twenty-six out of thirty-two). Are his metrical procedures here the same, or do they differ from what we find in the *Thebaid* and the *Achilleid*? Duff states that the hexameters of the *Silvae* attain "a facility suitable to the lighter and more sportive subjects in the collection."[29] This implies a somewhat different handling of the hexameter from that in his epic poetry.

I turn first to the patterns and their percentages in the three works. The first eight patterns in order of frequency are as follows:

	1	2	3	4	5	6	7	8
Thebaid:	dsds	dsss	ddss	ddds	dssd	dsdd	ddsd	sdss
Achill.:	dsds	dsss	ddds	ddss	dssd	ddsd	dsdd	
							sdds	
Silvae:	dsds	dsss	ddss	ddds	dssd	ddsd	dsdd	ssds

The similarities here are amazing: *dsds* and *dsss*, first and second respectively; *ddss* and *ddds* in third or fourth place; *dssd*, fifth in all three works; *ddsd* and *dsdd* in sixth or seventh position. The *Silvae* is actually closer than the *Achilleid* to the *Thebaid*; the first five patterns are identical; also, *sddd* is the fifteenth pattern in both the *Silvae* and the *Thebaid*, with *sssd* sixteenth in all three poems.

The percentages are the following:

	1st pattern	1st four	1st eight
Thebaid:	16.24	48.90	74.26
Achilleid:	17.11	46.17	71.48
Silvae:	16.47	47.29	73.64

These percentages, like the patterns, are almost identical, with the *Silvae* between the two epics and in two cases closer to the *Thebaid*.[30] In the first eight patterns the number of fourth-foot spondees (five) and first-foot dactyls (seven) is the same in all three poems; in the distribution of spondees and dactyls in the first four feet of the first eight patterns, the *Achilleid* is slightly more dactylic — fourteen spondees only, with fifteen in the *Thebaid* and the *Silvae*. But there are no significant variations here; the lighter themes of the *Silvae* obviously have not affected either Statius' choice of metrical patterns or their frequencies.

When we turn to the statistics on variety and repetition, we find again that Statius' "finger-prints" are as clearly marked on the *Silvae* as on the two epics. I cite a few examples where the *Silvae* (= *S*) resembles either the *Thebaid* (= *Th*) or the *Achilleid* (= *Ach*) or both: number of patterns per sixteen-line unit: *S*, 9.4; *Th*, 9.2; *Ach*, 9.5; percentage of units with eight or more patterns: *S*, 90.21; *Th* 90.20; percentage of fourth-foot homodyne: *S*, 38.41; *Th*, 40.18; *Ach*, 39.84; one repeat every *x* lines: *S*, 12.2; *Th*, 12.1; one repeat plus near repeat every *x* lines: *S*, 4.4; *Th*, 4.3; *Ach*, 4.5; most frequent repeat: *dsds* in all three works; percentage of total repeats: *S*, 33.21; *Th*, 30.88; *Ach*, 32.0; percentage of total *dsds*: *S*, 16.48; *Th*, 15.67; *Ach*, 16.67; one opposite every 20.0 lines in *S*, one every 21.8 in *Th*; one reverse every 41.5 lines in *S*, one every 41.6 in *Ach*.[31] There are also striking similarities in the various patterns preceded or followed by their opposites, as follows:

	S	Th	Ach
% of *sssd* with *ddds*:	17.78	19.87	18.75
% of *ssss* with *dddd*:	5.0	4.89	8.70
% of *sdss* with *dsdd*:	12.89	12.19	15.87
% of *sdsd* with *dsds*:	29.92	30.54	39.13
% of *ssds* with *ddsd*:	13.27	12.75	17.65
% of *sdds* with *dssd*:	12.88	14.80	15.81

Again we find the percentages of *S* almost identical with those of *Th*.

The themes and tone of the *Silvae* differ much from those of epic poetry, and one might expect this to be true also of the verse; Butler speaks of the "sprightly and dexterous handling of the hexameter" in this collection of short poems.[32] It is apparent, however, that Statius does not change his metrical technique when he turns to occasional poetry; the *Silvae* as a whole actually resemble the *Thebaid* somewhat more closely than does the fragmentary *Achilleid*.

The Metrical Artistry of Silius Italicus

Vergil and Ovid, the two great epic poets of the Augustan Age, represent two entirely different hexameter techniques, the former spondaic, with low frequencies and percentages; the latter dactylic, with less regard for variety and change in fourth-foot texture; in the Silver Age likewise, two epic poets are at opposite extremes — Silius Italicus, who follows the "Vergilian norm" but is even more spondaic than his master, and Valerius Flaccus, thoroughly Ovidian, but whose repetition is far more monotonous than that in the *Metamorphoses*.

At the beginning of Chapter 7, I compared a sixteen-line unit from Vergil with units from Cicero, Lucretius and Catullus; at the beginning of Chapter 9, I presented a sixteen-line unit from Ovid for a contrast with units from Vergil and Horace. Since Valerius Flaccus and Silius Italicus are so very different in their hexameter technique, it will be of interest to select arbitrarily sixteen lines from each and compare their procedures also *in parvo*; in the summary following the passages I shall add the corresponding figures from the sixteen-line units of Vergil (*Aen.* XII, 937-942) and Ovid (*Metam.* XV, 864-879) already presented in Chapter 9.

Valerius Flaccus, *Argon.* V, 1-16

(dsds)	Altera lux haud laeta viris emersit Olympo:	*(t)*
(dssd)	Argolicus morbis fatisque rapacibus Idmon	*(m)*
(dsds)	labitur extremi sibi dudum conscius aevi.	*(m)*

(ddds)	at memor Aesonides nimium iam vera locuti	*(t)*
(ddsd)	Phineos hinc alios rapto pavet Idmone luctus.	*(t)*
(ddds)	tum comiti pia iusta tulit caelataque multa	*(t)*
(ddss)	arte Dolionii donat velamina regis,	*(t)*
(dsds)	hospes humum sedemque Lycus. flens arma revellit	*(t)*
(dssd)	Idmonis e celsa Mopsus rate; robora caedunt	*(t)*
(ssss)	pars silvis portantque arae: pars auguris alba	*(t)*
(dsdd)	fronde caput vittisque ligant, positumque feretro	*(t)*
(dddd)	congemuere; dies simul et suus admonet omnes.	*(m)*
(sdss)	Ecce inter lacrimas interque extrema virorum	*(m)*
(dsdd)	munera, quem cursus penes imperiumque carinae,	*(m)*
(ddds)	Tiphyn agit violenta lues, cunctique pavore	*(t)*
(dsss)	attoniti fundunt maestas ad sidera voces:	*(t)*

Silius Italicus, *Pun.* IX, 1-16

(ssds)	Turbato monstris Latio cladisque futurae	*(t)*
(ddsd)	signa per Ausoniam prodentibus irrita divis,	*(m)*
(dsds)	haud secus ac si fausta forent et prospera pugnae	*(t)*
(dsss)	omina venturae, consul traducere noctem	*(t)*
(ssds)	exsomnis telumque manu vibrare per umbras,	*(t)*
(ddsd)	ac modo segnitie Paulum increpitare, modo acres	*(m)*
(sdsd)	exercere tubas nocturnaque classica velle.	*(m)*
(dsds)	nec minor in Poeno properi certaminis ardor.	*(t)*
(ssss)	erumpunt vallo, fortuna urgente sinistra,	*(m)*
(sdss)	consertaeque manus; nam sparsi ad pabula campis	*(m)*
(ssds)	vicinis raptanda Macae fudere volucrem	*(t)*
(ssss)	telorum nubem. ante omnes invadere bella	*(t)*
(ssss)	Mancinus gaudens hostilique unguere primus	*(t)*
(dddd)	tela cruore cadit; cadit et numerosa iuventus	*(m)*
(dsss)	nec pecudum fibras Varro et contraria Paulo	*(m)*
(dsds)	auspicia incusante deum compesceret arma,	*(t)*

The following table not only compares Valerius Flaccus and Silius Italicus, but shows Valerius' resemblances to Ovid and Silius' to Vergil:

	Ovid	Valerius	Silius	Vergil
No. of patterns:	9	10	8	9
Most frequent:	*dsss* (3)	*dsds* (3)	*dsds* (3)	*dsds* (5)
	ddsd (3)	*ddds* (3)	*ssss* (3)	
			ssds (3)	
First four feet,				
No. of spondees:	28	29	40	36
No. of dactyls:	36	35	24	28
% of spondees:	43.75	45.32	62.50	56.25
1st foot dact. (of 16):	14	14	8	12
4th-foot spond. (of 16):	6	11	12	14
Repeats in unit:	2	0	1	1
R + NR in unit:	2	3	1	2
Opposites in unit:	0	1	4	0
Reverses in unit:	2	0	1	1
4th-foot homodyne lines:	11	5	7	6
Homodyne % in unit:	68.75	31.25	43.75	37.50
Total homodyne %:	50.0	31.70	42.95	37.78

This brief survey of the units proves that even passages of sixteen lines display clearly the distinctions between the various poets — the dactylic nature of Valerius Flaccus and Ovid, and the spondaic nature of Silius Italicus and Vergil (with Silius more spondaic than Vergil). Also, with the exception of Ovid, the percentage of fourth-foot homodyne in each unit is almost identical with that in each poem as a whole. The number of patterns in the *Argonautica* passage is above average, that in the *Punica* below average; also, the unit from the *Punica* is abnormal in having four opposite combinations in sixteen lines (average frequency, one every 22.3 lines).

I return now to the total statistics for the *Punica* of Silius Italicus and Vergil's *Aeneid* (= V). Several similarities between the two poets have already been noted: the first eight patterns are the same, as is the resultant distribution of twenty spondees and twelve dactyls; the percentage of the first eight patterns is 72.64 (V, 72.78). The following resemblances are equally striking: patterns per sixteen-line unit, 9.5 (V, 9.4); percentage of units with eight or more patterns, 93.37 (V, 92.46); repeat clusters, one every 187.6 lines (V, 200.1); percentage of fourth-foot change in repeats, 46.09 (V, 44.49); increase over homodyne percentage, +3.14 (V, +6.71);[33] repeats plus near repeats, one every 4.6 lines (V, 4.6); percentage of change in repeats plus near repeats, 46.12 (V, 45.83); increase over homodyne percentage, +3.17 (V, +8.05); most frequent repeat, percentage of total repeats, 19.71 (V, 22.18),[34] and percentage of total pattern, 12.82 (V, 12.40); percentage of fourth-foot change in the most frequent repeat, 44.61 (V, 45.14); combination of the two patterns most often repeated: repeats, percentage of total repeats, 37.58 (V, 38.02); repeats plus near repeats, percentage of total repeats plus near repeats, 36.84 (V, 39.67);[35] opposites, one every 22.3 lines (V, 23.1); percentage of *sddd* with *dsss*, 27.12 (V, 29.38); percentage of *dsdd* with *sdss*, 18.86 (V, 18.41). Reverse combinations occur once every 29.0 lines (V, 38.9), and in using these to counteract the monotony of repeated patterns, Silius resembles Horace, where reverse combinations appear once every 29.4 lines.[36]

The metrical technique displayed in the *Punica* is identical with that in the *Aeneid* in far too many respects to be the result of accident. Silius must have studied Vergil's metrics with extreme care to have been able to imitate him so closely. This is certainly not true of the other three epic poets, who reveal no such metrical adherence to Vergil, however much they may be indebted to him for language, style, and poetic structure.[37]

The *Punica* has been much maligned in the handbooks of Latin literature, where we usually read that it is not only the longest but the worst of Latin epics.[38] Not all writers have agreed; almost a century ago Simcox said that Silius "is always dignified and often pathetic; he comes nearer — much nearer — to the noble grace of Vergil than any other Roman poet."[39] Perhaps, as Huxley maintains, "the time is ripe for a revaluation of his poetic gifts."[40] I agree with Duff that "scholars would think better of the poem if they would condescend to read it,"[41] and I am happy to find the *Punica* called "the most readable of the post-Augustan Latin epic poems."[42] Wallace's estimate seems very reasonable:[43]

> Silius' style...is not characteristic of the times in which he wrote. He is markedly different from Lucan and Statius. In his simplicity and good taste he is an anachronism, closer to Virgil than to his contemporaries.

Certainly, everything that I have discovered about Silius as a careful metrician and the amazing resemblances of his hexameter technique to that of Vergil supports the view that, as in many other respects such as simplicity, straightforwardness, and freedom from rhetoric, Silius is to be preferred to the other three epic poets of the Silver Age.

The Authenticity of *Punica* VIII, 144-223

The consistently spondaic nature of Silius Italicus is important for the controversial passage in *Punica* VIII, 144-223 (eighty-one lines, including 157a), which appears in no manuscript, and in no edition prior to the Aldine text of 1523. Duff says of the passage:[44]

> The source from which these verses are derived is a matter of dispute: some critics believe them to be the work of a forger; others hold that they were written by Silius and that the loss of them was due to some mutilation of S, the original MS. at St. Gall.

Heitland considers both the language of the passage and the imitations of Vergil to be characteristic of Silius Italicus.[45]

Metrically, these lines also have the "fingerprints" of Silius. In the first eight patterns we have a distribution of twenty or nineteen spondees and twelve or thirteen dactyls (total Silius, twenty and twelve); *dsss* is first, *ssss* third, and *ssds* tied (with *ddds*) for fifth place (total Silius, *dsss* first, *ssss* third, and *ssds* sixth). The pattern percentages for the disputed passage are slightly higher: first pattern, 17.28; first four, 54.32; first eight, 76.54; the corresponding percentages in the *Punica* as a whole are 13.04, 43.90, and 72.64. Silius has more variety than the other epic poets of the Silver Age, e.g., number of patterns per sixteen-line unit, 9.5; repeats, once every 11.8 lines; repeats plus near repeats once every 4.6 lines. The corresponding figures for VIII, 144-223, show even less repetition: 10.0, 16.2, and 5.1. In the *Punica* we find one opposite combination every 22.3 lines, in the disputed passage one every 20.3 lines.

Statistics based on short passages are often misleading, but the fact that there are so many similarities between the passage in question and the *Punica* as a whole argues strongly for the authenticity of *Punica* VIII, 144-223.

The Authorship of the *Ilias Latina*

A far more important problem involving Silius Italicus is that of the authorship of the *Ilias Latina*, which is described as "a meagre epitome devoid of artistic merit, characterized by free and uneven treatment, a straightforward style thickly embellished with Virgilian and Ovidian echoes, and careful versification."[46] On the basis of an acrostic signature at the beginning and end of the poem which reads (with minor emendations) ITALICUS SCRIPSIT,[47] the poem has been considered a youthful work of Silius Italicus,[48] or the composition of Baebius Italicus, mentioned as the author in a late manuscript of the fourteenth or fifteenth century.[49] It seems not improbable that the *Ilias Latina*, praised for its "careful versification," is actually by Silius, who is likewise noted for careful versification and who, as we have seen, is closer metrically to Vergil than any other epic poet of the Silver Age.[50]

The *Ilias Latina* (= *IL*) resembles the *Punica* of Silius Italicus (= *SI*) in certain respects: the first pattern *(dsss)* and the fourth *(dsds)* are the same, but the more Ovidian patterns, *ddsd* (fifth in *IL*) and *dssd* (seventh in *IL*), do not appear among the first eight patterns of *SI*. Lucan (= *L*) and *IL* are also similar: first pattern, *dsss;* sixth, *ddds;* seventh, *dssd;* and the distribution of spondees and dactyls in *IL* (eighteen or seventeen spondees, fourteen or fifteen dactyls) is that of *L* (eighteen and fourteen) rather than that of *SI* (twenty and twelve). But in the percentages of the most frequent patterns, *IL* is much closer to *SI* than to *L*, as follows:

	L	IL	SI
% of first pattern:	15.40	13.76	13.04
% of first four:	52.28	43.64	43.90
% of first eight:	78.61	69.92	72.64

If the *Ilias Latina* is the work of Silius Italicus, written in the age of Nero, it is not surprising that we should find the similarities to Lucan mentioned above. Also, the *Ilias Latina*, if written by Silius after the publication of Lucan's *De bello civili* I-III (62-63 A.D.), can hardly be called a "youthful work" since Silius (born in 26 A.D.) would by then be more than thirty-five years old.

The various categories of variety and repetition reveal a few instances where *IL* is likewise closer to *L* than to *SI:* repeat clusters, one every 95.8 in *IL*, 82.7 in *L*, but 187.6 in *SI;* one repeat every 11.3 lines in *IL*, 11.4 in *L*, 11.8 in *SI;* most frequent opposite, percentage of total opposites: *IL*, 25.42; *L*, 26.92; *SI*, 21.90; reverse combinations once every 37.6 lines in *IL*, every 40.7 in *L*, but every 29.0 in *SI*.

In most respects, however, *IL* is far more similar to *SI* than to *L* (or to any other epic poet of the period). This is seen in the fourth-foot homodyne percentages (*IL*, 45.45; *SI*, 42.95), and in the percentages of change in both repeats (*IL*, 44.09; *SI*, 46.09) and repeats plus near repeats (*IL*, 43.75; *SI*, 46.12). In the case of the most frequent repeat *(dsss)*, the percentages of the total repeats (*IL*, 21.51; *SI*, 19.71), of the total pattern (*IL*, 13.79; *SI*, 12.82), and of the change in fourth-foot texture

(*IL*, 40.0; *SI*, 44.61) are practically identical, and this is even more true of the three corresponding percentages when we include the *dsss* near repeats (*IL*, 21.43, 33.10, 45.83; *SI*, 19.30, 32.37, 44.47). If we add the second pattern most frequently repeated (*ddss* in *IL*, *sdss* in *SI*), the combination of the two repeated patterns produces the following percentages of the total repeats: 38.71 in *IL*, 37.58 in *SI*, with much higher percentages in the other Silver Age epic poets, from 46.96 in Statius' *Silvae* to 56.88 in Valerius Flaccus (51.24 in Lucan). These latter percentages are almost as high as in the Republican poets (Cicero, 57.15; Lucretius, 59.64; Catullus LXIV, 68.51), but *IL* and *SI* are similar to Vergil, *Aeneid*, 38.02. The two most frequent repeats, in relation to the totals of the two patterns, are as follows: *IL*, 26.10 per cent; *SI*, 25.19 per cent, and the other poets have a range from Statius, *Thebaid*, 28.20 (cf. Lucan, 29.33) to Valerius Flaccus, 34.38. Here again *IL* and *SI* are similar and resemble Vergil's *Aeneid*, 25.94 (and also Cicero, 26.27); the percentages in the other Silver Age epic poets are higher, but not as high as in Lucretius (37.84) and Catullus LXIV (41.08).

Also, as in the case of Statius above, the percentages of the individual opposite combinations will be relevant here: percentage of *sddd* with *dsss: IL*, 26.32; *SI*, 27.12; but *L*, 37.0 (the other epic poets of the age are either lower or higher, with Petronius 43.86); percentage of *sssd* with *ddds: IL*, 7.14; *SI*, 9.19; *L*, 9.63 (the range for the other poets is from the *Silvae*, 17.78, to the *Argonautica*, 21.21); percentage of *dddd* with *ssss: IL*, 24.32; *SI*, 22.73; this similarity seems very significant, since the percentage in *L* is only 8.20, and in the other poets the same combination (but *ssss* with *dddd*) ranges from 4.89 in the *Thebaid* to 13.21 in the *Argonautica*. In the case of the reverse combination *sddd-ddds*, the percentage of *sddd* preceded or followed by *ddds* is 10.53 in *IL*, 8.05 in *SI*, and 7.09 in *L;* the corresponding percentages in the other poets range from 14.29 in Petronius to 35.29 in Valerius Flaccus.

These additional figures show even more clearly the extent to which the metrical technique of the *Ilias Latina* is almost identical with that of the *Punica*. We can hardly assume that Silius Italicus imitated the author of the *Ilias Latina;* even less, that the *Ilias Latina*, usually dated in the time of Nero, is later than the *Punica* and metrically indebted to the longer poem. As to the few resemblances to Lucan, they are what we should expect of a poet writing in the age of Nero, but the differences are more numerous than the similarities. We have a situation here not unlike the problem of Calpurnius Siculus as the author of the *Laus Pisonis*, discussed above in Chapter 12. The *Ilias Latina* resembles the *Punica* far too closely to be assigned to anyone but Silius, to whom the acrostic ITALICUS SCRIPSIT must therefore refer.

1. On the storms in Lucan and their relation to the earlier Roman tradition, both literary and rhetorical, see now Morford, *The Poet Lucan,* pp. 20-58.

2. *History of Latin Literature,* p. 345.

3. As usual, these totals do not include spondaic verses and corrupt or bracketed lines. I discuss later Statius' incomplete *Achilleid* (1,122 verses).

4. Valerius Flaccus and Statius are thus as consistent in their use of *dsds* as first pattern as were Lucretius, Vergil *(Georgics, Aeneid),* Horace, and Manilius in their preference for *dsss;* in Ovid's *Metamorphoses,* the first pattern *(ddss)* ranges in the individual books from first to fourth place; the second pattern *(dsss)* ranges from first to fifth.

5. *Silver Age of Latin Literature,* p. 52.

6. *Post-Augustan Poetry,* p. 123; see also Heitland in Haskins, *M. Annaei Lucani Pharsalia,* pp. xcvi-xcvii.

7. *Silius Italicus,* I, p. xi; see Groesst, *Qua tenus Silius...videatur;* von Albrecht, *Silius Italicus,* pp. 166-184; von Albrecht says (p. 189): "Kein anderes Epos kann man mit grösseren Recht den Versuch einer Fortsetzung der Aeneis im geschichtlichen Raum nennen als die Punica."

8. The range in the *Aeneid* is from eighteen spondees and fourteen dactyls to twenty and twelve; only in *Georgics* IV does Vergil have a distribution of twenty-one and eleven.

9. *CPh* 53 (1958), p. 99. For other aspects of the influence of Ennius on Silius Italicus, see Woodruff, *Univ. of Mich. Stud.* 4 (1910), pp. 355-424; Mendell, *PhQ* 3 (1924), pp. 92-106. There are also numerous Ovidian reminiscences in the *Punica;* see Bruère, in Herescu, *Ovidiana,* pp. 475-499; also *CPh* 54 (1959), pp. 228-245.

10. Only Books I-III of Lucan's epic were published during the poet's lifetime; see Rose, *TAPhA* 97 (1966), pp. 379-396. Petronius echoes passages from IV-X also; his knowledge of these later books could well have come from private recitations, much in vogue at that time, before Lucan's death; cf. Baldwin, *Bellum Civile of Petronius,* pp. 27-32.

11. See Simcox, *History of Latin Literature,* II, p. 99; Butler, *Post-Augustan Poetry,* p. 103; Baldwin, *Bellum Civile of Petronius,* pp. 11-12; Walsh, *CPh* 63 (1968), pp. 210-211. Gaselee, "Petronius Arbiter" in *OCD,* p. 672, calls the poem "an enlightened and penetrating criticism of Lucan's treatment of the same theme."

12. In Ennius *dsds* is eighth, in Cicero's *Aratea* it is tied for seventh place, and it appears again in sixth position only in Avitus in the fifth century. Usually it ranges from first to fourth place.

13. It is also seventh in Juvenal, Ausonius' *Mosella* (but tied for fifteenth place in his *Cento Nuptialis),* and Arator.

14. The percentage in Petronius is also lower than in any poet of the Late Empire, with the exception of the amazingly low percentage of 9.38 in Ausonius' *Mosella* and 12.05 in the *Psychomachia* of Prudentius (11.31 in the *Psychomachia* and the *Hamartigenia* combined).

15. Among the late poets, the eight-pattern percentages lower than that in Petronius are the following: Avienus, *Aratea,* 68.61; Ausonius, *Mosella,* 62.50; Prudentius, *Psychomachia,* 70.87; Paulinus of Pella, 69.39; Paulinus of Nola, 69.96; Prosper (?), *De providentia Dei,* 70.48. On the other hand, in some of the late poets the first eight patterns have a percentage between 80 and 85; these include Claudian, Avitus, and Corippus; Cyprian's percentage is 91.06.

16. Repeats plus near repeats thus appear in Petronius more seldom than in any other Silver Latin epic poet; they are of course most frequent in Valerius Flaccus, one every 3.5 lines.

17. The closest to this is one opposite every 16.3 lines in Horace, *Epistles* II *(Epist.* II, 1, 15.0; *Ars Poetica,* 15.3), one every 16.8 in Grattius, one every 16.7 in Statius, *Achilleid;* in the Late Empire, one every 15.4 in Avienus, *Aratea,* one every 16.5 in Sidonius and Arator. The two Einsiedeln pastorals (average, 14.1) are too short to provide a basis for comparison.

18. Cf. Lucretius, one every 51.3 lines; Catullus LXIV, 53.9; Vergil, *Eclogues,* 55.0; *Ciris,* 65.0; *Moretum,* 60.0.

19. *Post-Augustan Poetry,* p. 103. The hexameters of Petronius have been considered *Vergiliani, non Lucaniani;* see Trampe, *De Lucani arte metrica,* p. 78; Stubbe, *Die Verseinlagen im Petron,* p. 103. Baldwin, *Bellum Civile of Petronius,* p. 55, disagrees: "these verses are utterly un-Vergilian in their effect, and resemble those of Lucan in many points, especially defects." My own statistics indicate that Petronius is closer to Vergil than to Lucan, with the exception of his treatment of fourth-foot texture.

20. *History of Latin Literature,* p. 449; cf. Butler, *Post-Augustan Poetry,* p. 192; Mozley, *Valerius Flaccus,* pp. xvii-xviii.

21. The average for the *De rerum natura* is one repeat cluster every 49.2 lines, with a range from 39.1 in Book V to 68.5 in II.

22. The homodyne percentages in Vergil, *Eclogue* IV and *Aeneid* I, are unusually low, 28.57 and 30.91 respectively.

23. *Valerius Flaccus*, p. xviii. Cf. Summers, *A Study of the Argonautica*, p. 50, who says that this tripartite hexameter "is used to excess — a fault due to Ovidian influence." But we should not blame Ovid for the excesses of Valerius.

24. Anderson, "Lucan" in *OCD*, p. 514, says that the "hephthemimeral jerk" is a conspicuous feature of Lucan's verse. It is far more characteristic of Valerius Flaccus.

25. Butler, *Post-Augustan Poetry*, p. 226.

26. Repeats are especially numerous in Books III, V, and VI of the *De rerum natura*, one every 7.5, 8.0, and 7.6 lines respectively.

27. Claudian I includes the panegyrics for the fourth and sixth consulships of Honorius and the two invectives in *In Eutropium*. The percentage of change in *In Eutropium* II is 9.09.

28. For clusters of the same pattern in nine or ten lines, see *Argon.* I, 546-555 (*dsds*, seven instances); III, 511-520 (*dsds*); V, 26-35 (*ddds*), 679-687 (*dsds*); VI, 45-54 (*dsds*); there is in these passages almost no shift in fourth-foot texture, from heterodyne *(t)* to homodyne *(m)*, or the reverse; in *Argon.* III, 708-721, *dsds* appears nine times in fourteen consecutive lines, with fourth-foot texture as follows: *tt..ttm.tt..tt.* In the other three poets similar clusters are also found in very short passages, but there is more variation in the fourth foot: e.g., Lucan I, 571-577 (six instances of *dsss* in seven lines: *mtm.mtt*); Silius II, 334-344 (seven instances of *ddss* in eleven lines: *m..t.mt.mtt*).

29. *Literary History of Rome in the Silver Age*, p. 396.

30. In the individual poems of the *Silvae*, the percentage range for the first pattern is from 10.81 (for each of the two patterns, *ddds* and *dsdd*, in II, 4, a poem of 37 verses) to 26.32 (V, 4, the famous poem to Somnus in 19 verses); for the first eight patterns, from 69.35 (III, 1) to 100.0 (again V, 4; next is V, 5, with 86.21 per cent).

31. We find considerable variation in the individual poems of the *Silvae*, but this is to be expected, since many are very short; e.g., the average for repeat clusters is one every 150.7 lines (cf. *Achilleid*, 160.3); fourteen of the twenty-six hexameter poems have no clusters, but I, 2, and V, 1, each have four, one every 69.0 and 65.5 lines respectively; the fourth-foot homodyne percentages (average, 38.41) range from 24.53 (III, 4) to 49.11 (III, 5); the average of reverse combinations is one every 41.5 lines (cf. *Achilleid*, 41.6), but five poems (I, 4; I, 5; III, 2; IV, 2; V, 4) have no reverses at all.

32. *Post-Augustan Poetry*, p. 228.

33. The smaller increase here and in the repeats plus near repeats results from Silius' higher fourth-foot homodyne percentage, 42.95 (V, 37.78). But his increase over the homodyne percentage is conspicuously greater than that in Lucan, Valerius, and Statius.

34. Cf. Lucan, 26.74; Valerius, 46.37; Statius, 30.88.

35. Cf. with Silius (37.58, 36.84) these corresponding percentages: Lucan, 51.24, 49.84; Valerius, 56.88, 54.16; Statius, 50.01, 46.90; in their concentration on two repeated patterns, these three writers follow the practice of the Republican poets, while Silius is in the tradition of Vergil, Horace, and Ovid.

36. The other epic poets are much less interested in reverse combinations, which appear every x lines as follows: Lucan, 40.7; Valerius, 48.6; Statius, 46.9.

37. Their imitation of Vergil's structure is of particular interest. On the parallelism of the two halves of the *Aeneid*, with numerous similarities and contrasts between the corresponding books (I and VII, II and VIII, III and IX, etc.), see Duckworth, *AJPh* 75 (1954), pp. 1-15; *Structural Patterns*, pp. 2-10. This same division into halves with similarities and contrasts appears in both the *Argonautica* and the *Thebaid*; on the former, see Frank, *CB* 43 (1966-67), pp. 38-39, and cf. Schetter, *Philologus* 103 (1959), pp. 297-308. It is therefore wrong to maintain, as do many scholars, e.g., Butler, *Post-Augustan Poetry*, p. 182, Dimsdale, *History of Latin Literature*, p. 447, and Mozley, *PVS* 3 (1963-64), p. 14, that Valerius had probably intended his epic, like the *Aeneid*, to consist of twelve books. On the parallelism of the two halves of the *Thebaid*, see Frank, *RIL* 99 (1965), pp. 309-318. For the indebtedness of Statius to Vergil in general, see Legras, *Étude sur la Thébaide*, pp. 30-144; Legras says (p. 348) that Statius "sait Virgile par coeur, et il l'imite partout, dans la composition, les caractères, les ornements et le style." On the structure of the *Punica*, see Wallace, *CPh* 53 (1958), pp. 99-103, who suggests a possible arrangement with IX the central book and eight books balanced on each side; but Wallace (p. 102) agrees with earlier scholars that Silius probably intended an epic in eighteen books (to parallel Ennius' *Annales*), with a division into two corresponding halves in the manner of Vergil's *Aeneid*.

38. See, e.g., Butler, *Post-Augustan Poetry*, p. 236; Dimsdale, *History of Latin Literature*, p. 456.

39. *History of Latin Literature*, II, p. 64.

40. In Platnauer, *Fifty Years of Classical Scholarship*, p. 424. Huxley adds: "the better passages of the *Punica* compare favourably in respect of strength, simplicity, and sentiment with much that a student accepts without question and reads

without initial bias derived from prejudiced and sometimes misinformed sources."

41. *Silius Italicus*, I, p. xiii. He says also that "the versification is in general pleasing, and much less monotonous than that of Lucan." Cf. Heitland in Haskins, *M. Annaei Lucani Pharsalia*, p. xciv: "The general effect of Lucan's verse is one of steady monotony."

42. Bruère, *CPh* 54 (1959), p. 244.

43. *HSPh* 62 (1957), p. 161. See also Mendell, *PhQ* 3 (1924), p. 106: "In an age of artificial rhetoric when epigram was at a premium and the purple patch held supremacy as perhaps never before or since, Silius...dared to utter an impressive protest, pointing the audience of his own day back to national models well nigh forgotten but greater than the brilliant failures which that audience was every day applauding."

44. *Silius Italicus*, I, p. xvii.

45. *JPh* 24 (1896), pp. 209-210.

46. Hudson-Williams, "Ilias Latina" in *OCD*, p. 449; Duff, *Literary History of Rome in the Silver Age*, p. 276, says that the versification possesses "a considerable share of easy grace."

47. See Doering, *Ueber den Homerus Latinus*, pp. 3-5; Butler, *Post-Augustan Poetry*, pp. 162-163; Duff, *Literary History of Rome in the Silver Age*, p. 275; Zarker, *Studies in the Carmina*, pp. 32-34.

48. So Doering, *Ueber den Homerus Latinus*, who discusses similarity of sources, language, and meter; see pp. 39-46 for numerous verbal parallels between the *Ilias Latina* and the *Punica*. See also Cosenza, *Petrarch's Letters*, pp. 184-185; Zarker, *Studies in the Carmina*, p. 33.

49. Hudson-Williams, "Ilias Latina" in *OCD*, p. 449, says: "The ascription of the work...to Silius Italicus on the ground of two acrostics is untenable; but the author may be a Baebius Italicus." Cf. also Campbell, "Silius Italicus" in *OCD*, p. 838.

50. Cf., however, Butler, *Post-Augustan Poetry*, p. 163, who says of the *Ilias Latina*: "the style of the verse is very different from that of the *Punica;*" so Duff, *Literary History of Rome in the Silver Age*, p. 275.

Chapter 14

THE SILVER AGE: SATIRE

The two satirists of the Silver Age are Persius and Juvenal and both differ in many respects from the earlier satirists, Lucilius and Horace. Persius' six poems are described as sermons on Stoic texts, and Juvenal, obsessed by the wickedness of his age, has an element of invective far stronger than anything in earlier satire, and this is especially true of the first three books (I-V, VI, VII-IX).

Butler says that the meter of Persius "represents almost the high-water mark of the post-Vergilian hexameter,"[1] and he considers Juvenal "almost untouched by the Ovidian influence"; he adds: "As far as his metre has any ancestry, it is descended from the Vergilian hexameter."[2] But what influence, if any, does the Horatian hexameter have on the metrical procedures of the two later satirists who in other respects are so indebted to Horace?[3] To what extent is Persius indebted to Ovid, or Juvenal to Persius? Also, do we have any traces of Lucilius' hexameter technique in either poet? Persius was inspired by reading Lucilius to compose satire,[4] and Lucilius is called "the predecessor whom Juvenal most admires."[5]

Persius and Juvenal

The first eight patterns in Persius and Juvenal are as follows:

	1	2	3	4	5	6	7	8
Persius:	*dsss*	*ddss*	*dsds*	*sdss*	*dssd*	*ddds*	*ddsd*	*ssss*
Juvenal:	*dsss*	*sdss*	*dsds*	*ddss*	*dssd*	*ssds*	*sdsd*	*ssss*

The favorite pattern in both Persius (= *P*) and Juvenal (= *J*) is *dsss*, as in the late Republican poets, Vergil and Horace, and, in the first century A.D., Grattius, Germanicus Caesar, Manilius, and the *Aetna* in didactic poetry, and Lucan, the *Ilias Latina*, and Silius Italicus in epic.[6] In both *P* and *J* the first four patterns are the same, but in different order; *P* has the same order as in the *Aeneid* and in this one respect he is the most Vergilian of all hexameter poets.[7] The order of the first four patterns in *J* is identical with that of Horace, and *sdss* is second in both; this latter feature is so unusual[8] that perhaps we have evidence here of the Horatian nature of Juvenal's versification. On the other hand, this prominence of *sdss* in both Horace and Juvenal may result from their indebtedness to Lucilius, where *sdss* occupies first place.

The second four patterns in *P* and *J* show greater variation; both have *dssd* in fifth place and thus resemble Horace (*dssd* in sixth position), and both have *ssss* as their eighth pattern (Horace, fifth, Lucilius third); *ddsd*, seventh in *P*, is perhaps due to Ovid's influence (fifth in the *Metamorphoses*), and the presence of *sdsd* among the first eight patterns in *J* (seventh place) is again a rarity, but may result from the fact that *sdsd* is eighth in Lucilius.[9]

When we examine the three percentages — first pattern, first four, and first eight — we find a striking difference between *P* and *J*. The percentage of the first pattern in *P* is 17.57, much higher than in most poets of the Silver Age (cf. Lucan, 15.40; Statius, *Thebaid*, 16.24; Silius Italicus, 13.04) and resembles that of Manilius, 17.33; on the other hand, the percentage in *J* is 13.66, almost identical with that in Horace's *Satires*, 13.44. The percentages for the first four and first eight patterns in *J*, 45.73 and 71.07 respectively, are likewise close to the corresponding percentages in the *Satires* of Horace, 43.78 and 69.99. This indicates that the percentages of *J* should be considered "Horatian" rather than "Vergilian."[10] The percentages of the first four and the first eight patterns in *P* are considerably higher; they are more typical of the Silver Age and perhaps show the influence of Ovid: first four in *P*, 53.16; cf. Manilius, 53.59; Lucan, 52.28; Valerius Flaccus, 54.36 (Ovid, 48.37); first eight in *P*, 77.50; cf. Manilius, 77.33; Lucan, 78.61 (Ovid, 81.62).

The distribution of spondees and dactyls in the first eight patterns of *P* is eighteen and fourteen; this is the same as in Lucan and should not necessarily be considered Ovidian; the truly

Ovidian poets are Columella, Valerius Flaccus, and Statius (fifteen spondees, seventeen dactyls) and, most Ovidian of all, Calpurnius Siculus (*Eclogues,* twelve or eleven spondees, and twenty or twenty-one dactyls; *Laus Pisonis,* thirteen spondees and nineteen dactyls). The distribution in *J* is unusually spondaic, twenty-one spondees and eleven dactyls, and this is identical with that in the fragments of Lucilius (Horace, twenty and twelve, but twenty-one and eleven in *Satires* I and *Epistles* I and II).[11]

The statistics on variety and repetition reveal only a few similarities between *P* and *J*, and these consist mostly in the fact that the percentages of fourth-foot change in total repeats and in total repeats plus near repeats (also in the pattern most often repeated, both repeats and repeats plus near repeats) are all well below the percentages of fourth-foot homodyne,[12] whereas the corresponding percentages in the *Satires* of Horace (and in Vergil) are all much higher. In this respect both satirists are typical of the Silver Latin poets, with the exception of Lucan and Silius Italicus.

There are many differences between *P* and *J*. The average number of patterns per sixteen-line unit in *P* is 8.8 (cf. Lucan, 8.9; Ovid, 8.9), but in *J* is 9.6, higher than in Vergil's *Aeneid* (9.4) and Horace (9.3). Repeat clusters are almost twice as numerous in *P* (one every 108.2 lines; cf. Ovid, 112.5) as in *J* (one every 199.2 lines; cf. *Aeneid,* 200.1). The percentage of fourth-foot homodyne in *P* is unusually high, 58.0 (cf. Calpurnius, *Eclogues,* 61.08, *Laus Pisonis,* 54.02; Petronius, 52.07), but in *J* we find 48.93, not much higher than in Horace's *Satires* (45.24). Repeats are frequent in *P,* one every 10.8 lines (Ovid, 10.7), but in *J* we find less concentration, one every 12.0 lines (*Aeneid,* 12.4); repeats plus near repeats occur in *P* once every 3.9 lines, and in all Silver Latin hexameter this high frequency is surpassed only by that in Valerius Flaccus, once every 3.5 lines; in *J* they appear once every 4.8 lines (cf. Horace, *Satires,* 4.5; Vergil, *Aeneid,* 4.6). When we combine the two most frequently repeated patterns, the repeats comprise 46.67 per cent of the total repeats in *P* (cf. Statius, *Silvae,* 46.96; *Achilleid,* 47.0), but 39.69 per cent in *J* (cf. *Aeneid,* 38.02); the combined repeats plus near repeats comprise 43.44 per cent of the total repeats plus near repeats in *P* (cf. Statius, *Achilleid,* 44.94), but 36.49 in *J* (cf. Horace, *Satires,* 35.47).

The figures for total opposite combinations show little variation, but the percentages of *ssdd* with *ddss* and of *sssd* with *ddds* are both 40.0 in *P;* in *J* the corresponding percentages are 17.95 and 11.21 (cf. Horace, *Satires,* 22.22 and 6.67). *P* shows little interest in reverse combinations, one every 49.9 lines (Valerius Flaccus, 48.6), whereas *J* has one every 37.5 lines (*Aeneid,* 38.9); the most frequent reverse *(ssds-sdss)* comprises 38.46 per cent of the total in *P* (cf. Statius, *Thebaid,* 38.16), but 51.49 per cent in *J* (cf. Horace, *Satires,* 52.78). The percentage of *sssd* with *dsss* is 40.0 in *P,* but 26.72 in *J* (Horace, *Satires,* 24.76); the reverse combination *sddd-ddds* does not occur in *P* and is rare in *J,* where the percentage of *sddd* with *ddds* is 4.44 (also 4.44 in the *Satires* of Horace).

To summarize the analyses given above, Persius is far more Ovidian than is Juvenal and in most respects is characteristic of the poets of the Silver Age; there is little metrical evidence to indicate his devotion to Lucilius and Horace. Juvenal, in his avoidance of repetition and his desire for greater variety, resembles Vergil and especially Horace. If we had enough of Lucilius preserved to give us adequate information on the various categories of variety and repetition, we might find that Juvenal was even closer to Lucilius than to Horace; certainly, in his choice of favorite patterns and the distribution of spondees and dactyls, he is as Lucilian as Horatian.

In one respect Juvenal is almost unique: unlike most Latin poets he evinces a definite fondness for a spondee in the fifth foot; we have thirty-five instances, one every 109.1 lines. Wilson says that this is "a larger proportion than is found in any poet after Catullus himself,"[13] where in LXIV one spondaic verse occurs every 13.6 lines. Wilson is hardly accurate here; even if we exclude the *Ciris* (possibly contemporary with Catullus), where the proportion of spondaic verses is three times that in Juvenal, or one every 35.7 lines,[14] we find a much higher frequency of spondaic verses both in Petronius (one every 58.8 lines) and later in Avienus (one every 64.7 lines in the *Aratea,* one every 48.0 lines in his *Descriptio orbis terrae*). But it is interesting to note that Juvenal has thirty-five spondaic verses and that the total in all the other Silver Age poets is also thirty-five.

Juvenal's Indebtedness to Horace

There is one final topic to discuss in connection with Persius and Juvenal. Horace changed his metrical procedures over the years, with greater variety and less concentration on the same patterns in his late *Epistles* than in *Satires* I, and I find nothing comparable in Lucretius, Vergil,[15] Ovid, or the epic poets of the first century A.D. But what about the later satirists? Are they influenced by Horace in this respect?

Persius composed his satires over a period of about twelve years, with I-IV in the years 50-56 and V-VI about 62.[16] I find the following differences:

	I-IV	V-VI
% of first pattern:	19.31	15.13
% of first eight patterns:	80.16	77.12
Spondees in first eight:	19	18 or 17
Dactyls in first eight:	13	14 or 15
Repeats, one every x lines:	9.7	12.9
R + NR, one every x lines:	4.2	3.6

Persius thus to some extent follows the practice of Horace; his two final satires have less concentration on the same patterns and fewer repeated patterns, but the proportion of repeats plus near repeats shows a marked increase. Also, the last two poems reveal a slightly greater emphasis on dactyls in the first eight patterns.

The poetic career of Juvenal extended over a much longer period, perhaps as much as thirty years. The publication of Book I (*Satires* I-V) is dated by some shortly after 100, by others about 110, but some of the satires may have been written by 100 or earlier; Book V (*Satires* XII-XVI) was published or left unfinished between 127 and 131.[17] The number of years which Juvenal devoted to writing satire is thus about the same as that covered by Horace's hexameter poetry, from the earliest satires of Book I to the late *Ars Poetica*. I shall now compare certain aspects of Juvenal's metrical technique in Books I and V, omitting the intermediate books; when I add the corresponding figures for Horace, *Satires* I and *Epistles* II (including the *Ars Poetica*), we discover that the changes over the years in Juvenal are amazingly similar to those in Horace:

	Juvenal		Horace	
	I	V	*Sat.* I	*Epist.* II
% of first pattern:	15.49	13.24	12.82	10.82
% of first eight:	72.41	71.12	71.16	67.22
Spondees in first eight:	18	21	21	21
Dactyls in first eight:	14	11	11	11
% of 4th-foot homodyne:	46.46	52.21	46.80	52.49
Repeats, one every x lines:	11.5	12.8	11.2	13.9
R + NR, one every x lines:	4.3	5.0	4.2	5.1
Favorite repeat:	*dsss*	*dsss*	*dsss*	*dsss*
% of total repeats:	36.47	17.74	15.22	21.74
R + NR, % of total R + NR:	30.69	20.63	17.70	17.20
Opposites, one every x lines:	21.7	22.0	32.1	16.3
Reverses, one every x lines:	37.5	37.6	34.3	31.0

Dimsdale points out that the satires of Juvenal's last two books differ in subject and tone from the three earlier books and resemble in a sense Horace's *Epistles*.[18] Perhaps it is not surprising that Juvenal in many respects shows between his first and last book the same changes which appear in Horace: the percentages of the first and the first eight patterns are lower in each, and the frequency of both repeats and repeats plus near repeats decrease in each, with a striking similarity in the figures: repeats, Juvenal from one every 11.5 lines to 12.8, Horace from 11.2 to 13.9; repeats plus near repeats, Juvenal from 4.3 to 5.0, Horace from 4.2 to 5.1. Such numerical identity is difficult to explain unless we assume that Juvenal was as familiar with Horace's metrical technique as he was with his language.

Equally astounding is the fact that the decreasing emphasis on the same patterns is accompanied by a corresponding increase in each poet in the percentage of fourth-foot homodyne: in Juvenal from 46.46 to 52.21; in Horace from 46.80 to 52.49. Juvenal at the beginning was less spondaic in his first eight patterns (eighteen spondees, fourteen dactyls) but, unlike Persius who became more dactylic in his final satires, Juvenal in his final book has the same distribution of twenty-one spondees and eleven dactyls that we find in Lucilius and in three of Horace's four hexameter books. In his use of opposites Juvenal shows little variation from I to V; Horace had used them more sparingly in *Satires* I (one every 32.1 lines) but in the second book of his *Satires* he increased them to once every 20.8 lines, and this is approximately what we find in Juvenal.

In this short comparison of Juvenal's metrical practices in Book I and Book V, we have strong additional evidence to prove his indebtedness to the hexameter technique of Horace. Duff and Butler are therefore wrong to speak of Juvenal's meter as "Vergilian" rather than "Horatian."[19]

Notes to Chapter 14

1. *Post-Augustan Poetry*, p. 94; Butler continues: "Here, as in other writers of the age, the influence of Ovid is traceable in the increase of dactyls and the avoidance of elision. But the verse has a swing and dignity, together with a variety, that can hardly be found in any other poetry of the Silver Age."

2. *Post-Augustan Poetry*, p. 318; cf. Duff, *Literary History of Rome in the Silver Age*, p. 497.

3. On Persius and Horace, see Dimsdale, *History of Latin Literature*, p. 423; cf. Duff, *Literary History of Rome in the Silver Age*, p. 230: "His Horatian debts are visible everywhere"; Butler, *Post-Augustan Poetry*, pp. 83-85, who says (p. 85): "Horace appears everywhere, but *quantum mutatus ab illo!*" On Juvenal and Horace, see Highet, *AJPh* 72 (1951), pp. 388-389, who points out that Juvenal quotes or echoes Horace at least forty times.

4. See Duff, *Literary History of Rome in the Silver Age*, p. 227; he says later (p. 230): "Along with Horace he adopted for imitation Horace's outspoken master in satire, Lucilius." Cf. Fiske, *TAPhA* 40 (1909), pp. 121-150, who concludes that "Lucilius is a source for Persius second only to Horace in importance."

5. Highet, *Juvenal the Satirist*, p. 235, note 10, where he lists the allusions to Lucilius in Juvenal's first satire; see also Highet, *AJPh* 72 (1951), pp. 388, 394.

6. In Persius *dsss* is first in five satires and tied (with *ddss*) for first in one (V). Juvenal in his individual poems is less consistent (and resembles Ovid in the *Metamorphoses*): *dsss* is first in ten satires, and tied (with *dsds*) for first place in one (VI); it is second in three (II and V, where *ddss* is first; XV, where *sdss* is first) and fourth in two (VII and XIII, where again *ddss* is first).

7. This same order of the first four patterns had earlier appeared in Lucretius; after Persius, the closest approach is in Marius Victor in the fifth century, where we find *dsss* first, *ddss* second, and *dsds* and *sdss* tied for third place.

8. As I said above, in connection with Silius Italicus, *sdss* is first only in Lucilius, the *Dirae*, Horace, *Epistulae* II, 1, and the *Halieutica*. It is tied for second place in Ennius, and is elsewhere second only in Catullus LXIV, the *Aetna*, Silius Italicus, and, in the late period, in Paulinus of Pella and Avitus.

9. In Horace's *Satires*, *sdsd* is in twelfth position (eleventh in the *Aeneid*, tenth in Ovid's *Metamorphoses*). The pattern *sdsd* is tied for sixth place in Grattius, and is seventh in Germanicus Caesar, Ausonius *(Mosella)* and Arator. In Petronius it is tied (with *dssd*) for fourth place.

10. The three corresponding percentages in the *Aeneid* are 14.39, 46.95, and 72.78. Juvenal thus stands between Vergil and Horace, but somewhat closer to the latter. Lucilius has higher percentages, 16.86, 47.60, and 74.21 respectively.

11. As I pointed out above, this distribution appears, after Lucilius and Horace, only in Germanicus Caesar, the *Aetna*, Petronius, Silius Italicus (six books; five are even more spondaic, with twenty-two spondees and ten dactyls), and later in Juvencus, Paulinus of Périgueux, and Avitus.

12. Persius is usually lower than Juvenal by far: e.g., difference between percentage of change in total repeats plus near repeats and fourth-foot homodyne percentage: *P*, -14.62; *J*, -5.65; *dsss* repeats plus near repeats: *P*, -15.78, *J*, -5.43; repeats plus near repeats in second most repeated pattern: *P*, -28.37; *J*, -5.41.

13. *D. Iuni Iuvenalis Saturarum libri V*, p. lxvi; Wilson explains Juvenal's preference for the *versus spondiacus* as the result of a desire for emphasis.

14. Spondaic verses occur once every 60.3 lines in the *Dirae*, to be dated also in the late Republic.

15. The fact that *Aeneid* X-XII differ in so many respects from I-IX (and the *Georgics*) is probably to be explained by lack of revision.

16. See Ballotto, *Cronologia ed evoluzione*, pp. 27, 38, 45, 61.

17. See Duff, *Literary History of Rome in the Silver Age*, pp. 481-482; Ercole, *Studi Giovenaliani*, p. 102; Highet, *Juvenal the Satirist*, pp. 11-16.

18. *History of Latin Literature*, pp. 499-500.

19. See above, note 2.

Chapter 15

THE LATE EMPIRE: SECULAR POETS

After Juvenal, we enter upon a barren period in the history of Latin poetry. Dimsdale says: "For a century after the death of Marcus Aurelius, Pagan Literature at least was practically extinct."[1] Hexameter verse shared in the general decline of literature in this period and is represented chiefly by the *Cynegetica* and *Eclogues* of Nemesianus and the medical treatise of Serenus.[2] We have also, between the Silver Age and the Late Empire, the second century Vergilian cento of Hosidius Geta, the tragedy *Medea*. This work totals 343 hexameter verses, exclusive of the choruses, the hemistichs,[3] and the lines which have either too few or too many syllables; the latter are called "over-loaded" lines.[4] The cento of Hosidius Geta is less Vergilian than the *Cento Nuptialis* of Ausonius and the religious *Cento Probae* (both will be analyzed below). In the first eight patterns we find a distribution of seventeen spondees and fifteen dactyls (Ausonius, twenty and twelve; Proba, nineteen and thirteen); although *dsss* is the first pattern, *ddsd* is fourth and *sdsd* is eighth; neither of these two patterns appears among the first eight in Vergil, Ausonius' *Cento*, or Proba, and the high position of *ddsd* is typical of Ovid and many poets of the Silver Age.

In the fourth century we have a poetic revival which lasts to the middle of the sixth century, with many writers composing hexameter verse on a variety of subjects, both secular and religious. This and the two following chapters will be devoted to an analysis and comparison of their metrical practices and an examination of their relation to the earlier classical poets, especially Vergil and Ovid.

Also, from this point on, my own procedure undergoes modification. My earlier statistics have been based on the complete hexameter works of each poet, even when, as in the case of Vergil, Ovid's *Metamorphoses*, Statius, or Silius Italicus, the total number of verses ranges from twelve to fourteen thousand. But for the late period, with eighteen writers to be considered, many of them minor and little known, such a procedure seems impracticable. Steele says: "Given the data in any work, book, or section, we cannot by multiplication get the schemata for larger units, nor can we by division of the larger get the facts for the smaller."[5] This is true to a degree; we have already seen that Lucretius is more dactylic and has less variety in his latest books, whereas in both Horace and Juvenal the later works reveal less concentration on the same hexameter patterns; also, the last three books of Vergil's *Aeneid* differ in many respects from the *Georgics* and *Aeneid* I-IX. On the other hand, we do reach from a smaller number of verses a close approximation of the patterns and percentages favored by the individual poets and their treatment of variety and repetition. The comparison of one or two books of Vergil's *Aeneid* with one or two of Ovid's *Metamorphoses* still gives an accurate idea of the differences between the two poets, and the same is true in the case of Valerius Flaccus and Silius Italicus. Likewise, when we turn to Cicero and Germanicus Caesar, we find little variation between the *Aratea* and the fragments of each, and even when a poet uses the hexameter for two entirely different literary genres, as in the case of Statius (*Thebaid* and *Silvae*) and Nemesianus (*Cynegetica* and *Eclogues*), the patterns and their percentages are almost the same, as are the frequencies of repeated patterns and reverse and opposite combinations.[6]

The analyses which follow, therefore, are based on a liberal sampling of each of the later poets, usually from a thousand to two thousand verses, but about thirty-five hundred in the case of Claudian whose output is unusually large and who is considered the best of the poets after Statius.[7] I have preferred to scan complete works or books rather than shorter and incomplete sections from a larger variety of poems. My material for the secular poets of the Late Empire is based on the following works: Avienus, *Aratea* and *Descriptio orbis terrae*; Ausonius, *Mosella* and *Cento Nuptialis* (which I list separately to show its Vergilian nature); Claudian, *In Eutropium* I and II, and the panegyrics on the fourth and sixth consulships of Honorius (these four poems I designate as Claudian I), and *De raptu Proserpinae* (= Claudian II); Sidonius, the panegyrics to Avitus and Anthemius; and finally, in the middle of the sixth century, Corippus, *Johannis* (or *De bellis Libycis*), Books I and VIII.

The order of the first eight patterns in these selected works is as follows:

	1	2	3	4	5	6	7	8
Avien., *Arat.*:	dsss	dssd	ddss	dsds	ddsd	sdss	dsdd	sdsd
Avien., *Descr.*:	dsss	dssd	dsds	ddss	sdss	dsdd	ddsd	sdsd
Auson., *Mos.*:	dssd	ddss		dsss	ssds	sdsd	dsdd	
		dsds			ddsd		dddd	
Auson., *Cento*:	dsss	ddss	ssds		ssss		sdss	
			sdds		ddds		dssd	
Claudian I:	dsds	dsss	sdss	ddss	ssds	ddds	sdds	dssd
Claudian II:	dsds	ddss	dsss	sdss	ssds	ddds	sdds	dssd
Sidonius:	dsds	dsss	ddss	sdss	ssds	ddds	sdds	dssd
Corippus:	dsds	ddss	dsss	ddds	sdss	ssds	ddsd	sdds
								dsdd

The percentages of the first, first four, and first eight patterns vary widely, as does the distribution of spondees and dactyls in the first eight patterns:

	1st pattern %	1st four %	1st eight %	Spondees	Dactyls
Avien., *Arat.*:	13.42	42.97	68.61	16	16
Avien., *Descr.*:	14.53	45.93	75.13	16	16
Auson., *Mos.*:	9.38	36.04	62.50	16-15	16-17
Auson., *Cento*:	13.74	41.98	70.99	20	12
Claudian I:	18.27	55.0	82.21	18	14
Claudian II:	18.93	57.07	84.06	18	14
Sidonius:	12.53	44.48	71.28	18	14
Corippus:	18.06	58.50	81.53	17-16	15-16

I shall discuss below the salient metrical features of these five poets and compare their treatment of variety and repetition.

Avienus: *Aratea* and *Descriptio orbis terrae*

I had originally planned to base my statistics for Avienus only on his *Aratea* (1,848 verses), but since I am changing my procedure with the hexameter poets of the Late Empire, and limiting my material to selected works, I have decided, as an additional test, to compare Avienus' *Aratea* with his *Descriptio orbis terrae* (1,363 verses).

The first eight patterns in these two didactic poems are the same, with almost no variation in order of preference: *dsss* first in both, *dssd* second, and *sdsd* eighth; *ddss* and *dsds* in third or fourth place, *sdss* in fifth or sixth, *dsdd* in sixth or seventh; *ddsd* is fifth in the *Aratea* and seventh in the *Descriptio*. With the first eight patterns identical, the distribution of spondees (sixteen) and dactyls (sixteen) is of course the same in both poems. The percentages of the patterns are somewhat higher in the *Descriptio*, especially in the first eight patterns: 75.13, but an unusually low 68.61 in the *Aratea*.

Another striking similarity in the two hexameter works of Avienus is the high incidence of spondaic verses, one every 64.7 lines in the *Aratea*, one every 48.0 in the *Descriptio*; this latter frequency is higher than we find in any other Latin hexameter poet, with the exception of Catullus LXIV, one spondaic verse every 13.6 lines, and the *Ciris*, one every 35.7 lines.

Avienus is the only poet in this group of late secular writers, with the exception of Ausonius in his *Cento Nuptialis*, who has *dsss* as his first pattern, and in this respect he follows the didactic poets of the early first century.[8] He is, however, more dactylic than the others, and resembles Columella (and Ovid) in his fondness for *dssd, ddsd,* and *dsdd* patterns. It is most unusual for *dssd* to be in second place, and its percentages in Avienus (*Aratea,* 10.71; *Descriptio,* 12.25) are higher than that of *dssd* in Ausonius' *Mosella* (9.38), where the same pattern is first, the only instance of this in a complete poem in all Latin hexameter poetry.[9] The pattern *dssd* does not appear among the first eight in Grattius, Manilius, or Nemesianus,[10] and *ddsd* and *dsdd*, the other dactylic (and Ovidian) patterns favored by Avienus, occur in neither Vergil's *Georgics*, Germanicus, Manilius, or Nemesianus, but are fifth and eighth respectively in Columella (fifth and seventh in Ovid's *Metamorphoses*).

Avienus' percentages in the *Aratea* (first pattern, first four, and first eight) are lower than those of the earlier didactic poets,[11] lower even than Vergil's, and approach those of Horace. In the *Descriptio*, the first pattern percentage resembles those of the *Aetna*, Columella, and Serenus; the percentage of the first four patterns is lower than that of the didactic poets, with the exception of Nemesianus, 45.23 (*Descriptio*, 45.93); but the percentage of the first eight patterns (75.13) is higher, with the exception of Manilius (77.33) and Columella (81.84).

When we turn to the frequencies and percentages for variety in sixteen-line units, fourth-foot texture, repeated patterns, and opposite and reverse combinations, we find that the *Aratea* and the *Descriptio* have many other similarities; these include the following (*A = Aratea, D = Descriptio*):

1. Patterns per sixteen-line unit: *A*, 9.6; *D*, 9.8; these averages are higher than in the earlier didactic poets, with the exception of Nemesianus (10.0), and likewise higher than in the other secular poets of the later period, with the exception of Ausonius (*Mosella*, 10.1; *Cento*, 10.6).

2. Percentage of sixteen-line units with eight or more patterns: *A*, 95.65; *D*, 93.83; the earlier didactic poets have lower percentages, again with the exception of Nemesianus (95.0), as do the late secular poets, with the exception of Ausonius (both *Mosella* and *Cento*, 100.0) and Sidonius (97.14).

3. Repeats plus near repeats, one every 5.1 lines in *A;* one every 4.8 in *D;* the earlier didactic poets and the late secular poets all have higher frequencies, with the following exceptions: Nemesianus, 5.2; Ausonius, *Mosella*, 5.3, and *Cento*, 6.0.

4. The *dsss* repeats plus near repeats comprise in *A* 20.33 per cent of the total repeats plus near repeats, in *D* 23.0 per cent; cf. *Aetna*, 21.09; Columella, 22.12; Nemesianus, 19.35 (but *dsds*, the most frequent repeat, 30.65); Serenus, 23.29; Sidonius *(dsds)*, 19.74.

5. The *dsss* repeats plus near repeats comprise in *A* 29.47 per cent of the total *dsss* patterns, in *D* 33.33 per cent; cf. *Aetna*, 33.70; the other didactic poets have higher percentages, with the exception of Nemesianus, 24.0 (but *dsds*, the most frequent pattern, 38.0); the late secular poets are also higher, with the exception of Sidonius *(dsds)*, 32.17.

6. In both poems, the percentage of fourth-foot homodyne is unusually high: *A*, 56.15; *D*, 51.15. The homodyne percentage in *A* is surpassed, in all Latin hexameter poetry, only by that in Catullus LXIV, 60.44; Calpurnius Siculus, *Eclogues*, 61.08; and Persius, 58.0.

7. Reverse combinations, one every 31.9 lines in *A*, one every 35.9 in *D*; cf. *Aetna*, 31.8; Germanicus, 32.2; Columella, 33.5. Reverse combinations appear less frequently in the other didactic poets, but Claudian (I, 34.7; II, 34.5) and Sidonius (35.6) resemble Avienus in this respect.

The *Aratea* and the *Descriptio* differ somewhat in certain categories, e.g., in *A* one repeat cluster every 205.3 lines (cf. *Aetna*, 212.0), in *D* one every 136.3 lines (cf. Vergil's *Georgics*, 145.5; Grattius, 134.8); one repeat every 13.1 lines in *A*, one every 12.0 in *D;* these are less frequent than in most didactic poets, with the exception of Grattius (16.3) and Nemesianus (14.8); one opposite combination every 15.4 lines in *A* (cf. Grattius, 16.8), one every 22.0 lines in *D* (cf. Vergil's *Georgics*, 20.9; *Aetna*, 22.7; Nemesianus, 21.7; Serenus, 22.9). Thus, even when we find variations between *A* and *D*, the different frequencies are well within the range of, and paralleled by, corresponding frequencies in the earlier didactic poets.

In both poems of Avienus the percentages of change in relation to the fourth-foot homodyne percentages are low, but much lower in *A* than in *D*. Nothing like this had appeared in the earlier didactic poets, with the exception of Nemesianus: *dsds* repeats, -31.69; *dsds* repeats plus near repeats, -26.43; the corresponding figures for *dsss* repeats and *dsss* repeats plus near repeats in

	A	*D*
Repeats:	-10.05	-3.78
R + NR:	-15.48	-5.51
dsss repeats:	-27.58	-7.40
dsss R + NR:	-31.49	-14.79

Germanicus are +32.92 and +11.67; in Manilius, +14.87 and +7.86. The fourth-foot homodyne percentages in these two poets are of course much lower (35.83 and 39.33 respectively), but we still have here a clear indication that Avienus in his two didactic works, and especially in the *Aratea,* had no desire to introduce variety by means of a change in fourth-foot texture. In this respect he closely resembles several Silver Age poets, such as Calpurnius Siculus (both *Eclogues* and *Laus Pisonis*), Valerius Flaccus, and Statius.[12]

In summary, despite occasional variations of a minor nature, the evidence from the *Descriptio* supports my findings for the *Aratea* and provides additional proof that the distinctions to be drawn below between the various poets of the Late Empire are sound, even though I have not scanned the total works of each.

Ausonius: *Mosella* and *Cento Nuptialis*

The *Mosella* of Ausonius is unique not merely because *dssd* appears only here as the favorite pattern in a complete poem, but also because nowhere else in Latin hexameter poetry do we find such low percentages: first pattern, 9.38; first four, 36.04; first eight, 62.50. For anything comparable we must go back to the Augustan Age, to Horace's *Ars Poetica*, where the corresponding percentages are 10.32, 36.84, 65.89. Ausonius' use of Vergilian rhythms in the *Cento Nuptialis* is very unlike his Ovidian fondness for dactyls in the *Mosella* (*ddsd* tied with *ssds* for fifth place, *dsdd* tied with *dddd* for eighth); in the *Cento* we have a more normal treatment of the patterns, with *dsss* first, and *sdss, ssss, ddds,* and *sdds* all among the first eight patterns (not the case in the *Mosella*). The percentages (first pattern, 13.74; first four, 41.98; first eight, 70.99) approach those of Vergil's *Aeneid* (14.39, 46.95, 72.78), and the distribution of spondees and dactyls (twenty and twelve) is also that of the *Aeneid* and quite unlike that in the *Mosella* (sixteen or fifteen spondees, sixteen or seventeen dactyls; cf. Avienus, sixteen spondees and sixteen dactyls in both the *Aratea* and the *Descriptio*).

In the categories of variety and repetition, we likewise find many differences between the *Mosella* (= *M*) and the *Cento Nuptialis* (= *CN*); e.g., percentage of fourth-foot homodyne, *M*, 51.97, but *CN*, 35.11 (*Aeneid,* 37.78): percentage of fourth-foot texture change in repeats in relation to fourth-foot homodyne, *M*, -1.97, but *CN*, +7.75 (*Aeneid,* +6.71); corresponding change in repeats plus near repeats, *M*, -4.72, but *CN*, +19.44 (*Aeneid,* +8.05). These and other similarities between the *Cento* and the *Aeneid* are probably the inevitable result of the use of Vergilian lines and half-lines, and the *Mosella* therefore gives us a better idea of Ausonius' metrical technique, both his unusually low frequency of patterns (and repeats) and his resultant lack of interest in fourth-foot texture change. But in some respects the *Cento* does not reflect Vergil's procedure: e.g., the average number of patterns per sixteen-line unit is the highest in Latin hexameter poetry, 10.6 (*Aeneid,* 9.4); repeats are less frequent than in any other Latin poet, one every 18.7 lines (cf. *Culex,* 18.5; Grattius, 16.3; Sidonius, 16.1; but *Aeneid,* 12.4); the same is true of repeats plus near repeats, one every 6.0 lines (*Aeneid,* 4.6). Reverse combinations occur once every 26.2 lines (*Aeneid,* 38.9; cf. *M,* 43.6); *CN* here resembles Cicero, 24.0; Horace, 29.4; Nemesianus, *Eclogues,* 24.4; and Silius Italicus, 29.0.[13]

Claudian: Public Poems and *De Raptu Proserpinae*

Claudian is very unlike Ausonius, and there is almost no difference metrically between his panegyrics and invectives (= Claudian I) and the three books of the *De raptu Proserpinae* (= Claudian II); *dsds* is first in both groups, also in the individual books and poems under consideration, and in this respect Claudian closely resembles the Silver Latin poets, Calpurnius Siculus, Valerius Flaccus, and Statius, who represent what I term the "post-Ovidian" hexameter.[14]

The first eight patterns are identical in both Claudian I and II, with a distribution of eighteen spondees and fourteen dactyls in each, the order of the second four patterns *(ssds, ddds, sdds, dssd)* is the same, the frequency percentages are equally high in both, with that of the first pattern 18.27 per cent in I and 18.93 in II. The high percentages of the first eight patterns (I, 82.21; II, 84.06) resemble those of Ovid (81.62), Columella (81.84), and Valerius Flaccus (83.85). It therefore seems impossible to agree with Dimsdale when he says of Claudian that "at times he reproduces the Virgilian rhythm";[15] the panegyrics and the invectives show the same metrical technique that appears in his mythological epic.

This is equally true of Claudian's handling of variety and repetition. I give the following details in outline form to show the amazing similarity between Claudian I and II and also to indicate again that he resembles Ovid and the Silver Age poets rather than Vergil:

1. Number of patterns per sixteen-line unit, 8.3 and 8.5; cf. Ovid, *Metamorphoses*, 8.9.
2. Percentage of units with eight or more patterns, 74.0 and 77.61; these percentages are unusually low; cf. Valerius Flaccus, 74.86.[16]
3. Repeat clusters unusually frequent, one every 67.8 and 78.9 lines; cf. Lucan, 82.7; Valerius Flaccus, 44.7.[17]
4. Low fourth-foot homodyne percentage, 33.96 and 31.86; cf. Valerius Flaccus, 31.70.
5. Repeats, one every 10.0 lines in both I and II; cf. Ovid, 10.7; Calpurnius Siculus, *Eclogues*, 10.1.
6. The most repeated pattern *(dsds)* comprises 36.63 and 35.45 of the total repeats; 19.59 and 18.66 per cent of the total pattern; in most poets the corresponding percentages are much lower, e.g., Vergil, *Aeneid*, 22.18 and 12.40; Ovid, 18.08 and 13.47; Silius Italicus, 19.71 and 12.82; Ausonius, *Mosella*, 11.76 and 9.30; but cf. Lucretius, 37.60 and 21.20; Manilius, 32.67 and 18.09; Valerius Flaccus, 46.37 and 23.72.
7. Opposite combinations, one every 21.7 and 20.4 lines (cf. Vergil, *Aeneid*, 23.1; Lucan, 22.0; Statius, *Thebaid*, 21.8, *Silvae*, 20.0; Silius Italicus, 22.3; Avienus, *Descriptio*, 22.0, etc.).
8. Reverse combinations, one every 34.7 and 34.5 lines (cf. Vergil, *Aeneid*, 38.9; Ovid; 39.3; Columella, 33.5; Avienus, *Descriptio*, 35.9; Sidonius, 35.6, etc.).
9. The favorite reverse *(ssds-sdss)* provides an unusually high proportion of the total reverses, 74.29 and 81.25 per cent.[18]

We have seen above that Statius' metrical technique shows almost no deviation in two different literary genres, epic *(Thebaid* and *Achilleid)* and occasional poetry *(Silvae)*. Claudian likewise is amazingly consistent both in his public poems and in his mythological epic. Also, in almost every aspect of his hexameter technique, Claudian must be classified as "post-Ovidian."

Sidonius and Corippus

Sidonius composed panegyrics which "follow the traditional manner and owe much to a study of Claudian."[19] Dimsdale calls him "a frigid and vastly inferior Claudian."[20] Metrically, he is very similar to Claudian; the first eight patterns are identical, as is the distribution of spondees (eighteen) and dactyls (fourteen). The order of the first eight patterns is almost the same: *dsds* in first position (as in Claudian I and II), *dsss* second (as in Claudian I), *sdss* fourth (as in Claudian II); the second four patterns are in the exact same order as in Claudian I and II. But Sidonius differs from Claudian in one important respect: he has far less concentration on the first eight patterns; the percentages (first, 12.53; first four, 44.48; first eight, 71.28) are lower even than those of Vergil, and he therefore reveals a much greater desire to avoid repetition than does Claudian.

Sidonius' greater interest in variety is seen also in many other categories: e.g., the number of patterns per sixteen-line unit, 9.5 (*C* I, 8.3; II, 8.5); percentage of units with eight or more patterns, 97.14 (*C* I, 74.0; II, 77.61); repeat clusters, one every 190.3 lines (*C* I, 67.8; II, 78.9); repeats, one every 16.1 lines (*C* I and II, 10.0); repeats plus near repeats, one every 4.9 lines (*C* I, 3.6; II, 4.0);[21] repeats and repeats plus near repeats both occur in Sidonius less frequently than in the *Aeneid*. The percentages of change in fourth-foot texture, in relation to the percentage of fourth-foot homodyne, are also much higher than in Claudian; e.g., *dsds* repeats, +0.56 (*C* I, -20.17; II, -8.78); *dsds* repeats plus near repeats, -9.06 (*C* I, -20.56; II, -15.19). With all his faults, therefore, Sidonius metrically is much less monotonous than Claudian.

Corippus, like Claudian and Sidonius, prefers *dsds* as his most frequent pattern,[22] and his percentages resemble those of Claudian: first pattern, 18.06; first four, 58.50; first eight, 81.53. His hexameters are somewhat more dactylic, however, with *ddsd* in seventh place and *dsdd* (tied with *sdds*) in eighth; neither *ddsd* or *dsdd* appear among the first eight patterns in Claudian or in Sidonius.

Corippus resembles Claudian far more closely than does Sidonius, not only in his frequencies of the first eight patterns, but also in such categories as the number of patterns per sixteen-line unit, the percentage of units with eight or more patterns, the frequency of repeats plus near repeats, the frequency of opposite combinations.[23] Repeat clusters are unusually numerous (one every 51.2 lines), even more so than in Claudian (I, 67.8; II, 78.9); Corippus has more repeat clusters than any poet after the late Republic (Lucretius, 49.2; Catullus LXIV, 29.0). His frequency of repeats (one every 8.7 lines) is therefore higher than in any other Latin poet with the exception of Catullus (7.0), Valerius Flaccus (8.6), and the Christian poet Cyprian (7.9).

In his choice and frequencies of metrical patterns and in his handling of variety and repetition Corippus thus differs much from Vergil, although the *Aeneid* in a sense is his model; Corippus claims that Johannes is a greater hero than Aeneas, but he realizes that he, as a poet, is inferior to Vergil: cf. *Praef.* 15-16:

> Aeneam superat melior virtute Iohannes,
> sed non Vergilio carmina digna cano.

He was a devout Christian, but I list him among the secular poets because his epic (in praise of the *magister militum* who had subdued the Moors) is not the usual versification of the Old or New Testament which we find so frequently among the Christian poets.

The end of the Roman Empire in the West is usually dated in 476, when Romulus Augustulus was deposed by the German Odoacer.[24] It is interesting that, seventy-five or more years later, Corippus could compose a long epic in quantitative hexameters which followed Vergil so closely in language and epic devices. Raby says: "The epic itself is well conceived, and is written without any parade of learning or of obscurity."[25]

One of Vergil's most famous verses is that in *Aen.* VI, 853:

> parcere subiectis et debellare superbos.

This appears in Corippus, I, 148-149, as follows:

> hic pietatis amor, subiectis parcere, nostrae est,
> hic virtutis honos, gentes domitare superbas.

Here, in two verses, we have four virtues — *pietas, clementia, virtus, iustitia* — and these are the virtues listed on the golden shield which Augustus received from the senate and the Roman people in 27 B.C. and which are stressed by both Vergil and Horace.[26] We should, therefore, consider Corippus as one of the most Vergilian of the late poets, in spite of his failure to follow the metrical practices of his avowed model.

Notes to Chapter 15

1. *History of Latin Literature*, p. 529.

2. For the *Eclogues* of Nemesianus, see above, Chapter 12; his *Cynegetica* and the *Liber Medicinalis* of Serenus are analyzed in Chapter 11.

3. Hosidius is the only later Latin poet to imitate Vergil in his use of half-lines.

4. See Mooney, *Hosidius Geta's Tragedy "Medea,"* pp. 26, note 2; 27, note 3.

5. *PhQ* 5 (1926), p. 219.

6. Ovid, in all his authentic works, both epic and elegiac (with the exception of the short *Medicamina*), has a distribution of twelve spondees and twenty dactyls in the first eight patterns; see above, Chapter 9, and cf. Appendix A.

7. Cf. Simcox, *History of Latin Literature*, Vol. II, p. 368; Dimsdale, *History of Latin Literature*, p. 538. Raby, *Secular Latin Poetry*, Vol. I, p. 88, says that Claudian is "by far the ablest of the secular poets of this time, and...the last authentic voice of the poetry of the old world." But, as we shall see below, Claudian is definitely "post-Ovidian" rather than "Vergilian."

8. These are Grattius, Germanicus Caesar, Manilius, and the author of the *Aetna*, all of whom show the influence of Vergil's *Georgics*; see above, Chapter 11.

9. In Ovid's *Metamorphoses, dssd* is first in Book IV and tied for first place with *ddss* in Book XI; *dssd* is also first in the sixth eclogue of Calpurnius Siculus.

10. All references to Nemesianus in this chapter are to his didactic poem on hunting, the *Cynegetica*.

11. With the exception of Grattius: percentage of first pattern, 12.99 (Avienus, *Aratea*, 13.42).

12. Petronius, although less dactylic than the "post-Ovidian" poets, likewise has very low percentages of change in fourth-foot texture in relation to the percentage of fourth-foot homodyne: repeats, -27.07; repeats plus near repeats, -9.21; *ddss* repeats, -35.40; *ddss* repeats plus near repeats, -28.99.

13. Cf. in this respect the late Christian poets, Prosper, *De ingratis*, 29.3; *De providentia Dei*, 27.3; Avitus, 26.1; Cyprian, 27.6.

14. In Ovid's *Metamorphoses, dsds* is in fourth position, less frequent than in Lucretius, Vergil, and Horace (third place in each).

15. *History of Latin Literature*, pp. 540-541; but cf. p. 539, where Dimsdale calls the *Rape of Proserpina* an "unfinished Ovidian hexameter poem"; so Duff, *Literary History of Rome in the Silver Age*, p. 526. Henry, "Epic Poetry, Latin," in *OCD*, p. 322, says that "in the *De raptu Proserpinae*, Claudian shows a perfect mastery of the epic style and metre;" obviously "epic" here is not to be equated with "Vergilian."

16. Cf. Corippus, 77.63; the percentages in the Christian poets are all higher, with the exception of Avitus (75.37) and Cyprian (50.62).

17. Repeat clusters are most frequent in the Republican period (Cicero, 59.6; Lucretius, 49.2; Catullus LXIV, 29.0) and in the Late Empire (Corippus, 51.2; Avitus, 65.3; Dracontius, 78.1; Cyprian, 54.0; Arator, 67.2).

18. These percentages are surpassed only by that of *sdss-ssds* in Cyprian, an astounding 95.74 per cent of the total reverse combinations. Other high percentages are those of *ssds-sdss*: Catullus LXIV, 71.43; Grattius, 71.43; Lucan, 70.05; of *dsdd-ddsd* in Ovid's *Metamorphoses*, 71.05. The following percentages are more normal: *sssd-dsss*: Lucretius, 39.86; Vergil, *Georgics*, 38.30; Germanicus, 38.10; *ssds-sdss*: Vergil, *Aeneid*, 40.08; Persius, 38.46; Sidonius, 43.75; *ddsd-dsdd*: Statius, *Thebaid*, 38.16.

19. Raby, *Secular Latin Poetry*, Vol. I, p. 77.

20. *History of Latin Literature*, p. 545. Cf. also Anderson, *Sidonius*, Vol. I, p. liii, who adds: "Sidonius observes all the pitiable conventions of the *genre*, and succeeds in writing three 'poems' which for prolonged insipidity, absurdity, and futility would be hard to beat."

21. Cf. also the following: most repeated pattern, percentage of total repeats, 19.72 (*C* I, 36.63; II, 35.45), and percentage of total pattern, 9.79 (*C* I, 19.59; II, 18.66). The favorite reverse combination comprises 43.75 per cent of the total reverses (*C* I, 74.29; II, 81.25).

22. The pattern *dsds* is also in first place in the "post-Ovidian" poets, Calpurnius Siculus, Valerius Flaccus, Statius, Nemesianus, and, in the late Christian poets, Paulinus of Nola, Sedulius, Paulinus of Périgueux, and Arator.

23. Corippus shows less interest than Claudian in reverse combinations, one every 49.2 lines (*C* I, 34.7; II, 34.5).

24. It is ironical that the last Roman emperor of the Western Empire bore the names of both Romulus and (in diminutive form) Augustus, the founders of Rome and its Empire.

25. *Secular Latin Poetry*, Vol. I, p. 144.

26. See Duckworth, *TAPhA* 87 (1956), pp. 299-308.

Chapter 16

THE LATE EMPIRE: CHRISTIAN "VERGILIAN" POETS

The Christian hexameter poets of the fourth and fifth centuries are surprisingly numerous and follow the epic tradition; they go back to the classical poets and especially Vergil. Raby says.[1]

> When Latin Christian poetry really began in the West, the main literary influence could hardly fail to be that of the Latin classical poets, the only possible models for men who had received their education in the public schools.... Virgil was their model, and their subjects were taken, as a rule, from sacred history.

My metrical analyses of the Christian poets include the following authors and works (in approximate chronological order):

Fourth century:
    Juvencus, *Libri Evangeliorum* I and IV
    Prudentius, *Psychomachia* and *Hamartigenia*
    Proba, *Probae Cento*
Fourth-fifth centuries:
    Paulinus of Nola (c. 355-431), *Carmina* V, XV, and XXIII
Fifth century:
    Prosper of Aquitaine, *De ingratis*
    De providentia Dei, often ascribed to Prosper
    Sedulius, *Paschale carmen* I, II, and V
    Marius Victor, *Alethia* I and II
    Paulinus of Pella, *Eucharisticus*
    Paulinus of Périgueux, *De vita Martini* I and IV
    Dracontius, *De laudibus Dei* I, and *De raptu Helenae*
    Avitus, *De spiritalis historiae gestis* I ("De mundi initio") and V ("De transitu maris rubri")
    Cyprian of Gaul, *Heptateuchos* II ("Exodus")
Sixth century:
    Arator, *De actibus Apostolorum* I[2]

I do not include Commodian in the list of Christian poets given above, because he writes in accentual rather than in quantitative hexameters. Raby suggests that "his neglect of quantity may perhaps be conscious and studied...[the verses] are only rhythmical in the sense that they were meant to be read according to their word-accent, as though they were prose."[3] The ending of each line is usually quantitative, but this results from the normal coincidence of word-accent and metrical ictus in the last two feet. To illustrate Commodian's accentual rhythm and his disregard of quantity, I quote the first six verses of his *Carmen Apologeticum*:

> Quis poterit unum proprie Deum nosse caelorum,
> Quis nisi quem sustulerit ab errore nefando?
> Errabam ignarus spatians spe captus inani.
> Dum furor aetatis primae me portabat in auras,
> Plus eram quam palea levior; quasi centum adessent
> In humeris capita, sic praeceps quocumque ferebar.

Rand says of Commodian that his "most interesting characteristic is his illiteracy — or his unmetricality. His little knowledge of the Virgilian hexameter was a dangerous thing for art; his verse is fearfully and wonderfully made."[4] Fortunately, the other Christian poets, from Juvencus to Arator, are quantitative and not accentual.

I discuss in this chapter the Christian poets who seem most Vergilian, with *dsss* the first pattern in each instance, and who usually have a high proportion of spondees in the first eight patterns.

These poets are Juvencus, Proba, Prosper (and the anonymous *De providentia Dei*), Marius Victor, Paulinus of Pella, and Avitus. Their choice of the first eight patterns is as follows:

	1	2	3	4	5	6	7	8
Juvencus:	*dsss*	*ddss*	*sdss*	*ssss*	*dsds*	*ssds*	*dssd*	*sdds*
Proba:	*dsss*	*dsds*	*ddss*	*sdss*	*ddds*	*sdds*	*ssss*	*dssd*
Prosper, *De ingr.*:	*dsss*	*dsds*	*sdss*	*ssss*	*ddss*	*ssds*	*dssd*	*ddds*
De provid. Dei:	*dsss*	*dsds*	*ddss*	*sdss*	*ssds*	*ssss*	*sdds*	*ddds*
Marius Victor:	*dsss*	*ddss*	*dsds*		*ssds*	*ddds*	*sdds*	*ddsd*
			sdss					
Paul. of Pella:	*dsss*	*sdss*	*ddss*	*dsds*	*dssd*	*ddds*	*ddsd*	*ssss*
Avitus:	*dsss*	*sdss*	*ssds*	*ssss*	*ddss*	*dsds*	*sdds*	*dssd*

All the poets in this group seem Vergilian to a decided degree, more so than the secular poets analyzed in the preceding chapter. Not only is *dsss* in first position in each instance, but seven of the first eight patterns are identical with the first eight in Vergil's *Aeneid*, with one exception, Paulinus of Pella (*dssd* and *ddsd*); in the *De providentia Dei*, the first eight are those of Vergil in slightly different order. The Vergilian nature of these poets is shown especially by the prominent position assigned to *ssss*, which among the secular poets of the Late Empire had appeared in the list of the first eight patterns only (and understandably) in Ausonius' *Cento*. All the poets in this group, with the exception of Marius Victor, include *ssss* among their first eight patterns, and it is in fourth place in Juvencus, Prosper, and Avitus.

The relevant percentages, with the distribution of spondees and dactyls in the first eight patterns, are also of interest:

	1st pattern	1st four		1st eight	
	%	%	%	Spondees	Dactyls
Juvencus:	15.28	48.89	76.85	21	11
Proba:	13.71	50.22	74.89	19	13
Prosper, *De ingr.*:	15.45	45.54	72.62	20	12
De provid. Dei:	13.62	43.71	70.48	20	12
Marius Victor:	14.26	48.96	75.66	17	15
Paul. of Pella:	12.93	44.35	69.39	18	14
Avitus:	18.09	52.73	82.30	21	11

These percentages are in the Vergilian range with two exceptions: Paulinus of Pella, who has less concentration on the first eight patterns and thus resembles Horace rather than Vergil; and Avitus, whose higher percentages are those of Ovid, Valerius Flaccus, and Claudian. Juvencus and Avitus are both heavily spondaic, with twenty-one spondees and eleven dactyls; this is the distribution found in Lucilius, Horace (*Satires* I, *Epistles* I and II), Germanicus Caesar, the *Aetna*, Petronius, and Juvenal.[5]

Juvencus and Avitus

Labriolle says that, if Commodian is put in the fourth or fifth century, "Juvencus should be reckoned the first Christian poet in the Latin tongue."[6] But the date of Commodian is not really important in this connection; Juvencus was the first of a long line of Christian poets to write in *quantitative* hexameters, and, as all agree, "Virgil is his great master."[7] It is Avitus, however, who is praised as the "Christian Vergil",[8] his *De spiritalis historiae gestis* is considered "the best of all the Biblical epics,"[9] and Raby considers his poetical talent to be "above that of Juvencus or indeed of any of the 'epic' poets of the Church."[10] In his heavy concentration on the first eight patterns, however, Avitus is definitely less Vergilian than is Juvencus.

When we turn to the various categories of variety and repetition, neither Juvencus nor Avitus seems particularly Vergilian. This lack of Vergilian variety may be seen, for example, in the number of patterns per sixteen-line unit (9.0 and 8.6); the percentage of units with eight or more patterns (84.69 and 75.37); the frequency of repeat clusters (one every 87.1 and 65.3 lines); the frequency of repeated patterns (one every 10.8 and 10.1 lines); the frequency of repeats plus near repeats (one every 3.9 and 4.0 lines); in every instance but the final one Avitus consistently has greater repetition and consequently is farther from the Vergilian norm. But in these same categories Prosper in the *De ingratis* is much closer to Vergil, and Paulinus of Pella has even less repetition; e.g., average number of patterns per sixteen-line unit, 9.4 and 9.7 respectively (*Aeneid*, 9.4); percentage of units with eight or more patterns, 88.71 and 89.21 (*Aeneid*, 92.46); repeat clusters once every 110.8 and 203.7 lines (*Aeneid*, 200.1); repeats once every 12.2 and 15.3 lines (*Aeneid*, 12.4); repeats plus near repeats, one every 4.3 and 5.6 lines (*Aeneid*, 4.6). In their desire for variety, therefore, both Prosper and Paulinus of Pella resemble Vergil more closely than do either Juvencus and Avitus, although both are praised as Vergilian.

Proba and Marius Victor

Prosper and Paulinus of Pella in their patterns and percentages seem as Vergilian as Proba, and in their categories of variety and repetition somewhat closer to the *Aeneid*, even though she composes her poem in Vergilian lines and half-lines.

Proba's Christian *Cento*, however, is more Vergilian in several respects than the secular *Cento Nuptialis* (= *CN*) of Ausonius, e.g., average number of patterns per sixteen-line unit, 9.3; *Aeneid*, 9.4 (*CN*, 10.6); one repeat every 11.2 lines; *Aeneid*, 12.4 (*CN*, 18.7); the most frequent repeat comprises 24.19 per cent of the total repeats; *Aeneid*, 22.18 (*CN*, 42.86); the favorite repeat plus near repeats comprises 20.57 of the total repeats plus near repeats; *Aeneid*, 23.15 (*CN*, 36.36); one opposite every 25.7 lines; *Aeneid*, 23.1 (*CN*, 18.7).

The poet in this group who resembles Proba (= *P*) most closely is Marius Victor: e.g., he has 9.1 patterns per sixteen-line unit (*P*, 9.3), 85.29 per cent of the units with eight or more patterns (*P*, 88.37), one repeat every 11.1 lines (*P*, 11.2), one repeat plus near repeat every 4.0 lines (*P*, 4.0); the favorite repeat comprises 24.24 per cent of the total repeats (*P*, 24.19) and 15.22 of the total pattern (*P*, 16.30); the favorite repeat plus near repeats provides 21.90 per cent of all repeats plus near repeats (*P*, 20.57) and 38.22 of the total pattern (*P*, 39.13); one opposite combination every 26.9 lines (*P*, 25.7). The percentage of change in the repeats differs from the homodyne percentage +11.98 (*P*, +10.53), a striking similarity paralleled in this group only by the corresponding figure in Juvencus (+8.21), but, in the case of the most repeated pattern, Marius Victor is very unlike Proba: repeats, +11.47; *P*, -7.96; repeats plus near repeats, +6.47; *P*, -4.07.[11]

The Authorship of the *De providentia Dei*

The anonymous *De providentia Dei* has been assigned by many scholars to Prosper of Aquitaine. McHugh in his recent edition discusses the frequency of the verse patterns in the *De providentia* and in Prosper's *De ingratis*, also the percentages of spondees and dactyls, and compares the two poems with the classical poets, especially Vergil.[12] He finds that the two poems are similar and reasonably close to the Vergilian norm, but on the question of authorship he concludes that "no final decision could be reached."[13]

New light can now be thrown on the problem by a comparison of these two works with the other late Christian poems. The *De ingratis* and the *De providentia* are the only two works in the Christian "Vergilian" group which have the Vergilian distribution of twenty spondees and twelve dactyls in the first eight patterns; not only is the first pattern *(dsss)* identical, but also the second *(dsds)* and the eighth *(ddds)*. This last is sufficiently unusual to justify added comment: *ddds* is in eighth position also in Cicero, Catullus LXIV, Horace, Silius Italicus, and Serenus, and it does not appear among the first eight patterns in Ennius, Germanicus Caesar, the *Aetna*, Petronius, Juvenal, nor, in the late period, in Avienus, Ausonius *(Mosella)*, Juvencus, Avitus, or Paulinus of Périgueux. But in all the other Roman poets, both classical (including Vergil and Ovid) and later, *ddds* has a normal range from fourth to sixth position. This similarity in the frequency of *ddds* in the *De ingratis* and the *De providentia* gives strong support to Prosper's authorship of the latter poem.

The categories of variety and repetition provide additional evidence of value. When we compare the metrical features of the *De providentia* with those of Prosper's *De ingratis*, we find several differences (especially in the percentages of the pattern most frequently repeated), but the similarities seem more significant and are more numerous — too numerous, I am convinced, to be the result of coincidence. In most instances the *De providentia* (= *P*) resembles the *De ingratis* (= *I*) and usually only the *De ingratis*; I summarize, in outline form, the most important similarities, and also comment on the corresponding technique of the other poets in this group:

1. Percentage of fourth-foot homodyne: *P*, 45.43; *I*, 44.76. Avitus, 44.06; the others range from 34.63 to 38.53, with the exception of Paulinus of Pella, 51.47.
2. Repeats, one every *x* lines: *P*, 11.8; *I*, 12.2. The others range from 10.1 to 11.2, except Paulinus of Pella, 15.3.
3. Percentage of change in fourth-foot texture: *P*, 39.19; *I*, 40.24. The others range from 42.72 to 50.51.
4. Differs from homodyne percentage: *P*, -6.24; *I*, -4.52. The others range from -1.34 to +11.98.
5. Repeats plus near repeats, one every *x* lines: *P*, 5.2; *I*, 4.3. The others 3.9 and 4.0, except Paulinus of Pella, 5.6.
6. Opposite combinations, one every *x* lines: *P*, 16.8; *I*, 19.2. The others range from 21.8 to 30.7.
7. Most frequent opposite, percentage of total opposites: *P*, 19.23; *I*, 19.23. Juvencus, 19.30; the others from 25.0 to 33.33.
8. Reverse combinations, one every *x* lines: *P*, 27.3; *I*, 29.3. Avitus, 26.1; the others from 30.3 to 55.5.
9. Most frequent reverse, percentage of total reverses: *P*, 43.75; *I*, 44.12. The others range from 35.71 to 36.36 and from 51.92 to 65.0.

To these convincing resemblances between the two poems may be added the following evidence based on the individual opposite combinations:

	% *ssdd* with *ddss*	% *dsdd* with *sdss*	% *sdsd* with *dsds*
De providentia:	25.64	20.0	23.53
De ingratis:	25.0	17.65	22.73
Juvencus:	25.0	28.95	9.26
Proba:	63.64	4.55	28.13
Marius Victor:	5.0	9.09	19.15
Paulinus of Pella:	8.33	5.56	9.38
Avitus:	12.50	35.29	26.83

Here, too, the variation among the other poets is so great and the *De providentia Dei* and the *De ingratis* are so similar that we need have no hesitation in asserting that Prosper of Aquitaine is the author of the *De providentia Dei*.

Notes to Chapter 16

1. *Christian-Latin Poetry*, pp. 4, 76. Rand, *TAPhA* 51 (1920), p. 81, refers to the "writers who, in a steady stream from the time of Juvencus, had essayed to turn the Holy Scriptures into Virgilian epic."

2. On the Christian poets in general, see Labriolle, *History and Literature of Christianity*, pp. 311-332, 446-494; Rand, *Founders of the Middle Ages*, pp. 181-217; Raby, *Christian-Latin Poetry*, pp. 44-120; Hudson-Williams, *PVS* 6 (1966-67), pp. 11-21.

3. *Christian-Latin Poetry*, p. 14. Commodian is to be dated about the middle of the third century, not in the fourth or fifth; see Raby, *ibid.*, p. 11, note 4.

4. *Founders of the Middle Ages*, pp. 181-182. On Commodian's complete ignorance of quantity, see Sturtevant, *Language* 2 (1926), pp. 223-237.

5. Silius Italicus is also heavily spondaic; of the seventeen books of his *Punica*, six have a distribution of twenty-one spondees and eleven dactyls, five have twenty-two and ten.

6. *History and Literature of Christianity*, p. 314.

7. Rand, *Founders of the Middle Ages*, p. 197; cf. Raby, *Christian-Latin Poetry*, p. 17, who says that the *Evangeliorum libri* are "thoroughly Virgilian"; see also Labriolle, *History and Literature of Christianity*, p. 316.

8. See Schippers, *Avitus, De mundi initio*, p. 3.

9. Rand, *Founders of the Middle Ages*, p. 203; cf. Labriolle, *History and Literature of Christianity*, p. 488: "the most remarkable poem inspired by the book of Genesis in the Vth century."

10. *Christian-Latin Poetry*, p. 78.

11. For other differences, cf. the following percentages: *sddd* with its opposite *dsss*, 36.36 (*P*, 16.67); *ssdd* with *ddss*, 5.0 (*P*, 63.64); *sdsd* with *dsds*, 19.15 (*P*, 28.13).

12. *Carmen de Providentia Dei*, pp. 215-225; cf. Labriolle, *History and Literature of Christianity*, p. 432, note 1.

13. *Carmen de Providentia Dei*, p. vii.

Chapter 17

THE LATE EMPIRE: CHRISTIAN "POST-OVIDIAN" POETS

The other seven Christian poets are less Vergilian and should perhaps be termed "post-Ovidian," since many favor *dsds* as their first pattern in the manner of the Silver Age poets (Calpurnius Siculus, Valerius Flaccus, and Statius) and in general they are more dactylic. This group consists of Prudentius, Paulinus of Nola, Sedulius, Paulinus of Périgueux, Dracontius, Cyprian, and Arator.

The first eight patterns are as follows:

	1	2	3	4	5	6	7	8
Prudentius:	*ddss*	*dsds*	*sdss*	*dsss*	*ddds*	*ddsd*	*dssd*	*ssds*
Paul. of Nola:	*dsds*	*dsss*	*ddss*	*sdss*	*dssd*	*ddds*	*ddsd*	*ssds*
Sedulius:	*dsds*	*ddss*	*ddds*	*dsss*	*dssd*	*sdss*	*sdds*	*ssds*
Paul. of Périg.:	*dsds*	*dsss*	*sdss*	*ddss*	*ssss*	*ssds*	*dssd*	*sdds*
Dracontius:	*ddss*	*dsds*	*ssds*	*dsss*	*ddds*	*sdss*	*ddsd*	*dssd*
Cyprian:	*ssds*	*dsss*	*ddss* *sdss*		*dsds*	*sdds*	*ddds*	*ssss*
Arator:	*dsds*	*ddsd*	*ddds*	*ddss*	*ssds*	*dsdd*	*sdsd*	*dsss* *sdds*

In the choice of patterns, we find much more variation here than in the Christian poets whom I have called "Vergilian." The first pattern is *dsds*, with the exception of Prudentius and Dracontius, who prefer *ddss*, and Cyprian, who in this respect is almost unique: his first pattern is *ssds*, and no poet in the entire range of Latin hexameter poetry before the fifth century so favors this pattern; it usually varies from fifth to eighth position, but is third in Avitus and Dracontius (and first in Dracontius' *De raptu Helenae*). The favorite pattern of the Vergilian Christian poets, *dsss*, is now second or fourth, with the exception of Arator, where it is tied with *sdds* for eighth place; only in the *Eclogues* of Calpurnius Siculus do we elsewhere find *dsss* in such a low position.

The pattern *ssss* ranges from fourth to eighth position in the Vergilian group (with the exception of Marius Victor); among these poets it appears among the first eight patterns only in Paulinus of Périgueux and Cyprian (cf. the late secular poets, where it occurs only in Ausonius' *Cento*); *ssss* is fifteenth in Sedulius and sixteenth in Prudentius and Arator. On the other hand, in this group, *dddd* appears among the last two patterns only in Paulinus of Périgueux; among the Christian poets of Chapter 16, *dddd* is fifteenth or sixteenth in all but Proba and Marius Victor.

The percentages in this final group of poets have an unusually wide range, as does the distribution of spondees and dactyls in the first eight patterns:

	1st pattern	1st four		1st eight	
	%	%	%	Spondees	Dactyls
Prudentius:	11.31	42.77	70.79	17	15
Paul. of Nola:	12.82	43.05	69.96	17	15
Sedulius:	15.72	48.07	75.37	18	14
Paul. of Périg.:	13.31	48.44	78.19	21	11
Dracontius:	13.66	47.87	74.04	17	15
Cyprian:	16.58	59.91	91.06	20	12
Arator:	16.19	49.77	76.56	15-14	17-18

The percentage of the first pattern in Prudentius (11.31) is lower than in any other poet of the Late Empire, with the exception of Ausonius in the *Mosella* (9.38). In the case of the first eight patterns, the percentages are low both in Prudentius and Paulinus of Nola, 70.79 and 69.96 respectively, and resemble those in the *De providentia Dei* (70.48) and Paulinus of Pella (69.39);[1] the percentages are average in the other poets of this group, from 74.04 to 78.19, with the exception of Cyprian, who has an amazingly high 91.06; there is nothing like this in all Latin hexameter poetry with the exception of Catullus LXIV (90.98) and Vergil, *Eclogue* IV (91.93). As to the distribution of spondees and dactyls in the first eight patterns, Paulinus of Périgueux and Cyprian are heavily spondaic (cf. Juvencus, Prosper, both *De ingratis* and *De providentia Dei*, and Avitus); the other poets of this group have a larger proportion of dactyls and thus resemble the Silver Age poets (though less dactylic than Calpurnius Siculus, and, with the exception of Arator, less so than Columella, Valerius Flaccus, and Statius).

Prudentius and Paulinus of Nola

Prudentius is praised not only as "the first great Christian poet,"[2] but also because "he has mastered the art of the Virgilian hexameter with more delicacy than those martial and resonant singers, Juvenal, Lucan, and Claudian."[3] But with *dsss* in fourth place and *ssss* in sixteenth, and with both *dssd* and *ddsd* included among the first eight patterns, Prudentius in his choice of patterns seems definitely more Ovidian than Vergilian, more so certainly than Lucan, Juvenal, or Claudian, none of whom includes *ddsd* among his first eight patterns. In Paulinus of Nola, *dssd* and *ddsd* appear in fifth and seventh position, respectively. In their lower percentages (first, first four, and first eight patterns), however, both Prudentius and Paulinus of Nola are more Vergilian than either Lucan or Claudian.

Not only do Prudentius and Paulinus of Nola have the lowest percentages in this group of Christian poets, but they are the most Vergilian in several other respects; this may be seen especially in the number of patterns per sixteen-line unit (9.6 and 9.4), their avoidance of repeat clusters (one every 311.0 and 170.3 lines), and the relative infrequency of repeats (one every 12.7 and 11.0 lines) and repeats plus near repeats (one every 4.8 and 4.6 lines).

From Sedulius to Arator

Sedulius also studied Vergil carefully,[4] but he likewise departs from his model in his dislike for *ssss* (fifteenth place); *dsss* is in fourth position, as in Prudentius and Dracontius. Arator, "the last important Italian poet of the sixth century,"[5] is also the most dactylic, with *ddsd* second and *dsdd* sixth, and in no other Christian poet does *dsdd* appear among the first eight patterns;[6] *dsss* is tied (with *sdds*) for eighth place, a position paralleled elsewhere in Latin hexameter poetry only in the *Eclogues* of Calpurnius Siculus, and *ssss* is sixteenth, as in Prudentius. We can therefore consider the last of the ancient Christian poets the most Ovidian of them all.

The Christian poets from Sedulius to Arator display almost no interest in any form of metrical variety: the average number of patterns per sixteen-line unit decreases from 9.0 in Sedulius to 7.6 in Cyprian; the repeat clusters increase in frequency from one every 98.9 lines in Sedulius to one every 54.0 lines in Cyprian, repeats increase from one every 10.4 lines in Sedulius to one every 7.9 in Cyprian, and repeats and near repeats from one every 4.1 lines in Sedulius and Dracontius to one every 3.2 in Cyprian. In the case of the most repeated pattern, the percentages of change in fourth-foot texture reach new and unheard-of lows, with the exception of Dracontius, whose percentages of change (repeats, 52.88; repeats plus near repeats, 58.33) are unusually high and resemble or surpass the corresponding percentages of several Christian poets in the "Vergilian" group (Prosper, Marius Victor, Paulinus of Pella, and Avitus).

We have seen above that Claudian's metrical technique in his mythological epic and in his public poems is practically identical; this is not true of Dracontius, whose secular poem, *De raptu Helenae* (= *H*) differs surprisingly from his religious work, *De laudibus Dei* (= *L*): the three most frequent patterns in *H* are *ssds, dsds, ddss*; in *L, ddss, dsds, dsss; ssds* as a preferred pattern is most unusual, and is paralleled only by Cyprian, where *ssds* is first, *dsss* second, and *ddss* tied with *sdss* for third place. In general *H* has less repetition than *L*: repeat clusters once every 93.4 lines in *H*, but once every 68.4 in *L*; one repeat every 10.2 lines in *H*, but one every 9.4 in *L*; one repeat plus near repeat every 4.3 lines in *H*, but one every 3.9 in *L*. The percentage of fourth-foot homodyne in *H* is a low 31.80, but 37.50 in *L*. Although *H* has fewer repeats, it also has much lower percentages of change in fourth-foot texture: repeats, *H*, 28.13; *L*, 41.25; repeats plus near repeats, *H*, 25.83; *L*, 39.79. In the case of the most repeated pattern (*dsds* in *H*, *ddss* in *L*), the percentages of change are as follows: repeats: *H*, 20.0; *L*, 54.17; repeats plus near repeats: *H*, 16.13; *L*, 58.82. The low percentages of change in fourth-foot texture produce in the *De raptu Helenae* a monotony similar to that found in Valerius Flaccus, Claudian, Corippus, Arator, and especially Cyprian.

Arator is less extreme in his desire for repetition than Cyprian, who is not only unusual in his choice of patterns and in his high percentage of the first eight patterns but who approaches the nadir of Latin hexameter variety; e.g., repeats once every 7.9 lines; repeats plus near repeats once every 3.2 lines; nothing like this had appeared since Catullus LXIV, in the first century B.C., where the corresponding frequencies are 7.0 and 3.0. But in percentage of change in fourth-foot texture, Cyprian is far lower than Catullus; this is seen especially in the pattern most frequently repeated:

	Catullus	Cyprian
% of fourth-foot homodyne:	60.44	34.16
Most frequent repeat:	*dsss*	*ssds*
% of change	37.50	2.63
Differs from homodyne %:	-22.94	-31.53
R + NR, % of change:	34.62	2.22
Differs from homodyne %:	-25.82	-31.94

These percentages of change in Cyprian's most repeated pattern (2.63 and 2.22) are almost incredible; out of thirty-eight *ssds* repeats, only one has a fourth-foot texture change; the *ssds* repeats plus near repeats total ninety, with a change in only two instances.

In one other respect Cyprian is abnormal: reverse combinations are more than twice as frequent as opposites, once every 27.6 lines to once every 59.0,[7] and his treatment of the reverse combinations is also unique; of the four possible reverses he has two instances of *sssd-dsss* and forty-five of *sdss-ssds;* these last comprise 95.74 per cent of the total reverses, and nothing like this had happened earlier in the whole history of Latin hexameter poetry.

Notes to Chapter 17

1. The percentages of Avienus, *Aratea*, and Ausonius, *Mosella*, are the lowest in this late period, 68.61 and 62.50 respectively.

2. Raby, *Christian-Latin Poetry*, p. 44; cf. p. 61: the *Psychomachia* "presents the first poetical Christian allegory, an original creation;" see also Rand, *TAPhA* 51 (1920), p. 81.

3. Rand, *Founders of the Middle Ages*, p. 184.

4. See Labriolle, *History and Literature of Christianity*, p. 476.

5. Raby, *Christian-Latin Poetry*, p. 117.

6. In this respect Arator resembles Ovid (*dsdd* seventh), Calpurnius Siculus (sixth), Columella X (eighth), Valerius Flaccus (seventh), Statius (sixth or seventh), Avienus (sixth or seventh); in Ausonius *(Mosella)* and Corippus *dsdd* is tied for eighth place.

7. After the Republican period (Cicero and the *Dirae*), reverse combinations appear more frequently than opposites also in Nemesianus *(Eclogues)*, Paulinus of Périgueux, and Avitus, but never twice as often; see above, Chapter 12 ("Calpurnius Siculus and Nemesianus").

Chapter 18

REPETITION IN LATE GREEK HEXAMETER POETRY

The poets of the Late Empire who have the greatest amount of repetition and are thus farthest from the Vergilian norm are Claudian and Corippus among the secular writers, Cyprian and Avitus among the Christian writers. With the exception of Cyprian, however, these poets differ little from Ovid and his imitators, especially Calpurnius Siculus, Valerius Flaccus, and Statius. The two Latin poets most conspicuous for their lack of metrical variety are the fifth century Cyprian and Catullus LXIV, of the first century B.C., but their monotonous repetition of the same metrical patterns is far less striking (and less offensive) than what we find in the Greek hexameter poets of the fourth and fifth centuries A.D.

Greek hexameter poetry from the very beginning is heavily didactic. The first four patterns in Homer are *dddd, dsdd, sddd,* and *ssdd,* and the distribution of dactyls and spondees in the first eight patterns is twenty-two dactyls, ten spondees, the exact opposite of that in the fragments of Ennius (ten dactyls, twenty-two spondees); Ennius' first pattern is *ssss,* which is sixteenth in Homer. The percentages in Homer are high: first pattern, 21.36; first four, 59.90; first eight, 85.42;[1] these are not unlike the corresponding percentages in the Roman poets Valerius Flaccus, Claudian, and Avitus. But the Greek poets of fourth and fifth centuries A.D. display an almost incredible amount of repetition.[2]

I now compare Catullus LXIV and Cyprian with three late Greek poets, Quintus of Smyrna, Nonnus, and Musaeus:

	Catullus	Cyprian	Quintus	Nonnus	Musaeus
First pattern:	*dsss*	*ssds*	*dddd*	*dddd*	*dddd*
% 1st pattern:	27.59	16.58	38.75	35.52	36.07
Second pattern:	*sdss*	*dsss*	*dsdd*	*dsdd*	*dsdd*
Third pattern:	*ddss*	{ *ddss*	*sddd*	*ddds*	*sddd*
Fourth pattern:	*dsds*	{ *sdss*	*ddds*	*sddd*	*ddds*
% 1st four:	67.90	59.91	81.77	84.78	82.99
% 1st eight:	90.98	91.06	96.15	99.79	98.83
Spondees:	20	20	10	10	10
Dactyls:	12	12	22	22	22
Patterns per 16-line unit:	7.0	7.6	6.0	5.5	6.0
% units with 8 or more:	30.43	50.62	13.33	0.	0.
Repeat clusters, 1 every *x* lines:	29.0	54.0	18.5	15.7	17.1
R, 1 every *x* lines	7.0	7.9	4.7	4.8	5.4
R + NR, 1 every *x* lines:	3.0	3.2	2.2	2.1	2.3
Most frequent repeat:	*dsss*	*ssds*	*dddd*	*dddd*	*dddd*
% total repeats:	44.44	23.17	66.50	56.50	71.43
% total pattern:	23.08	17.67	54.57	33.14	36.59
1 opposite every *x* lines:	37.7	59.0	320.0	960.0	341.0
1 reverse every *x* lines:	53.9	27.6	38.4	20.9	21.3

The late Greek poets avoid the more spondaic patterns; in 960 lines of Quintus of Smyrna, *dsss* and *ssss* do not appear at all, and there is only one instance of *ddss, sdss,* and *ssds.* Nonnus is even more limited in his choice of patterns: in 960 lines, *dssd* and *sdsd* are tied for eighth position with only *two* instances each; the following patterns do not appear: *dsss, ddss, sdss, ssss, ssds, sssd,* and *ssdd.* Musaeus in his *Hero and Leander* (341 verses) is almost as extreme: the eighth pattern, *sdsd,* occurs four times, *dssd* three, and *ssdd* once; again the more spondaic patterns

135

(dsss, ddss, sdss, ssss, ssds, and *sssd)* do not appear. As a result, the first four patterns have higher percentages than do the first *eight* in most Latin poets, and the percentages of the first eight patterns in these Greek poets (from 96.15 to 99.79) prove again that the other eight patterns are almost totally ignored. Also, *dddd,* the first pattern, has percentages from 35.52 (Nonnus) to 38.75 (Quintus); again there is nothing like this in Latin hexameter poetry. In the case of Quintus, the frequent use of spondaic verses (one every 14.3 lines) provides an additional type of variety, but there are no spondaic verses in either Nonnus or Musaeus.

The repetition of *dddd* in these three poets is almost unbelievable. In the Latin poets, the same pattern seldom appears more than four times in succession.[3] In the late Greek poets, we find numerous passages with the same pattern five and six times in succession; we have seven instances of *dddd* in Quintus XIV, 23-29, and eight in I, 112-119. As a result of the numerous *dddd* repeats and near repeats, there are fourteen instances of *dddd* in twenty lines, in I, 106-125, and fifteen instances in eighteen lines, in XIV, 18-35. Likewise, in Nonnus we find seven instances of *dddd* in ten lines (I, 133-142), ten in twelve (I, 163-174); eight in twelve in Musaeus (66-77), eleven in sixteen lines (184-199), etc. We have in both Nonnus and Musaeus no sixteen-line units with eight or more patterns, and in all three poets the frequencies both of repeats and of repeats plus near repeats rise to unheard-of highs.

Repetition of the same pattern can assuredly go little farther in hexameter poetry. Catullus and Cyprian, deficient in metrical variety as they are, still avoid the excessive monotony found in the late Greek poets.

Notes to Chapter 18

1. See above, Chapter 1, note 11.

2. In the Hellenistic period, Callimachus in his *Hymns* has less variety than Aratus, Theocritus, or Apollonius of Rhodes, and resembles the late Greek poets; see Table III.

3. In all Latin hexameter poetry I have found only nineteen instances of the same pattern repeated five times in succession; six (almost one-third of the total) in Lucretius, two in Vergil, one in Horace, one in Ovid, one in Germanicus Caesar, two in Manilius, three in Valerius Flaccus, one in Statius *(Silvae),* one in Juvenal, and one in Claudian. Only in Catullus LXIV (99-104) does the same pattern *(sdss)* appear in six lines in succession.

Chapter 19

FACTS AND FINDINGS: A RECAPITULATION

With Corippus and Arator (both dated in the mid-sixth century) we come to the end of ancient Latin hexameter verse. This is roughly seven and one-half centuries after Ennius introduced the quantitative hexameter into Latin poetry. We have traversed this entire period of Roman literature and have compared the metrical procedures of many poets; Vergil's *Aeneid*, renowned for its rhythmical perfection, has been used as a "norm," and the spondaic nature of his verse, followed by many later poets, provides a striking contrast to the dactylic rhythm of Ovid, who likewise had his imitators both in the Silver Age and the Late Empire.

Numerous criteria were established in Part I: the sixteen patterns and their percentages (first, first four, and first eight), variety in sixteen-line units, repeat clusters and repeated patterns, change in fourth-foot texture in repeated patterns, and opposite and reverse combinations. These criteria have been applied to the various hexameter poets in Part II with surprising results in many instances, and Part II thus becomes in a sense a history of Latin hexameter poetry, with new conclusions on the metrical practices of the individual poets and their indebtedness to their predecessors, and on the authenticity of several works of disputed authorship.

I have endeavored, as much as possible, to avoid all unnecessary and irrelevant statistics in the preceding chapters and have summarized my conclusions in the individual chapters or sections. On the other hand, I realize that the many percentages and frequencies given above often make for difficult reading, and it therefore seems advisable to present in a final recapitulation my most important findings concerning the forty or more Latin poets whom I have analyzed. The Arabic numerals in parentheses refer to the chapters in Part II, where detailed arguments are given to support the generalizations which follow.

The Poets of the Roman Republic

(6.) Ennius, the first of the Latin hexameter poets, is the opposite of Homer; he is spondaic, with *ssss* his most frequent pattern (Homer, *dddd*), and with a distribution of twenty-two spondees and ten dactyls in his first eight patterns (Homer, ten spondees and twenty-two dactyls). His percentages (first pattern, 15.35; first four, 41.34; first eight, 65.35) are much lower than those of Homer and all later Greek poets, and also lower than those of most Latin poets.

Lucilius likewise is heavily spondaic, with twenty-one spondees and eleven dactyls in his first eight patterns. His favorite pattern is *sdss*.

In the case of Cicero we have both his *Aratea* and numerous fragments, and the results are almost identical; this gives added support to my conclusions on Ennius and Lucilius, which are based on short fragments only.

Cicero's first pattern is *dsss* and the distribution in his first eight patterns is twenty spondees and twelve dactyls. In these and other respects Cicero anticipates the metrical technique of Vergil and Horace in the Augustan Age.

Books I, II, and V of Lucretius' *De rerum natura* are more spondaic and have greater variety than the other three books; this evidence supports the theory of Büchner and Bailey that Books I, II, and V were composed before the other books.

The percentages of the first, first four, and first eight patterns increase from Ennius and Lucilius through Cicero and Lucretius to Catullus LXIV, where we find amazingly high percentages (first pattern, 27.59; first four, 67.90; first eight, 90.98) and abnormally high frequencies of repeat clusters and repeated patterns.

The unusually high percentages and frequencies in Catullus (paralleled in Latin poetry only by those of the late Christian poet Cyprian) seem the direct result of his indebtedness to the Greek Hellenistic poets, and especially Callimachus.

137

The Augustan Age: Vergil, Horace, and Ovid

(7.) Vergil's metrical technique marks a revolt from the repetition of Lucretius and Catullus and, in part, a return to the procedures of Cicero.

Vergil's innovations include (1) less concentration on the most frequent patterns and, as a result, fewer repeat clusters and repeated patterns; (2) a decided decrease in the percentage of fourth-foot homodyne; (3) a greater change in fourth-foot texture to give variety to repeated patterns; and (4) an increased use of opposite patterns in adjacent lines.

The *Eclogues* are much more dactylic than the *Georgics* and the *Aeneid;* they show the influence of Theocritus, especially in the earliest pastoral (*Eclogue* II).

Eclogue IV, the famous Messianic poem, is quite unlike the other nine pastorals in its metrical structure, especially in the high percentages of its most frequent patterns; it resembles closely Catullus LXIV, as in so many other respects.

In the *Georgics* Vergil achieves his metrical maturity, but still lacks the perfection of the *Aeneid*.

Aeneid X-XII differ metrically in many respects from the *Georgics* and the first nine books of the epic; the most plausible explanation is that Vergil's sudden death in 19 B.C. left the final three books of the *Aeneid* without the metrical revisions which he had already made in the remainder of the poem.

Vergil's favorite pattern, *dsss* (normally about fourteen per cent) shows an amazing variation in percentage according to style and subject matter; from zero to six or eight per cent in emotional and dramatic episodes and speeches (passages to which Otis applies the term "subjective style"), but from twenty to thirty per cent in scenes of fighting, those in which the divinities appear and speak, and especially those dealing with Rome, Roman history, and Augustus.

(8.) Horace resembles his friend Vergil (and Cicero earlier) in his choice of patterns and in his distribution of spondees and dactyls in his first eight patterns, but his percentages of these patterns are lower, with a resultant greater variety in the sixteen-line units and a lower frequency of repeated patterns. Horace also favors reverse combinations to a greater degree than does Vergil, but he differs from the epic poet in returning to higher percentages of fourth-foot homodyne, and he shows little interest in change in fourth-foot texture.

Unlike most Roman poets, who are remarkably consistent in their percentages, Horace changes his hexameter technique over the years. His works in chronological order reveal a steady increase in variety from *Satires* I to *Epistles* II, and a greater desire for opposite combinations.

Since the changing trends in the many categories of variety and repetition reach their respective culminations in the *Ars Poetica*, we have decisive arguments to support the view of Dilke, Brink, and others that this is Horace's latest poem, to be dated in the final years of his life, 12-8 B.C.

(9.) Ovid resembles the Republican poets in his higher percentages of the first eight patterns and also in his high percentage of fourth-foot homodyne; his use of opposite combinations is similar to that of Lucretius.

Ovid's practice is that of Vergil and/or Horace in several respects; e.g., low percentage of the most frequent pattern; relation of the most frequent repeat plus near repeats to the total repeats plus near repeats. Ovid's frequency of reverse patterns in adjacent lines is similar to that in the *Aeneid;* his percentage of *sssd* with *dsss* resembles that in Horace.

Ovid's *Metamorphoses* is unlike all earlier Latin poetry (excluding, of course, his own previous works) in many important respects: the unusual treatment of *ddss* (his most frequent pattern), from first to fourth position in the different books, and of *dsss,* from first to fifth; the (almost Homeric) distribution of twelve spondees and twenty dactyls in the first eight patterns (the opposite of the twenty spondees and twelve dactyls which appear in Cicero, Catullus, Vergil, and Horace); the low percentage of change in fourth-foot texture in relation to fourth-foot homodyne (previously surpassed especially by that in Catullus LXIV); and the choice of *dsdd-ddsd* as the most frequent reverse combination (the inevitable result of his emphasis on dactylic patterns), with an abnormally high percentage of *dsdd* preceded or followed by *ddsd*.

The *Halieutica* is attributed to Ovid by writers both ancient and modern, but both the high proportion of spondees in the first eight patterns (nineteen to twenty-one) and the low percentages of the most frequent patterns seem conclusive proof that Ovid can not be the author and that Birt, Housman, Wilkinson, Richmond, and others are correct in their rejection of its authenticity. Ovid's distribution of twelve spondees and twenty dactyls appears consistently throughout his elegiac poetry, from early to late, as well as in the *Metamorphoses*.

The *Appendix Vergiliana* and Later Didactic Poetry

(10.) The hexameter poems of the *Appendix Vergiliana* could not be the work of Ovid, as Radford maintains.

The *Culex* has striking metrical similarities to the *Eclogues* and is probably a youthful work of Vergil; there are also differences which are difficult to explain if the *Culex* is the work of a later forger imitating Vergil's technique.

The *Moretum* resembles both the *Culex* and the *Eclogues* and is likewise probably by Vergil. It seems significant that Columella borrowed not only from Vergil's authentic works but also from both the *Culex* and the *Moretum*.

The *Ciris* is definitely not by Vergil but dates from the first century B.C. In its high frequency of spondaic verses, it resembles Catullus LXIV. If Cornelius Gallus is the author, Vergil may have borrowed phrases and lines from the work of his friend.

The *Dirae (Lydia)* can not possibly be the work of Vergil, but the metrical evidence favors the view that it is one poem rather than two and that it should be dated in the late Republic.

(11.) The *Aetna*, also in the *Appendix Vergiliana*, is likewise assigned by some scholars to Vergil, but it has the characteristics of other didactic poems of the early first century A.D., e.g., the *Cynegetica* of Grattius, the *Aratea* of Germanicus Caesar, and the *Astronomica* of Manilius; these works all resemble in varying degrees the *Georgics* of Vergil.

The metrical technique of the *Aetna* is especially close to that of Germanicus' *Aratea*. In the time of Nero, Columella composed the tenth book of his *Res Rustica* in hexameters as a tribute to and continuation of Vergil's *Georgics*, but his metrical procedures, especially his emphasis on dactyls and his high percentage of the first eight patterns, are those of Ovid and not of Vergil. The most plausible date for the *Aetna*, therefore, is in the second quarter of the first century A.D., after Germanicus and before Columella.

Two didactic poems of the third century, the *Cynegetica* of Nemesianus and the *Liber Medicinalis* of Serenus, are likewise far more spondaic than the hexameter book of Columella, and Serenus in particular is amazingly similar to Vergil (in the *Aeneid*) in his percentages and his categories of variety and repetition. This is a striking illustration of the extent to which Vergil's metrical technique influenced later writers, working in an entirely different literary genre.

The Silver Age

(12.) The two Einsiedeln pastorals are almost too short to provide reliable information, but the statistics for each favor the view that they are the work of two different authors; they are not to be assigned to either Lucan or Calpurnius Siculus.

In all post-Ovidian hexameter poetry we find no such emphasis on dactyls in the first eight patterns as in the *Eclogues* of Calpurnius Siculus and the *Laus Pisonis;* for this and other metrical reasons the *Laus Pisonis* should be considered the work of Calpurnius.

The four *Eclogues* of Nemesianus are metrically very unlike those of Calpurnius Siculus. Nemesianus is unusual in that repeated patterns are relatively infrequent and that reverse combinations occur more often than opposite combinations.

(13.) The four epic poets of the Silver Age are surprisingly consistent metrically from book to book; this is especially true of Valerius Flaccus and Statius.

Valerius Flaccus and Statius, in spite of their use of Vergilian themes and language, are "Ovidian" in their metrical technique, whereas Lucan follows Vergil, and Silius Italicus even more so.

Petronius, in his parody of Lucan, not only disapproves of Lucan's rhetoric and avoidance of divine machinery but perhaps shows what he considers to be proper hexameter procedure; he has less concentration on the same patterns and is much more spondaic, but displays no interest in fourth-foot texture change.

Valerius Flaccus, in his use of hexameter patterns, is the most repetitious and monotonous of the four epic poets; he goes far beyond Ovid in his lack of variety.

The hexameter technique of Statius in his *Silvae* is very similar to that in the *Thebaid* and the *Achilleid*, in spite of the fact that the themes of the *Silvae* are those usually found in elegy and epigram.

Silius Italicus is the most painstaking metrician of the four epic poets and displays more variety than any of the other three. In most respects he closely resembles Vergil, but in many books is even more spondaic (almost "Ennian").

The passage in *Punica* VIII, 144-223, which appears in no extant manuscript and in no edition prior to the Aldine text of 1523, is not a Renaissance forgery but the authentic work of Silius Italicus. These lines have the metrical "fingerprints" of Silius, especially in the choice of patterns and in the distribution of spondees and dactyls in the eight most frequent patterns.

The *Ilias Latina*, with an acrostic signature assigning it to a poet named Italicus, is so close metrically to the hexameter technique of Silius Italicus that we seem justified in ascribing it to Silius, written in the time of Nero, when Silius was thirty-five or forty years of age; it should not, therefore, be called a "youthful work." This date also explains the few similarities of the *Ilias Latina* to Lucan's epic.

(14.) The metrical differences between the satirists Persius and Juvenal are striking; Persius is far more Ovidian than Juvenal and is characteristic of the poets of the age of Nero.

Juvenal avoids repetition and has much greater metrical variety than Persius. He is less Vergilian than Horatian, and as Lucilian as Horatian.

Horace, unlike most hexameter poets, changed his metrical technique over the years, with an increasing interest in variety. Persius follows him to a degree, Juvenal much more so; such similarity in statistical details is difficult to explain unless we assume that Juvenal was as familiar with Horace's metrical procedures as he was with his language.

The Late Empire

(15.) Avienus follows to a degree the metrical practices of the didactic poets of the first century A.D. but he has less regard for change in fourth-foot texture (especially in the pattern most frequently repeated) and he resembles Columella in his preference for dactylic patterns. His *Aratea* and the *Descriptio orbis terrae* show almost no difference in metrical technique.

Ausonius in the *Mosella* is unique in his avoidance of repetition and in his desire for variety (percentage of first pattern, 9.38; first four, 36.04; first eight, 62.50; the closest approach to such low percentages appears in the *Ars Poetica* of Horace). In his *Cento Nuptialis* the percentages are higher and almost Vergilian, but the repeated patterns are less frequent than in the *Aeneid* and reverse combinations more so.

Claudian's metrical technique is the same in his public poems (panegyrics and invectives) and in his mythological epic, *De raptu Proserpinae*. In his choice of favorite patterns and in the high frequency of their occurrence, he resembles the Silver Age poets, especially Valerius Flaccus. He concentrates on one reverse combination *(ssds-sdss)* to a greater extent than any other Latin poet, with the exception of Cyprian.

Sidonius in his choice of favorite patterns closely resembles Claudian, but he shows a greater desire for variety; his percentages fall to a Vergilian range, and he has even fewer repeat clusters and repeated patterns than Vergil.

Corippus has the high percentages of Claudian and an even greater emphasis on dactylic patterns; also he has a higher frequency of repeats than any poet after Valerius Flaccus, with the exception of Cyprian. His *Johannis* in eight books is an avowed imitation of Vergil's *Aeneid*, but metrically he fails to follow the technique of his great predecessor.

(16.) The Christian hexameter poets fall into two groups: (1) those more spondaic and Vergilian: Juvencus, Proba, Prosper (including *De providentia Dei*), Marius Victor, Paulinus of Pella, and Avitus; (2) those more dactylic and "post-Ovidian": Prudentius, Paulinus of Nola, Sedulius, Paulinus of Périgueux, Dracontius, Cyprian, and Arator.

Commodian is omitted, since his verse is accentual rather than quantitative.

In the first group, Juvencus and Avitus are the most spondaic in their first eight patterns; Avitus, called the "Christian Vergil," has the high percentages of Valerius Flaccus and Claudian and is therefore less Vergilian metrically than Juvencus; his concentration on repeated patterns is also greater than that of Juvencus.

In their use of repeat clusters and repeated patterns, both Prosper of Aquitaine and Paulinus of Pella show greater restraint than either Juvencus or Avitus.

Proba in her *Cento* reproduces of necessity the rhythms of Vergil, but her patterns and percentages seem no more Vergilian than what we find in Juvencus and Prosper; they are, however, somewhat closer to Vergil than those of Ausonius' *Cento Nuptialis*. Marius Victor's metrical technique resembles that of Proba in a number of striking details.

Prosper's *De ingratis* and the *De providentia Dei*, of uncertain authorship, are amazingly similar in the most important aspects of their meter; e.g., choice of patterns, distribution of spondees and dactyls, percentage of fourth-foot homodyne, frequency of repeated, opposite, and reverse patterns. We find here strong arguments to support the view that Prosper of Aquitaine was indeed the author of the *De providentia Dei*.

(17.) Of the second group of Christian poets, Prudentius and Paulinus of Nola, though non-Vergilian in their choice of metrical patterns and their emphasis on dactyls, avoid repeat clusters and repeated patterns (Prudentius even more than Vergil); in the other poets there is a steady increase in repetition until we reach in Cyprian of Gaul a monotony unparalleled since Catullus LXIV.

Dracontius differs from the other poets in this group in one respect: his percentages of change in fourth-foot texture are unusually high and resemble or surpass the corresponding percentages of several poets in the first group. This is true only of *De laudibus Dei*, not of *De raptu Helenae*, where the percentages of change are unusually low; in the *De raptu*, however, repeat clusters and repeated patterns are less frequent.

Cyprian of Gaul is unique in several respects: choice of *ssds* as first pattern (elsewhere only in the *De raptu Helenae* of Dracontius); percentage of first eight patterns, 91.06; almost no shift in fourth-foot texture, especially in the pattern most frequently repeated; and no variety in reverse combinations.

Arator is less repetitious than Cyprian, but has a higher proportion of dactyls in his first eight patterns than any other poet of the Late Empire; in this respect he resembles Valerius Flaccus and Statius.

(18.) The two Latin poets with the greatest amount of repetition, Catullus LXIV and Cyprian, still have far more variety than the late Greek hexameter poets, Quintus of Smyrna, Nonnus, and Musaeus, where the percentages of the first eight patterns range from 96.15 to 99.79; only nine or ten of the sixteen possible patterns are used, and the same pattern (usually *dddd*) occurs six, seven, and even eight lines in succession. Nothing like this had ever happened in Latin hexameter poetry.

APPENDICES

Appendix A

THE DACTYLIC NATURE OF OVID'S ELEGIAC POETRY

I discussed in Chapter 9 the authenticity of the *Halieutica* and stated that the favorite patterns in this short poem are very unlike those in all of Ovid's authentic works, as is the percentage of the first eight patterns and their distribution of spondees and dactyls. The statistics are these:

	1st pattern	%	% 1st four	%	1st eight Spond.	Dact.
Her. I-XV:	ddsd	14.32	49.20	81.89	12	20
Amores:	ddss	13.25	48.94	78.84	12	20
Ars A. I-II:	dsds	13.72	47.49	82.19	12	20
Medicamina:	dsds	14.0	46.0	80.0	15	17
Ars A. III:	ddss	15.80	51.11	82.22	12	20
Remedia:	dsss	15.52	50.76	81.29	12	20
Her. XVI-XXI:	dssd	16.41	56.28	86.03	12	20
Fasti:	dsss	16.22	56.27	89.27	12	20
Metamorphoses:	ddss	13.08	48.37	81.62	12	20
Tristia:	dssd	17.50	55.96	86.87	12	20
Ibis:	ddsd	17.09	54.43	83.86	12	20
Epp. ex Ponto:	dsss	15.43	55.31	85.85	12	20
Halieutica:	sdss	17.32	48.82	73.23	21-19	11-13

This table proves that Ovid is amazingly consistent, from his earliest through his latest works, in his distribution of twelve spondees and twenty dactyls in the first eight patterns. But the *Halieutica* has nineteen to twenty-one spondees and thirteen to eleven dactyls, the variation resulting from three patterns being tied for seventh place.

The first eight patterns in each of Ovid's works (with the exception of the *Medicamina*, fifty hexameters only) all begin with dactyls; in the *Halieutica*, *sdss* is first, *ssss* tied with *ddss* for third place, *sdds* fifth, and *ssds* tied with *dssd* and *ddsd* for seventh. The positions of these four more spondaic patterns in Ovid's works are as follows:

	sdss	ssss	sdds	ssds
Her. I-XV:	11	14	10	15
Amores:	9	14	10	12
Ars A. I-II:	9	14	10-11	12
Medicamina:	7	--	12-14	12-14
Ars A. III:	10	13	9	15-16
Remedia:	9	16	13	12
Her. XVI-XXI:	10	11	12	15
Fasti:	9	12	11	13
Metamorphoses:	9	15	11	13
Tristia:	9	11	13	15
Ibis:	9	14	11	15
Epp. ex Ponto:	9	13	11	14

No poet who so consistently looks upon *sdss*, *ssss*, *sdds*, and *ssds* with such disfavor could possibly have written the *Halieutica*.

Finally, since the *Halieutica* is short and for this reason may not conform to Ovid's normal technique in either the elegiac poems or the hexameter *Metamorphoses*, I give statistics for the first 130 hexameters of the following works, including the *Nux* and the *Consolatio ad Liviam*, usually considered spurious:

| | % | 1st eight patterns | | % 4th-foot homodyne |
		Spond.	Dact.	
Heroides I-II:	86.15	12	20	44.62
Amores I:	83.85	12	20	44.62
Ars A. I:	82.31	13	19	32.31
Ars A. III:	80.0	15	17	36.15
Remedia:	86.15	12	20	39.23
Fasti I:	90.0	12	20	52.31
Metamorphoses I:	81.54	14	18	51.54
Metamorphoses II:	83.85	12	20	49.23
Metamorphoses XV:	87.69	12	20	50.77
Tristia I:	81.54	12	20	40.77
Tristia V:	90.77	14	18	49.43
Ibis:	83.85	12	20	47.69
Epp. ex Ponto I:	83.08	12	20	48.46
Epp. ex Ponto IV:	93.08	14-12	18-20	47.69
Nux:	84.62	16-12	16-20	46.15
Consolatio:	75.95	15	17	56.54
Halieutica:	73.23	21-19	11-13	36.22

Again we find almost no variation in Ovid's authentic poetry, and both the *Nux* and the *Consolatio ad Liviam* seem more Ovidian than the *Halieutica*.

Appendix B

A RARE TYPE OF FIRST-FOOT DACTYL (THREE WORDS)

I stated above in Chapter 4, note 2, that Bolaños had failed to include in his list of dactyls the two following types:

No. 14: a dactyl composed of one word and parts of two others, i.e., a monosyllable (or elided dissyllable) preceded by the end of one word and followed by the beginning of another; e.g., Ennius 36: *pul/cher per a/moena;* Lucr. I, 442: *pos/sint in e/o;* Verg., *Aen.* I, 10: *vi/rum tot ad/ire;* II, 476: *Peri/phas et e/quorum;* 647: *di/vis et in/utilis;* Hor., *Sat.* I. 1, 7: *poti/or quid e/nim;* 9, 4: *ma/nu quid a/gis;* Ovid, *Metam.* I, 93: *su/i sed e/rant;* 132: *ven/tis nec ad/huc.* Dactyls of this type appear usually in the third or fourth foot.[1]

No. 15: a dactyl composed of three words, monosyllables or elided dissyllables. When my article on variety and repetition in Vergil's hexameters appeared,[2] Professor Highet wrote and asked me what Bolaños did with three-word dactyls such as *hic vir hic* (*Aen.* VI, 791), and said: "There are a few, a very few, of those." Such dactyls are relatively rare in Vergil, but Bolaños' omission and my own oversight are both most regrettable since, in Latin hexameter poetry as a whole, these dactyls are far more numerous and more varied than is often realized. They occur almost always in the first foot of the hexameter.[3]

I have collected all the first-foot dactyls of this type in the Roman hexameter poets from Ennius and Lucilius (second century B.C.) to Corippus and Arator (mid-sixth century A.D.) and I have departed from my procedure elsewhere in this volume for the poets of the Late Empire, where my statistics are based on the scansion of selected poems or books. For my examination of three-word dactyls in the first foot, I use the complete works of these late poets.

The most common type of three-word dactyl is that composed of three monosyllables; we find 80 different dactyls, ranging from *an quod in* (Ovid, *Metam.* XIII, 34), *an sit et* (Ovid, *Metam.* X, 27), *aut quid in* (Verg., *Aen.* II, 746; Claud., *In Eutrop.* I, 253) to *ut vel in* (Dracont., *De laud. Dei* II, 298), *vel quod ab* (Lucan, X, 242) and *vis et in* (Lucr., IV, 423).[4] One dactyl of this type, *quid quod et,* is especially frequent; it appears in Ovid, *Metam.* IX, 595; XIII, 223; Juvenal, VI, 45; Claud., *In Eutrop.* II, 138; Prud., *Hamart.,* 279; Paulinus of Nola, XXXII, 113, 117; Sedulius, *Carm. Pasch.* III, 285; Dracont., *De laud. Dei* II, 726. The examples in Vergil's poetry of dactyls with three monosyllables are the following (in addition to *aut quid in* and *hic vir hic,* mentioned above): *hinc vel ad* (*Georg.* III, 202), *neu quis ob* (*Aen.* XII, 566), *quam sit et* (*Georg.* III, 290), *sed quis ad* (*Aen.* III, 186), and *si quis in* (*Aen.* IX, 211).

The various possible combinations of monosyllables (= M) and elided dissyllables (= D) provide a long list of additional three-word dactyls: e.g., DMM: *namqu(e) ut ab* (*Aen.* X, 148); DDM: *quar(e) ag(e) et* (*Aen.* VII, 429), *surg(e) ag(e) et* (*Aen.* III, 169), *vad(e) ag(e) et* (*Aen.* III, 462; V, 548); DMD: *ten(e) ut eg(o)* (Hor., *Sat.* II, 8, 67); MDD: *hunc quoqu(e) ub(i)* (*Georg.* III, 95); MMD: *sed quid eg(o)* (Ennius, 196, 315; Lucilius, 1100; Catullus LXIV, 116, 164);[5] MDM: *haec cap(e) et* (*Aen.* XI, 590); *quin ag(e) et* (*Georg.* IV, 329); *quod nis(i) et* (*Georg.* I, 155); *sol quoqu(e) et* (*Georg.* I, 438). Several of these dactyls, such as *vad(e) ag(e) et* (DDM), *sed quid eg(o)* (MMD), and *fit quoqu(e) ut* (MDM) appear with considerable frequency and, like *quid quod et* (MMM), acquire a character that is almost formulaic; this seems especially true of *fit quoqu(e) ut* which occurs eight times in Book VI of Lucretius alone (137, 300, 309, 443, 483, 830, 1,042, 1,123).

The variety in the three-word dactyls in the first foot is thus amazing. The total numbers of the different types are as follows: MMM, 80; DMM, 13; DDM, 13; DMD, 2; MDD, 7; MMD, 12; and MDM, 52. I have found no cases of three elided dissyllables (DDD). We have therefore 179 different patterns, 80 composed of three monosyllables, 99 of six different combinations of monosyllables and elided dissyllables; these 179 dactyls occur in Latin hexameter poetry a total of 243 times.

I turn now to a more important topic, the frequency of the three-word dactyls in the poets from Ennius to Corippus. The following list gives the totals of the dactyls in the poets (or poems), the total lines (including spondaic verses), and the relative frequencies. For purposes of comparison I include the poets (or poems) where dactyls of this type do not occur.

Poet (or poem)	MMM	Types of M & D	Total	Total verses	One every x lines
Ennius	0	2	2	412	206.0
Lucilius	0	4	4	607	151.8
Cicero	0	1	1	745	745.0
Lucretius	10	25	35	7,367	210.5
Catullus LXIV	0	2	2	407	203.5
Culex	1	0	1	408	408.0
Ciris	0	1	1	535	535.0
Moretum	1	0	1	120	120.0
Dirae	0	0	0	181	---
Vergil	7	10	17	12,844	755.6
Eclogues	0	0	0	828	---
Georgics	2	4	6	2,187	364.5
Aeneid	5	6	11	9,829	893.5
Horace, *Sat. & Epp.*	2	3	5	4,081	816.2
Ovid, *Metamorphoses*	9	10	19	11,970	630.0
Halieutica	0	0	0	127	---
Grattius	1	1	2	539	269.5
Germanicus Caesar	0	0	0	921	---
Manilius	2	4	6	4,183	697.2
Aetna	0	0	0	637	---
Columella X	0	1	1	436	436.0
Calpurnius Sic.	0	0	0	758	---
Laus Pisonis	0	0	0	261	---
Lucan	7	1	8	8,034	1,004.3
Petronius	0	0	0	294	---
Valerius Flaccus	5	13	18	5,586	310.3
Statius	15	20	35	14,149	404.3
Silvae	9	7	16	3,317	207.3
Thebaid	5	12	17	9,710	571.2
Achilleid	1	1	2	1,122	561.0
Ilias Latina	1	0	1	1,054	1,054.0
Silius Italicus	2	10	12	12,203	1,016.9
Persius	0	1	1	650	650.0
Juvenal	4	2	6	3,820	636.7
Serenus	0	2	2	1,106	553.0
Nemesianus	0	0	0	644	---
Avienus	1	1	2	3,270	1,635.0
Ausonius	4	4	8	2,640	330.0
Claudian	5	1	6	8,809	1,468.2
Juvencus	0	0	0	3,218	---
Prudentius	1	3	4	4,948	1,237.0
Proba	0	0	0	693	---
Paulinus of Nola	10	12	22	6,198	281.7
Sedulius	2	0	2	1,753	876.5
Paulinus of Pella	1	1	2	614	307.0
Prosper, *De ingrat.*	0	0	0	1,001	---
De provid. Dei	0	1	1	876	876.0
Marius Victor	0	1	1	1,894	1,894.0
Paulinus of Périg.	0	7	7	3,622	517.4
Sidonius	0	1	1	2,445	2,445.0
Cyprian of Gaul	0	0	0	5,375	---
Dracontius	4	0	4	5,720	1,430.0
Avitus	1	0	1	3,418	3,418.0

Poet (or poem)	MMM	Types of M & D	Total	Total verses	One every x lines
Arator	1	0	1	2,325	2,325.0
Corippus	1	0	1	6,345	6,345.0

SUMMARY OF RELATIVE FREQUENCIES

Although statistics based on fragments and short poems are less satisfactory than those on longer works which total five or ten thousand verses, it still seems evident that the poets of the Republic used three-word dactyls with considerable freedom, Cicero excepted. In this respect, as in many others, Cicero anticipates the metrical procedures of Vergil and Horace. The three-word dactyl occurs in Cicero once every 745.0 lines, less than one-third as often as in Lucretius and Catullus. The frequencies of Vergil and Horace (one every 755.6 and 816.2 lines respectively) provide a striking contrast to those of Valerius Flaccus and Statius (one every 310.3 and 404.3 lines; cf. Ovid, *Metamorphoses,* one every 630.0 lines). On the other hand, in Lucan and Silius Italicus, the three-word dactyl appears only once in 1,004.3 and 1,016.9 lines. This striking difference between Lucan and Silius on one hand and Valerius and Statius on the other is one more indication of the many metrical features which distinguish the two pairs of Silver Age epic poets. In the hexameter poets of the Late Empire, both secular and Christian, the three-word dactyl is very rare, with the exception of Ausonius and Paulinus of Nola. In Sidonius, Avitus, and Arator it occurs less than once every two thousand lines, and in all of Corippus (6,345 verses) I find only one instance. In their use of these dactyls, therefore, almost all the poets of the late period differ from the earlier classical poets.

The following additional points are of interest:

1. Lucretius has three-word dactyls once every 210.5 lines, but their distribution in the six books of the *De rerum natura* is highly irregular: of the thirty-five instances, eighteen (51.43 per cent) occur in Book VI, a frequency of one every 71.1 lines; on the other hand, Book I has only one instance in 1,103 lines. How is this discrepancy to be explained? Was Lucretius hurried or careless in the composition of his final book? Or did he develop an interest in "formulaic" expressions, such as *fit quoqu(e) ut,* which occurs eight times in Book VI? I pointed out in Chapter 6 that Lucretius' metrical procedures support the theory of Büchner and Bailey that Books I, II, and V were composed before III, IV, and VI. Lucretius' use of three-word dactyls gives added confirmation to this view; in I, II, and V we find eight instances only, one every 465.8 lines (cf. Cicero, one every 745.0 lines), but in III, IV, and VI dactyls of this type are more than three times as numerous (twenty-seven, 77.14 per cent of the total) and almost three and one-half times as frequent, one every 134.9 lines.

2. Three-word dactyls appear about two and one-half times as often in Vergil's *Georgics* (one every 364.5 lines) as in his *Aeneid* (one every 893.5 lines). The higher frequency in the *Georgics* may be due to the influence of Lucretius, or the avoidance of this type of dactyl in the *Aeneid* may result from Vergil's desire to give greater dignity and majesty to his epic hexameters.

3. We might expect three-word dactyls to appear more often in the colloquial hexameters of Horace's *Satires* and *Epistles,* but such is not the case; we have one instance every 816.2 in Horace, in Vergil as a whole one every 755.6 lines. Vergil and Horace both differ from the Republican poets in their use of the three-word dactyl, as in so many other aspects of their metrical technique.

4. Vergil's *Eclogues* contain no three-word dactyls in the first foot, and it is interesting to note that none appears in the later bucolic poetry of Calpurnius Siculus and Nemesianus. But the total verses in each collection are perhaps too few to give significant results.

5. In Statius' *Silvae* three-word dactyls occur far more often (once every 207.3 lines) than in his epic poetry (*Thebaid,* once every 571.2 lines; *Achilleid,* once every 561.0 lines). Like Vergil, Statius apparently disliked an excessive number of such dactyls in his more dignified and ambitious compositions. As I pointed out above (in Chapter 13), Statius' metrical procedures in the *Silvae* are the same in most respects as in the *Thebaid* and the *Achilleid.*

6. I also showed above (in Chapter 13) that the poet of the *Ilias Latina,* although resembling Lucan in some respects, is far closer in his technique to Silius Italicus; this confirms the theory

that Silius himself is the author of the *Ilias Latina* and composed it in his late thirties after the publication of the first three books of Lucan's *De bello civili*. The use of the three-word dactyl in the *Ilias Latina* gives added support to this view: one instance in 1,054 lines, whereas in Lucan we find it once every 1,004.3 lines, in Silius once every 1,016.9 lines.

7. Persius and Juvenal are remarkably similar in their use of three-word dactyls (one every 650.0 and 636.7 lines respectively; this is slightly more frequent than in Horace's hexameter poetry (one every 816.2 lines). But four of the five instances in Horace occur in the *Satires* (2,113 verses) with a resultant frequency of one every 528.3 lines. Neither Horace nor the later satirists follow the practice of Lucilius, who apparently favored this type of dactyl (four in 607 verses of fragments, or one instance every 151.8 lines).

8. When we survey the whole range of Latin hexameter poetry from Ennius to Corippus and examine the poems (or collections) of 2,500 verses or more, we find the three-word dactyl appearing with the greatest frequency in the following five poets: (1) Statius, *Silvae*, one every 207.3 lines; (2) Lucretius, one every 210.5 lines; (3) Paulinus of Nola, one every 281.7 lines; (4) Valerius Flaccus, one every 310.3 lines; (5) Ausonius, one every 330.0 lines.

9. For a final summary of the frequency in Latin hexameter poetry of a first-foot dactyl composed of three words, I present the following table with totals for the various literary periods:

Periods	MMM	Types of M & D	Total	Total verses	One every x lines
Republican period (Ennius to *Dirae*)	12	35	47	10,782	229.4
Augustan Age (Vergil to Manilius)	21	28	49	34,665	707.4
Silver Age (*Aetna* to Juvenal)	34	48	82	47,882	583.9
Classical period (Ennius to Juvenal)	67	111	178	93,329	524.3
Late Empire (Serenus to Corippus)	31	34	65	66,914	1,029.4
Total (Ennius to Corippus)	98	145	243	160,243	659.4

Notes to Appendix B

[1]For examples in the second foot, see Lucr. II, 395: *ide/o fit u/ti*; Hor., *Sat.* I. 1, 19: *habe/o quod a/gam*; and, with an elided dissyllable instead of a monosyllable, Ovid, *Metam.* III, 297: *ingemu/it nequ(e) e/nim*; 524: *eveni/et nequ(e) e/nim*.

[2]In *TAPhA* 95 (1964), pp. 9-65.

[3]Three-word dactyls are very rare in the other feet, since the frequent caesuras in the second, third, and fourth feet produce dactyls (or spondees) beginning with the ends of words. Lucretius in Book VI has eighteen instances of three-word dactyls in the first foot, but none in the other feet. I have not attempted, therefore, to collect these dactyls in the other feet, but I have noted in passing the following: *quo fit ut*, in Hor., *Sat.* II. 1, 32 (fifth foot); *hic quis ab*, in Stat., *Theb.* IX, 70 (second foot); for a few examples with elided dissyllables, see *si qua vi(a)*, in Verg., *Aen.* VI, 194 (third foot) and 367 (second foot); *sis quod eg(o)*, in Hor., *Sat.* II. 7, 40 (second foot); *nos rap(e) in*, in Verg., *Aen.* II, 675 (fourth foot). Also, I do not include elegiac poetry in this survey of the three-word dactyl, but it is important to note that we have here a very different situation: in elegiac poetry these dactyls regularly appear not only in the first foot of the hexameter but also at the beginning of each half of the so-called pentameter; for examples in the first foot of the pentameter, see Catull. LVI, 86; Ovid, *Heroid.* IV, 4; V, 100; XX, 122; *Fasti* I, 620; V, 558, 690; VI, 594; at the beginning of the second half, Catull. CXV, 6; Ovid, *Heroid.* IX, 24, 36; XVII, 34; *Fasti* VI, 18.

[4]For the complete lists of three-word dactyls in the first foot, see Duckworth, *AJPh* 89 (1968), pp. 439-444.

[5]This dactyl, *sed quid eg(o)*, is very frequent, occurring also in Columella, X, 215; Stat., *Theb.* I, 461; IV, 774; VIII, 65; Sil. Ital., VI, 110; Claud., *De bello Goth.*, 154; Prud., *Apoth.*, 741; *Hamart.*, 553; *Contra Sym.* II, 182; Paulinus of Nola, XXI, 25, 551; Paulinus of Pella, *Euchar.*, 55; Paulinus of Périg., *De vita Mart.*, VI, 71.

Appendix C

MAPHAEUS VEGIUS AND VERGIL

In 1428 Maphaeus Vegius (Maffeo Vegio), aged twenty-one, composed in 630 verses *A Supplementum to the Twelfth Book of the Aeneid (Libri XII Aeneidos Supplementum)*, usually known as the "Thirteenth Book of the *Aeneid*." Vegius apparently thought that Vergil had failed to make Aeneas' future sufficiently clear, so he included in his book the surrender of the Rutulians, the burial of Turnus, with laments by Latinus and Daunus, the marriage of Lavinia and Aeneas, the founding of Lavinium, the death of Latinus, and Aeneas' own death, with his spirit taken by Venus to join the immortals.[1] Also, believing that Aeneas was an allegorical figure, Vegius wished to stress his marriage to Lavinia, who is to be interpreted as the soul, and his apotheosis, the attainment of his heavenly goal.[2]

Vegius' *Supplementum* became famous. The youthful author was known by his contemporaries as "alter Maro" and "alter Parthenias"; the "Thirteenth Book" was first printed with the *Aeneid* in 1471, shortly after the editio princeps (1469?), and was usually included in editions of the *Aeneid* until about 1650. Vegius knew his beloved Vergil by heart and his language, style, and meter are praised as Vergilian. Maguinness says:[3]

> His Virgilianism is more a matter of form and expression and rhythm than of verbal reproduction. One has always the impression that his Virgilian phrases have not been culled from a text before his eyes, but have sprung from his memory.

In a sense, however, the *Supplementum* was a mistake. The *Aeneid* is structurally complete, with an unusually elaborate architecture: the alternation of the even-numbered books (more serious and tragic) and the odd-numbered books (providing an effective contrast with their lighter nature); the parallelism of the books in each half (I and VII, II and VIII, III and IX, etc.), with numerous similarities and contrasts in the corresponding books; and the arrangement of the epic in a trilogy, with V-VIII (more Roman and Augustan) framed by the story of Dido in I-IV and that of Turnus in IX-XII.[4] Vegius' addition of a "Thirteenth Book" reveals his failure to understand the close-knit unity of Vergil's twelve books.

Furthermore, the *Supplementum* was quite unnecessary, since the reader of the *Aeneid* already knows what is going to happen after the death of Turnus: there are numerous references throughout the poem to the marriage of Aeneas and Lavinia (II, 783-784; VI, 93-94, 764; VII, 96-101, 268-273, 314; XII, 821-822, 937). Vergil alludes to the founding of Lavinium (I, 258-259; XII, 193-194) and the union of Trojans and Latins (XII, 187-193, 834-840). Aeneas will rule only three years (I, 263-266; cf. IV, 618-620) and upon his death will become a god (I, 259-260; XII, 794-795).[5] As Blandford says,[6]

> Although excellent in itself, as an alternative ending to the Aeneid Vegio's Supplement is an anti-climax, a most undramatic conclusion, in a word a failure. We know these things are going to happen, and to take a whole book describing them is, as Pope observes, to "overshoot the mark."

According to Brinton, "the greatest flaw in the composition of the 'Thirteenth Book' is an excess of speeches. ... There are no less than thirteen harangues, laments, addresses, appeals, and prayers, ranging in length from four to forty-two lines."[7] Actually, the number of speeches in Vegius can hardly be considered either excessive or un-Vergilian, as the following comparison with *Aeneid* I and IV (two of the shorter books of the epic) will indicate:

	Vegius	*Aeneid* I	*Aeneid* IV
Total lines:	630	760	703
Number of speeches	13	24	21
One speech every *x* lines:	48.5	31.7	33.5

151

	Vegius	*Aeneid* I	*Aeneid* IV
Total lines in speeches:	282	329	332
Percentage of book:	44.76	43.29	47.23

Speeches thus occur with much greater frequency in both books of the *Aeneid,* and comprise, in the case of Book IV, an even greater proportion of the book.

Brinton also speaks of "the pleasant Virgilian cadences of the young Italian poet," and says that "it was second nature for Vegius to infuse Virgilian cadences into his own verse."[8] Maguinness is even more specific: "With regard to metre and prosody, the passages quoted will have revealed how Virgilian is the rhythmic structure both of periods and of verses, and what a sensitive ear the poet has for suitable variety both in the disposition of pauses and caesuras and in the mingling of dactyls and spondees."[9] But are the cadences of Vegius really Vergilian? Does he actually have a sensitive ear for variety in the mingling of dactyls and spondees? In other words, does he favor the metrical patterns used most frequently by Vergil, and does he show the same regard for metrical variety that is so conspicuous in Vergil's hexameters?

In the remainder of Appendix C I shall apply the same metrical criteria to Vegius' "Thirteenth Book" that I have used elsewhere in this volume and shall endeavor to show the extent to which his hexameter verse should or should not be considered Vergilian.

A comparison of the order of the eight most frequent patterns reveals that the Italian poet differs from his model in several important respects:

	1	2	3	4	5	6	7	8
Vergil:	*dsss*	*ddss*	*dsds*	*sdss*	*ssss*	*ddds*	*ssds*	*sdds*
Vegius:	*dsds*	*ssds*	*dsss*	*ssss*	*ddss*	*sdss*	*sdds*	*ddds*

Vergil's favorite pattern in the *Georgics* and the *Aeneid* is *dsss;* this is also first in many other hexameter poets: the lengthy list includes Cicero, Lucretius, Catullus LXIV, *Ciris, Moretum,* Horace, Grattius, Germanicus Caesar, Manilius, *Aetna,* Lucan, Persius, *Ilias Latina,* Silius Italicus, Juvenal, and, in the Late Empire, Avienus, Juvencus, Marius Victor, Paulinus of Pella, Avitus, and Prosper of Aquitaine.[10] It is, therefore, most surprising to find that Vegius in this respect is unlike Vergil and so many other Roman poets. Vergil's first pattern *(dsss)* is third in Vegius and his second *(ddss)* is fifth; on the other hand, Vegius' first pattern *(dsds)* never appears as a favorite until the Silver Age, where it is first in the *Eclogues* of Calpurnius Siculus, the *Laus Pisonis* (which I ascribe to Calpurnius), Valerius Flaccus, Statius, Nemesianus, and, in the later period, the secular poets Claudian, Sidonius, Corippus, and the Christian poets Paulinus of Nola, Sedulius, Paulinus of Périgueux, Arator. These are all writers whom I term "post-Ovidian" in their treatment of the hexameter. Vegius, therefore, in the use of *dsds* as his favorite pattern not only departs from Vergil but differs from all the earlier poets both Republican and Augustan.

When we turn to Vegius' second pattern, *ssds,* we have an even more unusual situation; *ssds* is in seventh place in Vergil and Horace, and almost never appears more frequently than in fifth position; the only exceptions are the following: Ennius, fourth place; Ausonius, *Cento Nuptialis,* tie with *sdds* for third; Dracontius, third (but *De raptu Helenae,* first); Avitus, third; and Cyprian of Gaul, first. Here again Vegius is most unlike Vergil and the other classical poets.

The Republican poets had concentrated heavily on the first four and the first eight patterns, but Vergil and Horace, both interested in greater metrical variety, reduced the percentages to a striking degree. Ovid again increased the concentration on the first eight patterns and also made his lines much more dactylic; in these respects he was followed by some later poets, but not by others. The following percentage lists are selective but show where Vegius stands in relation to the more important Roman poets:

	% 1st pattern	% 1st four	% 1st eight	Spond.	Dact.
Cicero:	18.28	57.39	82.26	20	12
Lucretius:	20.20	54.34	79.81	18	14

	% 1st pattern	% 1st four	% 1st eight	Spond.	Dact.
Catullus LXIV:	27.59	67.90	90.98	20	12
Vergil, *Aeneid*:	14.39	46.95	72.78	20	12
Horace:	12.67	42.16	67.97	20	12
Ovid, *Metam.*:	13.08	48.37	81.62	12	20
Lucan:	15.40	52.28	78.61	18	14
Valerius Fl.:	22.65	54.36	83.35	15	17
Statius, *Theb.*:	16.24	48.90	74.26	15	17
Silius Ital.:	13.04	43.90	72.64	20	12
VEGIUS:	14.44	49.21	79.68	20	12

Vegius' percentage for the first four patterns (49.21) resembles that in Ovid's *Metamorphoses* and in Statius' *Thebaid*. In his percentage for the first eight patterns (79.68), he is far closer to Cicero, Lucretius, and Ovid than to Vergil, and is higher than any of the Silver Age poets, with the exception of Valerius Flaccus (83.35). Among the many poets in the Late Empire, only Claudian, Avitus, Cyprian of Gaul, and Corippus have higher percentages for the first eight patterns.

In many other respects also Vegius differs strikingly from Vergil. The average number of metrical patterns per sixteen-line unit is 8.8 in Vegius, but 9.4 in the *Aeneid;* again Vegius is close to Cicero (*Aratea*, 8.5), Lucretius (8.6). and Ovid (8.9); cf. Manilius (8.8), Lucan (8.9) and Persius (8.8). The percentage of sixteen-line units with eight or more patterns is 82.05 in Vegius, but 92.46 in the *Aeneid;* again Vegius resembles Cicero in the *Aratea* (82.76) and shows greater repetition than Ovid (86.35) and most other hexameter poets; the only exceptions are Lucretius (76.10), Catullus LXIV (30.43), *Dirae* (70.0), Valerius Flaccus (74.86), and, in the late period, Claudian I (74.0), Claudian II (77.61), Avitus (75.37), Cyprian of Gaul (50.62), and Corippus (77.63).

Repeat clusters appear in Vegius once every 105.0 lines; this is almost twice as often as in the *Aeneid*, once every 200.1 lines. Vegius is here more restrained than the Republican poets (Cicero, *Aratea*, one every 59.6 lines; Lucretius, 49.2; Catullus, 29.0) and the frequency of his repeat clusters is almost identical with that in Ovid's *Metamorphoses*, one every 112.5 lines;[11] cf. Lucan (82.7), Statius, *Thebaid* (101.1), Persius (108.2), and, in the Late Empire, Sedulius (98.9) and Marius Victor (110.1).

Repeated patterns in adjacent lines are more frequent in Vegius than in the *Aeneid:* one every 10.7 and every 12.4 lines respectively, and it is interesting that repeats likewise average one every 10.7 lines in Ovid's *Metamorphoses;* cf. Persius (10.8), Claudian (10.0), Juvencus (10.8), Paulinus of Nola (11.0), Sedulius (10.4), etc. But Vegius varies the fourth-foot texture in his repeated patterns more often than Vergil does; the percentage of change (from homodyne to heterodyne, or from heterodyne to homodyne) is 52.54 in Vegius, 44.49 in Vergil. Since the percentage of fourth-foot homodyne is about the same in each (Vegius, 36.51; Vergil, 37.78), the difference between the percentage of change and the homodyne percentage is as follows: Vegius, +16.03; Vergil, +6.71; such a large increase over the homodyne percentage is most unusual, and is paralleled only by that in the *Eclogues* of Nemesianus (+16.07).

The favorite pattern of Vegius, *dsds*, has a frequency of 14.44 per cent, and Vergil's first pattern, *dsss*, is practically the same, 14.39 per cent. In Vegius, however, the *dsds* repeats comprise 28.81 per cent of the total repeats and 18.68 per cent of the total pattern; the corresponding percentages for the *dsss* repeats in the *Aeneid* are much lower, 22.18 and 12.40 respectively (cf. Horace, 20.06 and 12.19; Ovid, 18.08 and 13.47). In this higher proportion of repetition in his favorite pattern Vegius again shows his lack of interest in variety; the percentages in relation to total repeats and total pattern are not as high as in the Republican poets (Cicero, *Aratea*, 40.48 and 19.77; Lucretius, 37.60 and 21.20; Catullus LXIV, 44.44 and 23.08), but resemble those of certain Silver Age poets (Lucan, 26.74 and 15.30; Statius, *Thebaid*, 30.88 and 15.67; Persius, 30.0 and 15.79).

Opposite patterns in adjacent lines (e.g., *sssd-ddds*) occur in Vegius once every 26.3 lines; this frequency is midway between that in the *Aeneid* (23.1) and in Ovid's *Metamorphoses* (29.3). Vegius' favorite combination, *ddsd-ssds*, comprises 25.0 per cent of the total opposites; this is much higher than Vergil's favorite opposite, *sdsd-dsds* (16.04 per cent), higher even than *sdsd-dsds* in Ovid (22.11), and resembles the percentages of *sdsd-dsds* in Lucan (26.92) and in Statius' *Achilleid* (26.86) and *Silvae* (24.70); cf. Petronius (25.0) and *Ilias Latina* (25.42).

Reverse patterns in adjacent lines (e.g., *sssd-dsss*) are much more frequent in Vegius (one every 27.4 lines) than in the *Aeneid* (one every 38.9 lines); in this respect Vegius is close to Cicero, *Aratea* (24.0), Horace (29.4), and several later poets (e.g., Silius Italicus, 29.0; Avitus, 26.1; Prosper, *De ingratis,* 29.3, *De providentia Dei,* 27.3; Cyprian, 27.6). An unusually high proportion of Vegius' reverse combinations consists of *sdss-ssds;* the percentage is 73.91, as opposed to 40.08, the percentage of Vergil's favorite reverse *(ssds-sdss)* in the *Aeneid;* such high percentages are rare but occur in Catullus LXIV (71.43), Ovid's *Metamorphoses* (71.05), and Lucan (70.05); cf. also Claudian I (74.29), Claudian II (81.25), and Cyprian of Gaul (95.74).

In almost every important category, therefore, the hexameter technique of Vegius is very unlike that of Vergil. I do not wish to ignore the few metrical similarities between the *Supplementum* and the *Aeneid,* most of which have already been mentioned; these may be summarized as follows:

	Vegius	*Aeneid*
% of first pattern:	14.44	14.39
Spondees in first eight:	20	20
Dactyls in first eight:	12	12
% of fourth-foot homodyne:	36.51	37.78
Favorite R + NR, % total R + NR:	25.50	23.15
Opposites, one every *x* lines:	26.3	23.1

These similarities, however, are few in comparison to the many striking differences which I have already enumerated, and actually they mean little, since in most of these categories Vegius resembles other poets as well; the distribution of twenty spondees and twelve dactyls appears also in Cicero, Catullus LXIV, Horace, Germanicus Caesar, Manilius, Silius Italicus, Nemesianus' *Cynegetica,* Prosper of Aquitaine, and Cyprian of Gaul; the percentage of fourth-foot homodyne in Lucan is 37.08, in Statius' *Silvae* 38.41; the favorite repeat plus near repeats comprises 25.26 per cent of the total repeats plus near repeats in Lucan, and 27.75 in Statius' *Thebaid;* opposite combinations occur once every 25.2 lines in Horace's *Satires,* and once every 26.9 lines in Valerius Flaccus.

In summary, almost all the criteria prove conclusively that the "Thirteenth Book" of Vegius lacks the essential metrical features found in the *Aeneid;* in his choice of patterns, in the high percentage of the first eight patterns, in the abundance of repetition and especially in his high percentages of the most frequent repeats, opposites, and reverses, Vegius resembles at times the Republican poets, but more often Ovid and the later poets. It is surprising that a Renaissance poet so devoted to Vergil could miss so much of the latter's metrical technique and be so oblivious of the variety which Vergil (along with Horace) had introduced into hexameter poetry in the Augustan Age. It is erroneous, therefore, to speak of the cadences of Vegius as "Vergilian" and to say that he mingles dactyls and spondees in the manner of Vergil. The hexameter verse of Vegius is not unpleasing, but it is basically very unlike that in the *Aeneid* of Vergil.[12]

Notes to Appendix C

[1]See Brinton, *Maphaeus Vegius,* pp. 1-3. A synopsis of the *Supplementum* is given by Maguinness, *The Thirteenth Book,* pp. 4-8; for a brief outline of the book, cf. Duckworth, *Structural Patterns,* p. 248, and, for a comparison of mathematical symmetry in Vegius and Vergil, pp. 110-111. (There are "striking dissimilarities between his structural procedure and that of his revered master," p. 111.)

[2]For Vegius' own view of the *Aeneid* as an allegory, see Brinton, *Maphaeus Vegius,* pp. 27-29.

[3]*The Thirteenth Book,* p. 9.

[4]See, for bibliography and discussion, Duckworth, *AJPh* 75 (1954), pp. 1-15; *TAPhA* 88 (1957), pp. 1-10; *Structural Patterns,* pp. 1-19. Otis introduces a second parallelism between the halves (I and VII, but II and XII, III and XI, etc.); see his *Virgil,* pp. 217-218, 344, 391-392, 418; he also includes Book IX in the central portion of the trilogy; see pp. 274, note 1, 344-345, 419. Cf. Duckworth, *AJPh,* 88 (1967), pp. 141-147.

[5]See Duckworth, *Foreshadowing and Suspense,* p. 34; Blandford, *Vergilius* 5 (1959), p. 29.

[6]*Vergilius* 5 (1959), p. 30.

[7]*Maphaeus Vegius,* p. 4.

[8]*Ibid.,* pp. v and 4.

[9]*The Thirteenth Book,* p. 10.

[10]Also the *De providentia Dei,* which for metrical reasons I assign to Prosper (see above, Chapter 16). Ausonius' *Cento Nuptialis* and the religious *Cento* of Proba likewise have *dsss* as their most frequent pattern; this is perhaps inevitable, as both were composed from lines and phrases of Vergil.

[11]I have already noted several other metrical similarities to Ovid. Maguinness, *The Thirteenth Book,* p. 2, says of Vegius that it was Ovid "whom he admired next to Vergil." Metrically he is much closer to Ovid.

[12]Appendix C appears in a slightly different form in Duckworth, *CPh* 64 (1969), pp. 1-6.

TABLES

TABLE III. GREEK POETS

Patterns and Percentages, Distribution of Spondees and Dactyls, Frequency of Spondaic Verses, Variety in Sixteen-Line Units, Frequency of Repeats and Near Repeats, Opposite and Reverse Combinations

	HOMER. Iliad	HOMER. Ody.	HOMER. Total	Hesiod	Aratus	Theocr. I-XIII	Call. Hymns	Apoll.	Quint.	Nonnus	Musaeus
Patterns, 1st 8, last 2											
dsss	15	14-15	14-15	15	15	–	–	–	–	–	–
dsds	7	5	6	5-6	7	–	6	6	6	5	5-6
sdss	–	15-16	14-15	–	–	15	–	–	–	–	–
ssss	16	15-16	16	16	16	16	–	–	–	–	–
ddds	4	6	5	5-6	8	–	4	5	4	3	4
ssds	–	–	–	–	–	–	7	–	7	–	–
sdds	8	7	7	7	6	8	–	8	–	6	5-6
dssd	6	8	8	8	5	6	8	7	8	8-9	7
ddsd	–	–	–	–	–	5	–	–	–	7	8
sdsd	3	2	2	1	2	7	1	2	2	8-9	2
dsdd	5	4	4	4	4	2	5	4	5	2	1
ssdd	1	1	1	2	1	4	2	1	1	–	1
dddd	2	3	3	3	3	3	3	3	3	1	3
sddd	–	–	–	–	–	1	–	–	–	4	–
% 1st pattern	22.81	20.10	21.36	18.23	20.81	18.43	28.95	23.96	38.75	35.52	36.07
% 1st four	62.50	57.60	59.90	58.85	59.29	63.51	71.74	63.54	81.77	84.78	82.99
% 1st eight	86.77	84.06	85.42	81.56	83.96	84.35	93.14	89.48	96.15	99.79	98.83
Spondees	10	10	10	11	10	12	10	10	10	10	10
Dactyls	22	22	22	21	22	20	22	22	22	22	22
Spondaic verses, 1 every x lines	18.3	20.6	19.4	15.7	6.9	63.1	15.1	11.9	14.3	–	–
Patterns per 16-line unit	8.0	8.0	8.0	8.2	8.0	7.0	6.6	7.6	6.0	5.5	6.0
% units with 8 or more	68.33	69.49	68.91	68.33	60.66	68.92	18.87	56.67	13.33	0	0
R clusters, 1 every x lines	45.7	68.6	54.9	50.5	75.8	36.1	23.0	43.6	18.5	15.7	17.1
Repeats, 1 every x lines	7.4	10.9	8.8	9.2	9.5	8.2	5.4	7.7	4.7	4.8	5.4
R + NR, 1 every x lines	3.3	3.7	3.5	3.6	3.6	3.1	2.7	3.2	2.2	2.1	2.3
Most frequent repeat	dddd	dddd	dddd	dddd	dddd	dddd	dsdd	dddd	dddd	dddd	dddd
% total repeats	40.0	43.18	41.28	25.96	38.46	27.01	45.34	41.60	66.50	56.50	71.43
Opposites, 1 every x lines	45.7	56.5	50.5	53.3	70.4	58.9	174.8	87.3	320.0	960.0	341.0
Favorite Opposite	sdss-dsdd	sdsd-dsds	sdsd-dsds	sdss-dsdd	sdss-dsds dsdd	ssds-sdsd ddsd	ssds-sdsd dsds-dsds sdsd-dsds	sdds-dssd sdsd-dsds dsds-dsds	sdss-dsds	sdsd-dsds	sdsd-dsds
% total opposites	33.33	35.29	28.95	33.33	42.86	36.84	40.0 each	36.36 each	66.67	100.0	100.0
Reverses, 1 every x lines	23.4	32.0	27.0	41.7	26.6	37.3	23.6 each	18.1	38.4	20.9	21.3
Favorite reverse	ddds- sddd	ddds- sddd	ddds- sddd	ddds- sddd	ddsd- dsdd	ddsd- dsdd	ddds- sddd	ddds- sddd	ddds- sddd	ddds- sddd	ddds- sddd
% total reverses	58.54	56.67	57.75	52.17	54.05	63.33	59.46	62.26	72.0	73.91	87.50

ABBREVIATIONS

(The following abbreviations are used for references to periodicals and texts both in the Bibliography and in the notes to each chapter.)

AJPh	*American Journal of Philology*
BICS	*Bulletin of the Institute of Classical Studies*, University of London
BSGL	*Berichte über die Verhandlungen der königlich sächsichen Gesellschaft der Wissenschaften zu Leipzig*
C & M	*Classica et Mediaevalia*
CB	*Classical Bulletin*
CML	*Corpus Medicorum Latinorum*
CPh	*Classical Philology*
CQ	*Classical Quarterly*
CR	*Classical Review*
CSEL	*Corpus Scriptorum Ecclesiasticorum Latinorum*
CW	*Classical World* (formerly *Classical Weekly*)
G & R	*Greece and Rome*
HSPh	*Harvard Studies in Classical Philology*
JPh	*Journal of Philology*
JRS	*Journal of Roman Studies*
LCL	Loeb Classical Library
MGH	*Monumenta Germaniae Historica*
OCD	*Oxford Classical Dictionary*
OCT	Oxford Classical Tests
PhQ	*Philological Quarterly*
PLM	*Poetae Latini Minores*
PVS	*Proceedings of the Virgil Society*
RBPh	*Revue Belge de Philologie et d'Histoire*
RE	*Real-Encylopädie der classischen Altertumswissenschaft*
RhM	*Rheinisches Museum für Philologie*
RIL	*Rendiconti, Istituto Lombardo*
TAPhA	*Transactions and Proceedings of the American Philological Association*
UCCPh	*University of California Publications in Classical Philology*
WS	*Wiener Studien*

BIBLIOGRAPHY

I. TEXTS, COMMENTARIES, AND TRANSLATIONS

[The items marked with asterisks are the texts used for scansion and statistics. I give in square brackets the total verses of each poet (excluding spondaic verses and corrupt or bracketed lines), except for the Greek poets and the Latin poets of the Late Empire, where I give the totals of the selected works or poems on which my statistics are based.]

Aetna: W. Richter, [*Vergil*] *Aetna* (Berlin, 1963).

———: F. R. D. Goodyear, *Incerti Auctoris Aetna* (Cambridge, 1965).

*———: F. R. D. Goodyear; see *Appendix Vergiliana.* [636 verses]

*Apollonius Rhodius: R. C. Seaton, *The Argonautica* (LCL, 1921). [960 verses from I, 1-525, and IV, 1-523]

Appendix Vergiliana: ed. by W. V. Clausen, F. R. D. Goodyear, E. J. Kenney, J. A. Richmond (OCT, 1966).

*Arator: A. P. McKinlay, *De actibus Apostolorum* (*CSEL* 72, 1951). [Book I, 1,075 verses]

*Aratus: G. R. Mair, *Phaenomena* (LCL, 1921). [985 verses]

*Ausonius: H. G. Evelyn White (LCL, 1919, Vol. I). [*Mosella* (480 verses) and *Cento Nuptialis* (131 verses)]

*Avienus: A. Breysig, *Aratea* (Leipzig, 1882). [1,848 verses]

*———: P. van de Woestijne, *La Descriptio Orbis Terrae d'Avienus* (Brugge, 1961). [1,363 verses]

*Avitus: R. Peiper, *De spiritalis historiae gestis* (*MGH*, auct. ant. VI.2, 1883). [Books I, "De mundi initio," and V, "De transitu maris rubri." 1,045 verses]

———: A. Schippers, *De Mundi Initio* (Amsterdam, 1945).

*Callimachus: A. W. Mair, *Hymns* (LCL, 1921). [I-IV and VI, 874 verses]

Calpurnius Siculus: J. W. Duff and A. M. Duff, *Minor Latin Poets* (LCL, 1934).

*———: R. Verdière, *T. Calpurni Siculi De laude Pisonis et Bucolica et M. Annaei Lucani De laude Caesaris Einsidlensia quae dicuntur carmina* (Berchem-Bruxelles, 1954). [= *Collection Latomus,* Vol. 19.] [*Eclogues* = 758 verses]

Catalepton: R. E. H. Westendorp Boerma, *P. Vergili Maronis qui inscribitur Catalepton.* Pars altera (Assen, 1963).

*Catullus: R. A. B. Mynors, *C. Valerii Catulli Carmina* (OCT, 1958). [LXIV, 377 verses]

Cicero: W. W. Ewbank, *The Poems of Cicero* (London, 1933).

*———: A. Traglia, *Ciceronis Poetica Fragmenta* (Rome, 1950, 1952; two volumes). [*Aratea,* 479 verses; 265 verses of fragments]

Ciris: F. R. D. Goodyear; see *Appendix Vergiliana.* [520 verses]

*Claudian: M. Platnauer (LCL, 1922; two volumes). [Claudian I (2,429 verses) = *In Eutropium* I and II; Panegyrics on the Fourth and Sixth Consulships of Honorius. Claudian II (1,104 verses) = *De raptu Proserpinae*]

*Columella: E. S. Forster and E. H. Heffner, *Lucius Junius Moderatus Columella. On Agriculture and Trees* (LCL, 1945, Vol. III). [Book X, 435 verses]

*Corippus: M. Petschenig, *Johannis,* or *De bellis Libycis* (*Berl. Stud. für class. Philol. und Archaeol.* IV.2, Berlin, 1886). [Books I and VIII, 1,229 verses]

Culex: W. V. Clausen; see *Appendix Vergiliana.* [408 verses]

*Cyprian: R. Peiper, *Cypriani Galli Poetae Heptateuchos* (*CSEL* 23, 1881). [Book II, "Exodos," 1,297 verses]

De providentia Dei: M. P. McHugh, *The Carmen de Providentia Dei Attributed to Prosper of Aquitaine: A Revised Text With an Introduction, Translation, and Notes* (Washington, 1964). [= *Catholic Univ., Patristic Studies,* 98.] [874 verses]

Dirae: C. Van der Graaf, *The Dirae, with Translation, Commentary and an Investigation of its Authorship* (Leiden, 1945).

*———: E. J. Kenney; see *Appendix Vergiliana*. [178 verses]

*Dracontius: F. Vollmer, *Romulea*, VIII = *De raptu Helenae* (*MGH*, auct. ant. 14, 1905). [654 verses]

*———: J. F. Irwin, *Liber I Dracontii De Laudibus Dei, with Introduction, Text, Translation, and Commentary* (Philadelphia, 1942). [752 verses]

*Einsiedeln Eclogues: see under Calpurnius Siculus. [85 verses]

*Ennius: E. H. Warmington, *Remains of Old Latin. Vol. I. Ennius and Caecilius* (LCL, 1935). [404 verses of fragments]

*Germanicus Caesar: A. Breysig, *Aratea* (2nd ed., Leipzig, 1899). [*Aratea*, 677 verses; 239 verses of fragments]

*Grattius: R. Verdière, *Gratti Cynegeticon Libri I Quae Supersunt* (Vol. I, Wetteren, 1965). [539 verses]

*Halieutica: J. A. Richmond, *The "Halieutica" ascribed to Ovid* (London, 1962). [127 verses]

*Hesiod: H. G. Evelyn-White (LCL, 1914). [480 lines from *Works* and *Days*, 1-511; 480 lines from *Theogony*, 1-521]

*Homer: D. B. Monro and T. W. Allen, *Homeri Opera* (OCT, 1908). [1920 verses; 480 each from *Iliad* I, 1-503; XXIV, 1-513; *Odyssey* I and II, 1-61; XXIV, 1-505]

 Horace: E. C. Wickham, *The Works of Horace, Vol. II. The Satires, Epistles, and De Arte Poetica* (Oxford, 1891).

———: A. S. Wilkins, *The Epistles of Horace* (London, 1902).

*———: H. W. Garrod, *Q. Horati Flacci Opera* (OCT, 1912). [*Satires* and *Epistles*, 4,080 verses]

———: A. Kiessling — R. Heinze, *Q. Horatius Flaccus, Briefe* (5th ed., Berlin, 1957).

*Hosidius Geta: J. J. Mooney, *Hosidius Geta's Tragedy "Medea." A Vergilian Cento* (Birmingham, 1919). [343 verses]

*Ilias Latina: A. Baehrens (*PLM*, Vol. III, Leipzig, 1881). [1,054 verses]

 Juvenal: H. L. Wilson, *D. Iuni Iuvenalis Saturarum libri V* (Boston, 1903).

*———: W. V. Clausen, *A. Persi Flacci et D. Iuni Iuvenalis Saturae* (OCT, 1959). [3,785 verses]

*Juvencus: C. Marold, *Libri Evangeliorum IIII* (Leipzig, 1886). [Books I and IV, 1,577 verses].

*Laus Pisonis: see under Calpurnius Siculus. [261 verses]

 Lucan: C. E. Haskins, *M. Annaei Lucani Pharsalia* (London, 1887).

*———: A. E. Housman, *M. Annaei Lucani Belli Civilis Libri Decem* (Oxford, 1927; reprint, 1950). [8,021 verses]

*Lucilius: E. H. Warmington, *Remains of Old Latin, Vol. III* (LCL, 1938). [605 verses of fragments]

*Lucretius: C. Bailey, *T. Lucreti Cari De Rerum Natura Libri Sex, Vol. I* (Oxford, 1947). [7,335 verses]

*Manilius: A. E. Housman, *M. Manilii Astronomica* (ed. minor, Cambridge, 1932). [4,178 verses]

*Maphaeus Vegius: A. C. Brinton, *Maphaeus Vegius and His Thirteenth Book of the Aeneid* (Stanford, 1930). [630 verses]

*Marius Victor: C. Schenkl, *Alethia* (*CSEL* 16, 1888). [Books I and II, 1,101 verses]

*Moretum: E. J. Kenney; see *Appendix Vergiliana*. [120 verses]

*Musaeus: H. Färber, *Hero und Leander* (München, 1961). [341 verses]

*Nemesianus: J. W. Duff and A. M. Duff, *Minor Latin Poets* (LCL, 1934). [*Cynegetica*, 325 verses; *Eclogues*, 319 verses]

*Nonnus: R. Keydell, *Nonni Panopolitani Dionysiaca* (Berlin, 1959; two volumes). [960 verses from I, 1-480, and XLVIII, 1-480]

*Ovid: F. J. Miller, *Metamorphoses* (LCL, 1916; two volumes). [11,933 verses]

———: J. H. Mozley, *Ovid. The Art of Love, and Other Poems* (LCL, 1929).

———: A. G. Lee, *P. Ovidi Nasonis Metamorphoseon, Liber I* (Cambridge, 1953).

*Paulinus of Nola: W. de Hartel, *Carmina* (*CSEL* 30, 1894). [V, XV, and XXIII, 1,022 verses]

*Paulinus of Pella: H. G. Evelyn-White, *Eucharisticus* (in *Ausonius*, Vol. II, LCL, 1921). [611 verses]

*Paulinus of Périgueux: M. Petschenig, *De vita Martini* (*CSEL* 16, 1888). [Books I and IV, 1,059 verses]

*Persius: W. V. Clausen, *A. Persi Flacci et D. Iuni Iuvenalis Saturae* (OCT, 1959). [649 verses]

 Petronius: H. Stubbe, *Die Verseinlagen im Petron* (Leipzig, 1933). [= *Philologus*, Supplb. 25, Heft 2.]

*———: K. Müller, *Petronii Arbitri Satyricon* (München, 1961). [289 verses]

*Proba: C. Schenkl, *Probae Cento* (*CSEL* 16, 1888). [693 verses]

*Prosper: C. T. Huegelmeyer, *Carmen De Ingratis S. Prosperi Aquitani. A Translation with an Introduction and a Commentary* (Washington, 1962). [= *Catholic Univ., Patristic Studies,* 95.] [997 verses]

*Prudentius: H. J. Thomson (LCL, 1949, Vol. I). [*Psychomachia* and *Hamartigenia,* 1,866 verses]

*Quintus of Smyrna: A. S. Way, *The Fall of Troy* (LCL, 1913). [960 verses from I, 1-512, and XIV, 1-514]

*Sedulius: N. Scheps, *Paschale Carmen, Book I en II* (Delft, 1938); J. Huemer, *Paschale Carmen, Liber V* (*CSEL* 10, 1885). [1,088 verses]

*Serenus: F. Vollmer, *Quinti Sereni Liber Medicinalis* (Leipzig, 1916). [= *CML* II, 3.] [1,101 verses]

*Sidonius: W. B. Anderson, *Poems and Letters* (LCL, 1936, Vol. I). [Panegyrics to Avitus and Anthemius, 1,142 verses]

*Silius Italicus: J. W. Duff, *Punica* (LCL, 1949-50; two volumes). [12,197 verses]

*Statius: J. S. Phillimore, *P. Papini Stati Silvae* (OCT, 1905). [3,316 verses]

*———: H. W. Garrod, *P. Papini Stati Thebais et Achilleis* (OCT, 1906). [*Thebais,* 9,703 verses; *Achilleis,* 1,122 verses]

Theocritus: A. S. F. Gow, *Theocritus, edited with a Translation and Commentary* (Vol. II, second ed., Cambridge, 1952).

*———: A. S. F. Gow, *Bucolici Graeci* (OCT, 1952). [*Idylls* I-XIII, 1,118 verses]

*Valerius Flaccus: J. H. Mozley, *Argonautica* (LCL, 1934). [5,585 verses]

Vergil: A. Forbiger, *P. Vergili Maronis Opera* (Leipzig, 1872-75; three volumes).

———: Th. Ladewig, C. Schaper, P. Deuticke, *Vergils Gedichte. 1. Bukolika und Georgika,* 9th ed. by P. Jahn (Berlin, 1915).

*———: F. A. Hirtzel, *P. Vergili Maronis Opera* (OCT, 1900). [12,812 verses]

———: C. Knapp, *The Aeneid of Vergil* (Chicago, 1923).

———: R. G. Austin, *P. Vergili Maronis Aeneidos Liber Quartus* (Oxford, 1955).

———: J. Perret, *Virgile. Les Bucoliques* (Paris, 1961).

II. GENERAL

M. von Albrecht, *Silius Italicus: Freiheit und Gebundenheit römischer Epik* (Amsterdam, 1964).

W. B. Anderson, "Lucan," in *OCD* (1949), p. 514.

G. d'Anna, "Oraziani i primi versi della decima satira?" *Maia* 7 (1955), pp. 26-42.

A. H. Ashcroft, "Vergil's Hexameter Line," *G & R* 20 (1951), pp. 97-114.

B. Axelson, "Eine ovidische Echtheitsfrage," *Eranos* 43 (1945) pp. 23-35.

C. Bailey, "Virgil," in *OCD* (1949), pp. 949-951.

F. T. Baldwin, *The Bellum Civile of Petronius* (New York, 1911).

F. Ballotto, *Cronologia ed evoluzione spirituale nelle satire di Persio* (Messina, 1964).

C. Becker, *Das Spätwerk des Horaz* (Göttingen, 1963).

H. Bellen, "ADVENTUS DEI. Der Gegenwartsbezug in Vergils Darstellung der Geschichte von Cacus und Hercules (Aen. VIII 184-275)." *RhM* 106 (1963), pp. 23-30.

W. Berg III, *Vergil's Bucolic Hero: Origins and Development* (Ann Arbor, 1967). [= Princeton Univ. dissertation, microfilmed.]

T. Birt, *De Halieuticis Ovidio poetae falso adscriptis* (Berlin, 1878).

D. W. Blandford, "Virgil and Vegio," *Vergilius* 5 (1959), pp. 29-30.

J. M. Bolaños, S.I., "Virgilio, Rey del Hexámetro (Estudio de Métrica)," *Estudios Virgilianos* (Quito, 1931), pp. 70-121.

C. O. Brink, *Horace on Poetry: Prolegomena to the Literary Epistles* (Cambridge, 1963).

E. L. Brown, *Numeri Vergiliani. Studies in "Eclogues" and "Georgics"* (Bruxelles-Berchem, 1963). [= *Collection Latomus,* Vol. 63.]

R. T. Bruère, "*Color Ovidianus* in Silius *Punica* 1-7," in N. I. Herescu (ed.), *Ovidiana: Recherches sur Ovide* (Paris, 1958), pp. 475-499.

———, *"Color Ovidianus* in Silius *Punica* 8-17,"* CPh* 54 (1959), pp. 228-245.

K. Büchner, *Beobachtungen über Vers und Gedankengang bei Lucrez* (Berlin, 1936). [= *Hermes, Einzelschriften,* Heft 1.]

———, "Tullius,"* RE* 7A.1 (1939), cols. 827-1274.

———, *P. Vergilius Maro: Der Dichter der Römer* (Stuttgart, 1956). [= "Vergilius,"* RE* 8A.1 (1955), cols. 1021-1264; 8A.2 (1958), cols. 1265-1486.]

C. C. Bushnell, "The First Four Feet of the Hexameter in Horace's *Satires," TAPhA* 33 (1902), pp. lvi-lviii.

H. E. Butler, *Post-Augustan Poetry from Seneca to Juvenal* (Oxford, 1909).

D. J. Campbell, "Silius Italicus," in *OCD* (1949), pp. 838-839.

C. G. Cooper, *An Introduction to the Latin Hexameter* (Melbourne, 1952).

A. Cordier, *Les Débuts de l'Hexamètre latin. Ennius* (Paris, 1947).

M. E. Cosenza, *Petrarch's Letters to Classical Authors* (Chicago, 1910).

Tr. Costa, "Formele Hexametrului la Ovidiu," in *Publius Ovidius Naso* (Bucarest, 1957) [= *Bibliotheca Antică Studii,* II], pp. 211-332.

N. W. DeWitt, *Virgil's Biographia Litteraria* (Toronto, 1923).

O. A. W. Dilke, "When was the *Ars Poetica* Written?"* BICS* 5 (1958), pp. 49-57.

M. S. Dimsdale, *A History of Latin Literature* (New York, 1915).

R. Doering, *Ueber den Homerus Latinus* (Strassburg, 1884).

T. A. Dorey (ed.), *Cicero* (London, 1965).

F. L. Douglas, *A Study of the Moretum* (Syracuse, 1929).

M. W. Drobisch, "Ein statistischer Versuch über die Formen des lateinischen Hexameters,"* BSGL* 18 (1866), pp. 75-139.

———, "Weitere Untersuchungen über die Formen des Hexameter des Vergil, Horaz und Homer,"* BSGL* 20 (1868), pp. 16-65.

G. E. Duckworth, *Foreshadowing and Suspense in the Epics of Homer, Apollonius, and Vergil* (Princeton, 1933).

———, "The Architecture of the *Aeneid," AJPh* 75 (1954), pp. 1-15.

———, *"Animae Dimidium Meae:* Two Poets of Rome,"* TAPhA* 87 (1956), pp. 281-316.

———, "The *Aeneid* as a Trilogy,"* TAPhA* 88 (1957), pp. 1-10.

———, "Recent Work on Vergil (1940-1956),"* CW* 51 (1957-58), pp. 89-92, 116-117, 123-128, 151-159, 185-193, 228-235, reprinted in 1958 by the Vergilian Society of America under the title, *Recent Work on Vergil. A Bibliographical Survey, 1940-1956.*

———, "Vergil's *Georgics* and the *Laudes Galli," AJPh* 80 (1959), pp. 225-237.

———, "Mathematical Symmetry in Vergil's *Aeneid," TAPhA* 91 (1960), pp. 184-220.

———, "Tripartite Structure in the *Aeneid," Vergilius* 7 (1961), pp. 2-11.

———, review of J. Perret, *Virgile. Les Bucoliques, AJPh* 83 (1962), pp. 444-447.

———, *Structural Patterns and Proportions in Vergil's Aeneid* (Ann Arbor, 1962).

———, "Recent Work on Vergil (1957-1963),"* CW* 57 (1963-64), pp. 193-228, reprinted in 1964 by the Vergilian Society of America under the title, *Recent Work on Vergil. A Bibliographical Survey, 1957-1963.*

———, "Variety and Repetition in Vergil's Hexameters,"* TAPhA* 95 (1964), pp. 9-65.

———, review of B. Otis, *Virgil: A Study in Civilized Poetry, AJPh* 86 (1965), pp. 409-420.

———, "Horace's Hexameters and the Date of the *Ars Poetica," TAPhA* 96 (1965), pp. 73-95.

———, "Hexameter Patterns in Vergil,"* PVS* 5 (1965-66), pp. 39-49.

———, "The Non-Ovidian Nature of the *Halieutica," Latomus* 25 (1966), pp. 756-768.

———, "Vergil's Subjective Style and its Relation to Meter,"* Vergilius* 12 (1966), pp. 1-10.

———, "Studies in Latin Hexameter Poetry,"* TAPhA* 97 (1966), pp. 67-113.

———, "The Significance of Nisus and Euryalus for *Aeneid* IX-XII,"* AJPh* 88 (1967), pp. 129-150.

———, "Five Centuries of Latin Hexameter Poetry: Silver Age and Late Empire,"* TAPhA* 98 (1967), pp. 77-150.

———, "A Rare Type of First Foot Dactyl (Three Words),"* AJPh* 89 (1968), pp. 437-448.

———, "Maphaeus Vegius and Vergil's *Aeneid:* A Metrical Comparison,"* CPh* 64 (1969), pp. 1-6.

J. W. Duff, *A Literary History of Rome From the Origins to the Close of the Golden Age* (3rd ed. by A. M. Duff, London, 1960).

———, *A Literary History of Rome in the Silver Age* (2nd ed. by A. M. Duff, New York, 1960).

———, "Laus Pisonis," in *OCD* (1949), p. 484.

L. G. Eldridge, *Num Culex et Ciris Epyllia ab eodem poeta composita sint quaeritur* (Freiburg, 1914).

J. Elmore, "A New Dating of Horace's *De arte poetica*," *CPh* 30 (1935), pp. 1-9.

P. Ercole, *Studi Giovenaliani* (Milano, 1935).

G. Ferrara, *Calpurnio Siculo e il panegirico a Calpurnio Pisone* (Pavia, 1905).

G. C. Fiske, "Lucilius and Persius," *TAPhA* 40 (1909), pp. 121-150.

E. Fraenkel, "The Culex," *JRS* 42 (1953), pp. 1-9.

H. Fraenkel, *Ovid: A Poet between Two Worlds* (Berkeley, 1945).

E. Frank, "La composizione della Tebaide di Stazio," *RIL* 99 (1965), pp. 309-318.

———, "Structure of Valerius' *Argonautica*," *CB* 43 (1966-67), pp. 38-39.

T. Frank, *Vergil: A Biography* (New York, 1922).

G. K. Galinsky, "The Hercules-Cacus Episode in *Aeneid* VIII," *AJPh* 87 (1966), pp. 18-51.

———, "*Aeneid* V and the *Aeneid*," *AJPh* 89 (1968), pp. 157-185.

S. Gaselee, "Petronius Arbiter," in *OCD* (1949), p. 672.

R. J. Getty, "Classical Latin Metre and Prosody 1935-1962," *Lustrum* 8 (1963), pp. 103-160.

J. Granarolo, *L'Oeuvre de Catulle. Aspects religieux, éthiques et stylistiques* (Paris, 1967).

J. Groesst, *Qua tenus Silius Italicus a Vergilio pendere videatur* (Wiesbaden, 1887).

H. Hagen, "Zur lateinischen anthologie," *Philologus* 28 (1869), pp. 338-341.

W. R. Hardie, "A Note on the History of the Latin Hexameter," *JPh* 30 (1907), pp. 266-279.

———, "On Some Non-Metrical Arguments Bearing on the Date of the Ciris," *JPh* 30 (1907), pp. 280-289.

W. E. Heitland, Introduction to C. E. Haskins, *M. Annaei Lucani Pharsalia* (London, 1887), pp. xiii-cxxxi.

———, "The 'Great Lacuna' in the Eighth Book of Silius Italicus," *JPh* 24 (1896), pp. 188-211.

J. Hellegouarc'h, *Le monosyllable dans l'hexamètre latin. Essai de métrique verbale* (Paris, 1964).

G. L. Hendrickson, "Horace and Valerius Cato," *CPh* 11 (1916), pp. 249-269.

R. M. Henry, "Epic Poetry, Latin," in *OCD* (1949), pp. 321-323.

N. I. Herescu (ed.), *Ovidiana. Recherches sur Ovide* (Paris, 1958).

G. Highet, "Juvenal's Bookcase," *AJPh* 72 (1951), pp. 369-394.

———, *Juvenal the Satirist: A Study* (Oxford, 1954).

A. E. Housman, "Versus Ovidi de Piscibus et Feris," *CQ* 1 (1907), pp. 275-278.

J. Hubaux, *Les thèmes bucoliques dans la poésie latine* (Bruxelles, 1930). [= *Memoires, Académie Royale de Belgique*, 29.1.]

A. Hudson-Williams, "Ilias Latina," in *OCD* (1949), p. 449.

———, "Virgil and the Christian Latin Poets," *PVS* 6 (1966-67), pp. 11-21.

H. H. Huxley, "Silver Latin Poetry," in M. Platnauer (ed.), *Fifty Years of Classical Scholarship* (Oxford, 1954), pp. 413-431.

W. F. Jackson Knight, *Vergil's Troy. Essays on the Second Book of the Aeneid* (Oxford, 1932). [= *Vergil. Epic and Anthropology* (London, 1967), pp. 19-134.]

———, *Accentual Symmetry in Vergil* (Oxford, 1939).

———, "Ovid's Metre and Rhythm," in N. I. Herescu (ed.), *Ovidiana. Recherches sur Ovide* (Paris, 1958), pp. 106-120.

———, *Roman Vergil* (rev. ed., Peregrine Books, 1966).

F. P. Jones, "A Binary-Octal Code for Analyzing Hexameters," *TAPhA* 97 (1966), pp. 275-280.

F. Klingner, *Römische Geisteswelt* (3rd ed., München, 1956).

W. F. J. Knight. See under W. F. Jackson Knight.

I. Koltowski, "De poematis Ovidio falso adscriptis. II. De argumentorum fide in *Halieuticis* ab Ovidio auctore abiudicandis," *Eos* 51 (1961), pp. 109-118.

P. de Labriolle, *History and Literature of Christianity from Tertullian to Boethius*, trans. H. Wilson (London, 1924).

J. La Roche, "Zahlenverhältnisse im homerischen Vers," *WS* 20 (1898), pp. 1-69.

———, "Der Hexameter bei Vergil," *WS* 23 (1901), pp. 121-142.

S. Lederer, "Ist Vergil der Verfasser von 'Culex' und 'Ciris'? Zugleich ein Beitrag zur Geschichte des Hexameters," *Jahres-bericht über das K. K. Akademische Gymnasium in Wien* (Wien, 1890), pp. 14-30.

A. G. Lee, review of J. A. Richmond, *The Halieutica ascribed to Ovid*, *CR* 13 (1963), pp. 294-295.

L. Legras, *Étude sur la Thébaïde de Stace* (Paris, 1905).

W. S. Maguinness, *The Thirteenth Book of the Aeneid* (London, 1957).

J. Marouzeau, *Traité de stylistique latine* (2nd ed., Paris, 1946).

G. Martin, *Laus Pisonis* (Cornell Univ. diss., 1917).

P. Maury, "Le secret de Virgile et l'architecture des Bucoliques," *Lettres d'Humanité* 3 (1944), p. 71-147.

R. Maxa, "Lautmalerei und Rhythmus in Vergils Aeneis," *WS* 19 (1897), pp. 78-116.

C. W. Mendell, "Silius the Reactionary," *PhQ* 3 (1924), pp. 92-106.

W. A. Merrill, "The Lucretian Hexameter," *UCPPh* 5 (1922-23), pp. 253-334.

J. Mewaldt, "Lucretius," *RE* 13.2 (1927), cols. 1659-1683.

M. P. O. Morford, *The Poet Lucan. Studies in Rhetorical Epic* (Oxford, 1967).

J. H. Mozley, Virgil and the Silver Latin Epic," *PVS* 3 (1963-64), pp. 12-26.

V. P. Naughtin, "Metrical Patterns in Lucretius' Hexameters," *CQ* 2 (1952), pp. 152-167.

H. Nettleship, "The *De Arte Poetica* of Horace," *JPh* 12 (1883), pp. 43-61.

J. K. Newman, *Augustus and the New Poetry* (Bruxelles-Berchem, 1967). [= *Collection Latomus*, Vol. 88.]

——, *The Concept of Vates in Augustan Poetry* (Bruxelles, 1967). [= *Collection Latomus*, Vol. 89.]

E. G. O'Neill, Jr., "Word-Accents and Final Syllables in Latin Verse," *TAPhA* 71 (1940), pp. 335-359.

B. Otis, *Virgil: A Study in Civilized Poetry* (Oxford, 1963).

——, *Ovid as an Epic Poet* (Cambridge, 1966).

S. G. Owen, "Notes on Ovid's *Ibis, Ex Ponto Libri,* and *Halieutica,*" *CQ* 8 (1914), pp. 254-271.

——, "Ovid," in *OCD* (1949), pp. 630-632.

G. Pennisi, "Quando lo scrittore parla de se' stesso, ovvero Horat. *Serm.* I, 10, 1a-8a," *Helikon* 2 (1962), pp. 112-130.

J. Perret, *Horace* (Paris, 1959). English translation by B. Humez (New York, 1964).

C. Plésent, *Le Culex: Étude sur l'alexandrinisme latin* (Paris, 1910).

J.-G. Préaux, "Constatations sur la composition de la 4e bucolique de Virgile," *RBPh* 41 (1963), pp. 63-79.

F. J. E. Raby, *A History of Christian-Latin Poetry from the Beginnings to the Close of the Middle Ages* (2nd ed., Oxford, 1953).

——, *A History of Secular Latin Poetry in the Middle Ages,* Vol. I (2nd ed., Oxford, 1957).

R. S. Radford, "The Juvenile Works of Ovid and the Spondaic Period of His Metrical Art," *TAPhA* 51 (1920), pp. 146-171.

——, "The *Priapea* and the Vergilian Appendix," *TAPhA* 52 (1921), pp. 148-177.

——, "Tibullus and Ovid," *AJPh* 44 (1923), pp. 1-26, 230-259, 293-318.

——, "The Culex and Ovid," *Philologus* 86 (1930-31), pp. 68-117.

E. K. Rand, "Young Virgil's Poetry," *HSPh* 30 (1919), pp. 103-185.

——, "Prudentius and Christian Humanism," *TAPhA* 51 (1920), pp. 71-83.

——, *The Magical Art of Virgil* (Cambridge, Mass., 1931).

——, *Founders of the Middle Ages* (Cambridge, Mass., 1941).

J. A. Richmond, "On Imitation in Ovid's 'Ibis' and in the 'Halieutica' ascribed to him," *Atti del Convegno Internazionale Ovidiano*, Sulmona, Vol. II (Roma, 1959), pp. 9-57.

K. F. C. Rose, "Problems of Chronology in Lucan's Career," *TAPhA* 97 (1966), pp. 379-396.

M. Rothstein, "Die Anfangsverse der Satire I, 10 des Horaz," *Hermes* 68 (1933), pp. 70-83.

F. H. Sandbach, review of W. F. Jackson Knight, *Vergil's Troy*, *CR* 47 (1933), pp. 74-75.

J. J. H. Savage, "The Cyclops, the Sibyl and the Poet," *TAPhA* 93 (1962), pp. 410-442.

——, "The Art of the Seventh *Eclogue* of Vergil," *TAPhA* 94 (1963), pp. 248-267.

M. Schanz-C. Hosius, *Geschichte der römischen Literatur, II* (München, 1935).

W. Schetter, "Die Buchzahl der Argonautica des Valerius Flaccus," *Philologus* 103 (1959), pp. 297-308.

H. Schnepf, "Das Herculesabenteur in Virgils Aeneis (VIII 184 f.)," *Gymnasium* 66 (1959), pp. 250-268.

M. Schuster, "Valerius," *RE* 7A.2 (1948), cols. 2353-2410.

G. A. Simcox, *A History of Latin Literature from Ennius to Boethius* (New York, 1883). Two volumes.

F. Skutsch, *Aus Vergils Frühzeit* (Leipzig, 1910).
——, *Aus Vergils Frühzeit: II. Gallus und Vergil* (Leipzig, 1906).
O. Skutsch, "Ictus and Word-Accent in Virgil" [= review of W. F. Jackson Knight, *Accentual Symmetry in Vergil*], *CR* 54 (1940), pp. 93-95.
R. B. Steele, "Variation in the Latin Dactylic Hexameter," *PhQ* 5 (1926), pp. 212-225.
——, *Authorship of the Culex* (Nashville, 1930).
——, "The Authorship of the *Moretum*," *TAPhA* 61 (1930), pp. 195-216.
——, *Authorship of the Dirae and Lydia* (Nashville, 1931).
E. H. Sturtevant, "Commodian and Medieval Rhythmic Verse," *Language* 2 (1926), pp. 223-237.
W. C. Summers, *A Study of the Argonautica of Valerius Flaccus* (Cambridge, 1894).
W. S. Summers, *The Silver Age of Latin Literature from Tiberius to Trajan* (London, 1920).
G. B. Townend, "Oxytone Accentuation in Latin Elegiacs," *AJPh* 71 (1950), pp. 22-39.
——, "More Oxytones in Latin Dactylic Verse," *AJPh* 71 (1950), pp. 365-378.
——, "The Poems," in T. A. Dorey (ed.), *Cicero* (London, 1965), pp. 109-134.
E. Trampe, *De Lucani arte metrica* (Berlin, 1884).
B. L. Ullman, "The Text Tradition and Authorship of the *Laus Pisonis*," *CPh* 24 (1929), pp. 109-132.
F. Vollmer, "Coniectanea," *RhM* 55 (1900), pp. 520-530.
M. V. T. Wallace, "The Epic Technique of Silius Italicus," *HSPh* 62 (1957), pp. 159-162.
——, "The Architecture of the *Punica*: a Hypothesis," *CPh* 53 (1958), pp. 99-103.
P. G. Walsh, "Eumolpus, the *Halosis Troiae*, and the *De bello civili*," *CPh* 63 (1968), pp. 208-212.
H. Weinold, *Die Dichterischen Quellen des L. Iunius Moderatus Columella in seinem Werke De Re Rustica* (München, 1959).
F. Weissengruber, "Zur Datierung der 'Aetna'," *WS* 78 (1965), pp. 128-138.
R. E. H. Westendorp Boerma, "Vergil's Debt to Catullus," *Acta Classica* 1 (1958), pp. 51-63.
M. Wigodsky, "The Arming of Aeneas," *C & M* 26 (1965), pp. 192-221.
W. Wili, *Horaz und die Augusteische Kultur* (Basel, 1948).
L. P. Wilkinson, "The Augustan Rules for Dactylic Verse," *CQ* 34 (1940), pp. 30-43.
——, *Ovid Recalled* (Cambridge, 1955).
——, *Golden Latin Artistry* (Cambridge, 1963).
R. D. Williams, *Virgil* (Oxford, 1967). [= *Greece & Rome. New Surveys in the Classics, No. 1.*]
S. E. Winbolt, *Latin Hexameter Verse. An Aid to Composition* (London, 1903).
L. B. Woodruff, "Reminiscences of Ennius in Silius Italicus," *Univ. of Michigan Stud.* 4 (1910), pp. 355-424.
A. Woodward, "The Fourth Foot in Vergil," *PhQ* 15 (1936), pp. 126-135.
J. W. Zarker, *Studies in the Carmina Latina Epigraphica* (Ann Arbor, 1958). [= Princeton Univ. dissertation, microfilmed.]